The Changing Body

Humans have become much taller and heavier, and experience healthier and longer lives than ever before in human history. However, it is only recently that historians, economists, human biologists, and demographers have linked the changing size, shape, and capability of the human body to economic and demographic change. This fascinating and groundbreaking book presents an accessible introduction to the field of anthropometric history, surveying the causes and consequences of changes in health and mortality, diet, and the disease environment in Europe and the United States since 1700. It examines how we define and measure health and nutrition as well as key issues such as whether increased longevity contributes to greater productivity or, instead, imposes burdens on society through the higher costs of health care and pensions. The result is a major contribution to economic and social history with important implications for today's developing world and the health trends of the future.

SIR RODERICK FLOUD is Provost of Gresham College, London. He is editor of *The Cambridge Economic History of Modern Britain* (Cambridge 2004) and has published many books on British economic history including *Height, Health and History: Nutritional Status in the United Kingdom, 1750–1980* (with Kenneth Wachter and Annabel Gregory, Cambridge 1990). He is a research associate at the National Bureau of Economic Research, and has received a knighthood for services to higher education.

ROBERT WILLIAM FOGEL is a professor of economics and the Charles R. Walgreen Distinguished Service Professor of American Institutions at the University of Chicago Booth School of Business, where he is Director of the Center for Population Economics. His many published titles include *The Escape from Hunger and Premature Death, 1700–2100: Europe, America, and the Third World* (Cambridge 2004). He is a research associate at the National Bureau of Economic Research, and received the Nobel Prize in Economics in 1993.

BERNARD HARRIS is Professor of the History of Social Policy at the University of Southampton. His published titles include *The Health of the Schoolchild: A History of the School Medical Service in England and Wales* (1995) and *The Origins of the British Welfare State: Society, State and Social Welfare in England and Wales, 1800–1945* (2004).

SOK CHUL HONG is Assistant Professor of Economics at Sogang University, South Korea. His current research focuses on the innovation of medical and environmental technologies and their impact on human development from a long-term perspective.

NEW APPROACHES TO ECONOMIC AND SOCIAL HISTORY

SERIES EDITORS

Nigel Goose, *University of Hertfordshire*
Larry Neal, *University of Illinois, Urbana-Champaign*

New Approaches to Economic and Social History is an important new textbook series published in association with the Economic History Society. It provides concise but authoritative surveys of major themes and issues in world economic and social history from the post-Roman recovery to the present day. Books in the series are by recognized authorities operating at the cutting edge of their field with an ability to write clearly and succinctly. The series consists principally of single-author works – academically rigorous and groundbreaking – which offer comprehensive, analytical guides at a length and level accessible to advanced school students and undergraduate historians and economists.

NBER Series on Long-term Factors in Economic Development
A National Bureau of Economic Research Series

Edited by CLAUDIA GOLDIN

Relation of the Directors to the Work and Publications of the NBER

1. The object of the NBER is to ascertain and present to the economics profession, and to the public more generally, important economic facts and their interpretation in a scientific manner without policy recommendations. The Board of Directors is charged with the responsibility of ensuring that the work of the NBER is carried on in strict conformity with this object.

2. The President shall establish an internal review process to ensure that book manuscripts proposed for publication DO NOT contain policy recommendations. This shall apply both to the proceedings of conferences and to manuscripts by a single author or by one or more co-authors but shall not apply to authors of comments at NBER conferences who are not NBER affiliates.

3. No book manuscript reporting research shall be published by the NBER until the President has sent to each member of the Board a notice that a manuscript is recommended for publication and that in the President's opinion it is suitable for publication in accordance with the above principles of the NBER. Such notification will include a table of contents and an abstract or summary of the manuscript's content, a list of contributors if applicable, and a response form for use by Directors who desire a copy of the manuscript for review. Each manuscript shall contain a summary drawing attention to the nature and treatment of the problem studied and the main conclusions reached.

4. No volume shall be published until forty-five days have elapsed from the above notification of intention to publish it. During this period a copy shall be sent to any Director requesting it, and if any Director objects to publication on the grounds that the manuscript contains policy recommendations, the objection will be presented to the author(s) or editor(s). In case of dispute, all members of the Board shall be notified, and the President shall appoint an ad hoc committee of the Board to decide the matter; thirty days additional shall be granted for this purpose.

5. The President shall present annually to the Board a report describing the internal manuscript review process, any objections made by Directors before publication or by anyone after publication, any disputes about such matters, and how they were handled.

6. Publications of the NBER issued for informational purposes concerning the work of the Bureau, or issued to inform the public of the activities at the Bureau, including but not limited to the *NBER Digest* and *Reporter*, shall be consistent with the object stated in paragraph 1. They shall contain a specific disclaimer noting that they have not passed through the review procedures required in this resolution. The Executive Committee of the Board is charged with the review of all such publications from time to time.

7. NBER working papers and manuscripts distributed on the Bureau's web site are not deemed to be publications for the purpose of this resolution, but they

shall be consistent with the object stated in paragraph 1. Working papers shall contain a specific disclaimer noting that they have not passed through the review procedures required in this resolution. The NBER's web site shall contain a similar disclaimer. The President shall establish an internal review process to ensure that the working papers and the web site do not contain policy recommendations, and shall report annually to the Board on this process and any concerns raised in connection with it.

8. Unless otherwise determined by the Board or exempted by the terms of paragraphs 6 and 7, a copy of this resolution shall be printed in each NBER publication as described in paragraph 2 above.

The Changing Body

Health, Nutrition, and Human Development
in the Western World since 1700

RODERICK FLOUD
ROBERT W. FOGEL
BERNARD HARRIS
SOK CHUL HONG

National Bureau of Economic Research

CAMBRIDGE
UNIVERSITY PRESS

CAMBRIDGE UNIVERSITY PRESS
Cambridge, New York, Melbourne, Madrid, Cape Town,
Singapore, São Paulo, Delhi, Tokyo, Mexico City

Cambridge University Press
The Edinburgh Building, Cambridge CB2 8RU, UK

Published in the United States of America by Cambridge University Press, New York

www.cambridge.org
Information on this title: www.cambridge.org/9780521705615

First published 2011
Reprinted 2011

Printed in the United Kingdom at the University Press, Cambridge

A catalog record for this publication is available from the British Library

ISBN 978-0-521-87975-0 Hardback
ISBN 978-0-521-70561-5 Paperback

To the memory of Enid Cassandra Morgan Fogel, who dedicated her life to helping others.

Contents

Figures

Tables

Acknowledgements

This book has been long in gestation and we have therefore benefited from the support of a number of institutions and from the comments of many scholars at seminars and conferences in a number of countries. Much of the research which is reported stems from findings from the program project "Early Indicators of Later Work Levels, Disease, and Death," which is funded by grants from the National Institute on Aging, the National Science Foundation, the National Institutes of Health (grant no. P01 AG010120), the Walgreen Foundation, the National Bureau of Economic Research, and the University of Chicago. Other research has been supported by the Economic and Social Research Council (grant no. G00428325035), by the National Institute of Ageing (grant no. P30 AG-12857-08), London Metropolitan University, the School of Advanced Study of the University of London, the European Science Foundation, Gresham College, the University of Southampton, and Sogang University.

We are particularly indebted to our collaborators, colleagues, friends, and critics who include Brian A'Hearn, Robert Allen, George Alter, Jere Behrman, Tommy Bengtsson, Peter D. Blanck, David Blane, Hoyt Bleakley, Joseph Burton, Louis Cain, Christine K. Cassel, Dora L. Costa, Partha Dasgupta, Paul David, Lance E. Davis, Angus Deaton, Johanna T. Dwyer, Stanley Engerman, Jacob J. Feldman, Joseph P. Ferrie, Cynthia Floud, Enid M. Fogel, Patrick Galloway, Michael Haines, Ben Harris, Deborah Harris, Tim Hatton, Andrew Hinde, Jane Humphries, Matthew E. Kahn, John Kim, Merijn Knibbe, John Komlos, Anton Kunst, Elizabeth Lawler, Chulhee Lee, Kwang-sun Lee, Ronald D. Lee, Mary McInery, Robert Milward, Robert Mittendorf, Aviva S. Must, Louis L. Nguyen, Clayne L. Pope, Samuel H. Preston, Irwin H. Rosenberg, Ira M. Rutkow, Roger Schofield, T. Paul Schultz, T. W. Schultz, Nevin S. Scrimshaw, Samantha Shave, Michael Smith, Chen Song, T. S. Srinivasan, Richard Steckel, James M. Tanner, Peter Temin, Werner Troesken, James

Trussell, Athina Vlachantoni, Kenneth Wachter, Lawrence Weaver, Sven E. Wilson, Larry T. Wimmer, Len Winokur, and Tony Wrigley. Marilyn Coopersmith, Katherine A. Chavigny, and Susan E. Jones prepared and edited early drafts of some chapters. Lewis Meineke assisted with research and with verifying calculations in Chapters 2 and 3. Nathaniel Grotte has given invaluable help in preparation of the final text.

Our co-authors have, perhaps, been our sternest critics and we acknowledge, finally, the pleasure and intellectual profit which we have gained from our collaboration.

1 | *Our changing bodies: 300 years of technophysio evolution*

This book is based on the belief that changes in the size, shape, and capability of the human body since the beginning of the eighteenth century both reflect and illuminate economic and demographic change over those three centuries. Such change has been immense. To take the United Kingdom as an example, its population has risen from under 5.5 million in 1700 to over 61 million today; life expectation at birth has risen from about 38 years to 75 years for males and 80 years for women; and gross domestic product per capita has risen in real terms from £1,643 to £20,790 (Wrigley 2004). Despite the setback in the world economy at the time of writing, similar changes have occurred in every other country of the developed world and are now occurring in almost every country in the world as a whole. At the same time, humans have become much taller and heavier and now experience lives which are much healthier, as well as longer, than ever before in human history.

It is only recently that the full potential of linking these apparently disparate aspects of the human experience has been realized by historians, economists, human biologists, and demographers. It was a matter of common observation during the eighteenth and nineteenth centuries that men and women from the richer groups within a given society – be it France, Britain, Belgium, or the United States – tended to be taller and heavier than those from poorer backgrounds, to suffer less from chronic and debilitating diseases, to live as long or longer and to be capable of harder and more sustained work. But the elucidation of the exact mechanisms which led to these observations – and their generalization to wider changes within economies and societies – has been a task of the late twentieth and early twenty-first centuries which is not yet complete. This book surveys the current state of knowledge of these matters, discusses some of the evidential and statistical problems which have been encountered, and suggests further lines of enquiry.

In one sense, the thesis of this book is very simple. It is, in brief, that the health and nutrition of one generation contributes, through mothers and through infant and childhood experience, to the strength, health, and longevity of the next generation; at the same time, increased health and longevity enable the members of that next generation to work harder and longer and to create the resources which can then, in their turn, be used to assist the next, and succeeding, generations to prosper. But this relatively simple statement conceals great complexity and also requires simultaneous attention to many different aspects of human experience which have normally been considered separately by different groups of human, social, and natural scientists. Even the terms used in the simple statement above are problematic. How do we define and measure "health" or "nutrition?" What is "one generation?" Does increased longevity contribute to greater productivity or does it, as is sometimes argued, impose great costs on society through higher costs of healthcare and pensions for an ageing population?

It will be particularly surprising to many people that this book chooses to place at the center of its enquiries into these matters the size and shape of the human body. How tall or heavy, pretty or ugly, each person grows up to be is often a matter of intense interest to them and to their friends and families, but it is not widely known how much can be gleaned, from statistics arising from the measurements of groups of people, about the societies and economies from which they came, even if they lived in periods before the existence of written documents (Steckel and Rose 2002). Nor is it generally known that historians and economists are able, by linking together the many apparently disparate documents which exist from more recent periods about the bodies of men and women, to describe and analyze social and economic change, often in great detail and not only over time but over space.

There is a further feature of this book which needs to be emphasized. Like much interdisciplinary or multi-disciplinary enquiry, it seeks to link phenomena and findings of previous studies which are simultaneously obvious or taken for granted by some and a revelation to others. It is, for example, a commonplace among human biologists that improved nutrition will lead rapidly to taller, stronger and heavier children; but it comes as a surprise to some historians that humans have grown significantly taller and heavier over recent decades and that this is more likely to have been the result of improved nutrition than of evolution or of the effects of migration in changing the composition of populations. It is equally surprising to many economists that the mean height of a group within a population can be used to measure changes to the standard of living, since they conceive of that term as being exclusively about monetary income and expenditure. Finally, it comes as a surprise to many human biologists, used to the concept of the "secular trend" in height, that historical studies show that growth in average height has been uneven and sometimes actually reversed.

There is, however, one matter that is common to all disciplines and, indeed, to all living beings: the conversion of energy into work. Human beings, from conception to death, take in energy in the form of food and warmth and expend it in body maintenance, growth, exercise, and work – both physical and intellectual. Greater inputs of energy allow men and women to work longer but also more intensively. In addition, for much of human history, intellectual work has resulted in the invention and innovation of tools which enable men and women to convert their energy more efficiently into outputs, both physical and intellectual. These tools have enabled men and women to transcend the limitations of their own individual physical capacity for work and thus, over centuries, have expanded their productivity – their lifetime output – to an enormous degree. Much of that expanded productivity has occurred during the past three centuries and the subjects of this study – centered around the size and shape of the human body – are the linkages and interactions which have made it possible. Much of the evidence for this – growth in childhood, mortality, adult living standards, labor productivity, food, or manufacturing output – has hitherto been studied as discrete topics; the ambition of this book is to link them.

1.1 A schema: technophysio evolution

There are dangers, but also benefits, in simplification and the use of analogy. Put very simply, this book will – on the basis of studies within many different disciplines – attempt to justify the use of the following schema:

1. The nutritional status of a generation – shown by the size and shape of their bodies – determines how long that generation will live and how much work its members will be able to do.
2. The work of a generation, measured both in hours, days, and weeks of work and in work intensity, when combined with the available technology, determines the output of that generation in terms of goods and services.

3. The output of a generation is partly determined by its inheritance from past generations; it also determines its standard of living and its distribution of income and wealth, together with the investment it makes in technology.
4. The standard of living of a generation determines, through its fertility and the distribution of income and wealth, the nutritional status of the next generation.
5. And so on *ad infinitum*.

It might perhaps be prudent to replace the word "determines" in each of these statements by the word "influences" or "partially determines." The former word is probably too strong, the latter two probably too weak. An alternative form of caution, beloved by economists, is to append the words *ceteris paribus* – others things being equal. The schema is certainly not put forward as a deterministic model; there are, in its workings, many historical contingencies and also many uncertainties. This book seeks to make use of the voluminous literature on these topics to assign some magnitudes, at the least, to the effects of one variable on another.

Economists will recognize this schema as a simplified form of endogenous growth theory, in which technology develops partly through investment in human capital in the form of health and education (see, for example, Mankiw, Romer, and Weil 1992; López-Casasnovas, Rivera, and Currais 2005).[1] Like such models, the schema focuses attention on the central or salient features which need to be measured and related one to the other – nutritional status, morbidity, mortality, technology, output, productivity, standard of living, investment, fertility, distribution of income and wealth. It differs from contemporary growth theory, appropriately for a work which has its genesis in economic history, in emphasizing long period change and, in particular, in its focus on the concept of "generation," which has defied attempts at precise definition but still remains useful as an heuristic device; there is no such thing as a single generation of a society, since generations overlap in very confusing ways, but it remains useful to think of the

---

[1] Such models have not yet fully integrated changes in health. As Morand (2005, p. 251) puts it: "additional theoretical work is needed to incorporate other mechanisms into a unified model of the long-term interaction between economic growth, population health and longevity, and that further empirical work is also needed to test the hypothesis generated by these models."

transmission of health and wealth within society in a way analogous to similar transmission within a family, where the term "generation" can more easily, though still with some difficulty, be defined.

Whatever the problems of definition, there is no doubt that from 1700 to 2000, over the course of some 12–15 human generations, all the features of this schema have been transformed in ways never seen before in human history. In the process, humankind has gained equally unprecedented control over its environment – even if it has sometimes misused that control – through the invention and application of new forms of technology. One sign of that control is that, in most if not quite all parts of the world, the size, shape, and longevity of the human body have changed more substantially, and much more rapidly, during the past three centuries than over many previous millennia. There were, of course, evolutionary changes to our bodies during those past millennia, but the change that has occurred in recent times is of a different character. It has come about, within a timescale which is minutely short by the standards of Darwinian evolution, through the application of technology, in particular to food production and distribution and to the development of means of combating disease. Fogel and Costa have named this process "technophysio evolution," linking technological with physiological change and using the word evolution – by analogy with Darwinian evolution – to emphasize the magnitude and speed of the changes that have occurred (Fogel and Costa 1997; Fogel 2004b).

As Jones has explained in his best-selling attempt to "update" Darwin's *Origin of Species*, modern evolutionary theory rests on the two fundamental principles of variation and selection. Variation in sexual populations occurs because of recombination and mutation, while evolution occurs because some of these variations will prove more or less beneficial in the environments within which they find themselves. However, although the incidence of such variations may be quite high, the pace of evolutionary change is nevertheless slow. This is because most variations are, in themselves, of limited value and need to be maintained for several generations before acquiring a "fixed character" (Jones 2000; Ridley 2004, pp. 87–89, 590–611).

The theory of "technophysio evolution" differs from conventional theories of biological evolution because it emphasizes the extent to which human beings have a unique capacity to shape their own environments; it differs also because of the rapidity of the changes which it describes. As Fogel and Costa explained in 1997: "the theory of technophysio evolution rests on the proposition that, during the last three hundred years, particularly during the last century, humans have gained an unprecedented degree of control over their environment – a degree of control so great that it sets them apart not only from all other species, but also from all previous generations of *homo sapiens*" (Fogel and Costa 1997, p. 49). This "unprecedented degree of control" has led to dramatic improvements in the "physiological capital" of human beings and in their life expectancy.

The theory of technophysio evolution also draws on recent research into the relationships between early-life health and health at older ages. Although the ideas which lie behind this research are not new, they have become increasingly influential in recent work as a result of the work of Barker and others, who have drawn attention to the fetal origins of adult disease (Barker 1992; Barker 1998). This has encouraged a large number of researchers to adopt a "life-course" approach to the study of human longevity (e.g., Ben-Shlomo and Kuh 2002).

Some of the concepts used in discussion of technophysio evolution and in the schema which will be elucidated below – such as mortality, fertility, income, or wealth – are familiar, if not always free from problems. Two, however, are less familiar or less well defined but nevertheless so important in summing up the changes that have occurred that they demand special attention at this stage: the standard of living and nutritional status.

1.2 The "standard of living" and "nutritional status"

In 1848 Thomas Babington Macaulay (later Lord Macaulay) devoted the third chapter of *The History of England* to a description of the state of England in 1685 (Macaulay 1848, pp. 209–320). Although this chapter is described by the author of the *Oxford Companion to English Literature* as "superficial and discredited" (Drabble 1985, p. 599), Macaulay displays in it a clear sense of the change in living conditions of the population which had occurred, and would occur, the difficulty of measuring such changes in human welfare, and the need to take account in any historical narrative of many different aspects of those conditions and of the distribution of the rewards of economic growth. As he concluded (Macaulay 1848, pp. 320–321):

It is now the fashion to place the golden age of England in times when noblemen were destitute of comforts the want of which would be intolerable to a modern footman, when farmers and shopkeepers breakfasted on loaves the very sight of which would raise a riot in a modern workhouse, when men died faster in the purest country air than they now die in the most pestilential lanes of our towns, and when men died faster in the lanes of our towns than they now die on the coast of Guiana. We too shall, in our turn, be outstripped, and in our turn be envied. It may well be, in the twentieth century, that the peasant of Dorsetshire may think himself miserably paid with fifteen shillings a week; that the carpenter at Greenwich may receive ten shillings a day; that labouring men may be as little used to dine without meat as they now are to eat rye bread; that sanitary police and medical discoveries may have added several more years to the average length of human life; that numerous comforts and luxuries which are now unknown, or confined to a few, may be within the reach of every diligent and thrifty working man. And yet it may then be the mode to assert that the increase of wealth and the progress of science have benefited the few at the expense of the many, and to talk of the reign of Queen Victoria as the time when England was truly merry England, when all classes were bound together by brotherly sympathy, when the rich did not grind the faces of the poor, and when the poor did not envy the splendour of the rich.

Macaulay encapsulates, in this passage, the difficulty of measuring what was later to be called the "standard of living" of a population. He was writing at a time when many observers were concerned at the "condition of England" under the impact of industrialization and urbanization and when Marx and Engels had just begun to mount their challenge to emergent industrial capitalism. In the process, they were to challenge also Macaulay's presupposition, which became known as the Whig interpretation of history, one of continual progress toward a better society.

During the twentieth century, historians and economists focused their discussion of living standards on the measurement of wages, adjusted for changes in the cost of living. The wages of different groups of workers were aggregated and compared with movements in the prices of "baskets of goods" representing their consumption expenditure. This had the merit of simplicity and reasonable precision, particularly if the nature of the occupations whose wages were being measured had not changed significantly. The principal drawbacks of the method were that – being based entirely on monetary income – it could not incorporate such issues as changes to the length of human life, that it did not adequately reflect the advent of new "comforts and luxuries," that it was difficult to incorporate new occupations, and that it was always difficult to ensure that the whole, or even a majority, of the population was considered.

These deficiencies did not prevent the resultant measures of real wages being used as evidence in what has rightly been called "the most sustained single controversy in British economic history" (Mathias 1975, p. vii).[2] The controversy was essentially begun by Engels in *The Condition of the Working Class in England*, first published in Germany in 1845. During the course of the next hundred years, British economic historians became divided between the "optimists," who believed that economic growth during and after the Industrial Revolution had benefited the working classes at the time, and the "pessimists," who believed by contrast that industrialization had led to declining living standards or, worse, to the "immiseration" of the English proletariat. The controversy was so long lasting – it is, indeed, still in progress – for two main reasons. First, there was no general agreement on a definition of the "standard of living" and, second, measures of changes to real wages were ambiguous. As Von Tunzelmann put it at one stage of the debate, after examining several series of wages and prices, "the patterns of real wages ... range anywhere from an increase of 150 percent between 1750 and 1850 down to no increase at all" (1979, p. 48). While the later work of Feinstein (1998) has achieved general acceptance as to the course of changes to real wages, argument still remains on the scope of measures of living standards and the quality of life. This topic is discussed in more detail in Chapter 4 below, where account is also taken of recent contributions to the debate from Clark (2007) and Allen (2009).

In the middle of the twentieth century, living standards came to be defined by economists, even more narrowly than before, in terms of income per capita, in other words the total annual measured income of an economy divided by the number in the population. The measurement of national income, primarily due to the work of Simon Kuznets, represented an enormous step forward in the ability of economists to describe and analyze economic growth and to compare that growth over time and space. It also provided, in the shape of the calculation of real income or real gross domestic product per capita, a means of comparing the average living standards of the population of a particular

---

[2] Oddly, as Engerman (1997) points out, a similar controversy did not take place in Germany, France, or the United States.

country either with those of another country or with those of the past. It did not, however, remove the drawbacks of the previous calculations of real wages, in particular their exclusive concentration on monetary income. Thus, as has often been pointed out, it ignored the contribution of unpaid employment such as housework or gardening, did not value leisure time, could not incorporate improvements in the quality of goods and services unless they were reflected in prices, could not take account of changes in health and mortality, and, in general, did not measure changes to the "quality of life."[3] Nor could it reflect, without the addition of other statistics, changes in the distribution of income (both within and between households) in order to test, as Macaulay put it, whether increasing national income had "benefited the few at the expense of the many."[4]

In recent years, these problems with the use of national income analysis in the description of changes in the standard of living have been addressed in two entirely separate ways. First, a number of economists have followed Nordhaus and Tobin (1972) and Usher (1980) in seeking to make adjustments to measured income per capita so as to reflect elements of life which are not included within conventional measures of income per capita. The major such adjustments have been for non-paid work such as housework and gardening and for leisure. In similar vein, Williamson (1981; 1982) attempted to value changes to the quality of life, including morbidity and mortality, with particular reference to the growing cities of the United Kingdom in the nineteenth century. These adjustments, each dependent on a series of debatable assumptions, share the characteristic that – when put into practice – they are quite large, thus throwing further doubt on the value of the underlying calculation of income per head when making temporal and spatial comparisons.[5] The second approach has relied on the insights of Sen (see, for example, 1999) and in particular on his stress

---

[3] Economists such as Kuznets and Abramowitz, who devised and refined the methods of measuring the national accounts, were of course fully aware of these omissions and deficiencies and discussed them in a number of papers and books. The problem lies, however, in the use to which simple measures of GDP and other variables have been put in cross-national and temporal comparisons.

[4] In recent years, economists have paid increasing attention to the question of whether economic growth increases happiness and of how happiness can be best measured; see, for example, Layard 2006 and Bok 2010.

[5] For a very thoughtful and comprehensive account of the relationship between national income analysis and economic welfare, see Offer 2003.

on "capabilities" as the true definition of living standards. Rather than using a measure which stresses income and the command over resources which it gives at one point of time, he regards a greater standard of living as being given by an improved capability to live a rewarding and fulfilling life. Part of this is, of course, "freedom from want," and therefore in measures based on these insights, such as the Human Development Index (HDI) developed by the United Nations, income per head forms one input into the index, the others being the average expectation of life and the average literacy of the population or country being measured. This concept has been further developed by the addition, in some formulations, of measures of political and civil freedom, again because they are seen as conferring a capacity or capability (Dasgupta and Weale 1992). It is natural that the HDI, and these other formulations based upon it, produce somewhat different rankings of nations in terms of living standards from the simpler criterion of income per capita. This has the virtue of drawing attention to particular features of societies, such as the expectation of life in the United States, which is low compared to other nations with similar, or even smaller, incomes per capita.[6]

Income per capita – whether adjusted or not – reflects the output of an economy, and the command over resources which this gives to its citizens, at one point in time. The HDI, or any measure based on the concept of capability, is intended to reflect the capacity or potential of the economy and society and thus in a sense its future as well as its present.[7] The difference is not as large as it might seem, since income per capita also reflects the potential for using resources in the future, but the emphasis of the HDI is on the long term, of income per capita on the short term. Both, of course, reflect the past in the sense that income and capabilities today are both determined and constrained by their development over past decades or centuries.

For these and other reasons, it seems unnecessary or misleading to express a generalized preference for one type of measure over another. Each is designed to measure a particular feature, or set of features, of

---

[6] For an application of the Human Development Index to historical data for Europe, see Crafts (1997). The Human Development Index and similar indices are, of course, sensitive to the chosen, and inevitably arbitrary, weighting of the different components of the index.

[7] For a slightly different formulation, see Harris, Gálvez, and Machado 2009.

society and economy; what is important is that the measure should be appropriate to the question that is being asked. The search for an "ideal" measure of living standards is, in that sense, a search for a chimera; there are, instead, several different measures, each with their own virtues, implications, and correlates. The measures may, or may not, conflict in any given historical circumstance but conflict carries with it as much information as agreement.

The concept known to human biologists as "nutritional status," which is at the center of this book, can therefore easily take its place within the set of possible measures of living standards. Nutritional status, usually measured by the physical growth of infants, children, and young people, has to be clearly distinguished from nutrition, which is the amount and nature of energy ingested in the form of food and drink. Nutritional status is a net measure; it represents the energy which has been used for growth once the demands of body maintenance, resistance to disease, play, and work have been satisfied. If nutritional status is inadequate, a child or young person will not grow, either not at all or less than he or she would do under more favorable circumstances. This inadequacy results normally either from lack of food or warmth or the effects of disease – which act in tandem in so much of the developing world even today – but growth can also be affected if the child is expected to undertake significant manual work or even if it is deprived of love and psychological support. Inadequate growth will result in children and adults who are stunted – short compared with some recognized standard – or wasted – light by comparison with some such standard; it can also affect children in less obvious ways, affecting their intelligence or mental capacity. But the primary evidence of nutritional status lies in our bodies and particularly in our height and weight.

Poor nutritional status and its effects can be most clearly seen in the developing world, where human biologists and development economists have intensively studied it and its correlates. The results of studies of malnutrition are unambiguous. Dasgupta (1993, pp. 12–13) sums them up:

The general effects of persistent undernourishment and infections vary widely, but they all result in an impaired life. In expectant mothers it affects the growth of the foetus, and therefore its health status (e.g., weight) at birth. It affects ... the lactation performance of nursing mothers ... causes fatigue and lowers resistance to infections ... causes muscle wastage and growth retardation, and thus future capability ... increases morbidity and vulnerability to infections ... affect[s] brain growth and development ... influences mental capacities through damage to the nervous system ... reducing the energy that children have available for learning ... [A]mong adults [it] diminishes their muscular strength, their capacity to do physical work, and their protection against a wide range of infectious diseases ... it brings marked psychological changes ... [and diminished] life expectancy.

The converse is in each case true for children and adults born and brought up in more favorable circumstances. Nutritional status thus sums up the resources – monetary and other – available to the growing child and the use that is made of them. It particularly reflects the environment of the child over a relatively short period of time; although humans continue to grow in stature for nearly 20 years after birth and in weight for many years thereafter, it is in the fetal stage and in early infancy – and later in adolescence – that growth is particularly responsive to energy inputs and demands.

However, as the quotation from Dasgupta implies, nutritional status is influenced by events that occur long before the birth of a child and persist long after, in fact until its death even in old age many years later. Indeed, through the effect of the nutritional status of a mother upon her child, the influence may be felt through yet further generations. The same conclusion has been reached, in a different way, by human biologists studying the fetal origins of adult disease (see, for example, Barker 1992; Barker 1998). In these senses, therefore, the measure of nutritional status is analogous to measures of capability. It sums up both the historical influences on parents and children and the capacity of that population to live, thrive, and contribute to economy and society.

A number of factors exert different impacts at different stages of life. It seems likely, for example, that maternal nutrition has an effect on the nutritional status of a fetus, affecting both birth weight and the potential for growth of the child after birth. Diet and disease – and possibly demands for work – then also affect that growth, particularly at phases – infancy, early childhood, and adolescence – when normal growth would otherwise be most rapid. Finally, after growth in height has ceased, nutrition, work, and disease continue to affect weight and productivity.

Paradoxically, the very far-reaching and multiple causes and consequences of changes in measured nutritional status diminish its usefulness in explaining the causes of changes to the standard of living of a population or socioeconomic group. It is frustrating to historians and economists that it is rarely possible to ascribe a single cause to a movement in the average height of a population or even to date it very precisely.[8] Of course, few indicators of living standards – even life expectancy or literacy, which can be very precisely measured – are really free from such problems. Even movements in income per capita arise as the outcome of a multiplicity of causes operating throughout the economy, many of which are difficult to discern.

To some economists, nutritional status – measured for example by heights – suffers as a measure of living standards because height is not normally seen as an object of desire or something that can be bought.[9] In economic jargon, height is not an argument in a utility function.[10] People do not normally or consciously sacrifice current expenditure so that their children can be taller. This is certainly not an overwhelming argument against the use of nutritional status as a measure of living standards, since it can be made with equal force against other measures such as life expectancy and, even more obviously, civil and political freedom. In addition, parents certainly do desire health and growth for

---

[8] These difficulties are compounded by difficulties in measuring height and its correlates in the past, or even in the present. Schultz (2005, p. 279), for example, draws attention to problems of measurement error in contemporary studies in the developing world: "The major complexity posed by health, which is less of a problem with education, is that the indicators that represent health are multifaceted and are not always adequately justified by their correspondence with mortality, morbidity and the quality of life. Many of these health indicators may represent proxies for human capital, consuming current social resources and yielding increased potential over the life cycle of cohorts. These indicators are a mixture of exogenous measurement error and genetic components, on the one hand, and an endogenous (or human capital) component. This distinction is perhaps most evident in the case of adult height, which has been emphasized here. In all of these studies of height, community health services and the socioeconomic characteristics of parents account for only 2–10 percent of the variation in the population, and much of the unexplained variation in height is undoubtedly due to genotypic variation across individuals and survey measurement errors." How much worse are the problems faced by historians.

[9] This is not entirely true, as can be seen from the immense efforts and expense undertaken by some parents of particularly short children to lengthen their children by persuading surgeons to break their leg bones and then to stretch their legs as they heal.

[10] Or, as Engerman (1997, p. 39) puts it more precisely: "While we might believe that individuals maximize utility, not measured income, life expectation, food consumption or height, it is not clear how to determine what enters into different individual utility functions."

their children and are prepared to make sacrifices of income to attain this. Recently, indeed, some economists have seen the force of these arguments and have accepted that increased height, among other attributes, can be seen as one aspect of the accumulation of human capital. As Schultz (2003, p. 331) puts it:

Schooling, height, weight-for-height and migration are attributes of workers associated with their current productivity. These forms of worker heterogeneity are to some degree reproducible: schooling and migration are created by well-described processes, whereas height and weight-for-height are formed by the biological process of human growth … These worker attributes are viewed here as indicators of human capital because they can be augmented by social or private investments, but they also vary across individuals because of genetic and environmental factors that are not controlled by the individual, family or society.

Some economists have sought to counter objections to the use of anthropometric indicators as an indicator of the standard of living, which essentially come down to the non-monetized nature of such indicators as height and weight, by referring to "the biological standard of living" rather than "nutritional status" (Komlos and Baten 1998; Komlos and Cuff 1998). This is a distinction without a difference and serves merely to confuse. The problem in fact arises not from the inappropriateness of the term "nutritional status" but from the restricted definition of "standard of living" adopted by economists. As Eric Hobsbawm (1963, p. 131) once observed in a contribution to the standard of living debate, "men do not live by bread alone"; it is simply foolish to exclude from consideration matters which clearly contribute to welfare, such as health, longevity, and quality of life.

Standard of living, quality of life, nutritional status are, therefore, all different but intimately related concepts which are useful in measuring human welfare, either over time or between nations or political and social groups at one point of time. Other aspects of the schema presented above – such as mortality, morbidity, or productivity – may in practice be more relevant to, or more affected by, one method of describing welfare than another and it is important to choose the most appropriate method in any given circumstance. Historical analysis is rarely tidy, since one is dealing with the complexities of societies and economies which are undergoing constant change, so the most that one can hope for is clarity in any particular argument.

1.3 Understanding technophysio evolution

The schema set out earlier in this chapter describes the interconnections between different aspects of economy and society which have made technophysio evolution possible. To be useful, however, the schema has to be fleshed out, first in general terms and in relation to the condition of the economy at the start of the eighteenth century. This is done in the remainder of this chapter. Chapters 2 and 3 deal with the technical aspects of a number of measurement issues, especially the need to think in terms of distributions rather than means. Then the concept of tech-nophysio evolution is explored through studies of the process in Britain (Chapter 4), Europe (Chapter 5), and North America (Chapter 6) since the beginning of the eighteenth century.

The first, and crucial, proposition is that:

1. The nutritional status of a generation – shown by the size and shape of their bodies – determines how long that generation will live and how much work its members will be able to do.

The concept of nutritional status has been explained in the last section. But what was not explained there was how nutritional status determines the size and shape of bodies and what are its short-, medium-, and long-term consequences for health and productivity. Nor have the consequences of considering these issues within the framework of a generation been considered.

Human beings require energy to maintain their bodies, to grow and engage in activity such as work and play. While a child is in the womb, this energy is supplied by the mother and is a call upon her energy resources; if she is malnourished – lacking sufficient energy inputs for growth, body maintenance, and the tasks which she needs to perform – then the fetus will be deprived and will not grow as well as it could under better circumstances. The most obvious – but certainly not the only – manifesta-tion of this deprivation will be low weight at birth. This in itself affects the chances of the child surviving through infancy and childhood, but there is also increasing evidence to support the so-called Barker hypothesis, that the poor nutritional status of a fetus can pre-dispose that person to develop a number of diseases in adulthood. This pre-disposition is distinct from any effects of genetic disorders which may be passed on from mother to child; it reflects, instead, the environment of the mother while she is childbearing and, indeed, her own nutritional status since childhood.

The first measurable characteristic of nutritional status is birth weight. Birth weights were not routinely recorded until the nineteenth century (Ward 1993). There is, however, little doubt that average birth weight in 1700 was very low, by modern standards, as can be inferred from stillbirth and neonatal mortality rates.[11] As Wrigley puts it (2004, p. 73): "Analyses of the proximate determinants of stillbirth rates consistently show that by far the most important single factor is birth weight. Low birth weight babies, especially at full term, are subject to very much higher perinatal mortality rates than those close to the optimum weight, usually taken to be in the range 3500–3900 grams. The stillbirth rate at an average birth weight of 2500 grams (the conventional point for defining low birth weight) is between ten and thirty times higher than the rate at an average of 3500 grams." In England at the end of the seventeenth century, the stillbirth rate was "probably between 100 and 125 per 1000 (total births)" though it was to fall, over the next 150 years or so, to 40–50 per 1,000 total births (Wrigley 2004, p. 71).[12] Neonatal mortality also fell from 203 per 1,000 in 1710–1719 to 140 per 1,000 in 1830–1837. The perinatal mortality rate (stillbirths plus neonatal mortality) is extremely strong evidence of the poor nutritional status of much of the population, in all European countries, at the start of the eighteenth century. Indeed, although the English statistics appear horrifying to modern eyes, Wrigley *et al.* (1997, p. 217) point out that: "infant mortality in England was never high by the standards of many pre-industrial communities, or indeed by comparison with those widely prevalent in Europe in the nineteenth century."

Provided that the child survives birth and its immediate aftermath, its energy needs in infancy and childhood are for body maintenance, activity, and growth. Growth charts, now routinely used by pediatricians and others, show clearly the two peaks of rapid growth in a well-nourished child; the first is immediately after birth, the second the so-called "growth spurt" at the advent of adolescence. Such charts

---

[11] Stillbirths are deaths of the fetus in the womb. Neonatal mortality is the mortality of infants in the first month of their lives. Perinatal mortality is mortality that occurs at or around birth. Infant mortality is death which occurs in the first year of life.

[12] Woods (2009) has recently argued that the fall was less, from a figure close to 60 deaths per 1,000 births at the start of the eighteenth century, although still substantial. He is also skeptical of the strength of the link between stillbirths and maternal nutrition.

also show the cessation of growth, which occurs nowadays and in developed countries in late teenage years (Eveleth and Tanner 1976; Tanner 1978). Malnutrition disturbs these patterns; it diminishes and retards the growth process, as there is insufficient energy intake to cope with the demands of body maintenance and growth, even if – as will often happen – activity is also diminished. Although it is possible for the body to recover from a short period of malnutrition – and even, through the phenomenon known as catch-up growth, to recover to the size and shape that it would have had – prolonged malnutrition leads to both stunting and wasting.[13] One sign of this is that the growth process itself continues for longer than under more favorable circumstances. But normally, despite this, the malnourished child or young adult will be both shorter and lighter than a child with more abundant energy supplies.

Stunting and wasting can also occur through the existence of other demands on the body's energy supplies. In particular, if the child has to combat disease or if he or she has to work from an early age, then energy which would otherwise be available for growth will have to be used for these purposes. This accounts for the phenomenon, seen both in the developing world today and in historical evidence, of young people and adults from upper social classes, where it is unlikely that there was any shortage of food, who are nevertheless stunted and wasted compared to their peers in more favorable environments.

There is essentially no evidence about the height and weight of children in the early eighteenth century in Britain, the rest of Europe, or North America. However, Floud, Wachter, and Gregory (1990) studied the records of the Marine Society of London, which took boys from the slums of London and found them berths on the ships of the Royal and merchant navies. The earliest measurements are of boys born in 1755, at a time when the evidence of mortality statistics suggests that there may have been a small improvement in conditions of life since the start of the century. Despite this, "the boys of the Marine Society were extraordinarily short, particularly in the eighteenth century. Thirteen-

---

[13] Such effects can be observed today; even periods of economic dislocation, short of what would normally be seen as famine conditions, can affect child growth. See, for example, Dangour *et al.* (2003), who report that in the 1990s in Kazakhstan the growth of 4-year-old boys ceased, while the average height of successive cohorts of girls actually fell, probably as the result of decisions on the distribution of food within the household.

year-olds born in 1753–1780 average 51.4 in (130.6 cm), a full 10
inches (25.4 cm) less than the children of London measured by Tanner
and others in the 1960s" (Floud, Wachter, and Gregory 1990, p. 165).
The nearest equivalent, in the modern world, is the children of Papua
New Guinea (Eveleth and Tanner 1976).

It is clear, from these data, that some groups of children in England,
and presumably in other countries, in the early eighteenth century were
severely stunted and – although we have no direct evidence of weight –
wasted. It must also be remembered that these children were those who
had survived the high perinatal and infant mortality rates reported
earlier. Other data for England also suggest that young people from
the highest social groups, where presumably there were no income
constraints on diet, were still much shorter than similar groups today,
even if they were also much taller than their less fortunate contemporaries recruited by the Marine Society. Floud, Wachter, and Gregory
report that boys recruited, in their early teenage years, to the Royal
Military Academy at Sandhurst and drawn "from a narrow segment at
the top of the British class and income distribution" (1990, p. 174)
nevertheless had a mean height below the 25th centile of the modern
British height standard (1990, p. 179, Fig. 4.10). It seems likely that the
growth of these children was retarded by the disease environment in
which they had been brought up.

Although growth in height – and the demands on energy inputs for
this purpose – ceases in early adulthood, nutritional status remains a
useful concept even if it is no longer demonstrated by height. In fact,
height still remains a useful indicator, because the physical capacity of
the body – in terms of strength and resistance to disease – remains
affected by the stunting that has occurred; it was for this reason that
British army recruiters, in the eighteenth and nineteenth centuries,
rejected short applicants wishing to join the army (Floud, Wachter,
and Gregory 1990, pp. 30–83). If, and this is the most normal circumstance throughout much of the world, deprivation and malnutrition in
childhood and adolescence are succeeded by more deprivation and
continued malnutrition in adulthood, then nutritional status will still
be inadequate and the body will not have sufficient energy for body
maintenance and work. The most obvious sign of this will be continued
wasting, together with an enhanced susceptibility to infectious diseases.
While this is a general phenomenon, caused by bodily weakness, malnutrition appears to produce enhanced susceptibility to a number of

life-threatening diseases. In addition, there is increasing evidence, for example from studies of Union Army veterans, that deprivation in childhood will increase the chances of suffering from chronic and disabling diseases. For whatever reason, the capacity to work will be limited.

Evidence drawn from the heights of military recruits supports the view that large sections of the populations of the eighteenth century were severely malnourished. For the United Kingdom, Floud, Wachter, and Gregory estimate (1990, pp. 140–149, Table 4.1) that the average height of recruits aged 18 or 19 and born in the late 1740s or early 1750s was less than 64 inches (162.5 cm), although young men of that age were still growing and final heights were probably 2 inches (5 cm) greater. The earliest estimates for French army recruits aged 20 in 1804 suggest that their average height was 163.5 cm (Weir 1997, p. 191 and see Chapter 5 below). White, native-born recruits, born in the first half of the eighteenth century, to North American armies were significantly taller, at about 172 cm tall on average, but nevertheless much shorter than current standards (Costa and Steckel 1997, p. 51). In all three countries, military recruits were drawn from the working classes, but it is nevertheless notable that these British heights are 6 inches (15 cm) less than the modern standard for the whole population. Once again, it has to be remembered that these were survivors from a regime of high perinatal, infant, and child mortality.

Even if malnutrition in childhood is followed by improved economic circumstances in later life, so that there is then no lack of energy for current work and other activity, the earlier deprivation can have long-term consequences. Although this theory is still unproven, it is suggested (Osmani and Sen 2003) that the "western diseases" which now afflict South Asia – in particular coronary heart disease and diabetes – together with the obesity which is now a feature of all developed countries, arise from a rapid increase in consumption among people who were previously malnourished.[14] Although there was little apparent increase in the body mass index in many developed countries during the nineteenth and most

---

[14] Cameron (2003, p. 41) suggests that this phenomenon can also be seen in South Africa: Children who are "born small and then grow quickly are at an increased risk of obesity and risk factors for type II diabetes. This increased risk is probably due to post-natal exposure to high fat, low fibre, high-energy diets resulting from economic and consequent nutritional transition."

of the twentieth centuries, it is possible that this phenomenon of early deprivation succeeded by later abundance could be one of the causes of the high incidence of coronary heart disease in, for example, Britain and the United States in the second half of the twentieth century although other causes of death have different relationships with nutritional status.[15]

In past centuries, however, the more typical pattern was one of deprivation both in childhood and in adulthood. In such circumstances, it seems likely that poor nutritional status has a direct effect on labor productivity. This was taken for granted in past centuries, as shown by the imposition of minimum heights for recruitment to armies. Officers and recruiters assumed that a taller soldier would be a fitter soldier, better able to withstand the rigors of military life. This indirect evidence of the link between nutritional status – as measured by height – and health is paralleled by direct evidence from modern studies of the relationship between height and wages. These demonstrate, as Dasgupta puts it, that "the link between nutritional status, physical work capacity, endurance and physical productivity is an established fact" (1997, p. 19) and that "a person's physical work capacity is determined by his entire nutritional history" (1997, p. 20).

Modern studies assume that, if employers are prepared to pay higher wages to taller men, they must be doing so because those taller men are more productive. Strauss and Thomas (1998) report estimates of the relationship between height and hourly wages in the United States and in urban Brazil, while observing that similar relationships have been observed in "a wide range of countries across the world" (1998, p. 799).

There is a powerful association between height and wages in Brazil. Taller men earn more: a 1 percent increase in height is associated with an almost 8 percent increase in wages. While this dwarfs the magnitude of the correlation in the United States, even taller American men earn higher wages. This ranking probably reflects differences in the extent of poor nutrition in the two countries as well as differences in the nature of work that is commonplace in each society, since manual labor – and thus reliance on physical strength – is far more important in Brazil. (1998, p. 772)

---

[15] As Waaler (1984) originally demonstrated, the relationship between height or BMI and later disease differs between diseases. The same point is made by Davey Smith *et al.* (2000) who show that there is a negative association between height and certain causes of premature death, such as prostate cancer, lymphoma, and colorectal cancer.

Strauss and Thomas show that this relationship holds even for those with no education, with a 1 percent increase in height being associated with a 4 percent increase in wages within that group. In other words, height is not simply a proxy for education, although taller and healthier children may also have greater access to, and derive greater benefit from, education. Similarly, Schultz (2002, p. 351) shows that, after controlling for schooling, post-schooling experience, and residence:

Height is significantly positively associated with the log hourly wage for men and women aged 25–54 in Ghana during 1987–1989, aged 25–54 in Brazil in 1989, and among youth aged 20–28 in the United States during 1989–1993. Ethnic-language or race groups are controlled by dummies and the effect of height is derived from deviations from the ethnic/race group mean, as proposed by Francis Galton ... An additional centimeter in adult height is significantly associated with a 1.5% higher wage for men and a 1.7% higher wage for women in Ghana; 1.4% and 1.7% higher wages in Brazil, respectively; and 0.45 and 0.31 % higher wages in the United States. The percentage increase in wages associated with height in the United States is less than one-third of that in the two lower–income countries, and this may be due to diminishing returns to nutrition/health associated with height in the United States than in Ghana and Brazil.

In a more recent survey, Schultz (2005, p. 277) concludes that "an additional centimeter of height is associated with a gain in wage rates of roughly 5–10 percent."

In addition, in modern urban Brazil, Strauss and Thomas show that nutritional status also affects labor force participation. "It is clear that shorter men not only earn less, they are also less likely to be working. Over 10 percent of men who are 154 cm tall were not working at the date of the survey, but among those who are about 167 cm tall, the fraction is only 5 percent."

It is not only height, as an indicator of nutritional status, which is associated with wage and labor force participation. Strauss and Thomas show that there are equivalent relationships with Body Mass Index (BMI), which to some extent reflects current nutritional status, as opposed to height which reflects nutritional status during childhood.[16] The difference between the United States and Brazil persists.

---

[16] The Body Mass Index is defined as the ratio of weight in kilograms to height in meters squared. It is therefore a measure of weight standardized for height.

The magnitude of the differences in wages across the BMI distribution in the United States is dwarfed by the magnitude in Brazil, where the shape is also quite different. Among men whose BMI is less than 27, wages rise dramatically (in Brazil) as BMI increases, particularly for those above 22. Wages are essentially unrelated to BMI for the 13 percent of men whose BMI is above 27. (Strauss and Thomas 1998, p. 774)

Once again, the association persists even for those with no education, perhaps because "elevated BMI is associated with greater physical strength, which is of value for manual labor." In summary, the evidence reported by Strauss and Thomas – even if it is based on cross-sectional data – suggests that, particularly in less developed economies where manual labor is relatively important, improved nutritional status leads to higher labor productivity.[17] Very low levels of BMI have also been found to be associated with poor health and difficulty in performing physical labor (Kimhi 2003).

In addition, it seems likely that poor nutrition affects labor productivity because it diminishes cognitive ability and the capacity to undertake and to benefit from education. Behrman, Alderman, and Hoddinott (2004) sum up the modern evidence on childhood ability:

Poorly nourished children tend to start school later, progress through school less rapidly, have lower schooling attainment and perform less well on cognitive achievement tests when older, including into adulthood. These associations appear to reflect significant and substantial effects in poor populations even when statistical methods are used to control for the behavioural determinants of pre-school malnutrition. In productivity terms, the magnitudes of these effects are likely to be substantial, easily exceeding the effects of height on productivity even if the indirect effect of height on wages mediated by the relationship between height and schooling is included. (Behrman, Alderman, and Hoddinott 2004, pp. 372–373)

More broadly, severe malnutrition leads to "deficits in cognitive development ... Malnourished children score more poorly on tests of cognitive function, have poorer psychomotor development and fine motor skills, have lower activity levels, interact less frequently in their environments and fail to acquire skills at normal rates" (2004, pp. 368–369).

---

[17] It may therefore be expected that the relationship between height and earnings will diminish over time in a typical country which is undergoing economic development.

Such relationships between nutritional status and cognitive ability do not exist only in very malnourished populations. Richards *et al.* (2001, p. 199) use the 1946 British birth cohort to show that:

Birth weight was significantly and positively associated with cognitive ability at age 8 ... between the lowest and highest birthweight categories after sex, father's social class, mother's education and birth order was controlled for. This association was evident across the normal birthweight range (>2.5 kg) and so was not accounted for exclusively by low birth weight. The association was also observed at ages 11, 15, and 26, and weakly at age 43, although these associations were dependent on the association at age 8. Birth weight was also associated with education, with those of higher birth weight more likely to have achieved higher qualifications, and this effect was accounted for partly by cognitive function at age 8.

Case and Paxson (2008, p. 503) put the argument clearly, after surveying a range of evidence: "the height premium in earnings is largely due to the positive association between height and cognitive ability, and it is cognitive ability rather than height that is rewarded in the labor market." Similarly, some modern evidence suggests that the connection between early health and cognitive ability persists throughout life. As Case and Paxson (2009, p. 104) put it: "We find evidence that the burden of disease in early life – measured using either mortality rates by cause or the overall infant mortality rate – is significantly associated with performance on cognitive tests in old age."

On the basis of all this evidence from the modern world, it seems highly likely that populations in the past, with high levels of malnutrition, suffered from low productivity not simply because of diminished physical strength but also because of diminished cognitive ability or intelligence. The relative contribution of these two potential causes of low productivity may be impossible to determine, but they are likely to have reinforced each other.

This is such a potentially contentious statement – particularly when applied to differences in stature between and within modern populations – that the argument needs to be spelled out. It is assumed that all human populations have equal potential which will be fulfilled under conditions of optimal nutritional status – even if that state has possibly never been achieved. (As always, there will in every population be a range of ability around the mean.) For the reasons just discussed, poorer than optimal nutritional status will lead to stunting and wasting and to diminished cognitive ability among infants and children. Education and training can enhance capability, even among malnourished populations, but poor educational opportunities – typical of so much of the world – will exacerbate or at least fail to mitigate earlier disadvantage. Thus a combination of environmental circumstances are likely to lead to the observation that – on average – more stunted and wasted populations will have lower cognitive ability than less stunted and wasted populations. This will affect the relative productivity of those populations.

Nutritional status, finally, affects the time of death. This is both because malnutrition in old age can affect the body's ability to combat disease, but also because of the evidence of such studies as those by Barker (1998) and Waaler (1984) that very early life experiences, of the kind which lead to stunting and wasting, influence expectation of life. Even the deprivation experienced by disadvantaged sections of developed nations today, mild though it is by historical standards, has very large effects on expectation of life. As just one example among many, Kuh *et al.* (2002, p. 1080) utilize the 1946 British birth cohort to examine the mortality experience of men and women who have lived, throughout their lives, in a welfare state in one of the richest countries in the world. They find, nevertheless, that:

Estimates from a model including father's social class and adult social class and their non-significant interaction indicate that those in manual households in childhood and young adulthood have almost a threefold increase in mortality compared with those in non-manual households at each time. Study members who experienced upward social mobility or downward social mobility had intermediate rates. The contrast using home ownership was even more noticeable; those from manual origins who did not own their home as young adults had an almost fivefold increase in mortality compared with those from non-manual origins who became owner occupiers. When smoking was included in the model, the effects weakened slightly but remained significant.

Such a modern British cohort has a life expectation of over 70 years. The average expectation of life at birth of men and women born in England at the end of the seventeenth century was about 38 years. This was, in fact, a substantial improvement on the situation only 20 years earlier, since Wrigley estimates that the birth cohort of 1681–1685 had an expectation of life of only 31.27 years (2004, p. 64, Table 3.1). This improvement continued during the eighteenth century, but much more slowly and with substantial fluctuations – for example to a figure of only 25.34 for those born in 1721–1731 – through the eighteenth century. During that century, perinatal mortality and maternal mortality both improved substantially – Wrigley (2004, p. 83) describes it as a "remarkable" change in which "the period immediately before birth, birth itself and the period immediately after birth became radically less dangerous to both mother and child" – and there was significant change in infant but not in child mortality. Adult mortality as a whole greatly improved (Wrigley 2004, p. 80).

The demographers' symbol for expectation of life at birth, e_0, is not as illuminating in historical periods as it is today, because of the very high levels of mortality in early life. Provided a man or woman survived this early mortality, his or her average age at death was substantially higher; although in the 1680s in England men or women who had reached the age of 25 lived on average for only another 28 years, this improved to at least 38 years by the end of the eighteenth century (Wrigley 2004, p. 80). However, this does not imply that there was no connection between early life conditions and later life mortality; on the contrary, the experience of the survivors of early life mortality continued to affect their health, productivity, and life chances until their deaths. The increase in life expectancy, therefore, tells us something about the experience of those men and women during their infancy and childhood.

It is this insight – drawn from the epidemiological work of Barker and, more broadly, from the experience of a number of longitudinal studies – that leads to a reframing of economic and social history in terms of the histories of successive generations. Demographers are familiar, of course, with one of the stock tools of their trade, the life table, which sets out the demographic experience of a cohort. But life tables have normally been seen as descriptive rather than explanatory and, more important, economic and social historians have not utilized them in describing or analyzing the experience of groups of people. By contrast, most historical statistics are presented as annual snapshots, even if it is accepted that they are the outcome of dynamic processes. This is not the only way to depict reality.

The evidence which has been presented briefly above, about the long-term effects of nutritional status, the impact of nutritional status on labor productivity and labor-force participation, and the relationship between early life experience on mortality, suggests an alternative approach. This is to amalgamate evidence on health, longevity, and work effort so as to consider the potential output of successive generations.

The experience of England during the "long" eighteenth century from 1681 to 1841 is particularly interesting because of the unusually rapid increase in population which occurred. In the period as a whole, "the English population almost trebled in size, from 5.1 to 14.9 million" (Wrigley 2004, p. 65), but this was the product of extremely slow growth, of about 0.2 percent per annum, from 1681 to 1741, followed by very rapid growth, of 1.01 percent per annum, for the period from 1741 to 1841. Wrigley and Schofield argue that the main reason for this increase was changes in fertility, although changes in mortality – such as the reductions in perinatal and maternal mortality, and in stillbirths (described above) – were significant; this view of the process, though disputed by some, now represents the consensus. Whatever the balance of causes between fertility (including nuptiality) and mortality, it is clear that the English population of the early eighteenth century – malnourished as it was – was experiencing startling and probably unprecedented change, in which far more people came to live far longer than in the immediate past.

Despite the dramatic demographic events of the period, it has become the consensus among economic historians that economic growth, in the sense of the growth of real output per capita, was very slow indeed. Indeed, in a recent survey, Mokyr concludes that "little if any real per capita growth can be discerned in Britain before 1830 ... As a macro-economic phenomenon, then, the Industrial Revolution in its 'classical years', 1760–1830, stands today diminished and weakened" (2004, pp. 1–2).

On the other hand, if one employs – as is done in Chapters 4, 5, and 6 below – evidence on food inputs, nutritional status, mortality, and their correlates to examine the growth in output of successive generations in the eighteenth and nineteenth centuries, it is clear that it was considerable. Further research is needed, unfortunately, to be more precise about the change in output from generation to generation, but it is clear that the extent of technophysio evolution, and hence of rising productivity, in the eighteenth and early nineteenth century was considerable and perhaps greater than is implied by the conventional measures of per capita income or output.

It is possible to give an illustration of the potential benefits of exploring the historical evidence of changes in height and combining it with

Table 1.1 *Mean height of military recruits by birth cohort, 1745–1749 and 1800–1804 (cm)*

Age	Birth 1745–49	Birth 1800–04	% change	Absolute change (cm)
18	160.76	166.34	3.47	5.58
19	161.37	167.69	3.92	6.32
20	161.29	168.48	4.46	7.19
21	162.97	169.11	3.77	6.14
22	166.14	169.62	2.09	3.48
23	167.34	170.31	1.77	2.97
24–29	165.66	169.57	2.36	3.91
Mean change			3.12	5.08

modern evidence of the relationship of wages to productivity. Unfortunately, it is impossible to estimate the height of the English population in 1700, since the earliest reliable estimates from military records date only from recruits born in the first half of the 1740s (Floud, Wachter, and Gregory 1990, Table 4.1). At that time, however, average heights were as shown in Table 1.1, which also reports heights of cohorts born in 1800.[18]

While the percentage changes in heights appear small, they are large by historical standards. In addition, one can apply the modern evidence, compiled by Schultz and others (Schultz 2005) to illustrate their potential impact. The comparison is particularly apposite because the heights of British military recruits in the middle of the eighteenth century were considerably less than those of the male workers in West Africa and Brazil studied by Schultz (though more comparable to those from Vietnam). However, by the end of the eighteenth century, the absolute levels of heights in the historical and modern samples were very

---

[18] Komlos (1993a; 1993b; 2004) has thrown doubt on the height estimates by Floud, Wachter, and Gregory (1990) for the later eighteenth century. He uses an alternative statistical technique, which involves discarding a large proportion of observations, to conclude that English heights fell at the end of the eighteenth century, and attributes this to a Malthusian crisis. Floud, Wachter, and Gregory (1993) defend their estimates. See Chapter 2 for further discussion of this issue.

similar.[19] Even if, as is sometimes postulated, there are diminishing returns to nutritional improvements, it is unlikely that they can have operated at such low absolute height levels. Recall that Schultz concluded that an additional one centimeter of height was associated, in modern cross-sections, with an increase of wages of 5–10 percent. If, and they are two very large caveats indeed, such relationships between height and wages exist also over time and if wages are an accurate reflection of productivity, then Table 1.1 suggests that increases in height in the second half of the eighteenth century could have been associated with large increases in productivity.

Modern evidence can also be used to assess the implications of other features of change in the eighteenth century. Expectation of life at age 25 is estimated, for example, to have increased by 10 years. This compares well with the estimate by Barro and Sala-i-Martin that "a 13 year increase in life expectancy raises the annual growth rate by 1.4 percent" (Morand 2005, p. 243). All this evidence accords with the view that, during the eighteenth century, the economy was experiencing extensive rather than intensive growth; in other words, the overall output was growing through demographic, agricultural, and behavioral changes – the last in the sense of changes to the number of hours worked, although it is debatable whether working hours increased quite as dramatically as some authors have been inclined to suggest (cf. Voth 2000, p. 123; Voth 2001; and Chapter 2 below).

The period is clearly one of the substantial accumulation of human capital. This occurred through extensions in the average working life – increasing the return on educational and other infrastructure investment and allowing accumulated experience to be applied to economic activity – and through increases in health and stature arising from improved nutritional status, indicating improvements in cognitive ability. It is possible to speculate, as Mokyr has done from a different direction (1990; 2004), that it is this accumulation of human capital that allows for the subsequent achievements of the Industrial Revolution of the nineteenth century.

To sum up, work output in the past was limited by the amount of energy available for it, by the physical and intellectual capacity or

---

[19] The heights of male 25–29 year olds (Schultz 2005, p. 276, Table 10.3) were, for Ghana in 1987–1989, 169.46 cm; for Côte d'Ivoire in 1985–1987, 170.11 cm; for Brazil in 1989, 168.90 cm; and for Vietnam in 1992–1993, 162.10 cm.

inheritance of members of a generation, by the effects of disease during life, and by limited lifespans. All these are closely related to and, in past ages, limited by nutritional status. This implies, in its turn, that the work effort of past generations was limited by the food supply – interacting with the disease environment and sources of income – available to each and every member of that generation, both during infancy, childhood, and adolescence, and as an adult. This constraint was at its most obvious at times of famine, when climatic conditions or problems of distribution limited the supply of food and increased the impact of disease. It used to be thought that "mortality crises" caused by famine had significant demographic effects and, in some cases, they did. But far more pervasive and insidious was the simple fact that large sections of the population were permanently malnourished and therefore permanently unable to work to what would have been, in other more favorable circumstances, their full capacity. Food, in other words, must be seen not simply as an item of consumption, but as a fuel for future work effort, one which, in past centuries, was often inadequate. The food supply is therefore, for all kinds of reasons, crucial to the concept of technophysio evolution and is considered at more length below.

2. The work of a generation, measured both in hours, days, and weeks of work and in work intensity, when combined with the available technology, determines the output of that generation in terms of goods and services.

The work output of human beings does not spring simply from their physical and mental effort or from the food intake that makes this effort possible; it is crucially assisted by technology, the product of their, and previous generations', ingenuity and investment. This relationship forms the second proposition in the schema of technophysio evolution.

This proposition is much more familiar than the first, but still not entirely self-evident. Three aspects in particular deserve further discussion: the relationship between supply and demand; the definition of "the available technology"; the definition of "output." All have a long history of discussion by economists and historians, which needs to be rehearsed briefly for a wider audience.

First, the second proposition implies that output is determined by the supply of work effort and technology, rather than, in the short run, by the demand for goods and services in the economy. This often seems questionable in a world which is used to economic cycles of "boom and bust" and to the manipulation by governments of public expenditure and interest rates in an effort to maintain economic stability. A great deal of economic analysis, most famously by John Maynard Keynes in relation to the slump of the 1930s, has been devoted to the inadequacy in such circumstances of aggregate demand and the measures that can be taken to stimulate demand in order to produce economic growth. Fluctuations in demand clearly do affect the short- and medium-term behavior of an economy and, in so doing, produce significant periods of misery or depression, characterized by unemployment and waste of resources, as well as other periods of prosperity and full employment.

However, the focus of this book, and of this second proposition of technophysio evolution, is on the long term and, in such an analysis, it is appropriate to focus on the long-term capacity of the economy, which is constrained by supply-side factors such as the number of people, their ability to work, and the equipment which they have available. The first proposition, discussed above, suggested that nutritional status is a major constraint on the work of a generation throughout its life, and even further through the effects on future generations. Neither the nutritional status of a generation, nor the technology with which it works, can change rapidly and the focus, in discussion of such factors, is properly on the long term.

A possible source of confusion, in this connection, is that the symptoms of a deficiency of aggregate demand and of constraints of supply can, in certain circumstances, be the same. Many observers in the sixteenth and seventeenth centuries discussed what was later to be called unemployment, drawing attention to the number of beggars or those dependent on poor relief. They pointed also to what they regarded as the laziness of the laboring classes, prone to extend the weekend by taking "Saint Monday" off from work or seizing other excuses to reduce their working week; this occurred despite apparently low wages which might have encouraged the seeking of work whenever and wherever it could be found. This phenomenon, later called underemployment, has been explained in terms of poor organization of the economy, for example in an inability to deal with the effects of climate on the distribution of goods, but also as simple distaste for work or, in economic jargon, a "high leisure preference." Voth (2000) documents the extension of working hours in the eighteenth century and the demise of "Saint Monday" and indeed most religious holidays, ascribing the change principally to the desire of the working population to expand their money incomes in response to the increasing availability of durable consumption goods.[20]

However, it is also possible that unemployment and underemployment in the period was, at least in part, the result of constraints on the ability of the population to work, because of poor nutritional status and the ravages of infectious and chronic disease. The stunting and wasting of the population – described in the previous section – indicates that many people, particularly at the lower end of the income distribution, would simply have been incapable of sustained manual labor for all or a large part of a day. They would not have died, but they would have been able to work only for limited periods. This would have reduced even further an already low wage and, in its turn, limited food consumption to serve as fuel for further work effort.

Strauss and Thomas (1998) throw doubt on the existence of this phenomenon, sometimes known as that of the "efficiency wage," in the modern underdeveloped world, although this is disputed by Dasgupta (1997). In addition, cyclical unemployment, caused by demand deficiency, can still be superimposed on long-term underemployment; the condition of the working classes can be further worsened, on relatively rare occasions, by famines or plagues, but these have relatively short-term effects. What is really constraining and determining the long-term growth of the economy is the underlying supply of people and the work that, limited or enabled by their nutritional status, they are able to do.

The second feature of the second proposition is that it places considerable emphasis on "the available technology" without explaining what that is and how it has become available. The latter question will be taken up shortly in discussing the third proposition. Here, it is necessary to explain that by "the available technology" is meant the entire apparatus of the economy which helps to translate human brain and muscle power into work and then into goods and services. "Technology" in modern parlance is often associated with complex machines, but the word is being used here with much wider connotations, ranging from simple hand tools to complex astronomical instruments and incorporating the buildings, such as watermills or iron-foundries, in which the tools were used and in which work took place. To introduce another

---

[20] An earlier, but still highly influential, treatment of these topics is that of E. P. Thompson (Thompson 1967).

piece of terminology, the technology available to a society is made up of a series of techniques applied to the production of different goods and services.

It is important not to underestimate the technology available to Britain, Europe, and North America in the first half of the eighteenth century. Recent research has documented the impressive growth of a wide range of capital and consumer goods – buildings, clothing, foot-wear, pottery, glass, agricultural machinery, transport infrastructure, etc. – which became available in the eighteenth century, much of it associated with new production methods. In addition, the development over several centuries of an extensive network of world trade gave access, on the part of each of these economies, to technologies of production in many other parts of the world; the fashion among the upper classes of eighteenth-century Europe for "chinoiserie" is just one example of the way in which this global network altered consumption patterns and gave access to a new technology.

Technology is not, of course, evenly spread across an economy. Tools and machinery replaced or assisted human effort in some activities earlier than in others, so that in any economy there is a co-existence between highly labor-intensive activities – such as teaching – and highly capital-intensive activities – such as power generation. This was true in the early eighteenth century, as it is today, but what characterized the economy of that period was the low level, compared to today, of labor productivity – output per head or per worker employed – even when making use of the best available techniques of production. In addition, as described above, recent research suggests that, in Britain at any rate, the overall – though not necessarily the sectoral – growth of labor productivity was low, if not non-existent, for much of the eighteenth century.

The third feature of the second proposition which requires discussion is the definition of the word "output." As was described briefly in examining the concepts of nutritional status and standard of living, the success and utility of the development of national income analysis has had one unfortunate consequence in limiting the concept of output to matters which are the subject of monetized transactions. This is particularly problematic in a world such as that of the eighteenth century, in which much output in the form of, for example, food from gardens or home-made clothing, was produced within the household. It should, therefore, be included within the definition of output, if only because it contributed to the overall food supply and thus to the nutritional status of the population.

So too must the provision of services. Economists have been emphasizing for over two centuries, at least since the time of Adam Smith, that there is no distinction in principle between the production of food, such as a tonne of wheat, the production of manufactured goods, such as a car, or the production of a service, such as an accountant completing a tax return. All three represent the product of work effort and the available technology and all are done because someone is prepared to pay for them. It is therefore entirely meaningless for politicians to say, as they sometimes do – unconsciously harking back to the mercantilist theories which preceded Adam Smith – that our economy is "dependent" on the production and sale overseas of manufactures and that the sale of brainpower by teachers or lawyers is somehow inferior. Services must be included within the definition of output, both today and in an economy such as that of the early eighteenth century in which domestic and personal service, both within and outside the household, was so important a form of economic activity. Services were certainly not as important a component of work activity at the beginning of the eighteenth century as they were later to become. In all the economies considered in this book, the leading role in 1700 was taken by agriculture, although "Britain already had a relatively large proportion of people in non-agricultural activities, both full-time artisans and part-time in cottage industries" (Mokyr 2004, p. 17). The proportion of the population engaged in agriculture probably fell from 74 percent in 1500 to only 45 percent in 1750, a level among the lowest in Europe (Allen 2004, p. 116).

3. The output of a generation is partly determined by its inheritance from past generations; it also determines its standard of living and its distribution of income and wealth, together with the investment it makes in technology.

The implication of propositions one and two, combined with evidence about the state of the economies of Britain, Europe, and North America in the early eighteenth century, is that the standard of living of the population was low and constrained by its nutritional status, even with the application to production of an increasing range of techniques. A further implication is that low output levels constrained the investment that could be made in more techniques, so as to enhance output for current and future generations.

It is important to refer again, at this point, to the salience of the distribution of income and wealth across the different members of a given population. In much of the preceding discussion, this has been ignored in the interests of simplicity, although reference was made to the fact that nutritional status was particularly poor – to the point that it constrained work – among those at the bottom of the income distribution. Apart from this, the discussion has considered the total output of a generation and, on occasion, output per head – total output divided by numbers in the population.

In reality, however, societies at the beginning of the eighteenth century were highly unequal in very many ways, to the point that a simple average – such as income per head – can be seriously misleading as a way of describing the society, unless it is accompanied by information on distribution around the average – such as the distribution of income and wealth. Thus these societies were characterized, to take a simple example, by a very small number of the very wealthy, a larger number of the "middling classes," and a very large number of the poor and working classes. This was such an important feature of these societies, to those who lived in them, that the distribution of income was the subject of perhaps the first example of social science investigation, Gregory King's enumeration of the population of England in 1688 (King 1696 [1973], pp. 48–49). Although there is no similar contemporary description of other European societies, it is likely that they were at least as unequal as British society in the early years of the eighteenth century, although the society of North America may have been somewhat more equal (see Chapters 2 and 3 below). There was thus an enormous difference between the income of an aristocrat and an agricultural laborer, a difference which we know from later evidence to have been reflected in their nutritional status, the size and shape of their bodies.

Floud, Wachter, and Gregory (1990) document, for example, the wide variation in height by social class; while the most dramatic differences were found between young boys recruited to the Royal Military Academy at Sandhurst and those from the London slums recruited by the Marine Society, clear and marked gradients in height existed by social class and even within working-class occupations.

Substantial parts of the generations which lived in the early eighteenth century were living essentially from hand to mouth, with incomes which constrained physical growth in their children and limited their own ability to undertake normal physical activity, let alone sustained work.

Such people – constituting a large fraction of the population – had no surplus, in fact a deficit, of income above immediate consumption needs. Moreover, it is likely that there were significant inequalities in consumption by gender and age within the family. By contrast, a small part of these generations had far more income, derived in many cases from inherited wealth, than they could conceivably require for immediate needs, whether for food or other items of consumption. This inequality becomes particularly important in determining how these societies transformed themselves – through the processes of economic growth and technophysio evolution – into the developed societies of today.[21]

Economic growth requires the creation of a surplus, above immediate needs for consumption and renewal – such as seed to be used for next year's planting – which can be invested in new techniques which will then help the society to raise its productivity. The relationship between investment, technological change, and the genesis of sustained economic growth is, to say the least, a complex one which has enthralled and puzzled many generations of economists. It has been very difficult, despite many studies of the process of technological change, to prove that there is a clear and quantifiable relationship between investment and innovation – in the sense of the adoption of a new technique – let alone with its invention. This is partly because these studies have shown most invention and innovation to be continuous and incremental, best described in the phrase "learning by doing," rather than the occasion of a single inventor shouting "eureka."

Despite these difficulties, it would be perverse to conclude that the economic growth which occurred during the eighteenth century in all three of the geographical areas considered in this book – very slow though it was – did not, at least by the end of the century, have something to do with what has been described as the "wave of gadgets" known to economic historians as the Industrial Revolution. Even in North America, where growth may have been equally due to an increase in knowledge about how to make use of the abundant land resources of the country, the introduction of new crops like cotton was intimately bound up with their use in the developing textile industries of Europe. In all these cases, the economic growth that was ultimately – over two centuries – to provide for the "escape from hunger" owed something to

---

[21] Dasgupta (1997) proposes a mechanism by which malnutrition leads to inequality.

the possession by a small fraction of the population of resources which could be invested in technological improvement (Mokyr 1990). We have not tried to defend the inequality of these societies, such as that of pre-Revolutionary France – or the consequent immiseration of much of their population – from an ethical perspective, so the statement that it also provided the capacity to invest is not a signal of approval; it is simply a judgment on the means by which, in the particular historical circumstances, economic growth was achieved.

At the same time, there is increasing evidence that – even during the so-called classical period of the English Industrial Revolution after 1750 – changes in technology proceeded mainly through very small improvements to existing techniques, rather than from major or path-breaking inventions. By definition, these improvements did not require, individually, significant investment funds. As Bruland puts it (2004, p. 146): "innovation was a broad process, pervasively embedded in many industries, even those that were essentially matters of hand technology." There was, she suggests, a "general social propensity to innovate." It seems unlikely that this suddenly sprang into life in 1750 and likely, therefore, that English society of the early eighteenth century was already benefiting, in terms of increased efficiency and improved living standards, from a general willingness to try out new ideas. Where this came from, in contrast to the situation in other economies at the time, is a much more difficult issue to resolve.

4. The standard of living of a generation determines, through its fertility and the distribution of income and wealth, the nutritional status of the next generation.

The fourth proposition follows on from all that has gone before, but adds a new factor in drawing attention to the importance of fertility. Decisions by men and women, about marriage (or in modern times, cohabitation) and about the number of children they will have, affect the distribution of resources within the family and, potentially, the nutritional status of the children. These decisions are not taken in a vacuum; instead, the collective behavior of a generation, in its marriage and fertility patterns as in many other ways, reflects a series of decisions in response partly to economic circumstances and opportunities. One such influence is their current and expected standard of living, which will itself depend on the overall standard of living and on the prevailing distribution of income and wealth.

There is now a consensus that the primary determinant of population growth in England in the eighteenth century was changing fertility, although changes in mortality were by no means unimportant; Wrigley (2004, pp. 68–69) estimates that fertility change was responsible for about 64 percent of the increase in the intrinsic growth rate of the population between 1666 and 1841. Careful analysis through family reconstitution suggests that fertility rose through a combination of an increase in the fertility rates of both married and unmarried women, earlier marriage, and a reduction in the proportion of women who remained unmarried (Wrigley 1998; Wrigley 2004, p. 69). Particularly notable was an increase in illegitimacy and prenuptial conceptions. Together, fertility trends – and particularly the first marriage rate – in England follow what is thought to have been the upward trend in real wages, presumably because improving economic circumstances encouraged marriage and childbearing.

Despite the evidence of changing marriage age and thus the response in fertility behavior to economic circumstance, it is obvious that poverty and malnutrition do not stop people from having children or from seeking to care for them as well as possible. However, it is equally obvious that poor and malnourished adults will find it difficult to care for their children, that the resources of the family will be spread more thinly, and that the children will therefore have a larger than average chance of themselves being malnourished.

In addition, as was argued above, there is direct evidence that the well-being of a mother affects the life chances of a child. This occurs partly through the likelihood that a wasted and stunted mother will have a child of low birth weight; such a mother is likely to have a small pelvis, associated either with low birth weight or, in extreme cases, difficulties during the birth. Such children will have a lesser chance of survival in infancy; in addition, through the longer-term influences of deprivation in the fetal period they will suffer from an increased chance of developing life-threatening or chronic diseases in adult life. As Osmani and Sen (2003) point out, this situation is exacerbated, in the modern world, by gender inequality, in which female children and women suffer discrimination in the distribution of food and other resources within the family. This leads to maternal undernutrition, then to low birth weight and to poor health and increased mortality in the later life of the children. While this is a particular feature of South Asia today, demonstrated for example in the lowest average birth weights, it is likely to have been a much more widespread feature of societies in the past.

The mechanisms by which the standard of living of one generation affects the standard of living and nutritional status of the next generation are therefore clear. But in fact the process is one which lasts over several generations. Wasting and stunting in a mother are likely to have arisen partially from her own deprivation before and after birth and, therefore, to have been influenced by the nutritional status and standard of living of her own mother. It is therefore in no way fanciful to see the influence of the health and welfare of grandparents in the bodies of their grandchildren and the effect may be even longer lasting. As Horrell, Humphries, and Voth (2001, p. 352) conclude from their reanalysis of data about recruits to the Marine Society in London in the eighteenth century:

Analysis of this sample provides evidence that deprivation in childhood conditioned human capital acquisition, with ongoing adverse effects on labor market opportunities, which confined the child to low-paid, low-status jobs. But perhaps the effects go further; their disadvantaged labor market position implies that when these fatherless boys in turn become parents their children would be at a disadvantage in the acquisition of skilled, better–paid jobs. Regression analysis reveals that, when other factors are controlled for, the nearest relative's qualification level often has a significant effect on a boy's height with higher qualification levels feeding into greater height attainment. Again this demonstrates the impact of parental attainment on human capital acquisition and provides further evidence of the intergenerational transmission of disadvantage.

Deprivation and disadvantage can arise from biological, economic, or cultural factors or, in most cases, from the interaction of all three. Sometimes, indeed, different factors may work in different directions. Such processes may account for a phenomenon of child growth which has been observed on a number of occasions; it can take several generations of prosperity before a community throws off its history of deprivation. The most graphic illustration of this phenomenon can be found in the Japanese-American and Italian-American populations of the modern United States. In these communities, it is commonly at least two generations before the young people take on the bodily characteristics of the host population. They have clearly not been constrained by any genetic factor, since the time period of two or three generations during which they do attain the size or shape of the host community is far too short for any genetic modification. But it is therefore puzzling that the transformation – in these cases of several centimeters of average height – does not occur more rapidly. One possible social or cultural explanation lies in diet or other attributes of care, which persist within the immigrant community and take some time to change. An alternative, or complementary, biological explanation is that there is a limit to the amount of change that can take place between generations, presumably because the nutritional status and standard of living of one generation constrains the change that can take place within the next generation (Osmani and Sen 2003). An alternative biological mechanism is proposed by Cole (2003) who believes that there is a physiological limit on the amount of growth in a given generation. However, if this is so, it is becoming clear that the constraint does not apply to weight gain, since the intergenerational increase in weight among South Asian populations is now very considerable and rapid and is leading to a serious problem of obesity in the younger generations.[22]

5. And so on *ad infinitum*

The five propositions which make up the schema of technophysio evolution are essentially circular, a never-ending process of influence from one generation to the next, and the next, and the next. Even if the logic and evidence which supports these propositions – and they are

---

[22] The problem is not confined to South Asia. Ulijaszek (2003) shows that mean BMI of women in the Cook Islands rose from 27.2 in 1952 to 28.9 in 1966 to 33.8 in 1996 (pp. 128–129). Similarly, Smith *et al.* (2003) find in a study of children of Mayan origin in the United States that: "Immigration from low-income countries to the US generally increases immigrants' nutritional intake, access to health care and clean water, but it also introduces some unhealthy lifestyle patterns, such as diets dense in energy, especially fat, and little regular physical activity" (p. 146). Maya-American children are 10.2 cm taller than their Guatemalan counterparts and this difference is not due to genetic change nor selective migration, about 60 percent of the height gain being due to leg length (p. 149). Maya children have more stunting, but less overweight and obesity; Maya-Americans, by contrast, are likely to be overweight compared to white children. But children of parents who had not assimilated, shown by speaking Spanish, were less likely to be overweight, which suggests that those who had assimilated were at higher risk. "If we use language as an indicator of assimilation, then this result is consistent with the hypothesis that a bicultural assimilation path generally results in healthier children. It also suggests the greater assimilation to American culture may place immigrant children at risk of weight problems" (p. 159). See also Popkin and Udry 1998.

admittedly controversial – is accepted, there are two major caveats which must be made at this stage and then explored throughout the remainder of the book.

The first is that, since the schema is designedly circular, only historical circumstances can determine where on the circle any process of change begins. In the formulation above, changes to the size and shape of the body as indicators of nutritional status are given pride of place, but the circle could equally easily be formulated to begin with proposition two, or three, or four. In this sense, the schema does not answer the question: "where did it all begin?" or even "which feature is most important at any one period?" All that it can do is to point to a dynamic system, in which both positive and negative feedback is possible and in which both have almost certainly occurred within the past three hundred years.

The second caveat is that the schema, designedly, does not attempt at this stage to estimate quantitatively the influence of one factor within it on another. This gap will trouble most economists, used to estimating elasticities; they want to know, not just that nutritional status affects the ability to work, but how much work effort changes in response to a 1 percent increase in height. In very similar vein, historians want to know how much of the decline in mortality in the late nineteenth century can be explained by improvements in nutritional status, how much by declines in the virulence of infectious disease, how much by investment in the infrastructure of public health such as drains and clean water supplies.

The remainder of this book will attempt both to flesh out and to diminish the force of these caveats, by providing historical evidence of the changes which are described as technophysio evolution and the factors which have influenced those changes. Where it is possible to answer questions about elasticities or the respective influence of one or other factor, they will be answered. But it should always be remembered that this book is extremely ambitious in seeking to encompass so many different aspects of history, economics, demography, and human biology – all normally treated separately – and that it is almost inevitable that the arguments will fail to satisfy all or some adherents of those disciplines.

2 | Investigating the interaction of biological, demographic, and economic variables from fragmentary data

The previous chapter raised various methodological issues about the estimation of food supplies and the heights of past populations. This chapter introduces a number of tools that are useful in the evaluation of the nutritional status of populations in the past. The theoretical foundation for these tools is contained in Appendix A at the end of this chapter, which combines biological and economic variables into an integrated explanation of the physiological component of long-term economic development.

In this chapter, we consider several tools that can be used to reconstruct the historical interrelationship between biological and economic factors from patchy sources of data. Among these tools are energy cost accounting, the size distribution of calories, and Waaler curves and surfaces. The chapter concludes by evaluating some possible scenarios of the distribution of calories available for work in Britain circa 1800, which serve as examples of applications of our methodology.

2.1 Food consumption (diet) and energy cost accounting

Some studies of improvements in nutritional status and the correlated secular decline in mortality make the unfortunate implicit assumption that diet alone determines nutritional status. Epidemiologists and nutritionists, however, are careful to distinguish between these terms. *Nutritional status* denotes the balance between the intake of nutrients and the claims against it. It follows that an adequate level of nutrition is not determined solely by *diet* – the level of nutrient intake – but varies with individual circumstances. Whether the diet of a particular individual is nutritionally adequate depends, in part, on his or her level of physical activity, the climate of the region in which he or she lives, and the extent of his or her exposure to various diseases. Nevin Scrimshaw has pointed out that the adequacy of a given level of iron consumption depends critically on whether an individual has hookworm (private communication).

Thus, a population's nutritional status may decline even as its consumption of nutrients rises if the extent of its exposure to infection or the degree of its physical activity is rising even more rapidly. It follows that the assessment of the contribution of nutrition to the decline in mortality requires measures of food consumption in addition to measures of the balance between food consumption and the claims on that consumption. To avoid confusion, we will use the term *diet* to designate nutrient intake only. All other references to nutrition, such as *nutritional status, net nutrition, nutrition, malnutrition*, and *undernutrition* will designate the balance between nutrient intake and the claims on that intake.

The principal indicators of net nutrition among adults are height and weight (or BMI). For children, the indicators are height for age, weight for age, and weight for height (Tanner 1990). The emphasis that we have placed on measures of body size does not mean that diet is unimportant. The level of the consumption of calories (and other nutrients per capita) affects the body size that can be sustained in the long run.[1] For example, during the eighteenth and early nineteenth centuries, the shortage of calories per capita severely limited the body size of the French, which put them at a high risk for death (see Section 2.3, below).

Diet is important for another aspect of the investigation of techno-physio evolution: it determines the level of energy available for work. Low levels of energy intake severely limit the ability to work. Not only are hours of work restricted, but the average intensity of labor per hour is restricted. (See Chapter 1 for an outline of the tenets of technophysio evolution.)

One of the most important aspects of the post-World War II studies of the economics of slavery was the discovery that slaves not only worked long hours (about 2,800 hours per year for the master and several hundred hours per year on their own account), but that the intensity of labor per hour was very high, especially on big plantations. To sustain such heavy levels of activity, slaves (both male and female) had to consume about 4,200 calories per capita. Such levels of energy intake and expenditure far exceeded the energy expenditure of the British and the French during the eighteenth and early nineteenth centuries (Fogel and Engerman 1974b; Sutch 1976; Fogel 1989; Metzer 1992; Olson 1992).

---

[1] As used here, the word *calorie* refers to the amount of heat required to raise one kilogram of water by one degree Celsius; also referred to as a *kcal*.

Large bodies, longer hours of labor, and more intense labor per hour are central aspects of both technophysio evolution and the Industrial Revolution (de Vries 1994; Voth 2001). The changes in intensity of labor have yet to be explored. That challenge is addressed in Chapter 3, and elsewhere in this book.

2.1.1 Energy cost accounting

In developed countries today – and even more so in the less-developed nations of both the past and the present – the basal metabolic rate (BMR) is the principal component of the total energy requirement. The BMR, which varies with age, sex, and body weight, is the amount of energy required to maintain the body while at rest; it is the amount of energy required to maintain body temperature and to sustain the functioning of the heart, liver, brain, and other organs. For adult males aged 20–39 living today in moderate climates, BMR normally ranges between 1,350 and 2,000 kcal per day, depending on height and weight (Quenouille *et al.* 1951; Davidson *et al.* 1979, pp. 19–25; FAO/WHO/UNU 1985, pp. 71–72). Because the BMR does not allow for the energy required to eat and digest food or for essential hygiene, an individual cannot survive on the calories needed for basal metabolism. The energy required for these additional essential activities over a period of 24 hours is estimated at 0.27 of BMR. In other words, a survival diet is 1.27 BMR. Such a diet, it should be emphasized, contains no allowance for the energy required for earning a living, preparing food, or any activity beyond what is needed for eating and essential hygiene. It is not sufficient to maintain long-term health, but represents the short-term maintenance level "of totally inactive dependent people" (FAO/WHO/UNU 1985, p. 73).

Energy requirements beyond maintenance primarily depend on how individuals spend time besides sleeping, eating, and maintaining essential hygiene. This residual time will normally be divided between work and such discretionary activities as walking, community activities, games, optional household tasks, and athletics or other forms of exercise. For a typical well-fed adult male engaged in heavy work – who needs 3,490 kcal per day – BMR and maintenance require about 35 percent of the total energy, work 59 percent, and discretionary activity just 6 percent. For a well-fed adult male engaged in sedentary work (an office clerk, for example) – who needs 2,580 kcal per day – a typical distribution would be: BMR and maintenance 51 percent, work 28 percent, and discretionary activity 22 percent (note that numbers do not add up to 100 due to rounding). For a 25-year-old adult male engaged in subsistence farming in contemporary Asia – who needs 2,780 kcal per day – a typical distribution would be: BMR and maintenance 42 percent, work 44 percent, and discretionary activity 14 percent.[2] Similar distributions of energy requirements have been developed for women, children, and adolescents of both sexes. Another measure, the physical activity ratio (PAR), consists of the energy requirements for any of a large number of specific activities and is expressed as a multiple of the BMR requirement per minute of activity (see Table 2.1 for some examples).

In order to standardize for the age and sex distribution of a population, it is convenient to convert the per capita consumption of calories into consumption per equivalent adult male aged 20–39 (referred to as a *consuming unit*). This transformation involves weighting persons at each age and sex relative to adult males aged 20–39. Table 2.2 gives an example of this procedure for the French population of 1806. In this case, average consumption is about 0.7658 of an equivalent adult male aged 20–39 in 1806. Toutain (1971) has estimated that per capita caloric consumption in France circa 1806 was 1,848 calories (see Section 3.3 below for more details about Toutain's estimate and its adjustment), which is equivalent to about 2,400 calories per consuming unit $(1,848 \div 0.7658 = 2,413)$.[3]

Energy cost accounting is usually worked forward, going from a list of activities to an estimate of the average daily caloric requirement, but such accounting can also be worked backward, going from the average

---

[2] The level of BMR and distributions of energy requirements depend on the assumption of body weight, height, and BMI of a typical individual in each group. The assumption used in the above calculations is as follows: the well-fed adult male who engaged in heavy work was 35 years old, weighed 65 kg, had a height of 1.72 m and a BMI of 22; the well-fed adult male who engaged in sedentary work was 25 years old, weighed 65 kg, had a height of 1.72 m and a BMI of 22; and the adult male who engaged in subsistence farming in contemporary Asia was 25 years old, weighed 58 kg, had a height of 1.61 m and a BMI of 22.4 (Source: FAO/WHO/UNU 1985, Tables 9–11).

[3] There are similar ways to standardize for the number of population at various ages or convert female population into equivalent units of adult males. For example, Allen (2009) estimates that a British family of five in the period of the Industrial Revolution contained the equivalent of three adult males. See Section 4.4 in Chapter 4 for more discussion of Allen's work.

Table 2.1 *Examples of physical activity ratio (PAR) for males and females: energy requirements of common activities expressed as a multiple of the basal metabolic rate (BMR)*

Activity	Males	Females
Sleeping	1.0	1.0 (i.e., BMR * 1.0)
Standing quietly or eating	1.4	1.5
Strolling	2.5	2.4
Walking at a normal pace	3.2	3.4
Walking with a 10 kg load	3.5	4.0
Walking uphill at a normal pace	5.7	4.6
Sitting and sewing	1.5	1.4
Weaving	2.0	
Sharpening axes	1.7	
Sharpening machete	2.2	
Sweeping floor	1.7	
Scrubbing floor	3.2	
Cooking	1.8	1.8
Hunting birds	3.4	
Tailoring	2.5	
Carpentry	3.5	
Common labor in building trade	5.2	
Milking cows by hand	2.9	
Hoeing		5.3–7.5
Collecting and spreading manure	6.4	
Binding sheaves	5.4–7.5	3.3–5.4
Uprooting sweet potatoes	3.5	3.1
Weeding	2.5–5.0	2.9
Plowing	4.6–6.8	
Cleaning house		2.2
Child care		2.2
Threshing		4.2
Laundry work		3.4
Making fence	2.7	
Tying fence post	2.7	
Digging holes for post	5.0	
Felling trees	7.5	

Sources: Durnin and Passmore 1967; FAO/WHO/UNU 1985.

Table 2.2 *Example of the procedure for computing the factor to convert caloric consumption per capita to caloric consumption per equivalent adult male: France 1806*

		Average caloric consumption at given ages as a proportion of that of those males aged 20–39			
Age intervals (1)	Proportion of persons in each age interval in 1806 (2)	Males (3)	Females (4)	Both sexes combined 0.5 * (Col.3 + Col.4) (5)	Age-specific caloric consumption per equivalent adult males Col.2 * Col.5 (6)
0–4	0.1224	0.4413	0.4367	0.4390	0.0537
5–9	0.1067	0.7100	0.6667	0.6884	0.0734
10–14	0.0984	0.9000	0.8000	0.8500	0.0836
15–19	0.0908	1.0167	0.7833	0.9000	0.0817
20–39	0.2875	1.0000	0.7333	0.8667	0.2492
40–49	0.1170	0.9500	0.6967	0.8234	0.0963
50–59	0.0894	0.9000	0.6600	0.7800	0.0697
60–69	0.0553	0.8000	0.5867	0.6934	0.0383
70+	0.0324	0.7000	0.5133	0.6067	0.0197
Factor for converting to consumption per equivalent adult male (Σ Column 6)					0.7658

Sources: Column 2: Computed from Bourgeois-Pichat 1965: 498. Columns 3 and 4: Computed from FAO/WHO 1971.
Notes: Entries in Column 5 may not always be equal to 0.5 × Col. 3 + 0.5 × Col. 4 because of rounding errors.

caloric intake to the residual (after deducting the survival level of energy) available for work and discretionary activities.

2.1.2 Sources of information on diet

Historical estimates of mean caloric consumption per capita have been derived from several principal sources: national food balance sheets, household consumption surveys, food allotments in hospitals, poor-houses, prisons, the armed forces, slave plantation records, and other lower-class institutions; food entitlements to widows in wills; and food allotment in noble households, abbeys, and similar wealthy institutions. National food balance sheets estimate the national supply of food by subtracting, from the national annual production of each crop, allowances for seed and feed, losses in processing, changes in inventories, and net exports (positive or negative) to obtain a residual of grains and vegetables available for consumption. In the case of meats, the estimates begin with the stock of livestock, which is turned into an annual flow of meat by using estimates of the annual slaughter ratio and live weight of each type of livestock. To estimate the meat available for consumption, it is necessary to estimate the ratio of dressed-to-carcass weight, as well as the distribution of dressed weight among lean meat, fat, and bones (Fogel and Engerman 1974b).

Household surveys are based upon interviews with families who are asked to recall their diets for a period as short as one day (the previous day) or their average diet over a period of a week, a month, a year, or an undefined period designated by their "normal diet." In recent times, such surveys may be based on a daily record of the food consumed, which is kept either by a member of the family or by a professional investigator. Institutional food allowances are based on food allotments for each class of individuals, laid down as a guide for provisions purchased by the institution (as in the case of victualing allowances for military organizations and daily diet schedules adopted in abbeys, noble households, schools, workhouses, hospitals, and prisons) as well as descriptions of meals actually served and actual purchases of food for given numbers of individuals over particular time periods (Oddy 1970; Appleby 1979; Dyer 1983; Morell 1983). Food entitlements of widows and aged parents were specified in wills and in contracts for maintenance between parents and children or other heirs (in anticipation of the surrender of a customary holding to an heir). Such food entitlements have been analyzed for England, France, the United States, and other countries at intermittent dates between the thirteenth century and the present (Hémardinquer 1970; McMahon 1981; Dyer 1983; Bernard [1969] 1975; for some studies of other countries, see Hémardinquer 1970 and Fogel 1986a).

Analysis of the estimates of average daily caloric consumption for recent times in nations for which national food balance sheets and household consumption studies (HCS) both exist indicates that estimates based on food balance sheets generally exceed the HCS estimates of caloric consumption (FAO 1983; Dowler and Seo 1985; Srinivasan

1992). Household consumption studies, especially historical ones, have several problems. They focus largely on lower-class diets and are generally judgment samples – samples that rely on the investigator's judgment about the underlying distribution. Hence, it is often difficult to know their precise location in the national distribution of calories and other nutrients. When these surveys include information on the income of households, it is possible to relate consumption to the income (or expenditures) of households (Crafts 1980; Woodward 1981; Shammas 1983; Shammas 1984; Fogel 1987; Shammas 1990).[4] Even then, there are uncertainties about where these households fit in the national distribution of income (see Chapter 3, below).

Sources of information about food allotments in institutions and about food entitlements in wills often suffer from a lack of information about the ages and sexes of the recipients. As Table 2.2 indicates, caloric requirements vary so significantly by age and sex that failure to standardize for these characteristics may cause misleading interpretations of the adequacy of diets, and shifts in the age–sex structure over time may bias the estimated trends in nutrition. Food wasting also varied greatly by institutions, so the proportion of the food supply actually consumed was probably much lower in noble households than in poor households (cf. Heckscher 1954, pp. 21–22, 68–70).

The long debate over the relative merits of food balance sheets and consumer surveys was finally resolved in the 1990s with the development of the doubly labeled water method. This technique measures the energy expenditure of individuals engaged in normal activity over a period of about two weeks. A measured amount of isotopes is introduced into the diet and then compared with the elimination of the isotopes measured over the same period (Schoeller 1990). Hundreds of experiments using this technique have been evaluated, and it has been judged to be highly reliable, with a measurement error rate of just 1 percent (cf. Black, Coward, and Cole 1996). The development of the doubly labeled water method made it possible to assess surveys of energy intake based on food diaries, next-day recall, and similar

---

[4] There is no direct information about how calories may have been distributed within a household; however, some scholars have suggested that heads of households may have consumed a proportionately greater share of available calories, to the detriment of wives and mothers (Osmani and Sen 2003; especially Harris 2008 for additional discussion).

methods. The food surveys suggested that consumption levels were generally less than energy expenditures, although for individuals in energy balance (not persistently losing or gaining weight), energy intake and expenditure should be equal.

The margin by which energy expenditures exceeded reported energy consumption is similar to the margin between food balance sheets and food surveys. Food balance sheets are the principal technique used by the Food and Agricultural Organization (FAO) to assess the annual consumption of energy and other nutrients of the member nations of the United Nations.[5] The United States Department of Agriculture (USDA) has also long used the food balance sheet method to assess trends in nutrient intakes (US Department of Agriculture 1953; US Department of Agriculture Agricultural Marketing Service 1958; Fogel and Engerman 1974a, pp. 92–99; cf. Fogel, Galantine, and Manning 1992, pp. 291–304; cf. Crawford 1992). In other words, the evidence indicates that food balance sheets are the best method for assessing trends in nutritional intake for both modern and historical populations.

2.2 Size distribution of calories

Size distributions of caloric consumption are one of the most powerful instruments for assessing the plausibility of proffered estimates of average diets. They not only give information about the implications of a given level of caloric consumption for morbidity and mortality rates, but they also indicate whether the calories available for work are consistent with the level of agricultural output and with the distribution of the labor force between agriculture and non-agriculture (Fogel 1997). Although national food balance sheets, such as those constructed by Toutain (1971) for France over the period 1781–1952, provide mean values of per capita caloric consumption, they do not produce estimates of the size distribution of the consumption of calories. Some investigators have sought to construct size distributions of calories from household consumption surveys. As most of these surveys were focused on the lower classes during the nineteenth century, it is necessary when using them to know from what centiles of either the national caloric or the national income distribution the surveyed

---

[5] See FAOSTAT, http://faostat.fao.org

households were drawn (see Section 3.1 for more discussion, below). However, historical household surveys often omit information on the ages and gender of the household members.

Three factors make it possible to estimate the size distributions of calories from the patchy evidence available to historians. First, studies covering a wide range of countries indicate that distributions of calories are well described by the lognormal distribution (Fogel 1994).[6] A lognormal distribution is the distribution of a random variable whose natural logarithm is normally distributed. The lognormal distribution is therefore right-skewed in natural numbers, while the normal distribution is symmetric and has a bell-shaped density curve, as seen in Figure 2.1(a).

Second, the variation in the distribution of calories – as measured by the coefficient of variation $(s/\overline{X})$ or the Gini coefficient (G) – is far more limited than the distribution of income. For clarification, Figure 2.1(b) presents two possible shapes of distributions of caloric consumption (solid) and income (dashed). Both distributions have the same mean; the difference in variation makes caloric consumption densely distributed around the mean, but income widely distributed. The left tail of the caloric distribution is sharply restricted by the requirement for basal metabolism and the prevailing death rate; at the high end, it is restricted by the human capacity to use energy and the distribution of body builds. The first restriction is more binding and gives rise to a right-skewed shape that is well approximated by the lognormal distribution. Consequently, the extent of the inequality of caloric distributions is pretty well bounded by $0.2 \leq s/\overline{X} \leq 0.4$ or equivalently $0.11 \leq G \leq 0.22$ (Aitchson and Brown 1966; FAO 1977; US National Center for Health Statistics 1977; Lipton 1983; also Appendix B for its calculation), while the distribution of incomes is generally much more unequal, so its Gini coefficient is typically bounded by 0.2 to 0.6 or higher.[7]

Third, when the mean of the distribution is known, the coefficient of variation (which together with the mean determines the distribution) can be estimated from information in either tail of the distribution.

---

[6] Logan (2006) tested Fogel's (1994) statement that the distribution of calories per capita is described by the lognormal distribution. Although Logan's distributional tests reveal that it is not lognormal, his graphical test shows that the lognormal assumption is appropriate to explain the distribution of calories per capita, and that departures from log normality are quite modest (Logan 2006).

[7] See Appendix B in this chapter for the parameters of the lognormal distribution and its relation to the Gini coefficient.

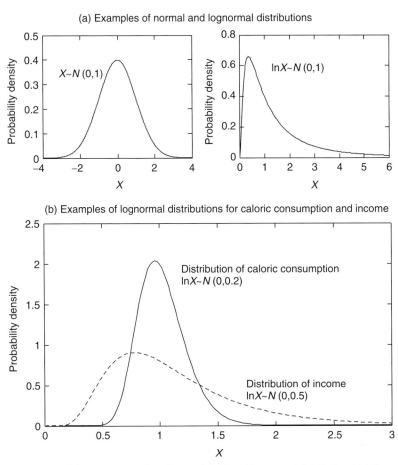

Note: Panel (a) shows examples of normal (left) and lognormal distribution (right). Panel (b) shows possible shapes of distributions of caloric consumption and income. In panel (b), we assume the same mean ($\mu = 0$) and different standard deviations ($\sigma_{calorie} = 0.2$ and $\sigma_{income} = 0.5$) in each log distribution as explained in the text.

Figure 2.1 Example of distribution

Fortunately, even in places and periods where little is known about ordinary people, there is a relative abundance of information about the rich. Although much remains to be learned about the ultrapoor of the eighteenth and nineteenth centuries, much has already been learned about them during the past quarter century, and such information is also helpful in resolving the problem of identifying the mean and coefficient of variation. However, at the bottom end, it is demographic information, particularly the death rate, that rather tightly constrains estimates of the proportion of the population whose average daily consumption of calories could have been below BMR or baseline maintenance. Estimates of consumption at the bottom end of the distribution are also constrained by the requirement that the energy available to the agricultural labor force is sufficient to produce the agricultural output.

Table 2.3 presents three possible size distributions of calories in France circa 1785 (see Appendix B for the procedures employed in the construction of these distributions). They are all lognormal distributions and are denominated in daily caloric consumption per consuming unit. They all have the same mean (2,413 kcal) but differ in their coefficients of variation. For reasons that will become clear in the discussion, distributions B and C are more egalitarian than the distribution of calories that now exists in the United States, although the US distribution of calories is itself far more egalitarian than that of its income or of the income of any major nation in the world today (Kuznets 1966; Paukert 1973; Sawyer 1976; Sayer and Cooper 2005). The degree of egalitarianism is measured by the coefficient of variation and the Gini ratio, which are closely related to each other (see Appendix B). Distribution A is the least egalitarian of the three distributions of calories, although with a Gini ratio of 0.22, it is far more egalitarian than the income distribution of any major nation. Distribution B, which has about the same coefficient of variation as the Philippines in 1965 (a Gini ratio of 0.17), is one of the most egalitarian of the known caloric distributions for less-developed nations today. Distribution C, with a coefficient of variation of 0.20 and a Gini ratio of 0.11, is considerably more egalitarian than any of the national distributions of calories currently available (FAO 1977; US National Center for Health Statistics 1977; Lipton 1983).

Consideration of Table 2.3 makes it possible to illustrate how the patchy evidence can be brought to bear in choosing which of the three distributions comes closest to representing the situation in France circa 1785. Even before we consider its consistency with the available historical evidence, Table 2.3 yields two important implications. The typical French adult male in circa 1785 was small with a height of 1.63 meters and a BMI of 19, which implies a weight of just 50.5 kg.[8] Then by Equation (A.7) in

---

[8] The trend of French adult male height is described in Table 2.5 below. As indicated in footnote 16 of Chapter 3, 19 is probably a least upper bound on the BMI of French consuming units in circa 1785.

Table 2.3 *Three alternative French distributions of the daily consumption of 2,413 kcal per consuming unit circa 1785, on the assumption of high, medium, and low levels of egalitarianism*

	Distribution A Low egalitarianism $\frac{s}{X} = 0.4$		Distribution B Medium egalitarianism $\frac{s}{X} = 0.3$		Distribution C High egalitarianism $\frac{s}{X} = 0.2$	
Decile Group (1)	Mean daily kcal consumption (2)	Cumulative % (3)	Mean daily kcal consumption (4)	Cumulative % (5)	Mean daily kcal consumption (6)	Cumulative % (7)
Highest	4,405	100	3,868	100	3,349	100
9th	3,350	82	3,141	84	2,910	86
8th	2,908	68	2,819	71	2,706	74
7th	2,600	56	2,589	59	2,554	63
6th	2,352	45	2,398	48	2,426	52
5th	2,134	35	2,227	38	2,308	42
4th	1,930	26	2,063	29	2,192	33
3rd	1,726	18	1,894	21	2,069	23
2nd	1,498	11	1,701	13	1,924	15
1st	1,139	5	1,381	6	1,671	7

Sources: The estimate of per capita consumption circa 1785 is from Toutain 1971: 1977.

Notes: His figure of 1,753 calories per capita was increased to 1,848 by taking account of some missing items and 10 percent gap between calories available for consumption and calories consumed, and then was converted into 2,413 calories per consuming unit on the assumption of 0.7658 consuming units per capita calculated in Table 2.2 (see Section 3.3 for discussion on Toutain's estimate). See Appendix A for the derivation of these figures. Columns 3, 5, and 7 show the percentage of total caloric consumption accounted for by consuming units at or below a given decile.

Appendix A, his BMR is estimated as 1,451 kcal and he requires at least 1,843 kcal for the body maintenance. Therefore, under distributions A and B, the individuals in the bottom 30 percent of French consumer units, and under distribution B, the bottom 20 percent, would have lacked the energy to participate regularly in the labor force. Those in the bottom 10 percent were below maintenance, and hence were starving to death.

Distribution A is unacceptable not only because it implies that the poorest 30 percent of French households had no energy available even for minimal sustained work, but also that most of those in the three bottom deciles were starving to death – about half of them quite rapidly because their intake was below basal metabolism. Such high proportions of starvation diets during normal times are inconsistent with what is known about the condition of the French lower classes during this period (Goubert 1973; Jones 1988; Dupâquier 1989). Distribution C, on the other hand, implies levels of consumption in the highest decile that are inconsistent with what is known about the conditions of rentiers as well as of the nobility and their retainers who made up that decile of consumers of calories. Not only did the type of food consumption (e.g., pickled, fresh, or aged) lead to significant losses of nutrients, but it is also likely that plate waste was high. Such losses probably reduced actual consumption by about 10 percent (to about 3,014 kcal per equivalent adult = 3,349 × 0.9). Thus, distribution C implies that France's richest tenth who, as young adults, spent much time in hunting and military activities, would have had only energy intake equivalent to about two and a half hours of work per day in the building trades (Quenouille *et al.* 1951; Goubert 1973; FAO/WHO/UNU 1985).[9] Thus, because of its implications about the diet of the rich, high egalitarianism is as implausible as low egalitarianism.

---

[9] If it is assumed that the distribution of BMI follows LN (19, 3), and that the distribution of stature follows N (1.63, 0.066), the mean height for the top decile is 1.75 meters and the average BMI of the group is 24.7. Since the BMI is the ratio of weight in kilograms to height-squared, measured in meters, weight is 75.3 kg. Using Equation (A.7) for predicting basal metabolic rate, BMR requires about 1,832 kcals/day, and the baseline for body maintenance is about 2,326 kcal/day. Then, eight hours of sleep requires 1,832 × 8 ÷ 24 = 611 kcal, 2.4-hour building trade labor requires 952 kcal (calculated from 5.2 BMR × 2.4 ÷ 24) (see Table 2.1 for the PAR of building trade labor); the remaining 13.6 hours used for maintenance requires 1,453 kcal (= 1.4 BMR × 13.6 ÷ 24). The sum of energy used for three activities (sleeping, building trade, and body maintenance) is 3,016 kcal which is similar to 3,014 kcal.

We are left with moderate egalitarianism (distribution B) as a plausible assumption. Under that distribution, only the bottom 20 percent of households is below baseline maintenance, and those subject to rapid starvation are about 5 percent of the population, a finding consistent with what is known about mortality rates during the *ancien régime* (Bourgeois-Pichat 1965; Goubert 1973; Flinn 1974; INED 1977; Flinn 1981; Weir 1984; Galloway 1986; Dupâquier 1989; Weir 1989b). Similarly, under distribution B, the richest decile of the population has on average enough energy for nearly nine hours a day of moderate activity – about the same amount of energy available for a moderately active adult male from the prosperous classes in developed nations toward the end of the twentieth century (US National Center for Health Statistics 1977; Lipton 1983).[10]

The French distribution is also consistent with what is known about the English consumption of calories circa 1800. Table 2.4 presents the probable English distribution, which was based on food balance sheets. The mean consumption was about 36 percent higher in England than in France, which is consistent with the taller stature and higher BMI of the English population (see Chapters 3, 4, and 5), and with the relative productivity of agriculture in the two countries (O'Brien and Keyder 1978; Wrigley 1987b; Hoffman 1988; Grantham 1992). Moreover, the average levels are not out of keeping with recent experiences in the less-developed nations. Low as it is, Toutain's estimates of the French supply of calories are above the average supply of calories in 1965 estimated for such nations as Pakistan, Rwanda, and Algeria, and only slightly less (by 39 calories) than that of Indonesia. The English estimate ranks it above the average of the middle income countries in 1965 (World Bank 1987). Compared to France, England in 1800 was awash with calories available for work.

The distributional implications of the two estimates are consistent with both qualitative and quantitative descriptions of the diets of various social classes (Cole and Postgate [1938] 1956; Drummond and Wilbraham 1958; Pullar 1970; Rose 1971; Tilly 1971; Goubert 1973; Wilson 1973; Hufton 1974; Tilly 1975; Blum 1978; Burnett 1979; Frijhoff and Julia 1979; Hufton 1983; Mennell 1985). In the French

---

[10] If the richest decile of the population spent eight hours sleeping (1 BMR), 7.6 hours for moderate activity like hunting birds (3.4 BMR, see Table 2.1), and 8.4 hours of body maintenance (1.4 BMR), total required energy for three activities is estimated 3,480 kcal using the BMR calculated in footnote 9. This figure is similar to 3,481 kcal that is the 10 percent discounted caloric consumption among the richest decile.

Table 2.4 *Comparison of probable French and English distributions of the daily consumption of kcal per consuming unit near the end of the eighteenth century*

	France circa 1785 $\frac{s}{\overline{X}} = 2,413$		England circa 1800 $\frac{s}{\overline{X}} = 3,271$	
Decile group (1)	Daily kcal consumption (2)	Cumulative % (3)	Daily kcal consumption (4)	Cumulative % (5)
Highest	3,868	100	5,244	100
9th	3,141	84	4,258	84
8th	2,819	71	3,822	71
7th	2,589	59	3,509	59
6th	2,398	48	3,251	48
5th	2,227	38	3,019	38
4th	2,063	29	2,797	29
3rd	1,894	21	2,568	21
2nd	1,701	13	2,305	13
1st	1,381	6	1,872	6

Notes: The French distribution is from Column 4 of Table 2.3. For the English distribution, the per capita caloric intake is from Table 4.13; conversion factors (France = 0.7658 and England = 0.7506) for consuming units were derived from Column 5 of Table 2.2 for France, and Wrigley and Schofield 1981: 529 for England; the distribution assumes $s/\overline{X} = 0.3$. Cf. Fogel 1987. Columns 3 and 5 show the percentage of total caloric consumption accounted for by consuming units at or below a given decile; they are identical because the two distributions have the same shape and coefficient of variation.

case, for example, Bernard's study of marriage contracts made in Gévaudan (Bernard [1969] 1975) during the third quarter of the eighteenth century revealed that the average ration provided for parents in complete pensions contained about 1,674 calories. Because the average age of a male parent at the marriage of his first surviving child was about 59, the preceding figure implies a diet of about 2,270 calories per consuming unit.[11] That figure falls near the 45th centile of the estimated

[11] From Column 5 of Table 2.2, average caloric consumption at ages 50–59 and 60–69 as a proportion of that of males aged 20–39 is estimated 0.7800 and 0.6934, respectively. Taking the average of two values for age 59, 1,674 kcal implies 2,272 kcal per consuming unit (= 1,674 kcal ÷ 0.7367).

French distribution, which is consistent with the class of peasants
described by Bernard.

2.3 Waaler curves and surfaces

A number of recent studies (see Chapter 1) have established the
predictive power of height and BMI with respect to morbidity and
mortality. The results of two of these studies are summarized in
Figures 2.2 and 2.3.

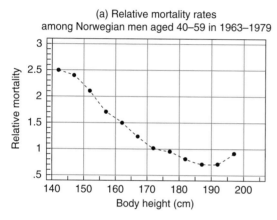

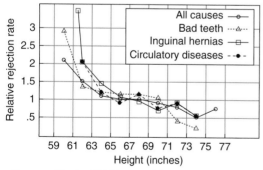

Sources: Waaler 1984 for part (a) and Fogel 1993b for
part (b).

Figure 2.2 Comparison of the relationship between body height and relative
risk in two populations

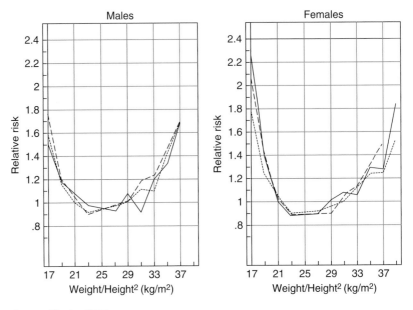

Source: Waaler 1984.
Note: Solid line shows the relationship among adults aged 50–54, dashed line is for ages 55–59, and dotted line is for ages 60–64.

Figure 2.3 Relationship between BMI and prospective risk among Norwegian adults aged 50–64 at risk (1963–1979)

Part (a) of Figure 2.2 reproduces a diagram by Waaler (1984). (Appendix A discusses the methods of constructing such curves.) It shows that short Norwegian men aged 40–59 between 1963 and 1979 were much more likely to die than tall men. Indeed, the risk of mortality for men with heights of 165 cm (65.0 inches) was, on average, 71 percent greater than that of men who measured 182.5 cm (71.9 inches). Part (b) shows that height is also an important predictor of the relative likelihood that men aged 23–49 would be rejected from the Union Army in the American Civil War during 1861–1865 because of chronic diseases (Fogel 1993b, pp. 14–15). Despite significant differences in mean heights, ethnicities, environmental circumstances, the array and severity of diseases, and time, the functional relationship between height and relative risk is strikingly similar. Both the Norwegian curve and the US all-causes curve have relative risks that reach a minimum of between 0.6 and 0.7 at a height of about 187.5 centimeters. Both reach a relative risk of about 2 at about 152.5 centimeters. The similarity of the two risk curves in Figure 2.2, despite the differences in conditions and attendant circumstances, suggests that the relative risk of morbidity and mortality depends not on the deviation of height from the current mean but from an ideal mean: the mean associated with full genetic potential.

Waaler (1984) has also studied the relationship in Norway between BMI and the risk of death in a sample of 1.7 million individuals. Curves summarizing his findings for both men and women are shown in Figure 2.3. Although the observed values of the BMI (kg/m²) ranged between 17 and 39, over 80 percent of the males over age 40 had BMIs within the range 21–29. Within the range 22–28, the curve is fairly flat, with the relative risk of mortality hovering close to 1.0. However, at BMIs of less than 22 and over 28, the risk of death rises quite sharply as the BMI moves away from its mean value. The BMI curves are much more symmetrical than the height curves in Figure 2.2, indicating that high BMIs are as risky as low ones.

Although Figures 2.2 and 2.3 are revealing, neither singly nor together are they sufficient to shed light on the debate about the "small but healthy" issue – whether moderate stunting impairs health when weight-for-height is adequate. Figure 2.2 is only partially controlled for weight, and Figure 2.3 is only partially controlled for height (Fogel 1987). To get at this small-but-healthy issue, one needs an iso-mortality surface that relates the risk of death to both height and weight simultaneously.[12] Such a surface, presented in Figure 2.4, was fitted to Waaler's data by a procedure described in Appendix A. Transecting the iso-mortality map are lines that give the locus of BMI between 16 and 34. The heavy black curve running through the minimum point of each iso-mortality curve gives the weight that minimizes risk at each height.

Figure 2.4 shows that even when body weight is maintained at what Figure 2.3 indicates is an "ideal" level (BMI = 25), short men are at substantially greater risk of death than tall men. Thus, an adult male with a BMI of 25 who is 164 centimeters tall is at about 55 percent greater risk of death than a male who is 183 centimeters tall and also has a BMI of 25. Figure 2.4 also shows that the "ideal" BMI varies with height. A BMI of 25 is "ideal" for men in the neighborhood of 175

[12] For further discussion of the small-but-healthy debate, see Fogel 2004b.

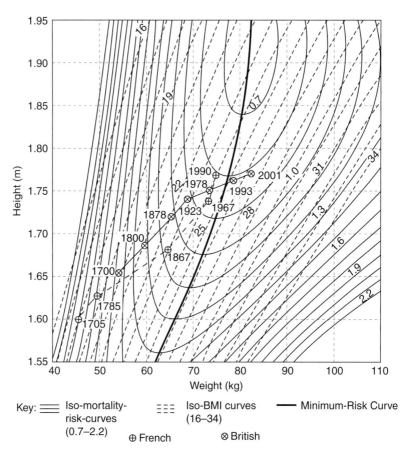

Key: ═══ Iso-mortality-   ≡≡≡ Iso-BMI curves   ──── Minimum-Risk Curve
risk-curves   (16–34)
(0.7–2.2)   ⊕ French   ⊗ British

Sources: French: The data points for 1705 and 1785 are based on the discussion in Section 3.3 of Chapter 3. For 1867 and 1967 see Figure 2.4 in Fogel 2004b; the point for 1867 is from Baxter 1875, 1: 58–59; the point for 1967 is from Eveleth and Tanner 1976. The height for the 1990 data point is from Cavelaars *et al.* 2000; the BMI for 1990 is assumed to be the same as the 1980 BMI in Rolland-Cachera *et al.* 1991. *British*: The data points for 1700 and 1800 are based on the discussion in Section 3.5 of Chapter 3. For a brief description of the procedure used to estimate the British point for 1800, also see Fogel 1997. Points for 1838, 1878, 1923, and 1978 are from Floud 1998, Table 6. The points for 1993 and 2001 are from the Health Survey for England (see Tables 4, 5, and 6 at www.doh.gov.uk/stats/trends1.htm).

Figure 2.4 Waaler surface of the relative mortality risk for height and weight among Norwegian males aged 50–63 with a plot of estimated French and English heights and weights since 1700 at ages 25–39

centimeters, but for tall men (greater than 183 centimeters) the ideal BMI is between 22 and 24, while for short men (under 168 centimeters) the "ideal" BMI is about 26.

2.3.1 Issues in the construction of Waaler curves and surfaces

Data on height began to become plentiful around the middle of the eighteenth century. Most of the early height data are derived from military records because military authorities found such data useful in connection with control over the quality of recruits, the procurement of uniforms, and the identification of runaways. Information on the heights of slaves was collected from the early nineteenth century onward, largely as a result of abolitionist efforts to suppress the international slave trade. Scattered height data on students may be found in the eighteenth and early nineteenth centuries but do not become widespread in western Europe or the United States until the last quarter of the nineteenth century. Due to the work of reformers, there are some bodies of data, especially in England, on the heights of child laborers and other working-class children that go back to the mid eighteenth century. Scattered measurements of birth length from the mid eighteenth century exist, but such measurements did not start to become routine practice in hospitals in Europe and the United States until the second half of the nineteenth century. Numerous investigators have collected height data from these sources since the mid 1970s.[13] At present, the number of observations on height in machine-readable form for the period between 1700 and World War I, covering twenty-six nations or ethnicities in Europe, Africa, and the Americas, is over half a million (Tanner 1981; Eltis 1982; Higman 1984; Fogel 1986a; Fogel 1986b; Steckel 1986; Åkerman, Högberg, and Danielsson 1988; Komlos 1989; Floud, Wachter, and Gregory 1990; Komlos 1990; Mokyr and O'Gráda 1991; Fogel, Costa, and Burton 2008).

Data on weight during the eighteenth and nineteenth centuries are scarcer than those on height. Military organizations, the principal

---

[13] Other scholars have used prison records and records of transportees to Australia (Nicholas and Steckel 1991; and Riggs 1994; Johnson and Nicholas 1995; Nicholas and Oxley 1996; Baten and Murray 1997; Johnson and Nicholas 1997; Baten and Murray 2000; Horrell, Meredith, and Oxley 2009).

source of the early height data, did not begin to weigh recruits routinely until late in the third quarter of the nineteenth century. However, early medical reformers and investigators of human growth (auxologists) began collecting data on weight in the second quarter of the nineteenth century – Quetelet for Belgium, Villermé for France, and Chadwick and his associates for working-class children in England. A small percentage of recruits were occasionally weighed before the late 1860s, and scattered estimates of birth weights are available going back to the mid eighteenth century (Gould 1869; Tanner 1981; Ward 1988; Goldin and Margo 1989; Komlos 1990). The records of benevolent societies in both Europe and North America, which are just beginning to be exploited, are another important source of data on anthropometric measures and appear to have included information on weight during the second half of the nineteenth century.

Inferring mean population heights from these historical datasets poses a number of complex problems, especially when the source is military records. Use of military data raises questions about the extent to which soldiers and sailors were representative of the populations from which they were drawn. The problem is more severe in volunteer than in conscript armies. Volunteer armies, especially in peacetime, are selective in their admission criteria and often have minimum height requirements. Consequently, even if information on rejected volunteers exists, there remains the question of the extent to which applicants are self-screened.

In many conscript armies, virtually every male of eligible age, including those who offered substitutes or were otherwise excused, was examined and measured. Clear evidence of self-selection bias in volunteer armies exists, however. Because there are significant differences in height among various groups of nativity, birthplace, and socioeconomic status in early life, it is necessary to standardize for these characteristics in estimating the trend in average heights. The necessary weights are obtainable from federal censuses and similar sources. Much of the interest turns on secular trends in the heights of particular groups that, even if underrepresented, are nevertheless present in numbers sufficient to permit analysis.

Another issue is whether the volunteers in particular subgroups (e.g., blue-collar urban laborers aged 20–25) are representative of the class from which they are drawn. One approach to this question is to compare the characteristics of the volunteers in the peacetime army with individuals of the same subgroups in three other types of datasets. In the US case, for example, there have been wartime armies subject to conscription (World War II), armies in which a very high proportion of those of military age were examined (the Civil War), and scientifically designed random samples such as the US national sample of 1960–1962 (US National Center for Health Statistics 1965). For the Union Army, information on height and social characteristics is available not only for those actually recruited but also for those rejected, for those who provided substitutes, and for the substitutes. Analysis of these data revealed that the recruits from farm households, for example, covered virtually the full range of household wealth in this sector, and that the mean of the sample of parental wealth (adjusted for age) differed from that of a random sample of farm households in the 1860 census by less than 0.25 of a standard deviation (Fogel 1986a; Fogel 1986b; cf. Floud, Wachter, and Gregory 1990).

The finding that subgroups in military organizations are socially representative of the classes from which they were drawn does not imply the absence of a height bias. Indeed, the curve of rejection by height shown in part (b) of Figure 2.2 implies not only that such a bias exists but also that the degree of overestimation of the population heights from military heights will vary with the mean height of the underlying population. In the case of the Union Army, in which about 30 percent of the examinees were rejected for chronic diseases, rejectees were about 0.6 inches shorter than the recruits, implying that the true population mean is about 0.18 inches (0.46 centimeters) less than the mean of the recruits. Even if uncorrected, biases of this magnitude will not seriously distort the evaluation of secular trends. Moreover, if the proportion of eligible males who were rejected is known, the curve in part (b) of Figure 2.2 can be used to estimate and correct the rejection bias.

In addition to sample selection biases, there is a series of measurement issues pertaining to the use of military data. Some relate to the accuracy of the age information and some to the accuracy of the information on height. Issues regarding age include whether ages were heaped, were reported to the nearest or the last birthday, or were arbitrarily assigned on the basis on height. Issues regarding height include whether heights were rounded to the nearest inch (or fraction of an inch) rather than to the last full inch (or fraction thereof), and whether individuals were measured with or without shoes.

Accuracy in age has little bearing on the determination of the secular trend in final heights; it is of little importance whether a person classified as 30 is actually 28 or 32. But such heaping is of some importance during the growing years. There is evidence of age heaping at ages 10 and 20 and at the minimum age for recruitment into military organizations. Although such heaping will add perturbation to the height–velocity profile, it does not usually affect the determination of the age at which the profile peaks. A more serious issue is posed by the datasets, such as those involving slaves, where it has been suggested that ages were arbitrarily assigned on the basis of height. If that was true, however, the standard deviation of height would not have the characteristic pattern of increasing and then decreasing as the peak of the growth spurt is approached and surpassed (Trussell and Steckel 1978). Thus, by examining the variation of the standard deviation of height by age it is possible to determine whether ages were arbitrarily assigned according to height.

Heaping on even inches is evident even when the measurement is conducted by qualified personnel (as in US National Center for Health Statistics 1965). In military organizations with minimum height requirements, there is further evidence of heaping at the inch just above the cutoff. Simulation models indicate that even-number heaping does not introduce a systematic bias. Even large amounts of heaping, in the range of 15–30 percent, only affect the mean by around one-tenth of an inch, although they may affect the standard error of the mean. With respect to rounding, from the earliest date for which records are available, the standard practice was to round to the nearest inch or fraction of an inch. A study of actual practice in World War II revealed a slight tendency to round downward, thus introducing an average error of –0.2 inches (–0.5 centimeters). There is no reason to assume that this tendency was different in the eighteenth and nineteenth centuries. Analysis of the data in the Union Army records indicates that the bias may be due mainly to a tendency to round the heights of tall persons (who should have been measured at fractional inches) downward to the nearest inch. In this case, as in the case of the rejection bias, the magnitude of the error is too small to distort secular trends, and it should not significantly affect the cross-sectional analysis of the relationship between height and economic or demographic factors (cf. Karpinos 1958; US National Center for Health Statistics 1965; Floud, Wachter, and Gregory 1990). It is worth noting that the rounding bias almost exactly offsets the rejection bias.

From the mid eighteenth century on, military regulations required the measurement of recruits without shoes. Two samples in which it was thought that these regulations were ignored were tested against corresponding groups known to have been measured without shoes. The tests revealed no significant difference between the control groups and the suspected samples. Tests of the heights of slaves reported in the US coastwise manifest against ex-slaves of the same birth cohorts measured in the Union Army also resulted in the rejection of the hypothesis that the slaves were measured in shoes. Indeed, it seems unlikely that shoes would have been kept on in those cases where the recording of height was intended for purposes of later identification. However, measurements for insurance purposes and of students were often made with shoes on. Such datasets require estimates of average heel heights when statistics calculated from them are employed (US Department of Agriculture Human Nutrition Research Division Agricultural Research Service 1960; Fogel *et al.* 1983).

The most difficult problems of estimation arise from measurements made by organizations that had varying minimum height requirements for entry. This situation prevailed not only in military organizations such as the regular armed forces of Great Britain but also in such charitable organizations as the Marine Society of London, whose records contain the longest continuous series on the heights of adolescents in the eighteenth and early nineteenth centuries. These organizations set minimum height limits at different times, varying with needs, sometimes shifting frequently, and sometimes ranging above the mean height of the populations from which they were recruiting. Minimum height standards were flexibly enforced, so very sharp cutoffs are not usually apparent in the data. It appears that, in some cases, 30 or 40 percent of the smaller heights in the underlying distribution may be missing. Such undersampling would destroy the usefulness of the data unless reliable statistical procedures are employed to correct for the problem.

The development of estimators capable of performing reliably in the presence of large undersampling of small heights (accompanied by such additional distortions as heaping on even inches and flexible enforcement of standards) was approached at two levels. One issue was the estimation of the mean of an underlying distribution for men old enough to have attained their final heights. A normal distribution for final heights – which looks like the distribution of the left panel of Figure 2.1(a) – is both well established for contemporary data and consistent with the examination of the historical data. Thus the assumption of normality for the underlying distribution places the problem into a well-defined parametric framework. Somewhat more complex was the problem of how to estimate the mean of a distribution of height at a given age during the ages of growth. Modern data indicate that the underlying distributions during adolescence are at first skewed to the right, as early maturers attain peak growth velocity, and then skewed to the left, when only late maturers still await their growth spurt.

The two principal methods developed for correcting left-tail truncation, the Quantile Bend Estimator (QBE), and the Reduced Sample Maximum Likelihood Estimator (RSMLE), are described in Wachter (1981) and Wachter and Trussell (1982). Extension of the RSMLE method to regression analysis is reported in Trussell and Wachter (1984). These methods have been tested extensively by both Monte Carlo techniques and simulation techniques on actual distributions of heights.[14] The tests have shown that both methods are generally reliable, both in the presence of moderate skewing and when such skewing is combined with pronounced heaping (Fogel *et al.* 1983).

Komlos has criticized our application of these procedures in the estimation of trends in the heights of mature British males. He argued that the pooling of samples obtained from the British Army and the Royal Marines obfuscated the underlying distribution of heights among the British male population. He contends that, because the Army and Marines had different height requirements, combining the two samples would lead to biased estimates of both the mean and standard deviation of the underlying population. The difficulty with this argument is that it presupposes that if two or more distributions are scrambled together, there is no way of disentangling them. However, such unscrambling can be effectively accomplished with the QBE and RSMLE procedures (Floud, Wachter, and Gregory 1990; Floud, Wachter, and Gregory 1993; Komlos 1993b).

---

[14] In the tests, Fogel *et al.* (1983) selected a sample of the heights of London schoolchildren for 1965 that consisted of nontruncated distributions at each age during the growing spurt. They randomly generated truncated samples under various assumptions of truncation from the lower end (Monte Carlo techniques), used the methods of QBE and RSMLE, and statistically tested the extent to which both methods allowed the true mean of the distribution to be inferred.

A key issue is whether different military organizations had different target heights. If, for example, the infantry had a high target height, the Marines a medium target height, and the Navy a low target height, each organization would generate a normal distribution around its target (cf. Fogel *et al.* 1983). Then, if each of these distributions were plotted on normal probability paper (the equivalent of a QBE plot), they would each appear as a straight line until each unit's truncation point, after which each curve would bend. If there were upper and lower truncations, the plot would be straight as one moved from the mean toward the upper and lower truncation points, and it would bend at the beginning of each truncation point, displaying the degree of truncation at each end. There is still the question of how to work back from the height distribution of different units to the underlying normal distribution of adult British males from which particular military units drew their recruits. That task involves developing estimates of the share of each military organization in the total pool of adult British males of military ages and whether there were systematic differences in the preferences of recruiters by regional or socioeconomic characteristics. To answer these questions, Floud, Wachter, and Gregory (1990) examined the directives to recruiters and experimented with the sensitivity of the results to different weighting schemes.[15]

The statistical issues involved in exploiting weight data are analogous to heights but generally less severe, partly because measurement of weight generally began at a later date. When instituted in military organizations, weight was measured on high-quality platform scales calibrated to the nearest quarter pound. Men were sometimes weighed in pants and underwear, but samples of the clothing were weighed to obtain adjustment factors (Gould 1869). Although there were often upper and lower weight limits, these were generally far less constraining than height limits. For example, fewer than two out of one hundred men were rejected from the Union Army for unsatisfactory body build (Baxter 1875). Weights taken in schools and for insurance purposes, however, involved errors introduced by the wearing of shoes and varying amounts of outer garments (US Department of Agriculture Human Nutrition Research Division Agricultural Research Service 1960).

---

[15] For a more detailed discussion of technical issues discussed here, see Floud, Wachter, and Gregory (1990; 1993).

2.3.2 Uses of anthropometric measures to explain secular trends in mortality rates

The available anthropometric data tend to confirm the basic results of the analysis based on energy cost accounting: chronic malnutrition was widespread in Europe during the eighteenth and nineteenth centuries. Furthermore, such malnutrition seems to have been responsible for much of the very high mortality during this period. Moreover, nearly the entire decline in mortality rates in England and France between 1750 and 1875 appears to be explained by the marked improvement in whatever caused changes in anthropometric measures of malnutrition. This section summarizes some findings on the relationship between mortality and two anthropometric measures – height at maturity and BMI – that are discussed in more detail elsewhere (Fogel 1986a; Fogel 1987; Fogel 1991; Fogel, Galantine, and Manning 1992, Chapter 47; cf. Kim 1993).

Because height-specific and weight-specific mortality rates are measured relative to the average crude death rate (CDR) for the population as a whole, short-term shifts in the CDR by themselves will not necessarily shift the surface. However, fundamental shifts in the environment, including changes in medical technology, may shift the risk surface. One way of ascertaining whether there has been a shift in the risk surface is to determine what part of the decline in mortality rates can be explained merely by movements along the surface (i.e., by changes in height and weight on the assumption that the surface has been stable since 1750).

Table 2.5 contains estimates of the final (or near-final) heights of men in several European countries from 1750 to modern times. It appears that, during the eighteenth century, these Europeans were severely stunted by modern standards. The most stunted population appears to have been the French cohort of 18-IV, measuring only 163 cm (64.2 inches) at the age of 20. Although these men may not have finished growing, our estimates still place them below the third centile of the heights of eighteen-year-old US males in 1977 (Steckel 1995a, p. 16). There was a growing divergence between the heights of British and French men during the late eighteenth and early nineteenth century, and although some allowance needs to be made for differences in age-at-measurement, the gap between French heights and British heights was almost 7 cm during the second quarter of the nineteenth century. However, this gap narrowed during the second half of the

Table 2.5 *Estimated average final heights (cm) of men who reached maturity between 1750 and 2000 in six European populations, by quarter-centuries*

	Date of maturity by century and quarter	Denmark	France	Great Britain	Hungary	Norway	Sweden
1	18-III			165.5	167.4	165.6	168.1
2	18-IV	165.7	163.0	168.6	166.6	165.5	166.7
3	19-I	166.2	163.7	167.9	163.1	166.6	166.7
4	19-II	166.7	164.3	171.2	163.5	167.4	167.3
5	19-III	165.3	164.7	167.2	162.3	168.7	168.0
6	19-IV	167.8	165.4	168.0	163.8	169.6	169.5
7	20-I	169.3	166.3	168.2	165.4	171.0	171.9
8	20-II	171.5	168.0	170.0	168.4	173.8	173.9
9	20-III	175.5	171.2	175.0	170.7	177.6	177.2
10	20-IV	183.2	174.7	176.6		179.5	179.2

Sources: Denmark: Rows 1–9: Floud 1994: 16; Row 10: Statistics Denmark 2009: Table 47.

France: Rows 3–7: Weir 1997: 197; Rows 8–10: Demoulin 1998: 110.

Great Britain: Rows 1–6: Floud, Wachter, and Gregory 1990: 145–147 (22-year-olds); Rows 7 and 9: Rosenberg 1988: 282 (20–24-year-olds); Row 8: Floud 1998: 34 (heights of men born in 1900–19 and aged 26–30 at the time of measurement); Row 10: Department of Health 2004: Table 4 (heights of men aged 16–24, 1993–2000).

Hungary: Komlos 1989: 242 (QBE estimates for 21- and 22-year-olds).

Norway: Row 1: Kiil 1939: 71, 73; Row 2: Kiil 1939: 73; Row 3: Kiil 1939: 73, 80, 122, 127–128; Row 4: Kiil 1939: 80, 122, 127–128; Rows 5–6: Kiil 1939: 13; Rows 7–10: Statistics Norway 2000: Table 4.22.

Sweden: Rows 1–3: Sandberg and Steckel 1987: 106; Rows 4–9: Sandberg and Steckel 1997: 129; Row 10: Lindgren 1998: 322.

Notes: France: 18-IV: The figure for 18-IV has been estimated using Weir's (1997: 197) data for 1804–12. The figures in rows 2–7 are for men aged 20 at the time of their last birthday.

Norway: All data were derived from military recruiting statistics. The data in rows 1–6 are for 22-year-olds. The recruitment cohorts of 1913–15 included 21- and 22-year olds, and the recruitment cohorts of 1916 and 1917 included men aged 20, 21, and 22. The recruitment age was lowered to 20 in 1918 (Kiil 1939: 12–14).

Sweden: All data are from military recruiting statistics. Before 1898, recruits were admitted in the year they turned 21. The recruitment age fell to 20 in 1898, 19 in 1930, and 18 in 1936 (Sandberg and Steckel 1997: 158).

nineteenth century, and was less than 2 cm in the final quarter of the twentieth century (Fogel 2004b, Fig. 3.2).[16]

Over the last century, the three Scandinavian countries (shown in Table 2.5) and the Netherlands (Chamla 1983) have had the most vigorous and sustained increases in stature in the western world, outpacing Britain and the United States (Fogel 1986b). Hungary's growth pattern (Komlos 1990) differs from that of the other European nations, although the reasons remain unclear.[17] (See Section 5.1 for further discussion of recent changes in stature in European countries.)

Data on BMIs for France and Great Britain during the late eighteenth and most of the nineteenth centuries are much patchier than those on stature, so attempts to compare British and French BMIs during this period are necessarily conjectural. We have estimated that the average English BMI for males at ages 20–30 was about 21 circa 1800, which is about 15 percent below current levels.[18] The corresponding figure for French males circa 1785 may only have been about 19, which is approximately 20 percent below current levels (Fogel 2004b). The conjectural nature of these figures makes the attempt to go from the anthropometric data to differential mortality rates more illustrative than substantive. However, Figure 2.4 indicates the apparent location of French and English males of 18-IV on the iso-mortality map

---

[16] However, as Figure 2.4 shows, the British BMIs were larger than those of the French.

[17] Our figures are based on Komlos's QBE estimates for men who were aged 21–22 at the time of measurement. In addition to publishing QBE estimates for men aged 23–45 at the time of measurement, he also published estimates based on the mean values of the heights of 21–22-year-old recruits and on the mean values of both the original samples and truncated samples of the heights of 23–45-year-old recruits. For men who were born between the 1740s and 1810s, the extent of the decline suggested by the QBE estimates is significantly greater than the declines suggested by the mean values of either the original samples of Hungarian recruits or the truncated samples. We have discussed our reasons for preferring the QBE procedure elsewhere in this chapter (see Section 2.4.1) and in Chapter 4.

[18] See Table 4.14 in Chapter 4. A BMI of 21 under the estimated per capita daily caloric consumption in England (2,439 kcal) in circa 1800 is consistent with BMIs from modern data. According to the WHO and FAO online database, the BMIs of adult males in many underdeveloped countries have been between 20 and 21 in recent years, and the levels of their per-capita caloric consumption (Cal) are between 2,000 and 2,500 kcal; for example, Gambia (BMI 20.8, Cal 2,270 kcal), Kenya (20.6, Cal 2,110 kcal), Uganda (BMI 20.6, Cal 2,360 kcal), Vietnam (20.8, Cal 2,530), and Sri Lanka (20.9, Cal 2,390 kcal) (source: WHO, http://apps.who.int/bmi/index.jsp; FAO, ftp://ftp.fao.org/docrep/fao/008/a0205m).

generated from Waaler's data. These points imply that the French mortality rate should have been about 33 percent higher than that of the English, which is quite close to the estimated ratio of mortality rates for the two countries.[19] In other words, the available data suggest that in 18-IV both France and Great Britain were characterized by the same mortality risk surface (i.e., the same mortality regimen) and that differences in their average mortality rates are explained largely by differences in their distributions of height and weight-for-height.

This observation raises the question as to how much of the decline in European mortality rate since 18-IV can be explained merely by whatever caused increases in stature and BMIs, that is, by movements along an unchanging mortality risk surface. For the three countries for which even patchy data are currently available – England, France, and Sweden – it appears that most of the decline in mortality between 18-IV and 19-III was attributable to movements along the Waaler mortality surface, because the estimated changes in height and BMI appear to explain about 75 to 90 percent of the decline in mortality during this three-quarters of a century. Movements along the Waaler surface appear to explain only about 50 to 60 percent of the decline in mortality rates after 1875, however. After 1875, increases in longevity were more affected by factors other than those that exercise their influence through stature and body mass, including the direct effect of improvements in public health and sanitation and the introduction of new medical technologies as discussed in later chapters.

Movements along the Waaler surface measure the impact of net nutrition but do not indicate how much of the improvement in net nutrition was due to improvements in the diet and how much was due to reductions in claims on the diet. Much work remains before this issue can be resolved. At present, we only have preliminary work illustrating lines of research that may ultimately succeed in producing reliable findings. Based on patchy aggregate data, we have previously suggested (Fogel 1992b; 2000; 2004b) that in the US case reductions in exposure to disease were probably more important than improvements in the diet, accounting for perhaps half the nutritional effect on mortality. Applied to the European case, this proportion would imply that

---

[19]   The English CDR for eleven years centered on 1800 is 26.1 and 1.33 times that number is 34.7, which is close to the French CDR in circa 1785 derived from INED 1977, pp. 332–333 and Mitchell 2003, pp. 106–119; cf. Weir 1984.

improvements in the diet per se may have accounted for 35 to 45 percent of the mortality decline before 1875 but only for about 25 to 30 percent of the mortality decline after 1875.

2.4 Scenarios of the possible distribution of the calories available for work in Britain

At the end of the eighteenth century, Britain had about 3,271 calories per consuming unit (see Table 4.13 of Chapter 4), about 36 percent more than was available to the French circa 1785. According to Table 2.5, the average height of British men in their twenties and thirties was about 1.68 meters. If we are correct in assuming that the average BMI of English males who were aged about 30 in circa 1800 was approximately 21, this would imply that their average weight was around 59.3 kg (Fogel 1997; 2004b). Men with these body builds would require about 1,586 calories per day for basal metabolism, which is calculated from Equation (A.7) in Appendix A. The implied average physical activities level (PAL) – a person's daily physical activity level as a multiple of BMR – is 2.06.[20] Table 2.6 presents the English size distribution of caloric consumption circa 1800 (Column 6), based on the medium egalitarianism assumption. The estimated distribution of PAL among consuming units is also given in Table 2.6

The first thing to note about Table 2.6 is that those in the bottom tenth of PAL distribution lack the energy for any regular work. They are close to the maintenance level of 1.27 BMR and are slowly starving to death. A person in the second-lowest decile would need to sleep or be inactive for about two-thirds of a day. About one-sixth of the day could be spent in light activity, and the other sixth in moderate activity. Table 2.7 gives one scenario for the daily activity of a person in the second-lowest decile. The last column lists each activity's PAR, the energy required for the activity as a ratio of basal metabolic rate. The average PAR throughout the day, which is the time-weighted average of PARs of all activities engaged in, must be no greater than the PAL achievable by someone in that decile. The scenario in Table 2.7 implies

---

[20] PAL is the ratio of calories used for physical activities to BMR. Thus, the implied average PAL is calculated from average calorie consumption per consuming unit divided by the implied BMR for the average body size (3,271 kcal ÷ 1,586 kcal = 2.06)

Table 2.6 *The distribution of PAL (physical activity level) among British adult males circa 1800*

| | | | | | Medium egalitarianism $\frac{s}{\bar{X}} = 0.3$ | |
Decile (1)	BMI (2)	Stature (m) (3)	Weight (kg) (4)	kcal for BMR (5)	kcal consumption (6)	PAL (7)
Highest	26.68	1.80	86.04	1,995	5,244	2.63
9	24.12	1.75	73.77	1,808	4,258	2.36
8	22.89	1.72	68.09	1,721	3,822	2.22
7	21.96	1.71	63.88	1,656	3,509	2.12
6	21.16	1.69	60.33	1,602	3,251	2.03
5	20.42	1.67	57.06	1,552	3,019	1.95
4	19.68	1.65	53.86	1,503	2,797	1.86
3	18.88	1.64	50.49	1,452	2,568	1.77
2	17.92	1.61	46.51	1,391	2,305	1.66
Lowest	16.20	1.56	39.63	1,285	1,872	1.46

Notes: PAL means a person's daily activity level as a multiple of BMR. It is assumed that the log of BMI is normally distributed with mean 21 and standard deviation 3 [BMI~LN (21, 3)], and that stature is normally distributed with mean 1.68 meters and standard deviation 0.066 meters [Stature~N (1.68, 0.066)]. Column 4: Col. 2 × (Col. 3 squared), Column 5: computed from Equation (A.7), Column 6: The size distribution of calories is from Column 4 in Table 2.4, and Column 7: Col. 6 ÷ Col. 5. Note that some figures are subject to rounding.

Table 2.7 *A scenario for the second-lowest decile*

Activity	Hours	PAR
Sleeping	8	1.0
Inactive	8	1.4
Sweeping floor	1	1.7
Cooking	1	1.8
Strolling	2	2.5
Milking cow by hand	2	2.9
Scrubbing floor	2	3.2

Note: PAL is Σ(Hours × PAR) ÷ 24 = 1.66. PARs are from FAO/WHO/UNU 1985.

Table 2.8 *A scenario for the highest decile*

Activity	Hours	PAR
Sleeping	8	1.0
Eating	1	1.4
Sharpening axes	2	1.7
Weaving	1	2.0
Strolling	2	2.5
Making fence	2	2.7
Tying fence posts	2	2.7
Weeding	2	3.8
Digging holes for post	2	5.0
Felling trees	2	7.5

Notes: PAL is Σ(Hours $\times$ PAR) $\div$ 24 = 2.63. PARs are from FAO/WHO/UNU 1985.

a PAL of 1.66 that is statistically identical to the PAL of the second-lowest decile in Table 2.6.

A man in the top decile with a PAL of 2.63 has enough energy to spend most of his waking hours in moderate and heavy work. Table 2.8 is a possible scenario for a man in the top decile of Table 2.6.

In the manual of FAO/WHO/UNU (1985), 1.7 BMR is the gross energy expenditure on occupational work at light level, 2.7 BMR is moderate work, and 3.8 BMR is heavy work. Which of the deciles in Table 2.6 is consistent with heavy labor that is more than sporadic? That question can be answered with the aid of Equation (2.1):

$$D_i = 1.7\alpha + 3.8(1 - \alpha) \tag{2.1}$$

where:

D_i = the decile mean
α = the proportion of light labor
$1 - \alpha$ = the proportion of heavy labor.

If Equation (2.1) is applied to the eighth decile we obtain:

$$2.22 = 1.7\alpha + 3.8(1 - \alpha) \tag{2.2}$$

Solving for α in Equation (2.2), we obtain: $\alpha = 0.75$. Hence, for those at the eighth decile, only 25 percent of work was heavy, and the balance of work was light. If the same procedure is applied to the fourth decile, just 8 percent of energy is regularly available for heavy labor. In the second decile, there is only enough energy for light and moderate labor. Heavy work on a regular basis is precluded.

Voth (2001) has estimated that, in 1800, English workers were working for 3,328 hours per year, or 9.12 hours per day.[21] Assuming that there are 16 waking hours, an additional 6.88 hours were spent in other activities. According to Table 2.6, average energy expenditure in the top nine deciles was about 3,419 kcal per day, of which 544 were for sleep.[22] This leaves 2,876 kcal per day for activities or about 180 per waking hour. If the working day was divided solely between light and moderate activity, about 60 percent would be light.[23]

There is still the question of how the calories available for activities (2,876 kcal) were divided between work (9.12 hours) and other activities (6.88 hours) as Voth suggests. Table 2.9 shows some possibilities.

Rows 4, 5, and 6 are not plausible because the PARs of "other activities" are too high, and those of work are too low. Row 1 is implausible because no energy is available for other activities beyond maintenance. Row 2 is also dubious because it only allows light work for other activities – but many of these other activities were labor intensive.

---

[21] Voth (2001) estimates that the number of working hours in London was 3,319 hours per year and 3,411 hours for the north of England. The above figure, 3,328, is the population-weighted average. On the other hand, Voth (2000) states that the number of working hours in London was either 3,152 hours per year (varying mealtimes) or 3,366 hours per year (constant hours), while the equivalent figures for the north of England were 2,981 hours and 3,036 hours, respectively. But the selection of the estimates does not change the main implications of this section.

While such longer and harder work during the Industrial Revolution is related to the rise of labor-intensive industries, de Vries (2008) looks for the reason from the variety in the consumption basket and the rise of consumption for them at that period. He also argues that, as the demand for household productions like health-related cleanliness increased, the working hours of household heads and males increased.

[22] We assume that those in the bottom decile lack the energy for any regular work. Because the average BMR in the top nine deciles is 1,631 kcal, the energy expenditure for eight hours of sleep is estimated as: 1,631 kcal × 8 hours ÷ 24 = 544 kcal.

[23] The PAL is estimated as 3,419 kcal ÷ 1,631 kcal = 2.10. Thus, Equation (2.1) gives $2.17 = 1.7\alpha + 2.7(1 - \alpha)$, where α denotes the proportion of light labor, and $1 - \alpha$ denotes that of moderate labor. Then, $\alpha = 0.60$.

Table 2.9 *Alternative scenarios for Voth's work year*

	Work		Other activities	
Scenario	(1) kcal	(2) PAR	(3) kcal	(4) PAR
1.	2,240	3.61	636	1.36
2.	2,105	3.40	771	1.65
3.	1,785	2.88	1,091	2.33
4.	1,545	2.49	1,331	2.85
5.	1,280	2.07	1,596	3.41
6.	1,015	1.64	1,861	3.98

Notes: PAR in Column (2) is calculated from [Column (1) ÷ 1,631 kcal] × [24 ÷ 9.12 hours for working] and that in Column (4) is calculated from [Column (3) ÷ 1,631 kcal] × [24 ÷ 6.88 hours for other activities].

Consequently, row 3 of Table 2.9 appears to be a reasonable esti- mate, with other activities at an average PAR of 2.33, roughly midway between light and moderate activity levels. The average PAR for work is 2.88, slightly above the moderate level. If 30 percent of time was devoted to heavy labor, 55 percent could be spent at moderate labor and 15 percent at light labor.[24]

The foregoing analysis suggests that Voth's estimate of a 3,328-hour work year is plausible only if the bulk of hours at work were devoted to light or moderate labor. While such a pattern is plausible for urban jobs conducted mainly in sitting positions, it is not plausible for the work of typical agricultural laborers or for urban jobs that required a great deal of walking or lugging (stevedores or construction workers).

The preceding discussion points to a dimension of long-term economic growth that is often overlooked: the increase in the intensity of work. The use of the word "work" is not confined to effort aimed at producing goods and services that enter into GDP, but is meant to apply to all activities that require energy above BMR. One of the overlooked char- acteristics of economic growth is that it permitted energy-intensive leisure-time activities, including jogging, baseball, football, soccer,

---

[24] Considering three levels of labor together, Equation (2.1) can be expressed as $D_i = 1.7\alpha + 2.7(1 - \alpha - \beta) + 3.8\beta$, where α and β denote the proportions of light and heavy labor, respectively. For $D_i = 2.88$ and $\beta = 0.3$, the equation gives $\alpha = 0.15$, implying $1 - \alpha - \beta = 0.55$.

swimming, bicycling, basketball, tennis, and golf. Thus, despite the shift from menial to sedentary occupations, energy used per consuming unit today in western Europe is a third more than it was in 1800 (Chapter 5, Table 5.5, below). The great technological advances since 1700 have not freed humankind from toil; today, we toil not just out of necessity, but out of choice, and largely in activities we relish (cf. Fogel 2000).

Appendix A   A theoretical model of the interaction of biological, demographic, and economic variables

The aim of this appendix is to develop a theoretical model that integrates the four types of evidence discussed in Chapter 1 (caloric content of the diet, stature, body mass index (BMI), and mortality rates) into as consistent a picture as possible of the physiological component of economic development over the past 300 years. In so doing, we make extensive use of Waaler surfaces, which were first suggested in Waaler (1984) and have been implemented and explored by Kim (1995 and 1996). Kim has brought into a single diagram iso-mortality curves that relate relative mortality rates to height and weight, iso-BMI curves, and a curve that gives the weights that minimize the relative odds of dying at each height for mature adults. These Waaler surfaces are one of the principal analytical devices that we employ in our effort to integrate the four types of evidence into a consistent whole.

A.1   Some theoretical considerations

The basic relationships between the variables of interest are inherent in the aggregate production function, which postulates a single output produced by land, capital, and labor. Labor, however, is a produced input that depends on the intensity of effort (the energy expended in a particular activity) and on the efficiency with which the energy input is transformed into work output (which is measured by stature and BMI). The validity of the use of stature and BMI as measures of the efficiency of caloric utilization has been demonstrated in recent econometric studies of labor in Brazil, the Philippines, and India (see Chapter 1, above).

The theoretical basis for using stature and BMI as measures of the efficiency of the human engine rests on the first law of thermodynamics, which holds that energy output cannot exceed energy input; on nutritional science, which has estimated the extent to which the body can metabolize various foods (the "Atwater factors"); and on physiology that has shown that chronic malnutrition impairs the functioning of various vital organ systems, changing the chemical composition of tissues, reducing the strength of electrical signals across membranes, impeding the operation of the endocrine and immune systems, and reducing the capacity of the central nervous system as well as the ventilatory capacity of the lungs.

From the economist's point of view, stature and BMI are, at least in part, forms of human capital that are established early in life. Moreover, early physiological impairments affect productivity later in life. Some of these impairments take place *in utero* or during the first three years after birth, even though their effects may not become evident until later in life. When growth is primarily through increases in the number of cells, as is the case during the first trimester *in utero* for the circulatory and respiratory systems, such impairments may be irreversible in the sense that shortages of cells due to insults *in utero* cannot be made up by later nutritional programs. In the case of the central nervous system, the main period of vulnerability runs from the beginning of the third trimester to the end of the third year after birth.

The economic component of the model consists of four sectors. The three sectors producing products which enter into GDP are food, other agricultural output, and manufacturing (which includes construction, mining, and services). The fourth sector is called the *household sector*. Although this sector produces a variety of products and activities that require energy inputs (including child-rearing and play), the outputs of the household sector are, by convention, omitted from gross domestic product (GDP). The nutritional component of the model includes an equation that relates height and weight (and therefore, by implication, BMI) to the basal metabolic rate (BMR), which is the amount of energy required to maintain body temperature and to keep vital organs functioning when the body is completely at rest. There is also an equation that relates the calories required for BMR to the maintenance requirement, which is the sum of BMR and the energy needed for the digestion of food and for vital hygiene. The demographic/epidemiological component of the model contains a number of equations relating height, weight, and BMI to the odds of developing chronic diseases and of dying during given intervals. It thus links back to the economic component of the model since it has a bearing on the efficiency with which the body converts energy inputs into work outputs.

A.1.1 The economic component of the model

The economic component of the model is as follows:

$$Q_a = f_a(T_a, K_a, L_a) \quad \text{Production function of food measured in calories}$$

$$(A.1)$$

$$Q_o = f_o(T_o, K_o, L_o) \quad \text{Production function of other agricultural products}$$

$$(A.2)$$

$$Q_m = f_m(T_m, K_m, L_m) \quad \text{Production function of manufacturing}$$

$$(A.3)$$

where:

T = land input quality adjusted and measured in physical units
K = capital input quality adjusted and measured in physical units
L = labor input measured in calories
Q = total output of a given sector measured in physical units except for Q_a which is measured in calories.

$$K_n = k(T_k, K_k, L_k) \quad \text{Production function of capital} \qquad (A.4)$$

where K_n is the annual gross output of capital.

Land (T) is assumed to be a gift of nature, measured in units of equivalent quality.

$$G = g(T_g, K_g, L_g) \qquad (A.5)$$

is the production function for household output and activities not included in *GDP*, where the subscript g indicates an input into the household sector.

It follows that:

$$GDP = P_a Q_a + P_o Q_o + P_m Q_m \qquad (A.6)$$

where P_a, P_o, and P_m are the prices of the respective outputs. Note that K_n is not included in *GDP* since it is part of the outputs of the *a*, *o*, and *m* sectors. Food is not considered an intermediate good, even when it is used to produce other output, and K_g and T_g are also considered consumption.

A.1.2 The nutritional component of the model

Notice that Q_a is greater than $L_a + L_o + L_m + L_g$ even if it is assumed that net changes in food inventories (I) and in food exports (X) are both zero. Indeed, the bulk of Q_a is used for basal metabolism and for maintenance.

When all individuals in society are converted into equivalent adult males aged 20–39 (which we call consuming units), the requirement for basal metabolism per consuming unit (B) is given by equation (A.7):[25]

$$B = 15.3W + 679 \qquad\qquad (A.7)$$

where:

B = kcal required for basal metabolism per consuming unit per day
W = average weight measured in kg.

The relationship between maintenance (M) and BMR is also empirically derived and is given by

$$M = 1.27 \text{ BMR per day.}^{26} \qquad\qquad (A.8)$$

Now the average amount of calories that needs to be ingested to yield M is

$$M' = \frac{M}{A} \qquad\qquad (A.9)$$

where:

A = the proportion of ingested calories that are metabolized (which we will refer to as the "proportional Atwater factor").

It follows that the identity that relates the annual output of calories to the annual consumption is

$$Q_a = \frac{L_{GDP}}{A} + \frac{L_g}{A} + N_c M' + V + X + I \qquad\qquad (A.10)$$

where:

V = aggregate waste, excluding human excrement
$L_{GDP} = L_o + L_m + L_g$ = calories used to produce GDP
X = net annual exports of food
I = net annual changes in food inventories,
N_c = the number of consuming units

---

[25] Considering height, Equation (A.7) can be expressed as $B = 15.4W - 27H + 717$, where H is height measured in meters. See FAO/WHO/UNU 1985.
[26] Assuming 8 hours of sleep (1 BMR) and 16-hour body maintenance such as washing, dressing, and short periods of standing (= 1.4 BMR), M is calculated from 1.27 BMR = 1 BMR × (1/3) + 1.4 BMR × (2/3).

and all the variables in Equation (A.10), except for A and N_c, are measured in kcal.

It should be kept in mind that Q_a refers only to food intended for human consumption. The production of animal feed as well as the production of work animals, seeds, and the building up of the breeding stock are covered by Equations (A.2), (A.3), and (A.4). Notice also that L_k was not included in Equation (A.10) since that would involve double counting (L_k represents the parts of Q_a, Q_o, and Q_m that are used as capital). In other words L_k is a subset of the sum of L_a, L_o, and L_m.

When Q_a and L_a are both measured in calories, the ratio Q_a/L_a is the amount of food calories produced per unit of calories used by labor to produce that output. We refer to that ratio as "caloric productivity." It plays a central role in evaluating the consistency between estimates of Q_a, L_a, L_{GDP}, M', and BMI (i.e. height and weight) at given points in time.

A.1.3 The demographic/epidemiological component of the model

The demographic/epidemiological component of the model is also based on empirically derived relationships. It has been shown that the odds of dying or of contracting chronic diseases are related to height, weight, and BMI (see Kim (1995) and the sources cited there). Figure 2.4 presents a set of iso-mortality curves. This Waaler surface relates the relative odds of dying to both height and weight. Superimposed on the iso-mortality map is a set of iso-BMI curves which show the various combinations of height and weight that yield a given BMI. Moving along any given BMI curve shows how changes in height and weight change the relative odds of dying when BMI is held constant. The heavy line running through the iso-mortality curves at their minimum slope is the locus of weights at each height that minimizes the relative odds of dying.

The relative odds of dying, with respect to height and weight, are defined separately for men and women. For each sex it is given by

$$R = R(H, W) + u \tag{A.11}$$

and

$$R(H, W) = \sum_{0 \leq i+k \leq 3} \beta_{ik} H^i W^k \tag{A.12}$$

where:

R = relative mortality risk
H = height in meters
W = weight in kilograms
u = a random disturbance term.

The iso-BMI curve for BMI = b is by definition

$$W - bH^2 = 0. \tag{A.13}$$

The minimum risk curve is defined as the locus of (H, W) pairs such that W minimizes the relative mortality risk, given H. Hence, given an estimated Waaler surface $\hat{R} = \hat{R}(H, W)$, its equation is derived as

$$0 = \frac{\partial R}{\partial W} = \frac{\partial}{\partial W} \hat{R}(H, W), \tag{A.14}$$

and an iso-risk curve in which all combinations of H and W give the same risk level r is

$$\hat{R}(H, W) - r = 0. \tag{A.15}$$

Equation (A.12) is normally estimated as a cubic function. The quadratic form imposes the restriction that the minimum risk curve is linear, which biases the estimated locus of optimal weights upward. Polynomials of degree 4 and higher improve the fit marginally at additional computational expense, yielding surfaces whose contour plots are all almost identical to the cubic.

Figure A.1 is a Waaler surface for chronic diseases that was fitted to the data of the National Health Interview Survey (NHIS) for the years 1985–1988. The equations that describe it are identical to Equations (A.11)–(A.15), except that the R is interpreted as the relative risk of having poor health due to chronic conditions or of having specific chronic diseases.

It is possible to define a Waaler surface in H and BMI, instead of H and W. Its equations are analogous to Equations (A.11)–(A.15), except that BMI is substituted for W in (A.11), (A.12), and (A.15); the iso-BMI curves in Figure A.1 become iso-weight curves, and the minimum risk locus (Equation A.15) is defined with respect to BMI.[27]

---

[27] For further discussion of the usefulness of this alternative see Kim (1995).

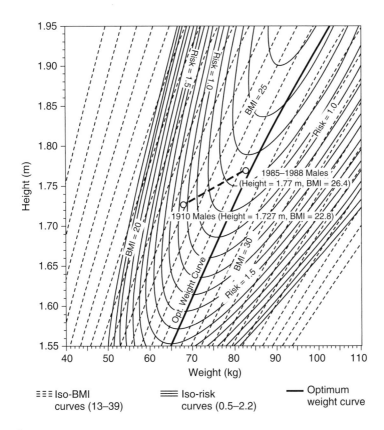

Figure A.1 Health improvement predicted by NHIS 1985–1988 health surface

Source: Kim 1993.
Note: All risks are measured relative to the average risk of morbidity (calculated over all heights and weights) among NHIS 1985–1988 white males aged 45–64.

It is also possible to define marginal risk distributions, one of which is shown in Figure 2.2 with respect to height. In Figure 2.2, the relative risk at each height is obtained by summing over all weights, with each weight multiplied by the share of persons at that weight. Thus, Equation (A.11) becomes

$$R(H = h, W) = \sum_{w \in W} R(h, W) \cdot \frac{N(h, w)}{N(h)} \qquad (A.16)$$

where N denotes the number of samples in the height–weight intervals.

In Figure 2.3, the relative risk with respect to BMI is again defined separately for men and women. For each sex it is

$$R(H, BMI = b) = \sum_{h \in H} R(h, b) \cdot \frac{N(h, b)}{N(b)}. \tag{A.17}$$

A.1.4 Interpretation of the model

Although equations (A.1)–(A.17) are interrelated, they do not form a closed system, nor are all of the variables simultaneously determined (see Figure A.2, below). Parts of the model are recursive. The mature heights used to predict mortality in the Waaler surfaces are to a large extent determined early in life, including *in utero*. Moreover, the mature height of an individual is also influenced by the health of his or her mother and maternal grandmother. Recent studies also indicate that BMI at middle and later adult ages may be, to some degree, controlled by environmental conditions of the mother, and of the child *in utero*.

It is possible to close the model, or parts of it, by taking certain variables as given, or by adding additional constraints. Both procedures are followed in Chapter 3 in a demonstration of the utility of the model by exploring the consistency between estimates of the supply of food, average stature, and average BMI in France and England since 1700. Among the variables not explicitly included in the preceding model but brought into consideration as constraints are: the distribution of workers between sectors; the increased allocation of energy to the production of food made possible by reducing maintenance (as a result of practices that lead to stunting and to low BMIs) and by the reallocation of energy among the a, o, m, and g sectors; and the consistency of estimated mortality rates with body builds.

Perhaps the most versatile constraint that we employ is the condition that the calories available to produce the food supply ($\hat{L}_a$) must be such that

$$f_a(\hat{L}_a | \hat{K}_a, \hat{T}_a) \geq \hat{Q}_a + \varepsilon \tag{A.18}$$

that is, estimates of the labor input, given the estimates of capital and land, used in the production of food must be large enough, within a small error, to yield the estimated food output ($\hat{Q}_a$). Another way of putting the same constraint is: the estimated caloric productivity ratio (Q_a/L_a) must be consistent with what is known about the technical capacity of agriculture and the level of inputs at given times and places.

The model also indicates the set of feasible equilibria that can prevail between a population and a food supply. Any value of the ratio of Q_a/N_c is feasible in a closed society as long as the constraint given by Equation (A.18) is met, without reducing H and BMI to the point that they violate Equation (A.19) in the long run:

$$F - M = r \begin{cases} > 0 \text{ usually} \\ \leq 0 \text{ in certain cases} \end{cases} \tag{A.19}$$

where:

M = the mortality rate
F = the fertility rate
r = the natural rate of increase.

Social choices, such as the level and rate of growth of urbanization or the redistribution of income, often through mechanisms of domestic and international exchange, may exacerbate chronic malnutrition and hence lead to small average body builds. Small average body builds imply high normal death rates. However, as long as constraints (A.18) and (A.19) are met, population and the food supply are in equilibrium in the sense that such conditions can continue indefinitely.

There are aspects of the model that we have not yet interpreted, particularly Equations (A.9) and (A.10), which are critical to linking changes in human physiology to the theory of economic growth and to certain aspects of economic forecasting. We defer that task to when we dynamize and extend the model presented so far (see Chapter 3, below). However, we point out those aspects of the model that are central to the demonstration in Chapter 3, that the relationship between population and the food supply has involved multiple equilibria. Which of these equilibria has prevailed at particular times and places is, as we will demonstrate, the outcome of complicated interactions between technological, economic, political, cultural, demographic, ecological, and physiological factors.

Appendix B: Lognormal distribution

In estimating the means and bounds of each decile in caloric distributions A, B, and C in Table 2.3, use was made of the following relationships between the parameters of the lognormal distribution and the mean and standard deviation of the corresponding distribution of the logs (Aitchson and Brown 1966, pp. 8–9):

$$M_d = e^{\mu} \tag{B.1}$$

$$\overline{X} = e^{\mu + \frac{1}{2}\sigma^2} \tag{B.2}$$

$$s^2 = e^{\sigma^2 + 2\mu}(e^{\sigma^2} - 1) \tag{B.3}$$

$$\frac{s}{\overline{X}} = (e^{\sigma^2} - 1)^{\frac{1}{2}} \tag{B.4}$$

$$M_o = e^{\mu - \sigma^2} \tag{B.5}$$

where:

μ = the mean of the distribution of logs
σ = the standard deviation of the distribution of logs

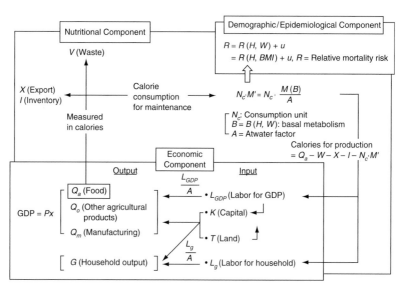

Note: See Appendix A.

Figure A.2 Flow diagram of the model

M_d = the median of the lognormal distribution
$\overline{X}$ = the mean of the lognormal distribution
s = the standard deviation of the lognormal distribution
M_o = the mode of the lognormal distribution.

It follows that if the coefficient of variation in the lognormal distribution is known, σ follows immediately from Equation (B.4). If $\overline{X}$ and σ are known, μ follows immediately from Equation (B.2). Once σ and μ are known, M_d and M_o follow from Equations (B.1) and (B.5). The lower bounds of deciles 2–10 in the lognormal distribution can be obtained from the unit normal distribution, making use of the following relationships:

$$\frac{\ln d_i - \mu}{\sigma} = Z_i \tag{B.6}$$

where:

d_i = the lower bound of the ith lognormal decile
Z_i = the Z score of $\ln d_i$.

Since Z_i, σ, and μ are known, $\ln d_i$ follows immediately from Equation (B.6). The mean of each decile of the lognormal distribution is obtained from:

$$Z_{mi} = \frac{N}{(2\pi)^{0.5}} \int\limits_{Z_i}^{Z_{i+j}} Z \cdot e^{-0.5Z^2} dZ \tag{B.7}$$

$$\overline{X}_i = e^{Z_{mi} \cdot \sigma + \mu} \tag{B.8}$$

where:

Z_{mi} = the Z score of the mean of the ith decile (or other interval) in the normal distribution
$\overline{X}_i$ = the mean of the ith decile (or other interval) in the lognormal distribution
N = the reciprocal of the area between Z_i and Z_{i+j} (which, in this case, is 10).

Equation (B.8) implies that the values Z_{mi} for each of the ten deciles are as follows:

Decile	Z_{mi}
Highest	1.7549
Ninth	1.0448
Eighth	0.6773
Seventh	0.3865
Sixth	0.1260
Fifth	−0.1260
Fourth	−0.3865
Third	−0.6773
Second	−1.0448
First	−1.7549

Some values of Z_{mi} for the areas above the highest decile are:

Above the 0.999 quantile	3.3675
Above the 0.99 centile	2.6655
Above the 0.95 centile	2.0626

Finally, the Gini coefficient G of $LN(\mu, \sigma)$ is given by $G = 2\phi\left(\frac{\sigma}{\sqrt{2}}\right) - 1$, where $\phi(.)$ is the distribution function of the standard normal cumulative distribution.

3 | *The analysis of long-term trends in nutritional status, mortality, and economic growth*

In Chapter 2, we developed techniques for the estimation of the supply of calories as well as techniques for choosing among competing estimates of caloric consumption. We also described the way in which data on height and weight (or BMI) can be used to assess long-term changes in the risk of dying at specific ages for men and women.

In this chapter, we apply these and related techniques to evaluate and propose resolutions to issues under debate by economic and social historians concerned with long-term trends in health, longevity, and other aspects of human welfare. Section 3.1 considers the nature of the samples contained in the Davies and Eden surveys. Section 3.2 evaluates the biases that arise from using cross-sectional data in estimating longitudinal income elasticities of demand for food. Section 3.3 assesses French productivity in food production during the eighteenth century. Section 3.4 examines the nature of European famines. Section 3.5 deals with the effect of variations in body size on the balance between population and the food supply. Section 3.6 evaluates the impact of improved nutrition on the growth of labor productivity. Section 3.7 discusses the impact of thermodynamic and physiological factors on long-term economic growth.

3.1 Estimating the income distribution of households and identifying the location of the ultrapoor and the average income of households in England for 1759 and 1801

Although the British lower classes were severely malnourished (Table 2.6), they were even worse off in other aspects of consumption, since calories were more equally distributed than income as discussed in Chapter 2. Studies of household consumption of agricultural and non-agricultural rural laborers in the second half of the eighteenth century by two reformers, David Davies and Frederick Eden, allow us to reconstruct the income of the British lower classes. The mean annual expenditure on all items in the Davies study (1795) was £27.00 per household circa 1790 (about 72 percent of which went for food) and £39.84 per household in the Eden study circa 1794 (about 74 percent of which went for food) (Stigler 1954).[1]

The expenditures must be adjusted for inflation, since prices rose rapidly over the period covered by the two, especially after the outbreak of the French Revolutionary Wars. The adjustment for inflation depends on the price index used. Using the Schumpeter–Gilboy index of consumer prices, the index number is 100 for 1759, 124 for 1790, and 136 for 1794 (Mitchell and Deane 1962). The annual expenditure figures in 1759 prices, then, are £21.80 in the Davies survey and £29.30 in the Eden survey according to the Schumpeter–Gilboy index. Using the Feinstein (1998) cost of living index (which uses a different base year), the price index is 100 in 1759, 104.9 in 1790, and 110.8 in 1794. In that case, the annual expenditures in 1759 prices are £25.70 in the Davies survey and £36 in the Eden survey.[2]

English political arithmeticians produced estimates of the social distribution of income in England circa 1759 (Massie, in Mathias 1957) and circa 1801 (Colquhoun 1814). These tables have been revised and converted

---

[1] These two studies used different sample surveys. Davies undertook a postal survey and asked his fellow ministers of the Church of England for detailed household budget information of poor families in their parish. Eventually, he received responses from 34 parishes and used a sample of 134 household budgets based on about 20 items of expenditure. But the postal survey caused a self-selection problem. Eden followed the survey model of Arthur Young – who toured the whole of England collecting a vast amount of data on all aspects of rural economy – to avoid the self-selection problem. He sent a researcher around England to survey the state of the poor population in 16 parishes, and eventually collected 53 household budgets.

But these studies omitted the very poor and the prosperous; none of the households in these samples had an annual income of less than £15 or as much as £70 per year. Although the households in both samples represented lower classes, they were living in settled residences and in their own homes rather than in workhouses, and so they were neither vagrants nor indoor paupers. In addition, they did not receive any form of outdoor relief. See Brunt (2001) for a discussion of the methods of Davies and Eden.

[2] The price indices of Schumpeter–Gilboy and Feinstein are also discussed in Chapter 4.

into size distributions of income by Lindert and Williamson (1982). We have corrected the Lindert and Williamson estimate of the proportion of ultrapoor households in 1759. They put the figure at 12.5 percent,[3] although they put the proportion at 24.2 percent in 1688 and 19.9 percent in 1801 – both of these proportions are downward revisions of those estimated by King (Laslett 1971) and Colquhoun (1814). This large implied drop in the English proportion of the ultrapoor during the mid eighteenth century appears to be an artifact of their estimating procedure. They assumed that the paupers and vagrants omitted by Massie were equal to their estimate of Massie's overstatement of households in manufacturing and agriculture, less Massie's understatement of households in the building trades and mining. However, there is little evidence to support the implication that the proportion of the ultrapoor dropped sharply from 1688 to 1759 and then rose nearly as sharply between 1759 and 1801. Given the large military drain on manpower during 1801, one would expect the proportion of the ultrapoor to have been relatively low. Various studies indicate that the 1750s and 1760s were a troubled period for labor with the condition of the ultrapoor unabated (Barnes 1930; Thompson 1963; Marshall 1968; Lipson 1971; Rose 1971; Schwarz 1985). Consequently, we have reestimated the proportion of the ultrapoor for 1759 as 21.4 percent by interpolating geometrically between the proportions for 1688 and 1801.

Figure 3.1 displays the estimated size distribution of income by households for 1759, using the corrected proportion of the ultrapoor as explained above. It also locates the average household income (as measured by expenditures in 1759 pounds and the Schumpeter–Gilboy index of consumer prices) in the Davies and Eden surveys. Figure 3.1 shows that, in both surveys, average income is close to the median of the estimated English income distribution during the third quarter of the eighteenth century (= £24.50), with one of the means falling somewhat above it, and the other somewhat below it.

---

[3] In Lindert and Williamson's article (1982, Table 3), the revised number of families that belonged to the classes of paupers and vagrants are 178,892 and 13,418, respectively. The total number of families is estimated 1,539,140 in 1759.

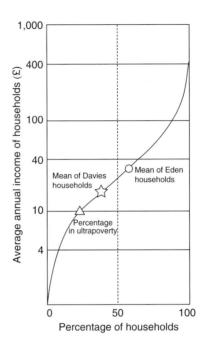

Source: Fogel 2000.
Notes: The income distribution is constructed using the revised proportion of the
ultrapoor and the average income estimated by Lindert and Williamson (1982).
The income of the ultrapoor was assumed less than £10 in 1759 pounds.
The estimated mean of income distribution in 1759 is £46.37 and its median is £24.5.
The means of the Davies and Eden surveys are £21.8 and £29.3, respectively,
in 1759 pounds. The price was adjusted by the Schumpeter–Gilboy index of
consumer prices.

Figure 3.1 The income distribution of English households in 1759

Since the median income was only about 53 percent of the mean
income (£24.5 ÷ £46.37 = 0.528), the households selected for the two
surveys straddled the poverty line, where poverty is defined as an
income less than half of that of the mean household, as was the typical
definition in the United States prior to the 1960s.[4] (These standards

---

[4] The method of estimating poverty – a relative poverty threshold here – has
changed over time. For example, the European standard of poverty threshold
today is the percentage of the population whose income falls below 60 percent
of the median income for the population as a whole.

are apparently quite similar to standards used by reformers who conducted the surveys [cf. Smolensky 1971].) However, none of the households were so poor that they fell below the ultrapoverty line, which encompassed paupers and vagrants. The ultrapoor (the bottom 21 percent) had incomes below £10.00, which was barely a fifth of the mean. The average income of the ultrapoor in 1759 was about £5.30, almost the same in purchasing power (£9.70 in the prices used by Colquhoun) as the ultrapoor had to spend, on average, circa 1801 (£10.00). So the first four decades of the Industrial Revolution did little to change either the proportion of the English ultrapoor or the level of their real earnings.

The finding that households in the two surveys had incomes well below the English national average does not imply that their calorie consumption was also below the average for England. In eighteenth- and nineteenth-century Britain, the poorest households were often able to augment their meager resources with the aid of what several authors have called the "economy of makeshifts" (Hufton 1974), including such activities as poaching, gleaning, the use of allotments and gardening, as well as applications for both charitable aid and poor relief (King 1991; Broad 1999; King and Tomkins 2003; Reay 2004, pp. 72–92; Williams 2005).

The relationship between the size distribution of incomes and the size distribution of calories is also complicated by the fact that, in cross-section (though not longitudinally), very poor households have a high propensity to purchase additional calories as their income increases, which initially leads the consumption of calories to increase more rapidly than income. However, as calorie consumption approaches the societal mean, the propensity to purchase additional calories declines sharply, even though incomes are still quite low. Thus, at average levels of calorie consumption similar to those found in the Davies and Eden surveys, when calories are sufficiently cheap and the distribution of income sufficiently skewed, the mean consumption of calories might well be achieved by households that are below the median of the income distribution. In rural India in 1971–1972, for example, the average consumption of calories was achieved by households in the 49th centile of the income distribution. Since calories usually were relatively cheap in England during the last half of the eighteenth century, and England's income distribution was far more skewed than that of rural India in the 1970s, the calorie consumption

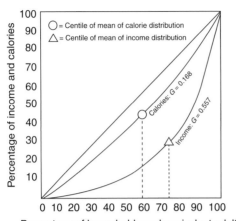

Source: Fogel 2000.

Figure 3.2 Comparison of the Lorenz curves for calories and for income in England during the second half of the nineteenth century

of median-income families was probably well above the mean calorie consumption of English households in 1759 (estimated from the data in Lipton [1983] by fitting a lognormal curve to the income distribution).

We also discussed the relationship between variations in the distributions of calories and income in Section 2.2. The extent of the inequality of each distribution or its variation can be measured by the Gini coefficient, and its cumulative distribution can be graphically represented by the Lorenz curve as seen in Figure 3.2, which is estimated from English data in the second half of the nineteenth century. The figure shows that the mean of caloric distribution is closer to its median level than is that of income distribution; the cumulative distribution of calories is closer to the (diagonal) line of perfect equality than is that of income. These imply that size distributions of calories are generally more equal than those of income.

The procedure for identifying the parameters of the lognormal distribution that fits the revised Massie table (income distribution) is somewhat different from the procedure employed in the construction of the size distribution of calorie consumption in Tables 2.3 and 2.4.

There, the specification of the coefficient of variation determined the standard deviation of the distribution of logs, σ; and σ together with estimated mean calorie consumption (2,413 per consuming unit for France and 3,271 for England) determined the mean of the distribution of logs, μ. (See Appendix B of Chapter 2 for further treatment of the lognormal distribution and the derivation of the equations used in the following discussion.) The two equations used for Tables 2.3 and 2.4 are:

$$\frac{\sigma^2}{2} + \mu = \ln \overline{X}, \tag{3.1}$$

$$\frac{s}{\overline{X}} = (e^{\sigma^2} - 1)^{\frac{1}{2}}. \tag{3.2}$$

In the case of the revised Massie social table, $s/\overline{X}$ is not known. However, recalling the discussion in Section 2.2, we can use the information we have about the proportion of ultrapoor population to approximate it. We have estimated that 21.4 percent of English households were ultrapoor, and that this class was defined by incomes of £10 or less. Since the natural log of income (ln X) follows the normal distribution, i.e., ln $X \sim N(\mu, \sigma)$, the Z score (standardized values in the normal distribution) can be expressed as follows:

$$Z[\Pr(X \leq X_i)] = \frac{\ln X_i - \mu}{\sigma}. \tag{3.3}$$

Then, given the cutoff income of the ultrapoor group ($X_i = £10$), the equation becomes:

$$-0.7926 = \frac{2.3026 - \mu}{\sigma}. \tag{3.4}$$

where 2.3026 is the natural log of 10, and –0.7926 is the Z score corresponding to 21.4 percent. Since $\overline{X}$ is known (£46.37) and its natural log is 3.8367, Equations (3.1) and (3.4) imply the following quadratic in σ:

$$\sigma^2 + 1.59\sigma - 3.07 = 0. \tag{3.5}$$

Solving Equation (3.5) gives $\sigma = 1.13$, which, when substituted in Equation (3.4), yields $\mu = 3.20$.

This procedure for fitting the lognormal retains the estimates of the mean income and the household count reported by Lindert and Williamson (1982). Under these circumstances, the revised estimate of the proportion that was ultrapoor produces an adjustment in the share of income received by the upper classes.

An alternative procedure is to assume that the 137,066 families added to the ranks of the ultrapoor represent an addition to the population (rather than a redistribution of a fixed total population).[5] The new assumption increases the total of English families by 8.91 percent (= 137,066 ÷ 1,539,140; not an implausible figure) and changes the variance of the distribution in a direction that depends on the estimate of the mean and the standard deviation of the income in the previously omitted ultrapoor households. If one assumes that the additional ultrapoor households had the same distribution of income as the ultrapoor originally specified by Lindert and Williamson, Equation (3.1) implies:

$$\frac{\sigma^2}{2} + \mu = 3.7544. \tag{3.6}$$

Here, 3.7544 is the log of the new mean income (£42.71); it is less than the previous mean (£46.37) because the added households had incomes well below the mean (the mean income of this group is £5.3).[6] In addition, the Z score in Equation (3.3) implies:

$$-0.8542 = \frac{2.3026 - \mu}{\sigma} \tag{3.7}$$

where the new Z score (-0.8542) is further below zero than the score in Equation (3.4) because adding persons to the denominator slightly reduces the share of the population that is ultrapoor.[7] Solving Equations (3.6) and (3.7) yields $\mu = 3.20$ and $\sigma = 1.05$.

The consequence of the alternative procedure is to slightly reduce σ, which measures the inequality of the income distribution, but this

---

[5] The estimated total number of families in Lindert and Williamson (1982) is 1,539,140, and the number of ultrapoor families is 192,310. Thus, the difference of ultrapoor families between their estimate and our adjustment is 137,066 = 1,539,140 × 0.214 – 192,310.

[6] The value of £42.71 comes from 0.0891 × £5.3 + 0.9109 × £46.37.

[7] Because an additional 8.91 percent of populations are added, the new proportion of ultrapoor group becomes 19.65 percent (= 21.4 percent/1.0891). Its Z score is –0.8542.

change does not affect any of the major points discussed here. For example, the median of the income distribution (£24.5) is unchanged to three significant places, and the mean income of the ultrapoor is also virtually unchanged (£5.5). Other reasonable alternatives for fitting the distribution demonstrate that the principal points at issue here are robust to the fitting procedure.

The procedure used to compare the real average income of the English ultrapoor circa 1759 and circa 1801 is as follows. The Davies sample indicates that less than 0.5 percent of the servants in husbandry, the class that it describes, had household incomes below £10.9 in 1759 prices. Since none of the households in the Davies sample were characterized as ultrapoor (i.e., as paupers or vagrants), the upper-bound income for the ultrapoor is below that figure. So we have chosen £10, the next lower whole number, as the upper income bound of the pauper class.

To compare the mean income of the ultrapoor in 1759 prices with the comparable figure in Colquhoun's table for 1801–1803, it was necessary to develop an appropriate price deflator. This deflator was obtained by projecting the mean average income estimated by Lindert and Williamson (1982) for 1759 (£46.37) to 1801 by using Crafts's (1985a) estimate of the average annual real rate of growth in per capita income between 1759 and 1801. The procedure yielded a figure of £50.01 for the 1801 average household income in 1759 prices. Lindert and Williamson's revisions of Colquhoun's table yielded a per household income of £91.63 in 1801–1803 prices. Consequently, the implied national income deflator is 1.83 (91.63 ÷ 50.01 = 1.83), which makes the mean income of the ultrapoor in 1801–1803 pounds about £9.7 (£5.30 × 1.83).

It follows that the real rate of increase in the average earnings of the ultrapoor, $(10 \div 9.7)^{1/42} - 1 = 0.00073$ or 0.073 percent per annum, was less than that of society as a whole, $(50.01 \div 46.37)^{1/42} - 1 = 0.00180$ or 0.18 percent per annum.

3.2 Problems in estimating the income elasticity of demand for food from cross-sectional data rather than longitudinal data

It is common to attempt to estimate the income elasticity of the demand for food and/or calories from cross-sectional data. Such approaches leave something to be desired. In principle, although not necessarily in practice, time-series data are more appropriate than cross-sectional data for estimating income elasticities. We illustrate the problem by exploiting the food balance sheets currently available for England and Wales for 1700, 1750, 1800, and 1850.

The following are our current estimates of average calories available, rather than ingested, for daily consumption in England and Wales.

The demand for calories may be represented by:

$$Q = DY^{\phi}P^{-\varepsilon}. \tag{3.8}$$

When Equation (3.8) is reduced to rates of change, Equation (3.9) follows:

$$\phi = \frac{\overset{*}{Q} + \varepsilon\overset{*}{P}}{\overset{*}{Y}} - \frac{\overset{*}{D}}{\overset{*}{Y}} \tag{3.9}$$

where

Q = total calories consumed daily in England and Wales
Y = real national income
P = the relative price of calories
D = other variables that may shift demand
ε = the price elasticity of demand
* = the rate of change of a variable.

The annual rate of decrease in per capita caloric consumption between 1700 and 1750 was −0.055 percent per annum (essentially constant) and the rate of population growth was 0.265 percent (Table 3.1); $\overset{*}{Q}$ is the sum of these two growth rates, 0.21. Over the same period, Crafts (1980) indicates that the rate of growth in aggregate real income was 0.69 percent per annum. Hence, if $\overset{*}{P}$ and $\overset{*}{D}$ are presumed to equal zero, the income elasticity of demand for calories is:

$$\phi = \frac{0.21}{0.69} = 0.30. \tag{3.10}$$

If we use Deane and Cole's (1967) estimate of the rate of growth of total income ($\overset{*}{Y}$ = 0.663) instead of Crafts', the value of ϕ would become 0.32.

The relative price of grains, the main source of calories, was declining between 1701 and 1750 (Mitchell and Deane 1962). Using the price of

Table 3.1 *Average calories available for daily consumption in England and Wales and annual growth rates of daily caloric consumption and population, 1700–1850*

Year	Per capita	Per consuming unit	Annual rate of increase, per capita	Annual rate of increase of total population (percent)
1700	2,229	2,951		
1750	2,169	2,867	−0.055	0.265
1800	2,456	3,271	0.249	0.816
1850	2,524	3,337	0.055	1.325

Sources: The daily average calorie consumption was calculated as the mean of Grand total (A) and Grand total (B) in Table 4.9.

wheat as a proxy for a price index of all grains and deflating by the Schumpeter–Gilboy index of consumer prices other than cereals, the annual rate of decline in real grain prices ($\overset{*}{P}$) was 0.364 percent. Assuming that the price elasticity of demand (ε) was 0.18 (Fogel 1992a), the new value of ϕ becomes 0.21, if we use Crafts's figure for $\overset{*}{Y}$, and 0.22, if we use the Deane and Cole figure for $\overset{*}{Y}$.

When the same exercise is undertaken for the period 1751–1800, the estimated value of ϕ becomes relatively large. The relative price of grain (and hence calories) appears to have risen fairly sharply: $\overset{*}{P} = 0.76$. However, even if changes in relative prices are ignored and ϕ is estimated by $\overset{*}{Q}/\overset{*}{Y}$, its value is fairly high, either 1.05 or 0.76, depending on whether the Crafts or the Deane and Cole estimate of rates of change in income are used in the denominator ($\overset{*}{Y}_{\text{Crafts}} = 1.010$ and $\overset{*}{Y}_{\text{Deane and Cole}} = 1.404$ for the 1751–1800 period).

These figures are augmented by the rise in the relative prices of grains, taken as a proxy for the cost of calories. Again, assuming that $\varepsilon = 0.18$, ϕ becomes either 1.19 or 0.86.

What is to be taken from these computations? Mainly, that the range of plausible estimates of income elasticities derivable from the currently available time series is fairly wide, ranging from 0.21 to 1.19. The computation of ϕ in time series is quite sensitive to which time series on population is used, to the estimate of ε, to whether the calculation is done in total or per capita income, the conflicting estimates of Q and Y, and to the time period used for the estimates.

There is another way of conceptualizing Equation (3.8), which separates the income elasticity of the demand for calories into two parts, ϕ' and ψ. Then

$$Q = D\overline{Y}^{\phi'} N^{\psi} P^{-\varepsilon}. \tag{3.11}$$

Now $\overline{Y}$ is per capita income, ϕ' is the elasticity of demand for calories with respect to $\overline{Y}$, N is the number of people, ψ is the elasticity of demand for calories with respect to the number of people. Since ψ is the elasticity of calories with respect to numbers, *holding $\overline{Y}$ constant*, it seems reasonable to set $\psi = 1$

Then, dividing both sides of Equation (3.11) by N, differentiating totally, and rearranging terms yield Equation (3.12).

$$\phi' = \frac{\overset{*}{\overline{Q}} + \varepsilon \overset{*}{P}}{\overset{*}{\overline{Y}}} - \frac{\overset{*}{D}}{\overset{*}{\overline{Y}}} \tag{3.12}$$

where $\overset{*}{\overline{Q}}$ is the rate of change in per capita calorie consumption. In this case, the several estimates of ϕ' vary between −0.30 and 1.99. Now the range is even wider and (implausibly) includes the possibility of a negative elasticity.

In their thoughtful 1995 article "A British food puzzle, 1770–1850," Clark, Huberman, and Lindert observed an apparent contradiction with the conventionally understood income elasticity of demand for food. As the British population increased by 165 percent between 1750 and 1850, and income per head increased (according to their estimates) by 65–123 percent, they argued that "domestic agricultural output would have to have grown by between 172 percent and 228 percent from 1770 to 1850" in order to keep pace with the demand which these figures implied (Clark, Huberman, and Lindert 1995, pp. 216–218). However, in practice, the output of domestic agriculture fell some way short of this. According to Holderness (1989, p. 174), it "rather more than doubled between 1750 and 1850." They explained this contradiction in several ways. First, they observed that the evolving economy of Britain influenced trends in food consumption. They noted a trend toward food products that were increasingly processed and transported, reflecting increasing urbanization. Second, they identified a leveling of the demand for food among the middle and upper classes. They presumed that the income elasticity of the demand for food was about 0.6, a figure previously adopted by Crafts and others. Moreover, while most food prices rose with the cost of living, the prices of tea and sugar dropped by more than 50 percent, which may have shifted demand away from other sources of calories. Prices for coal and clothing, two alternative sources of body heat, dropped as well.

The most critical of their points was their assumption that the income elasticity of the demand for food was 0.6. Indeed, the British food puzzle is a puzzle only if one postulates that the true income elasticity, derived from cross-sectional data, is about 0.6 and if one also assumes that the trend in food prices can be overlooked or treated lightly. Clark, Huberman, and Lindert (1995) bypassed the problems of the estimation of ϕ' from time series. Instead, they hoped to finesse these issues by using the Eden/Davies and other studies of food consumption of lower-class households to estimate cross-sectional income elasticities. But how are such elasticities to be interpreted?

One way of getting at this issue is to consider the following identity using the daily consumption for calories per consuming unit:

$$C = B + M + W + A + L. \tag{3.13}$$

The rate of change of Equation (3.6) is:

$$\overset{*}{C} = \gamma_1 \overset{*}{B} + \gamma_2 \overset{*}{M} + \gamma_3 \overset{*}{W} + \gamma_4 \overset{*}{A} + \gamma_5 \overset{*}{L} \tag{3.14}$$

where

C = average daily calories per consuming unit
B = calories required for BMR
M = additional calories required for baseline maintenance
W = calories required for work (which includes all discretionary activities requiring energy)
A = calories excreted in urine and feces (often called the Atwater factor when expressed as a share of calories ingested)
L = calories lost (as with plate waste)
$\gamma_1, \gamma_2, \gamma_3, \gamma_4, \gamma_5$ = the shares of B, M, W, A, and L in C, respectively
* = the rate of change of a variable.

Our approximate estimates of the γ_i for England and Wales during the eighteenth and early nineteenth century are as follows:

$$\overset{*}{C} = 0.47 \overset{*}{B} + 0.13 \overset{*}{M} + 0.20 \overset{*}{W} + 0.10 \overset{*}{A} + 0.10 \overset{*}{L}. \tag{3.15}$$

The last two terms of Equation (3.15) represent food that is wasted (not metabolized). If one considers only the distribution of energy that is metabolized, the three coefficients would be about 0.59, 0.16, and 0.25. Note that nutritional manuals take account of the current level of A when reporting the caloric value of a unit of food. Hence $\gamma_4 \overset{*}{A}$ refers to the extra losses of ingested calories such as those incurred during eighteenth-century Britain.

Which variables in Equation (3.15) would be correlated with changes in current income (i.e., are endogenous during the period at issue)? That is the implicit question that is posed when one assumes that a cross-sectional regression of calories available for consumption on income *at a point in time* provides an estimate of how caloric consumption will increase with the changes in real income *over time.*

Recent biomedical evidence indicates that the mechanisms controlling not only adult height but also adult weight (the determinants of B and M) are, to a considerable degree, established *in utero* and during the first three years after birth. Barker and Clark (1997) report that measures such as weight at birth and weight at age one predict not only adult BMI but also the ratio of hip to waist circumferences (a measure of the distribution of body fat). Hence the current (as opposed to early age) income elasticity of adult B and M are both quite low, and, as a first approximation, will be put at zero.

The elasticity of A with respect to current income is also very low, since physiological studies indicate that A depends on exposure to disease, the amount of non-starch polysaccharides (dietary fiber) in the diet, and the absorptive capacity of the mucosal cells of the gastro-intestinal tract, which is influenced by nutritional status.[8] One would not expect L, losses of nutrients in cooking, spoilage, and losses to rodents and other small animals to be significantly correlated to changes in current income during the periods at issue. Moreover, the income elasticity of W in cross-section is approximately 0.63, i.e., $\overset{*}{W} = 0.63\overset{*}{\overline{Y}}$.[9] Consequently, Equation (3.15) can be reduced to

---

[8] The extent to which the consumption of non-starch polysaccharides may have been affected by variations in income is not presently known.

[9] The income elasticity of W was calculated by running a regression of the logarithm of W on the logarithm of $\overline{Y}$. W (calories available for work) was obtained from Table 2.6 in Chapter 2, where $W = $ Col. (6) − 1.27 × Col. (5). The size distribution of $\overline{Y}$ (income per capita) was calculated using the income distribution parameters

$$\overset{*}{C} = 0.20 \times 0.63 \times \overset{*}{\overline{Y}}. \tag{3.16}$$

Hence, the income elasticity of calorie consumption for work (say, $\tilde{\phi}$) is estimated by

$$\tilde{\phi} = \frac{\overset{*}{C}}{\overset{*}{\overline{Y}}} = 0.126. \tag{3.17}$$

On the other hand, a regression of ln C directly on ln $\overline{Y}$ in cross section yielded the income elasticity of total calorie consumption (say, ϕ) as follows:

$$\ln C = 7.2184 + 0.26 \ln \overline{Y} \text{ or } \phi = \frac{\overset{*}{C}}{\overset{*}{\overline{Y}}} = 0.26 \tag{3.18}$$

where the $\overline{Y}$ column is calculated from $\mu = 3.20$, $\sigma = 1.13$, and the C column is from column 4 of Table 2.4 in Chapter 2.

The difference between the values of ϕ and $\tilde{\phi}$ derived from Equations (3.17) and (3.18) may be taken as an index of the elasticity of calorie consumption with respect to B, M, A, and L combined, designated by ϕ_X. Thus,

$$\phi - \tilde{\phi} = 0.59\phi_B + 0.16\phi_M + 0.125\phi_A + 0.125\phi_L = \phi_X = 0.134 \tag{3.19}$$

where ϕ_B, ϕ_M, ϕ_A, and ϕ_L denote $\overset{*}{C}/\overset{*}{B}, \overset{*}{C}/\overset{*}{M}, \overset{*}{C}/\overset{*}{A}$, and $\overset{*}{C}/\overset{*}{L}$, respectively, or

$$\phi = \tilde{\phi} + \phi_X = 0.126 + 0.134 = 0.26. \tag{3.20}$$

We are now in a position to consider the interpretation of cross-sectional regressions of calories (or food) on income, the so-called Engel curves, so insightfully discussed by Stigler (1954). The key point arising from Equations (3.13)–(3.20) is that cross-sectional regressions of calories (or food) on income reflect mainly the overwhelming influence of biological constraints, which are relatively fixed for particular individuals within a population at a point in time, although there is considerable variation from one person to another in that population. Consequently,

($\mu = 3.20$, $\sigma = 1.13$) estimated in Equation (3.5) of Section 3.1. The estimated $\overline{Y}$ (in 1759 pounds) for each decile group is as follows: 178.22 (top decile), 79.89 (9th), 52.74 (8th), 37.97 (7th), 28.29 (6th), 21.28 (5th), 15.85 (4th), 11.41 (3rd), 7.53 (2nd), and 3.38 (bottom).

what these cross-sectional regressions reflect primarily are differences in the levels of these constraints when individuals are grouped by income. They do not imply that mature individuals with low incomes who have low requirements for B and M will be able to alter these requirements merely by gaining income. Even when they have the resources (income) to do so, we know that many normally lean people find it very difficult to gain weight permanently, while many normally obese people find it difficult to lose weight permanently.

These biologically constrained requirements have changed slowly over time, mainly as a result of changing nutritional status both *in utero* and during developmental ages after birth, especially before age 3. The slave case (Fogel 1989; Fogel and Engerman 1992) shows that even when individuals are fed abundantly after early childhood, full catch-up is not possible. Slaves who were well fed only after they entered the labor force (mainly after age 10) exhibited considerable catch-up, but were still stunted at maturity by about 4 inches when compared to current NCHS standards (or close to 6 inches by current Dutch standards). We do not know how the BMIs of these slaves were affected by the improvements in their diets during developmental ages, but at maturity, though higher in BMI than comparable whites, they were still below current levels of US blacks by about 3 BMI points (about 21 pounds at the current mean height) (Fogel and Engerman 1992).

The point is that there are limits to the extent that the negative physiological consequences of malnutrition *in utero* and early childhood can be reversed during later life. Indeed, animal experiments have shown that some insults *in utero* require several generations of good feeding before the influence of the original insult becomes undetectable (Chandra 1975).

What about Equation (3.20)? Can we still accept the income elasticity of W obtained from household budget studies for time-series analysis? The answer depends on how quickly and how fully a small adult person existing habitually at very low work levels can upgrade health, improve muscle tone, increase the absorptive capacity of his or her mucosal cells, and generally raise his or her efficiency in transforming energy intake into work output. The cross-sectional regression tells us how much more energy people at higher levels of income, each of whom is more or less in long-term thermic equilibrium,[10] and fixed in stature, have available

---

[10] These individuals may be above or below the long-term equilibrium from day to day, month to month, or season to season.

Table 3.2 *Income elasticities of the demand for calories*
in eight nations (computed from time-series data)

Country	Time period for calculation	Elasticity
1. China	1962–2000	0.26
2. India	1961–2000	0.20
3. Japan	1961–2000	0.07
4. Germany	1961–2000	0.23
5. Italy	1961–2000	0.21
6. United States	1961–2000	0.30
7. France	1807–2000	0.22
8. England/UK	1800–2000	0.15

Sources: FAOSTAT Consumption Database; Maddison 1995;
Maddison 2001; Fogel 2004b.

for work than people at lower levels of income. It does not tell us by how much the energy used for work will increase with income for people fixed in stature (and relatively fixed in build) who are *in transition* from a low level of income to a higher one.

The difficulty with much of the Engel-curve literature is that it often fails to appreciate the role of biological constraints in the demand for energy (Dasgupta [1993] is a major exception). That caveat also applies to the argument of Clark, Huberman, and Lindert (1995), which assumes that a cross-sectional regression provides the same information as one in time series. They come back to this assumption later on (pp. 232–233), recognizing that it is a problem, but assign only 10 percent of the gap (their food puzzle) to it. However, had they used an elasticity of 0.26 (see Equation [3.20]) instead of 0.6 nearly all of the unexplained puzzle would have been resolved (see Table 3.2). What remained would have been due to errors in the estimation of the time series on the production of food, which should be measured by calories available for human consumption.

3.3 Assessing the productivity of food production in France, 1705 and 1785

The model which we have outlined operates in the long run, and its implications are worked out over generations. Today's changes in one variable, most notably the food supply, depend on the labor input generated partially by the environment which applied to the mothers of current agricultural workers, while those workers were still in the womb. Similarly, today's change in the food supply and in the disease environment will affect generations yet unborn.

Such long-run processes need to be investigated with long-run data which can only be gathered by historical research. We begin with France because, due to the work of Toutain (1971), we have a more complete time series of the average daily level of calories available for consumption for France than for any other country. Toutain's series, which extends back to circa 1785, was derived from national food balance sheets.[11] His estimate for circa 1785 is 1,753 kcal per capita daily (or 2,289 kcal per consuming unit). This estimate has been criticized as being too low because Toutain omitted calories coming from wine and from wild foods. Johansson (1994) has suggested adding 300 kcal per day to Toutain's estimates, which would raise the circa 1785 figure for average daily calories available for consumption to about 2,053 kcal per capita (or about 2,681 kcal per consuming unit) (cf. Weir 1989a).

On the other hand, Toutain's figure refers to calories available for consumption (total output less seed, feed, changes in inventory, net exports, and losses in distribution) and not to calories actually consumed.[12] Although he allowed for losses in milling, he did not take account of losses in spoilage, in distribution, in processing, and in plate waste. To be conservative we have set the difference between calories available for consumption and calories consumed at 10 percent, which implies that after correction for the omitted items, about 1,848 kcal per capita (= [1,753 + 300] × 0.9 or equivalently 2,413 kcal per consuming unit) were consumed daily. The last figure is very close to Grantham's (1993) estimate that French per capita consumption averaged 1,850 kcal daily, which he based on a collection of estimates made by knowledgeable contemporaries near the end of the *ancien régime*.

3.3.1 Labor productivity in food production

Toutain argued, on much less evidence than was available for later years, that the French aggregate output of food in 1705 was only 62

---

[11] National food balance sheets are created by estimating the total annual production of food plus inventory changes and imports less exports, and then subtracting feed, seed, and losses in processing and distribution. The procedure involves the estimation of such factors as the share of the slaughter weight of animals that is edible.

[12] The changes in inventory are not net of inventory spoilage.

percent of the circa 1785 level. Since the French population of 1705 was about 78 percent of the circa 1785 level, Toutain's implied estimate of average daily food consumption in 1705 is about 1,469 kcal per capita (= 1,848 kcal × 0.62 ÷ 0.78) or about 1,918 kcal per consuming unit assuming the same conversion factor (= 0.7658) that we used for 1785. That finding was challenged by Le Roy Ladurie (1979b) who argued that 1705 production was about 70 to 80 percent of the circa 1785 level, implying that on a per capita basis consumption in 1705 was, at worst, about 1,658 kcal per capita (= 1,848 kcal × 0.7 ÷ 0.78) or 2,165 per consuming unit.

One approach to the resolution of this issue is to consider whether the growth rate in consumption is consistent with what is known about changes in labor productivity in agriculture. If the share of food in agricultural output was constant and the share of output that was wasted remained constant, then Equation (3.21) would be the applicable identity for rate-of-change analysis:

$$\frac{C_a}{N} = \left(\frac{C_a}{A_a}\right)\left(\frac{A_a}{N_a}\right)\left(\frac{N_a}{N}\right) \tag{3.21}$$

where

C_a = calories consumed by people
N = the size of the population
N_a = the size of the agricultural population
A_a = the number of agricultural laborers.

Differentiating equation (3.21) totally yields

$$(\overset{*}{C_a} - \overset{*}{N}) = (\overset{*}{C_a} - \overset{*}{A_a}) + (\overset{*}{A_a} - \overset{*}{N_a}) + (\overset{*}{N_a} - \overset{*}{N}) \tag{3.22}$$

where an asterisk over a variable indicates the percentage rate of change in that variable.

Toutain's hypothesis implies that the growth rate of per capita calorie consumption $(\overset{*}{C_a} - \overset{*}{N})$ was about 0.29 percent per annum.[13] Wrigley (1987a) has estimated that between 1700 and 1800 $(\overset{*}{N_a} - \overset{*}{N})$ was about −0.07 percent per annum. If we assume that the labor force participation rate within agriculture was constant, i.e. $(\overset{*}{A_a} - \overset{*}{N_a}) = 0$,

[13] $\left[\left(\frac{1,848\,\text{kcal}}{1,469\,\text{kcal}}\right)^{\frac{1}{80}} - 1\right] \times 100.$

the preceding estimates imply that growth in labor productivity in food production in France during the eighteenth century, $(\overset{*}{C}_a - \overset{*}{A}_a)$, was about 0.36 percent per annum. The last figure may seem modest since it is less than half of the rate of growth of labor productivity in English agriculture (food plus nonfood) during the same century (Allen 1994). Hoffman's (1991) analysis of productivity growth in the Paris basin during the eighteenth century, however, indicated that between circa 1700 and circa 1785 labor productivity in agriculture grew by less than 0.15 percent per annum.

A potential difficulty with postulating a 26 percent increase (from 1,918 kcal to 2,413 kcal per consuming unit, following Toutain's estimates) in the French consumption of calories per capita between circa 1705 and circa 1785 is that it might imply a level of caloric availability in 1705 that was too low to provide the dietary energy required for the work involved in producing the national product of that year. The salience of this point becomes evident when labor productivity is measured by calories of food produced per calorie of labor input $(Q_a \div L_a)$. This "caloric productivity ratio" will be discussed more fully in Section 3.3.2, below. The implications of such a calculation are reported in Tables 3.3 and 3.4. Table 3.3 presents three distributions of calories that indirectly reflect three alternative assumptions about caloric availability. Distribution A is based on Toutain's assumption that consumption of food per consuming unit was 20 percent less in 1705 than in circa 1785. Distribution B is based on Le Roy Ladurie's suggestion that the rise in per capita consumption between these dates may have been 10 percent. Distribution C is that which prevailed in circa 1785 (i.e., the no-rise distribution).

Which of these three possibilities is most plausible for 1705? We approach this problem by evaluating the three distributions with respect to Equation (A.18) in Appendix A of Chapter 2, above: Are there, under each distribution, enough calories to make it possible for food workers to produce the output of food? To get at this question, we must first estimate the calories available for work, assuming that the typical adult male in circa 1705 was small with a height of 1.63 meters[14] and a BMI of 19, which implies a weight of just 50.5 kg.[15]

---

[14] Table 2.5 above estimates the heights of French men in the final quarter of the eighteenth century, but does not provide data for an earlier period. The current calculations are based on the assumption that the average height of French men

Table 3.3 *Three alternative distributions of the daily French consumption of calories per consuming unit circa 1705 (s/$\overline{X}$ = 0.3)*

Decile (1)	Distribution A A 20 percent cut in consumption $\overline{X}$ = 1930 kcal (2)	Distribution B A 10 percent cut in consumption $\overline{X}$ = 2171 kcal (3)	Distribution C No cut in consumption $\overline{X}$ = 2413 kcal (4)
1. Highest	3,094	3,481	3,868
2. Ninth	2,512	2,826	3,141
3. Eighth	2,255	2,537	2,819
4. Seventh	2,071	2,329	2,589
5. Sixth	1,918	2,158	2,398
6. Fifth	1,781	2,004	2,227
7. Fourth	1,650	1,856	2,063
8. Third	1,515	1,704	1,894
9. Second	1,360	1,530	1,701
10. First	1,104	1,242	1,381

Notes: See Appendix B, Chapter 2, above. $\overline{X}$ denotes caloric consumption per consuming unit. Decile entries in this and all other columns are at decile means. The distribution for the 20 percent cut (compared with circa 1785) was computed from LN (1,930; 579). The distribution for the 10 percent cut was computed from LN (2,171; 651). The distribution for no cut was computed from LN (2,413; 724).

According to Table 3.4, under the hypothesis of no cut in consumption (Distribution C), the physical activity level (PAL) – a person's daily energy expenditure expressed as a multiple of BMR – of the bottom decile is less than 1.27, which is not enough for body maintenance. Average daily energy expenditure of the top nine deciles

who were alive in 1705 was the same as the estimated value of French heights in circa 1785. We consider the implications of an alternative assumption at the end of this section.

[15] A weight of 50.5 kg implies a BMR of 1,451 kcal, and PAL of 1.66, which is lower than the required energy level for light work (1.7 BMR) and so would be inadequate for agricultural workers. Moreover, as indicated by Figure 2.4 above, a height of 1.63 m and a BMI of 19 imply that French mortality rates were about 33 percent higher than British mortality rates of the period, which is consistent with direct estimates (cf. Fogel 1992c, Table 9.1; see Section 2.3.2, above). On the other hand, if the French BMI is put at 21, BMR would be 1,533 kcal, and PAL would be 1.53, which is far too low for any but the lightest work, and would require inactivity for much of the working day (see Table 2.7, above).

Table 3.4 *The distribution of PAL among French adult males circa 1705*

Decile (1)	BMI (2)	Stature (m) (3)	Weight (kg) (4)	kcal for BMR (5)	Distribution A PAL (6)	Distribution A PAL (7)	Distribution B PAL (8)	Distribution C PAL (8)	Distribution A PAL: under the assumption of reduced body size (9)
Highest	24.72	1.75	75.34	1,832	1.69	1.90	2.11		1.77
9	22.11	1.70	63.82	1,655	1.52	1.71	1.90		1.59
8	20.87	1.67	58.54	1,575	1.43	1.61	1.79		1.50
7	19.94	1.66	54.65	1,515	1.37	1.54	1.71		1.43
6	19.14	1.64	51.38	1,465	1.31	1.47	1.64		1.37
5	18.40	1.62	48.39	1,419	1.26	1.41	1.57		1.32
4	17.66	1.60	45.47	1,375	1.20	1.35	1.50		1.26
3	16.88	1.59	42.41	1,328	1.14	1.28	1.43		1.20
2	15.93	1.56	38.82	1,273	1.07	1.20	1.34		1.12
Lowest	14.25	1.51	32.67	1,179	0.94	1.05	1.17		0.98

Notes: Column 2: BMI~LN (19, 3); Column 3: Stature~N (1.63, 0.066); Column 4: Col. 2 × (Col. 3 squared) and the sample mean is 50.5 kg; Column 5: computed from Equation (A.7) in Chapter 2; Column 6: Col. 2 of Table 3.3 ÷ Col. 5; Column 7: Col. 3 of Table 3.3 ÷ Col. 5; Column 8: Col. 4 of Table 3.3 ÷ Col. 5. Column 9: calculated under the assumption of BMI~LN (18, 3) and Stature~N (1.60, 0.066). Note that some figures are subject to rounding.

(Table 3.3, column 4) was 2,522 kcal. Because the average height and weight of the top nine deciles were estimated at 1.64 m and 53.2 kg respectively, men with these body builds would require about 1,493 kcal per day for basal metabolism (see Equation [A.7] in Chapter 2), implying that 498 kcal were required for eight hours of sleep (= 1,493 kcal ÷ 24 × 8 hours). This leaves 2,024 kcal per day for activities, or about 127 per waking hour (= 2,024 kcal ÷ 16 hours). Thus, the French only had the energy per consuming unit to perform about 74 percent of the work performed by the English around 1800.[16] Table 3.4 also indicates that in order for the top nine deciles in Distribution C to have been in the labor force, consuming units could have engaged only in light labor because their average PAL is around 1.69.[17] In the case of Distribution B with only 90 percent of the caloric consumption of circa 1785, the average PAL of the top eight deciles is 1.55. This implies that only 65 percent of the waking day could have been devoted to light activity. For 35 percent of the waking day, the average consuming unit had to be inactive.[18]

It follows that the 20 percent cut in caloric consumption in 1705 (compared to the circa 1785 level) shown as Distribution A in Tables 3.3 and 3.4 is untenable. Such a drastic cut would have left the bottom five deciles of consuming units below maintenance, with most of them starving to death quite rapidly. Even the consuming units in the highest decile (PAL = 1.69) would have had barely enough energy for about 2 hours of heavy labor, providing that they were completely inactive during the remaining 14 hours of the waking day, limited to maintenance only.[19] This calorie deficit is too large, even considering calorie transfers from non-working household members

---

[16] According to Section 2.4, Britain had about 3,271 kcal per consuming unit in 1800. Considering their typical body size, the estimated BMR for the English in 1800 was 1,586 kcal. This implies that 529 kcal were used for eight hours of sleep, and 2,742 kcal per day were available for activities, or about 171 kcal per waking hour.

[17] In the manual by FAO/WHO/UNU (1985), 1.7 BMR is the gross energy expenditure on occupational work at a light level, 2.7 BMR is for moderate work, and 3.8 BMR is for heavy work.

[18] Calculated by solving $1.55 = 1.27(1 - \alpha) + 1.7\alpha$ for α, where α denotes the proportion of light labor and 1.27 is the BMR for body maintenance, $\alpha = 0.65$.

[19] Solving $1.69 = 1.27(1 - \alpha) + 3.8\alpha$ for α, where α denotes the proportion of heavy labor and 1.27 is the BMR for body maintenance, $\alpha = 0.14$. This implies that out of 16 waking hours, 14 percent (2.2 hours) can be used for heavy work, and 86 percent (13.8 hours) for inactive body maintenance.

to those engaged in the labor force; this issue will be taken up later in Sections 3.5 and 3.6.

Of course, more of the consuming units could have been active in 1705 if we allowed for the possibility that they were smaller than so far assumed – say, with an average BMI of 18 and statures of 1.60 meters, which implies a weight of just 46.1 kg, the weight of a 13-year-old boy today, by the standards of the US Center for Health Statistics.[20] Under this assumption, the bottom four deciles of consuming units would be below maintenance level (Table 3.4, Column 9). The consuming units in the highest decile of Distribution A (PAL = 1.77) would have had energy for about 3 hours of heavy labor, providing that they were completely inactive during the remaining 13 hours of the waking day.

However, adjusting to diminished caloric availability by reducing the body builds of the consuming units would have involved a heavy cost. As indicated in the Waaler surface (Figure 2.4 in Chapter 2, above), the reduction from a BMI of 19 to 18, and stature from 1.63 to 1.60 meters, would increase the risk of death by about 15 percent.

3.3.2 *The caloric productivity ratio over the eighteenth century*

The caloric productivity ratio is the ratio of the total caloric consumption of a nation to the calories used for agricultural work. It is possible to estimate a caloric productivity ratio for France circa 1785 by making use of Wrigley's (1987a) division of the population between agriculture and non-agriculture for 1700 and 1800. According to Wrigley, about 58.7 percent of the French population of 1800 and 63.3 percent of the population of 1700 lived on farms. Interpolating geometrically yields a figure of 59.4 percent for circa 1785. If we assume that 35 percent of agricultural consuming units were in the agricultural labor force and that of this number, 80 percent were engaged in the production of food, then about 16.6 percent of all consuming units – $0.594 \times 0.35 \times 0.80 = 0.166$ – would have produced all of the calories consumed in France in circa 1785. We also assume that the size distribution of calories in circa 1785 follows Distribution C in Table 3.3 with a caloric consumption per

[20] Source: www.cdc.gov/growthcharts

consuming unit of 2,413 kcal. We also assume an average height of 1.63 meters, and an average BMI of 19. The consuming units who were engaged in agriculture produced 18.75 trillion kcal annually in circa 1785, and required about 0.753 trillion kcal to do so, implying a caloric productivity ratio of about 24.9 (see model 1 in Table 3.5 for detailed calculations).

There were about 19.3 million consuming units with energy available for work (= total consuming units × the proportion of consuming units with PAL > 1.27), and they consumed a total of 4.107 trillion kcal for work annually. Using the notation of Appendix A in Chapter 2, $L_a + L_o + L_m + L_g$ amounts to 4.107 trillion kcal. Of this amount, 1.437 trillion calories were used to produce GDP ($L_{GDP} = L_a + L_o + L_m$) annually, and the balance, 2.670 trillion kcal, were consumed in the household sector (L_g) in such activities as childbearing, child-rearing, food preparation, other forms of housework, physical growth, and play (see model 1 in Table 3.5 for detailed calculations). Altogether, 21.9 percent of calories consumed were available for work and the balance was available for BMR and maintenance.

Despite the low level of nutrition in circa 1785, which resulted in stunting, low BMI, and high mortality rates, the supply of calories was not only adequate to produce the estimated level of food production, but also to sustain the output of the other sectors of the economy. Could the same be said of a diet with twenty percent fewer calories (1,930 kcal per consuming unit) that is considered as a scenario for the year of 1705, as is the case with Distribution A of Table 3.3?

Assuming that the body builds, the share of consuming units in the labor force, and the share of labor devoted to food production remained constant, only about 0.329 trillion kcal would have been available for producing a food supply of 11.76 trillion calories. Under these circumstances (model 2 in Table 3.5), the caloric productivity ratio would have been about 37.0, about 48 percent higher than in circa 1785. This is contrary to what agricultural historians (cf. Grantham 1993; Allen 1994; Hoffman 1998) have discovered about the course of productivity growth during the eighteenth century.

As already discussed, maintenance requirements could have been reduced by following practices that increased stunting and reduced BMI. In other words, consuming units could have had more energy for work by reducing body size. According to models 3 and 4 in Table 3.5, the reduction from a BMI of 19 to 18, and stature from

Table 3.5 Caloric Productivity Ratio in France c. 1785 and 1705

Year	1785	1705	1705	1705
Size Distribution of Calories Scenario	Distribution C Model 1	Distribution A Model 2	Distribution A Model 3	Distribution A Model 4
(1) Daily caloric consumption per consuming unit	2,413	1,930	1,930	1,930
Panel A: For All Consuming Units: Assumption of Body Build, BMR and PAL				
(2) Height (meters)	1.63	1.63	1.60	1.60
(3) BMI (kg/m^2)	19	19	18	18
(4) Weight (kg)	50.5	50.5	46.1	46.1
(5) Average BMR	1,462	1,462	1,394	1,394
(6) Average PAL	1.61	1.29	1.35	1.35
Panel B: Calculation of Annual Total Caloric Consumption				
(7) Total population	27,800,000	21,800,000	21,800,000	21,800,000
(8) Consuming units	21,289,240	16,694,440	16,694,440	16,694,440
(9) Annual total caloric consumption (trillion kcal)	18.75	11.76	11.76	11.76
Panel C: For Consuming Units with Energy Available for Work (PAL>1.27): Proportion, BMR and PAL				
(10) Consuming units with PAL>1.27	19,309,341	8,714,498	10,550,886	10,550,886
(11) Proportion of total consuming units	0.91	0.52	0.63	0.63
(12) Average BMR	1,491	1,601	1,495	1,495
(13) Average PAL	1.66	1.45	1.49	1.49
Panel D: Calculation of the Number of Consuming Unit Engaged in Food Production				
(14) Consuming units engaged in food production	3,540,230	2,948,171	2,948,171	2,948,171

(15) Proportion of population in agricultural sector	0.594	0.631	0.631	0.631
(16) Labor force participation rate in agricultural sector	0.350	0.350	0.350	0.350
(17) Proportion of agricultural laborers engaged in food production	0.800	0.800	0.800	0.800

Panel E: Calculation of Caloric Productivity Ratio

(18) Daily calories available for work (kcal)	583	296	323	579
(19) Annual calories used for food production (trillion kcal)	0.753	0.318	0.348	0.623
(20) Caloric productivity ratio	24.9	37.0	33.8	18.9

Panel F: Total Calories Used for Work (Trillion kcal) and Decomposition by Sector

(21) Total calories used for work	4.107	0.940	1.246	1.246
(22) L_{GDP}	1.437	0.329	0.436	0.634
(23) L_a	0.753	0.318	0.348	0.623
(24) L_o+L_m	0.684	0.011	0.088	0.011
(25) L_g	2.670	0.611	0.810	0.611

Notes:
Row 1: See Table 3.3. Rows 2 and 3: See pp. 108–9, notes 15–16. Row 4: $(2)^2 \times (3)$. Row 5: Models 1 and 2: Calculated from Table 3.4, col. 5 (the reported value is the mean of the values for each decile). Models 3 and 4 have been recalculated on the same basis using the assumption of reduced body size. Row 6: Model 1: Calculated from Table 3.4, col. 8 (the reported value is the mean of the values for each decile; Model 2: Calculated from Table 3.4, col. 6. Models 3 and 4 have been recalculated on the same basis using the assumption of reduced body size. Row 7: Calculated from Wrigley 1987b: 184. Row 9: $(1) \times (8) \times 365$ days. Row 10: $(8) \times (11)$. Rows 11–13: Calculated using the methodology described in Table 2.6. Row 14: $(8) \times (15) \times (16) \times (17)$. Row 15: Calculated from Wrigley 1987b: 184. Rows 16 and 17: See text. Row 18: Models 1–3: $((13)-1.27) \times (12)$. Model 4: See text. A reduction in body size from 1.63 m and 50.5 kg to 1.6 m and 46.1 kg would reduce the number of calories required for BMR and therefore increase the number of calories available for work by 0.305 trillion calories for the population as a whole. If all these calories were allocated to the population which was engaged in food production (row 17), the number of calories available for this section of the population would increase by $(0.305 \times 10^{12})/(2{,}948{,}171 \times 365) = 283$ calories per day. The number of calories available for work in Model 2 is 296 calories, so $296 + 283 = 579$. Row 19: $(18) \times (14) \times 365$. Row 20: $(9) \div (19)$. Row 21: $(10) \times (18) \times 365$. Row 22: $(23) + (24)$. Row 23: (19); Model 4: Model 2 + 0.305×10^{12}. Row 24: Models 1–3: $(21) - (23)$. Model 4: As all the 'additional' calories have been allocated to the population engaged in food production (see row 18), this figure is the same as the figure for Model 2. Row 25: $(21) - (22)$.

1.63 to 1.60 meters would have increased the annual amount of energy available for work $(L_a + L_o + L_m + L_g)$ from 0.940 to 1.246 trillion kcal (model 3). If all of the increased calories were shifted to agriculture only (L_a), then the caloric productivity ratio would be 18.9, a figure that is more consistent with Hoffman's (1998) findings of a small rate of increase in productivity during the eighteenth century (model 4).[21]

3.4 The nature of European famines

If body size was varied to bring the food supply into equilibrium with the population, why did Europe continue to have national or even continental famines into the nineteenth century? At least from the beginning of the seventeenth century, when seed yields were well in excess of four and carryover inventories of food averaged between 33 and 42 percent of annual consumption, famines were man-made rather than natural disasters.

This hypothesis, and the evidence that supports it, has emerged from recent efforts to assess the types of inferences that can be made validly about the supply of food from data on grain prices. Attempts to make such inferences date back beyond Gregory King, although he was the first to explicitly propose something approaching a demand curve – the famous King's Law. After King, a host of political mathematicians and economists proposed variants of King's Law to predict the shortfalls in annual grain yields from the annual deviations of grain prices around their trend (Labrousse 1944; Slicher Van Bath 1963; Hoskins 1964; Hoskins 1968).

The problem with this approach to the measurement of subsistence crises lies not in its logic but in the difficulty of estimating the price elasticity (ε). If the elasticity of the demand for grain were known, the shortfall in the supply would follow directly from the deviation in price. Efforts to estimate that parameter from King's Law or variants of it (such as the formulas of Davenant, Jevons, and Bouniatian) imply values in the neighborhood of 0.4 (Wrigley 1987a; Fogel 1992c). The problem with these estimates is that they are based on the implicit

---

[21] The implied annual growth rate of caloric productivity ratio in 1705–1785 is 0.3 percent, while Hoffman's (1998) estimate for French agricultural annual Total Factory Productivity (TFP) growth in the late eighteenth century is 0.31 percent for the Paris Basin, 0.13 percent for Lorraine, and 0.21 percent for the southeast region.

assumption that the annual supply of grains varied directly with the annual per acre yield. That assumption would be correct only if carry-over inventories at the beginning of the harvest were zero, yet carryover inventories ran between four and five months of annual consumption. When King's Law is reestimated allowing for the effect of these stocks, the value of ε declines from 0.4 to 0.25. Additional evidence bearing on the exceedingly inelastic demand for inventories by those who held them indicates that the best estimate of ε is in the neighborhood of 0.18 (Fogel 1992c).

A price elasticity of 0.18 implies that even relatively small declines in supply would lead to sharp rises in prices. Moreover, because of large differences in the elasticity of demand for grain between the upper and lower classes, a reduction in the supply of grain by as little as 5 percent would set off a spiral rise in prices that would cut the consumption of the laboring classes by a third (Fogel 1992c). Thus, the typical English subsistence crises after the ascendancy of Henry VIII took place not because there was not enough grain to go around, but because the demand for inventories pushed prices so high that laborers lacked the cash to purchase the grain (cf. Sen 1981). Even the largest deviation of wheat prices above trend during Hoskins's (Hoskins 1964; Hoskins 1968) entire 280-year period or Wrigley and Schofield's (1981) 331-year period involved a manageable shortfall in the supply of food. Although carryover stocks were diminished, more than two-thirds the normal amount – more than a three months' supply – remained over and above all claims for seed, feed, and human consumption.

During the late Tudor era, authorities recognized that famines were man-made rather than natural disasters because the available sur-pluses were more than adequate to feed the lower classes. The basic strategy of the Crown was to leave the grain market to its own devices during times of plenty. But in years of famine for the lower classes, the state became increasingly bold in overriding the complaints of traders, merchants, brewers, bakers, and other processors about its meddling in the market. Since mere denunciations of engrossers did not work, in 1587 the Privy Council issued a "Book of Orders" which instructed local magistrates to determine the extent of the private inventories of grain and to force their owners to supply grain to artificers and laborers at moderate prices.

Although it took more than a decade to overcome local resistance to these orders, by 1600 local authorities were vigorously responding to the directives of the Crown. But this situation did not last long. The paternalistic system began to unravel with the Civil War of the 1640s, when Parliament developed a legislative program aimed at unshackling farmers, producers, and merchants from the restraints that had been imposed on them (Fogel 1992c).

Whatever the motivation for the switch in policy, it was the abandonment of the Tudor–Stuart program of food relief, not natural disasters or the technological backwardness of agriculture, that subjected England to periodic famines for two extra centuries. Analysis of variance of wheat prices – measured as percent deviations from trend (S^2) – indicates that during the period from 1600 to 1640, when government relief efforts were at their apogee, the variance of wheat prices around trend declined to less than a third of the level of the preceding era (from $S^2 = 935$ in 1541–1599 to 270 in 1600–1640). The large drop cannot be explained plausibly by chance variations in weather, since the F-value for $S^2_{1600-40}/S^2_{1541-99}$ is statistically significant at the 0.0001 level. Nor is it likely that the sharp rise in the variance of wheat prices during the last six decades of the seventeenth century (S^2 in1641–1699 = 625) was the result of chance variations in weather (Fogel 1992c).[22]

In the absence of government action to reduce prices during grain shortages, workers took to the streets and price-fixing riots became a standard feature of the eighteenth century. During the late 1750s, however, after food riots of unprecedented scope and intensity, proposals reemerged for the government to intervene vigorously in the grain market (to return to the Tudor–Stuart policies), including proposals to reestablish public granaries. As the battle over these questions ebbed and flowed during the next half century, the government, at local and national levels, gradually shifted toward more vigorous intervention in the grain market. By the start of the nineteenth century, famines had been conquered in England, not because the weather had shifted, or because of improvements in technology, but because government policy (at least with respect to its own people) had unalterably shifted back to the ideas and practices of commonweal that had prevailed during 1600–1640 (Barnes 1930, pp. 31–45; Post 1977).

---

[22] The F-value for $S^2_{1641-99}/S^2_{1600-40}$ is significant at the 0.004 level (see Fogel 1992c).

3.5 How variations in body size brought the population and the food supply into balance and affected the level of mortality

This section explores the proposition that variations in the sizes of individuals were a principal mechanism for equilibrating the population with the food supply, in determining the level of mortality, and in determining the level of work.

During the 1980s, the typical American male in his early thirties was about 177 cm tall and weighed about 78 kg (US Department of Health and Human Services 1987). Such a male required about 1,872 calories per day for basal metabolism and 2,378 calories per day for maintenance. If the French had been that large at the start of the eighteenth century, most of the energy produced by their food supply would have been required for maintenance and relatively little would have been available to sustain work. The implication of the energy cost accounting permitted by the recent work of agricultural historians is that to have the energy necessary to produce the national products of France, and even England, circa 1700, the typical adult male must have been quite short and light, weighing perhaps 25 to 40 percent less than his American counterpart today.

How Europeans of the past may have adapted their size to accommodate their food supply is shown by Table 3.6, which compares the average annual consumption of calories in England and Wales in 1700 and 1800 by two economic sectors: agriculture and non-agriculture. Within each sector, the estimated amount of energy required for work is also shown. The caloric productivity ratio represents a measure of the efficiency of the agricultural sector in the production of dietary energy. That measure is the number of calories of food output per calorie of work input in the food productivity sector.

Model 1 of Table 3.6 presents the situation in 1800, when calories *available* for consumption were quite high by prevailing European standards (about 3,271 kcal per consuming unit daily). At that time adult male stature made the British the tallest national population in Europe (168 cm or 66.1 inches at maturity) and relatively heavy by the prevailing European standards with an assumed BMI of about 21, which implies an average of about 59.3 kg at prime working ages. Food was abundant because in addition to a substantial domestic production Britain was able to import about 8 percent of its dietary

Table 3.6 *Caloric Productivity Ratio in England and Wales in 1700 and 1800*

	Year	1800	1700	1700
	Scenario	Model 1	Model 2	Model 3
(1)	Daily caloric consumption per consuming unit	3,271	2,951	2,951

Panel A: For All Consuming Units: Assumption of Body Build, BMR and PAL

(2)	Height (meters)	1.68	1.65	1.68
(3)	BMI (kg/m^2)	21	20	21
(4)	Weight (kg)	59.3	54.5	59.3
(5)	Average BMR	1,597	1,523	1,597
(6)	Average PAL	2.00	1.90	1.81

Panel B: Calculation of Annual Total Caloric Consumption

(7)	Total population	8,664,490	5,057,790	5,057,790
(8)	Consuming units	6,503,566	3,820,149	3,820,149
(9)	Annual total caloric consumption (trillion kcal)	7.765	4.115	3.774

Panel C: For Consuming Units with Energy Available for Work (PAL>1.27): Proportion, BMR and PAL

(10)	Consuming units with PAL>1.27	6,458,041	3,762,847	3,717,005
(11)	Proportion of total consuming units	0.99	0.99	0.97
(12)	Average BMR	1,600	1,529	1,607
(13)	Average PAL	2.01	1.91	1.83

Panel D: Calculation of the Number of Consuming Units Engaged in Food Production

(14)	Consuming units engaged in food production	660,112	588,303	588,303
(15)	Proportion of population in agricultural sector	0.363	0.550	0.550
(16)	Labor force participation rate in agricultural sector	0.350	0.350	0.350
(17)	Proportion of agricultural laborers engaged in food production	0.800	0.800	0.800

Panel E: Calculation of Calorie Productivity Ratio

(18)	Daily calories available for work (kcal)	1,183	973	892

Table 3.6 (*cont.*)

Year	1800	1700	1700
Scenario	Model 1	Model 2	Model 3
(19) Annual calories used for food production (trillion kcal)	0.285	0.209	0.192
(20) Caloric productivity ratio	27.2	19.7	19.7
Panel F: Total Calories Used for Work (Trillion kcal) and Decomposition by Sector			
(21) Total calories used for work	2.789	1.336	1.211
(22) L_{GDP}	0.976	0.468	0.424
(23) L_a	0.285	0.209	0.192
(24) $L_o + L_m$	0.691	0.259	0.232
(25) L_g	1.813	0.869	0.787
Panel G: Total Energy Consumed for All Purposes (Work + Other Activities + Maintenance)			
(26) In the agricultural sector	3.006	2.370	2.370
(27) Outside the agricultural sector	4.758	1.745	1.404
Panel H: Energy Consumed for Maintenance			
(28) In the agricultural sector	1.745	1.483	1.555
(29) Outside the agricultural sector	3.068	1.213	1.272

Notes:
Row 1: See table 4.13. **Rows 2 and 3:** See text. **Row 4:** $(2)^2 \times (3)$. **Rows 5 and 6:**
Model 1: Calculated from Table 2.6, col. 5 (BMR) and col. 7 (PAL). Models 2 and 3:
Based on assumptions described in the text, using the methodology described in
Table 2.6. **Row 7:** Wrigley and Schofield 1981: 533–4 (figures are for 1701 and 1801).
Row 8: 1700: (7) × 0.7553; 1800: (7) × 0.7506 For calculation of conversion factors,
see Table 4.12. **Row 9:** Models 1 and 2: (1) × (8) × (365). Model 3: This calculation
assumes that the caloric productivity ratio was the same as in Model 2, but that
body size was the same as in 1800 (model 1). **Row 10:** (8) × (11). **Rows 11–13:**
Calculated using the methodology described in Table 2.6. **Row 14:** (8) × (15) × (16) ×
(17). **Row 15:** Calculated from Wrigley 1987b: 170. **Rows 16–17:** See text. **Row 18:**
((13) – 1.27) × (12). **Row 19:** (18) × (14) × 365. **Row 20:** Models 1 and 2: (9) ÷ (19).
Model 3: Assumes that the caloric productivity is the same as in model 2. **Row 21:**
(10) × (18) × 365. **Row 22:** (23) + (24). **Row 23:** (19). **Row 24:** (21) × (16) × (23).
Row 25: (21) – (22). **Row 26:** (1) ÷ ((15) + (1 – (15)) × 0.9) × (8) × (15) × 365.
Row 27: (9) – (26). **Row 28:** 1.27 × (5) × (8) × (15) × 365. **Row 29:** 1.27 × (5) × (8) ×
(1 – (15)) × 365.

consumption. However, as model 1 indicates, British agriculture was very productive. English and Welsh farmers in the food-producing sector produced 27.2 calories of food output (net of seeds, feed, inventory losses, etc.) for each calorie of their work input. Assuming that food consumption per consuming unit was about 10 percent lower in the non-agricultural sector than in the agricultural sector, about 39 percent of this bountiful output was consumed by the agricultural workers and their families (3.006 trillion kcal ÷ 7.765 trillion kcal = 0.39).[23] The balance of their dietary output, together with some food imports, was consumed by the non-agricultural sector, which constituted about 64 percent of the English population in 1801 (Wrigley 1987b, p. 170). Food was so abundant that even the English paupers and vagrants, who accounted for about 20 percent of the population circa 1800 (Lindert and Williamson 1982), had about three times as much energy for begging and other activities beyond maintenance as did their French counterparts.

The food situation was tighter in 1700, when only 2,951 calories were available daily per consuming unit (see Tables 3.1 and 4.13). The adjustment to the lower food supply was probably made in three ways. First, the amount of energy used for work and production per equivalent adult worker was reduced both inside and outside agriculture, although the reduction was somewhat greater outside of agriculture (see variables (23) and (24) in model 2 of Table 3.6). Second, compared to 1800 the share of total dietary energy consumed in the non-agricultural sector in 1700 was reduced by about two-thirds, a reduction that was accomplished partly by constraining the share of the labor force engaged outside agriculture (see variable (27) in model 2 of Table 3.6). Third, the energy required for basal metabolism and maintenance was reduced by "shrinking" people (see variables (28) and (29) in model 2 of Table 3.6). If the average adult male in 1700 was 3 cm shorter and 4.8 kg lighter than their 1800 counterpart (i.e. they had a BMI of 20 rather than 21), the number of calories required for daily maintenance would have been 74 calories lower (1,597 − 1,523 = 74 kcal).

The last figure may seem rather small. However, it accounts for about 23 percent (74 ÷ 320 = 0.23) of the total shortfall in daily caloric

---

[23] The assumption is explained by the greater caloric demands of agricultural labor. We include the aristocracy and other members of the governing classes in the non-agricultural sector even though their wealth was mainly in land since they were not engaged in farming.

consumption (3,271 − 2,951 = 320 kcal). That figure is large enough to sustain the proposition that variations in body size were a principal means of adjusting the population to variations in the food supply. Since body height is determined in infancy and childhood, individuals cannot adapt to lower levels of food supply by changing their height, but populations can do so by exposing children to the level of food availability they are likely to encounter in adulthood. For a population to be in equilibrium with its food supply at a given level of consumption, the labor input (measured in calories of work) must be large enough to produce the requisite amount of food (also measured in calories). Moreover, a given reduction in calories required for maintenance will have a multiplier effect on the number of calories that could be made available for work. The multiplier is the inverse of the labor force participation rate. Since only about 35 percent of equivalent adults were in the labor force, the potential daily gain in calories for work was not 74 calories per equivalent adult worker, but 211 calories per equivalent adult worker (74 kcal ÷ 0.35 = 211 kcal).

The importance of the last point is indicated by considering models 2 and 3 of Table 3.6. Model 2 shows that the annual total of dietary energy used for GDP production in 1700 was 0.468 trillion calories, with 0.209 trillion expended in agriculture and the balance in non-agriculture. Model 3 indicates what would have happened if all the other adjustments had been made but body size remained at the level of 1800, so that maintenance requirements were unchanged. We also assume the same caloric productivity ratio of 19.7.[24] The first thing to note is that energy available for food production (L_a) would have declined by about 8 percent (1 − [0.192 ÷ 0.209] = 0.083) because agricultural workers used more energy for maintenance but had the same productivity ratio. Then, the national supply of dietary energy would have declined to 3.774 trillion calories, of which nearly 63 percent would have been consumed within the agricultural sector (2.370 ÷ 3.774 = 0.63). Similarly, those in the non-agricultural sector would have reduced the energy available for work due to the necessity

[24] The increase in the caloric productivity ratio from 19.7 to 27.2 implies that the annual growth rate of productivity is about 0.32 percent, which is close to the annual TFP growth in agriculture between 1700 and 1800 estimated by Deane and Cole (1967).

of greater maintenance. But our simulation result suggests that most of the energy available for non-agriculture would have been used for the maintenance requirements of that sector (1.272 trillion calories out of 1.404 trillion calories, i.e., about 90 percent). This leaves little energy for work in non-agriculture, on average. In this example, the failure to have constrained body size would have reduced the energy for work by about 10 percent $(1 - [0.232 \div 0.259] = 0.104)$.

Chronically malnourished populations of Europe universally responded to food constraints by varying body size. Such variation in height is displayed in Table 2.5 of Chapter 2; the cases of England and Hungary have been discussed in much greater detail in Floud, Wachter, and Gregory (1990) and Komlos (1990), respectively. Some may want to debate whether the size mechanism was more important than variations in fertility in equating population and the food supply. That interesting question should be pursued, but here we focus on the implication of the size mechanism for the explanation of the secular decline in mortality.[25]

It should be noted that subsistence is not located at the edge of a nutritional cliff, beyond which lies demographic disaster. Rather than one level of subsistence, there are numerous levels at which a population and a food supply can be in equilibrium, in the sense that they can be indefinitely sustained. However, some levels will have smaller people and higher "normal" (non-crisis) mortality than others.[26]

---

[25] Other assumed distributions of the supply of food to the non-agricultural sector yield more output. If persons outside of the labor force were squeezed, some of their calories could have been diverted to production. However, even a substantial impairment of the household economy would not have closed the gap in GDP originating in the non-agricultural sector.

[26] Moreover, with a given population and technology, changes in the allocation of labor between agriculture and other sectors may lead to changes in body size and mortality. In an ancien régime economy, the lower the share of the labor force that is in agriculture, *ceteris paribus*, the lower the share of caloric production that can be devoted to baseline maintenance. The reasoning behind this statement is as follows: Assume that one worker in agriculture feeds himself plus three persons outside of agriculture. Hence, a movement of 1 percent of agricultural workers to non-agriculture would reduce the per capita availability of food to the increased non-agricultural sector by about 1.33 percent. If baseline maintenance accounts for 75 percent of caloric consumption and if per capita calories reserved for work remain constant in the nonagricultural sector, calories available for baseline maintenance in that sector would decline by about 1.8 percent (assuming that within the agricultural sector per capita production and consumption is unchanged).

3.6 Contribution of improved nutrition and health to the growth of labor productivity

The neglect of the relationship between body size and the food supply has obscured one of the principal sources of the long-term growth in labor productivity. Reconsideration of the issue starts with the first law of thermodynamics, which applies as strictly to the human engine as to mechanical engines. Since, moreover, the overwhelming share of calories consumed among malnourished populations is required for BMR and essential maintenance, it is quite clear that in energy-poor populations, such as those of Europe during the second half of the eighteenth century, typical individuals in the labor force had, by modern standards, very small amounts of energy available for work.

This observation does not preclude the possibility that malnourished French peasants worked hard for relatively long hours at certain times of the year, such as at harvest time. Such work could have been sustained either by consuming more calories than normal during such periods, or by drawing on body mass to provide the needed energy. That level of work, however, could not have been sustained over the entire year. On average, the median individual in the French caloric distribution of 18-IV had only enough energy, over and above maintenance, to regularly sustain about 2.5 hours of heavy work per day.[27]

It is quite clear, then, that the increase in the amount of calories available for work over the past 200 years must have made a nontrivial contribution to the growth rate of the per capita income of countries such as France and Great Britain. That contribution had two effects. First, it increased the labor force participation rate by bringing into the labor force the bottom two deciles of the consuming units, who, even assuming highly stunted individuals and low BMIs, had previously had only enough energy above maintenance for a few hours of strolling each day – about the amount needed for a career in begging – but less on

---

[27] In 1785, total caloric consumption per consuming unit has been estimated 2,413 kcal. We have assumed a height of 163 cm, a BMI of 19, and a weight of about 50.5 kg. These assumptions imply a BMR of 1,451 kcal and 1,843 kcal for maintenance (= 1.27 BMR). Thus, the estimated PAL is 1.66 = 2,413 kcal ÷ 1,451. Assuming eight hours of sleep, hours of heavy work is calculated as about 2.5 hours per day (= 16 hours × α) by solving $1.66 = 3.8\alpha + 1.27(1 - \alpha)$ for α, where α denotes the proportion of heavy labor. See Section 2.4 for calculations.

average than that needed for just one hour of heavy manual labor.[28] Consequently, the elimination of the large class of paupers and beggars, which was accomplished in England mainly during the last half of the nineteenth century (Lindert and Williamson 1982; Himmelfarb 1983; Lindert and Williamson 1983b; Williamson 1985), contributed significantly to the growth of national product. The 25 percent increase in the labor force participation rate over the past two centuries made possible by raising the food consumption of the bottom 20 percent of consuming units above the threshold required for work, by itself, contributed 0.11 percent to the annual British growth rate between 1800 and 2000 ($1.25^{1/200} - 1 = 0.0011$).

In addition to raising the labor force participation rate, the increased supply of calories raised the average consumption of calories by those in the labor force from 3,271 calories per consuming unit in circa 1800 to 4,428 calories per consuming unit in 2000.[29] Of these amounts, 1,257 calories were available for work in circa 1800 and 1,936 calories in 2000, so that calories available for work increased by about 54 percent during the past two centuries.[30] We do not know exactly how this supply of energy was divided between discretionary activities and work circa 1800 but we do know that the pre-industrial and early-industrial routine had numerous holidays, absentee days, and short days (Thompson 1967; Landes 1969). If it is assumed that the proportion of the available energy devoted to work has been unchanged between the end points of the period, then the increase in the amount of energy available for work contributed about 0.22 percent per annum to the annual growth rate of per capita income ($1.54^{1/200} - 1 = 0.0022$).

---

[28] In the British case, Table 2.6 in Chapter 2 shows that the caloric intake of the lowest decile group in 1800 was too low on energy for any sustained work above maintenance, but that the next decile of consuming units were 161 cm tall, with a weight of about 46.5 kg, which implies a BMR of about 1,390 kcal and 1,766 calories for maintenance. A scenario of daily calorie use for the second-lowest decile is presented in Table 2.7.

[29] Source: FAO 2010, 3,400 kcal per capita. The estimated conversion factor in 2000 is 0.7678, based on the 2000 England and Wales population distribution in the UK national statistics online database. Then, the caloric consumption per consuming unit is estimated to be 4,428 kcal.

[30] For the calculation of energy available for work, we use the following assumptions of average adult male's height and weight at the prime age. For 1800, height is 1.68 m and BMI is 21, or weight is 59.3 kg (see Section 2.3.2). For 2000, height is 1.77 m and weight is 83.7 kg (source: NHS 2010). The calories available for work are calculated from total caloric consumption less 1.27 BMR.

Between 1800 and 2000, British per capita income grew at an annual rate of about 1.2 percent (Maddison 1982; Crafts 1985a). The combination of bringing the ultrapoor into the labor force and raising the energy available for work by those in the labor force therefore can explain about 30 percent of the British growth in per capita income over the past two centuries ($[0.11 + 0.22] \div 1.2 = 0.28$).

At the present stage of research, the last figure should be considered more illustrative than substantive since it rests on two implicit assumptions that have yet to be adequately explored. The first is that the share of energy above maintenance allocated to work was the same in circa 1800 as in 2000. It is difficult to measure the extent or even the net direction of the bias due to this assumption. On the one hand, absenteeism appears to have been much more frequent in the past than at present, due either to poor health or a lack of labor discipline (Landes 1969). On the other hand, work weeks are shorter today than in the past and a large share of energy above maintenance can be devoted to recreation or other activities whose values are excluded from the national income accounts. Although it is our guess that these two influences tend to cancel each other out, it may be that the share of energy above maintenance allocated to work (measured GNP) is lower now than in the past. In that event the estimate of the share of British economic growth accounted for by improved nutrition and health would be overstated. The other implicit assumption is that the efficiency with which tall people convert energy into work output is the same as that of short people. An enormous literature has developed on this question but the evidence amassed so far is inconclusive.

However, even if both of these assumptions tend to bias upward the share of British economic growth attributed to improved nutrition, it is quite unlikely that the bias could be as much as 50 percent. Hence it appears that improved nutrition and health accounted for at least 20 percent of British economic growth and the best estimate could be as high as 30 percent.[31]

---

[31] Of course, there are biases that run in the opposite direction. As Kim has pointed out, "Depending on how the caloric requirement for BMR and basic maintenance are defined and estimated, it is possible that the actual contribution of improved nutrition and health might be greater than the estimated 30 percent. Provided that changes in height and BMI affect not only mortality but also morbidity, shorter and lower-BMI people will have a higher incidence of disease

3.7 Some implications for the theory and measurement of economic growth

Recent findings in the biomedical area call attention to what may be called the thermodynamic and physiological factors in economic growth. Although largely neglected by theorists of both the "old" and the "new" growth economics, these factors can easily be incorporated into standard growth models. Viewed in the human-capital context, both factors may be thought of as labor-enhancing technological changes that were brought about by developments in the agricultural, public health, medical services, and household sectors. They may also be thought of as adjustments for the mismeasurement of the labor input, when labor is measured only in person-hours.

We referred to the thermodynamic factor indirectly when we indicated that as much as 30 percent of the British growth rate over the past 200 years could be attributable to improvements in gross nutrition. That computation was based on the first law of thermodynamics, which holds that energy output cannot exceed energy input. Since that law applies as much to human engines as to mechanical ones, it is possible to use energy-cost-accounting techniques to estimate the increase in the energy available for work over the past two centuries. In the British case, that increase had two effects. It raised the labor force participation rate by bringing into the labor force the bottom 20 percent of consuming units in 1800 who had, on average, only enough energy for a few hours of strolling. Moreover, for those in the

and illness, which would increase the caloric claims against diet, leaving less calories available for work and also leading to a higher number of sick days. If BMR and basic maintenance fail to take full account of such greater caloric demands by the higher incidence of disease and illness in a shorter and lighter population, estimates of the effect of improved nutrition and health on economic growth will be biased downward.

"The shorter and lighter British population of 1790 [1800 here] would have had a higher incidence of disease and illness than the 1980 [2000 here] population, requiring that a greater (negative) adjustment be made to the estimated calories available for work. This leads to a higher estimate of the increase in calories available for work between 1790 and 1980 and hence, the contribution of improved health and nutrition would be greater than the estimated 30 percent" (from a memorandum by John M. Kim dated November 4, 1991).

Moreover, we have to consider other channels in which improvement in nutritional status affects economic growth, especially through human capital accumulation like school attendance and cognitive development.

labor force, the intensity of work per hour has increased because the number of calories available for work increased. This change in the intensity of effort, by itself, appears to have accounted for about 18 percent of the long-term growth rate.

The contention that the British intensity of effort increased over time may seem dubious since the work day, week, and year (measured in hours) declined significantly over the past two centuries. However, the British (and other Europeans) could not have worked at the same average intensity per hour in 1800 as they do today, since that would have required a considerably larger supply of dietary energy per capita than was actually available. Increases in the intensity of labor per hour were also a factor in the American case, where food supplies were far more abundant than in Europe. Even if it is assumed that the daily number of calories available for work was the same in the United States in 1860 as today, the intensity of work per hour would have been well below today's levels, since the average number of hours worked in 1860 was about 1.75 times as great as today. During the mid nineteenth century, only slaves on southern gang-system plantations appear to have worked at levels of intensity per hour approaching current standards (cf. Fogel and Engerman 1974b; Olson 1992; Fogel 1993a; Fogel 1997).

The physiological factor pertains to the efficiency with which the human engine converts energy input into work output. Nutritionists, physiologists, and development economists have contributed to the extensive literature on this topic. Since some important issues are still unresolved, a firm assessment of the physiological contribution to economic growth is not yet possible. However, some aspects of the contribution can be indicated.

Changes in health, in the composition of diet, and in clothing and shelter can significantly affect the efficiency with which ingested energy is converted into work output.[32] Reductions in the incidence of infectious diseases increase the proportion of ingested energy that is available for work, both because of savings in the energy required to mobilize the immune system and because the capacity of the gut to absorb nutrients is improved, especially as a consequence of a reduction in diarrheal diseases. Thermodynamic efficiency has also increased because of

---

[32] The discussion in this paragraph draws on Dasgupta (1993) and the sources cited there.

changes in the composition of the diet, including the shift from grains and other foods with high fiber content to sugar and meats. These dietary changes raised the proportion of ingested energy that can be metabolized (increased the average value of the "Atwater factors," to use the language of nutritionists). Improvements in clothing and shelter have also increased thermodynamic efficiency by reducing the amount of energy lost through radiation. Individuals who are stunted but otherwise healthy at maturity will be at an increased risk of incurring chronic diseases and of dying prematurely. To evaluate the significance of changes in the rate of deterioration of the capacity to work over the life cycle, one needs to calculate the effect of changes in stature and weight on the discounted present value of the difference between earnings and maintenance over the life cycle (cf. Dasgupta 1993). A procedure for estimating this effect is set forth in Appendix C, below, along with illustrative estimates of the key variables. The exercise indicates that the discounted revenues would have increased by about 47 percent. This last figure, combined with a guess on the effect of the shifting of Atwater factors, suggests that the average efficiency of the human engine in Britain increased by about 65 percent between 1800 and 2000. The combined effort of the increase in dietary energy available for work, and of the increased human efficiency in transforming dietary energy into work output, appears to account for about 54 percent of British economic growth since 1800.

Focusing on the thermodynamic and physiological aspects of economic growth calls attention to the long lags that frequently occur between the time that certain investments are made and the time that their benefits occur. Much of the gain in thermodynamic efficiency that occurred in Britain and other OECD countries between 1910 and 1980 was due to a series of investments made as much as a century earlier. Failure to take account of these extremely long lags between investments and payoffs leads to puzzling paradoxes. During the Depression decade of the 1930s, for example, the US unemployment rate was never less than 16 percent; for half the period unemployment ranged between 20 percent and 25 percent. Yet life expectation between 1929 and 1939 increased by four years, and the heights of men reaching maturity during this period increased by 1.6 cm (Karpinos 1958; US Bureau of the Census 1975b).

The resolution of the paradox turns on the huge social investments, by both government and private enterprise, made between 1870 and

1930, whose payoffs were not counted as part of national income during the 1920s and 1930s even though they produced a large stream of benefits during these decades. We refer, of course, to the social investment in biomedical research (which included the establishment and expansion of modern teaching and research hospitals) whose largest payoffs came well after the investment was made. Also included in this category are such public health investments as the construction of facilities to improve the supply of water, the cleaning up of the milk supply, the draining of swamps, the development of effective systems of quarantines, and the cleaning up of the slums, which we will discuss more in later chapters.

Appendix C Estimating the effect of changes in stature and weight on the discounted present value of the difference between earnings and maintenance over the life cycle

The discounted present value of the age–earnings profile for n years beginning with the age x at which earnings peak is given by

$$P_x = E_x \int_0^n e^{-(\mu+\phi+r)t} dt \tag{C.1}$$

where μ is the rate of decline in the survivorship function (the l_x curve of the life table that describes the probability of surviving to age x), ϕ is the rate of decline in annual net earnings after age x, r is the discount rate (which, for convenience, is set at 6 percent), x is the age at which earnings peak, E_x is net earnings at that age, n is the average number of years that elapsed between x and the average age at which a living male ceased to be in the labor force regularly (for convenience, n will be taken to be equal to 35), and P_x is the discounted present value of the net earnings stream.

The value for μ for 1800 was computed from Wrigley and Schofield (1981), taking their e_0 for 1801 (which is 35.89) and interpolating between levels 8 and 9 in their family of English life tables to obtain the proper l_x curve for circa 1800. The value of μ for ages 35–70 in that schedule is 0.0413.

The projected shift in the l_x curve was based on the Waaler surface in Table A.1 in Fogel (Fogel 1993b). Using 1.68 m and 59.3 kg (or equivalently BMI 21) for 1800, and 1.77 m and 83.7 kg for 2000, yields a predicted decline of 33.1 percent in the mortality rate. The corresponding l_x schedule was obtained from Coale and Demeny's (1966) life table (Model North Male Level 13), using $_{35}m_{35} = 0.6932$ as the basis for the fit where $_t m_x$ denotes the mortality rate between age x and age $x + t$. The value of μ over ages 35–70 in that l_x schedule is 0.0221.

The changes in E_x associated with changes in height and weight were estimated from an equation reported by Robert A. Margo and Richard H. Steckel (1982). The data they used pertained to slaves seized as booty of war by the Union Army in 1863. The traders who related the value of slaves to their height and weight appear to have focused only on the differences in the location (not the slope) of the age–earnings profile, showing no apparent awareness of the relationship of stature and BMI to mortality and chronic diseases (cf. Fogel 1992a). The Margo–Steckel equation is:

$$\ln V = 2.73 + 0.032S + 0.17A - 0.005A^2 + 0.000046A^3 + 0.053H + 0.019W - 0.00027(H \times W)$$
$$\quad (1.47) \quad (0.92) \quad (2.22) \quad (-2.23) \quad\quad (2.10) \quad\quad (2.16) \quad (1.79) \quad\quad (-.173)$$
$$(n = 523, \ \overline{R}^2 = 0.20)$$

$$(C.2)$$

where V is the value of a slave, S is a dummy for skin color, A is age, H is height (in inches), and W is weight (in pounds); t statistics are in parentheses. For 1800, we used 66.1 inches and 130.7 pounds; for 2000, we used 69.7 inches and 185 pounds. The figures indicate that E_x increased by about 7 percent as a result of changes associated with body size.

The value of ϕ for circa 1800 between ages 35 and 70 was computed from data reported in Fogel and Engerman (Fogel and Engerman 1974b). These data indicate that net earnings at age 70 were about 17 percent of peak earnings, which was attained at age 35. Thus, the estimated ϕ is 0.0494 ($= 1 - 0.17^{1/35}$).

With the foregoing information and an initial assumption that ϕ remained constant, the increase in P_x can be computed from the data shown in Equations (C.3) and (C.4):

$$P_{x,1800} = \frac{E_x[1 - e^{-(0.0413 + 0.0494 + 0.06) \times 35}]}{0.1507} = 6.60E_x \qquad (C.3)$$

$$P_{x,p} = \frac{1.07 \times E_x[1 - e^{-(0.0221 + 0.0494 + 0.06) \times 35}]}{0.1315} = 8.06E_x, \qquad (C.4)$$

where $P_{x,1800}$ is the present value of the 1800 earnings profile and $P_{x,p}$ is the present value of the profile projected from the changes in height and BMI. Equations (C.3) and (C.4) imply that P_x increased by 22 percent ($8.06 \div 6.60 - 1 = 0.22$).

It is now necessary to take account of the effect of changes in body size on the rate of decline in the net earnings function (the value of ϕ). If it is assumed that net earnings at age 70 rose from 17 percent to 40 percent of peak-age earnings as a result of physiological improvements – $\phi = 0.0258$ for Equation (C.4), P_x increases by 47 percent. However, even the last figure is probably too low since it does not take account of the secular shift in the peak of the age–earnings profile from the mid-thirties to the mid-forties. Moreover, studies of the profiles of manual workers in recent times suggest that net earnings now decline much more slowly after the peak than in the past (cf. Fogel and Engerman 1974b; Jablonski, Rosenblum, and Kunze 1988; Murphy and Welch 1990).

In Section 3.6, we discussed that bringing the bottom 20 percent of the caloric distribution of circa 1790 into the labor force increased the labor force participation rate by 25 percent. Among those in the labor force, the average number of calories available for work increased by 60 percent between circa 1800 and 2000. Hence, the total increase in output per capita as a result of the increased availability of calories for work was about 100 percent ($1.25 \times 1.6 = 2.00$). Dasgupta's (1993) discussion suggests that reductions in diarrheal and other diseases combined with a shift in the composition of the diet increased the Atwater factors by about 12 percent. Since the above exercise implies that the reduction in chronic diseases and premature mortality increased thermodynamic efficiency by 47 percent, the combined increase in thermodynamic efficiency is about 65 percent ($1.12 \times 1.47 = 1.65$). In combination, then, increased calories available for work and the increased thermodynamic efficiency increased per capita income between 1800 and 2000 by 230 percent ($2.00 \times 1.65 = 3.30$) or by 0.6 percent per annum ($3.30^{1/200} - 1 = 0.0060$), which is about half of the annual British growth rate ($0.60 \div 1.12 = 0.54$). For further details, including discussion of possible upward and downward biases in this computation, see Fogel (1987).

4 | Technophysio evolution and human health in England and Wales since 1700

In the first three chapters of this book, we have outlined a theory of "technophysio evolution" and examined various techniques for estimating key elements of this theory, including the calculation of food supplies and the heights and weights of past generations. We have applied these insights to a range of practical problems, including the distribution of calories in Britain and France in the eighteenth and nineteenth centuries, the relationship between food availability and physical size, and the contributions made by changes in diet and physique to economic growth. We have also emphasized the critical importance of other factors, such as the quality of the sanitary environment, in helping to explain changes in the health of western populations over the last three hundred years.

This chapter examines the history of health and mortality in Britain in the light of these ideas. Section 4.1 examines changes in the heights and weights of both adults and children in Britain over the last three hundred years, and Section 4.2 summarizes the main trends in the history of mortality. Section 4.3 presents new evidence on the availability of food in Britain and Section 4.4 explores some of the implications of these findings for the history of work intensity. Section 4.5 considers a range of other factors which have been associated with improvements in health, including the roles of sanitary intervention and medical provision. Section 4.6 examines the history of morbidity and the concluding section explores the implications of these changes for the health of Britain's population in the future.

4.1 Height, weight, and body mass

Although measurements such as height and weight are, in themselves, much more straightforward than measurements of morbidity, there are also serious technical problems which need to be overcome before one can extrapolate from the height or weight of a sample of the population to the population as a whole. Nevertheless, there is now a broad consensus surrounding the main changes in these measurements since the mid nineteenth century. The most controversial sections of the anthropometric record, so far as modern British history is concerned, relate to the period between circa 1740 and 1820.

The first attempt to measure changes in the heights of British children over a continuous period was conducted by Floud and Wachter in 1982. Their analysis of the heights of poor London boys who were recruited by the Marine Society in the late eighteenth and early nineteenth centuries suggested that these children were extraordinarily small by modern British standards, and this continued to be the case even after a substantial increase in average heights among those born between circa 1800 and 1820 (Floud and Wachter 1982, pp. 431–436; Floud, Wachter, and Gregory 1990, pp. 165–171). The Marine Society children were also much smaller than upper-class children who attended the Royal Military Academy at Sandhurst during the same period. This work therefore provided an early indication of the capacity of anthropometric history to shed new light, not only on the effects of deprivation in the past, but also on the extent of social – and physical – inequalities (Floud, Wachter, and Gregory 1990, pp. 163–175).

Floud, Wachter, and Gregory were also able to construct a more representative picture of the heights of the male working class as a whole by examining changes in the heights of military recruits. These data suggested that although there were undoubtedly fluctuations in the average heights of army recruits between the birth cohorts of the 1740s and the 1820s, the overall trend was nevertheless an upward one, but it was thrown into reverse by the impact of urbanization during the second quarter of the nineteenth century, so that average heights only resumed their upward trend after about 1850. However, these conclusions have been attacked from a number of standpoints, most notably by Nicholas and Steckel (1991), Johnson and Nicholas (1995), and Komlos (1993b; 1993a).

Nicholas and Steckel (1991, p. 942) challenged Floud, Wachter, and Gregory's findings, partly on the basis of doubts about the technical problems involved in dealing with the exclusion of short men from military service, but primarily because they believed that "army volunteers ... typically included proportionately more individuals from the lower classes." In contrast to Floud *et al.*, they argued that the average heights of convicts who were transported to Australia between 1817 and 1840 showed that there was a sharp decline in the average heights of men born between 1780 and 1789, and a further decline in the heights of men born in urban areas between 1793 and 1802, and in rural areas between 1801 and 1812; but it is important to remember that only a small proportion of the convicts in this study were born in the 1770s (an average of twelve observations per year), and the representativeness of the convict data themselves has also been called into question (Shlomowitz 1990; Shlomowitz 1991; Jackson 1996).[1]

In a series of related articles, Nicholas and others have also compared trends in the average heights of male and female convicts (Nicholas and Oxley 1993; Johnson and Nicholas 1995; 1997). Nicholas and Oxley (1993) argued that the average heights of female convicts who were born in rural areas between 1790 and 1820 declined more rapidly than the average heights of either urban-born women or rural-born men, and they suggested that this may have been caused by changes in the way in which resources were allocated within rural households as a result of a decline in female employment opportunities in these areas. However, both Jackson (1996) and Harris (1998, p. 424; 2008, pp. 164–165; 2009, pp. 71–73) have questioned the representativeness of some of these data, and Harris has queried Nicholas and Oxley's account of the timing of changes in female employment rates. He has also highlighted the absence of any direct evidence of discrimination in the allocation of household resources to female children in these areas during this period.

Komlos (1993b) criticized Floud *et al.*'s analysis of both the Marine Society data and the military recruiting data. He argued that the analysis of the Marine Society data was flawed because it used an inappropriate statistical technique to estimate the height of the underlying population from truncated samples, and he criticized the analysis of the military recruiting data because it involved pooling data from different sources. He also claimed that his own analyses of both the

---

[1] Although Nicholas and Steckel criticized the representativeness of the army data, their own analysis of the occupational background of the convict data showed that these individuals also included a disproportionate number of men from the semi- and unskilled working class. The convicts also appear to have been unusually literate for such a population, and it is interesting to note that the men who were born in the 1770s must have been substantially older than the men who were born at the end of their period, since nobody was measured before 1817. It is possible that this fact may have contributed to the downward trend which their data revealed (Nicholas and Steckel 1991, pp. 940, 942–943; see also Nicholas and Oxley 1993; Jackson 1996; Nicholas and Oxley 1996; Johnson and Nicholas 1997, pp. 209–210).

Marine Society data and the military recruiting data were supported by other studies and by independent contextual evidence.

One of the main problems associated with the analysis of both the Marine Society data and the military data is that they are based on truncated samples. This is because both organizations applied minimum height standards which meant that they excluded the shortest members of the populations from which they were drawn. In the case of the Marine Society data, Floud, Wachter, and Gregory (1990, pp. 118–119) attempted to overcome this problem using a technique known as Quantile Bend Estimation. This technique relies on the fact that individual heights are normally distributed, but Komlos (1993b, pp. 118–131) argued that the technique had been applied inappropriately because the distributions of the heights of the Marine Society children violated the principle of normality. He therefore advocated an alternative procedure, based on the original means of the truncated samples (Komlos and Kim 1990); in order to allow for the fact that the minimum height standards changed over time, he disregarded all values which fell below the maximum value of the minimum height standards. However, as Floud, Wachter and Gregory (1993, pp. 153–154) pointed out, Komlos's own procedure relied on the assumption that the standard deviation of the heights of the underlying population was itself unchanging (see also Komlos 2004, p. 165). This assumption is not true of modern adult populations (Cole 2000a, p. 402) and is even less true of adolescent populations, and therefore the conclusions drawn from Komlos's analysis should be treated with considerable caution.

Komlos (1993b, p. 132) also criticized some of the assumptions which Floud, Wachter, and Gregory made when they analyzed the military data. He argued that they were wrong to pool the data for the Army and Royal Marines because the two branches selected their recruits according to different principles, and this argument has recently been repeated by Cinnirella (2008). However, as Floud, Wachter and Gregory (1993, pp. 147–8) pointed out when these arguments were raised initially, the crucial issue is not whether the recruits were allocated to different services on the basis of different principles, but whether they were drawn from different populations. They argued that "there is a striking similarity between Royal Marine and army recruits in occupational origins and, to a lesser but explicable extent, in geographical origins," and this led them to conclude "that it is reasonable to regard the Marines and the Army … as all drawing their recruits from the same broad spectrum of the working class ... rather than from distinct sub-populations" (Floud, Wachter, and Gregory 1993, p. 147).

When Komlos replied to Floud, Wachter, and Gregory's response to his original criticisms, he suggested that "instead of focusing on technicalities," it might be better to consider some of the contextual evidence which supported his notion of an "incipient Malthusian crisis in the late-eighteenth century." He cited Crafts' (1985a) observation that "per capita food consumption only regained its 1760 level at around 1840," and concluded that "agricultural output and food imports did not keep pace ... [with] the rate of growth in the number of mouths to feed" (Komlos 1993a, p. 365). Some authors have also suggested that average heights may have declined over the course of this period as a result of increases in work intensity and an increase in the incidence of child labor (de Vries 2008, pp. 110–111; Humphries 2010).

These arguments do not necessarily undermine Floud, Wachter, and Gregory's original results. We have already raised doubts about some of the estimates on which arguments about the increase in the total number of working days are based (see Chapter 2), but it is also worth noting that these arguments appear to be largely concerned with an increase in the number of days worked by adults, and there is no direct evidence to suggest that this led to a change in the relationship between diet and workload at younger ages, when heights are most responsive to changes in circumstances (cf. Voth 1995). It may therefore be more plausible to suggest that the average heights of successive birth cohorts declined as a result of a reduction in the ages at which children entered the workforce, but this argument is also called into question by the fact that when children did start work, they also became entitled to a larger share of household resources (Humphries 2010, pp. 243–244). However, the most important objections come from new evidence which contradicts Crafts' claims of a decline in per capita consumption. Our own investigations suggest that the average number of calories available per head increased between 1750 and 1800 (see below), and evidence from other sources suggests that real earnings increased over the course of this period (albeit very slowly) and that average mortality rates fell, at least up until circa 1820 (Harris 2004b, pp. 383–388).

Despite the controversial nature of the debate over changes in average height before 1820, most commentators agree that there was a decline in the average heights of both men and women between circa 1820 and

1850. In 1990, Floud, Wachter, and Gregory suggested that average heights of 21–23-year-old men may have declined by as much as 1.9 inches (4.8 centimeters) between the birth cohorts of the mid 1820s and the mid 1850s,[2] and this conclusion has been reinforced not only by Komlos (1993b), but also by Riggs (1994) and by Johnson and Nicholas (1995; 1997). However, even though average heights began to increase again after 1850, men born at the end of the nineteenth century were still comparatively short by modern standards. Men who were born in the mid 1880s and measured toward the end of the first decade of the twentieth century were more than two inches (5 cm) shorter than the men whose heights were published in the first official study of *The Heights and Weights of Adults in Great Britain* at the beginning of the 1980s (Knight and Eldridge 1984, p. 9; Floud, Wachter, and Gregory 1990, pp. 148, 203).

Although the increase in average heights began among those born during the second half of the nineteenth century, it is likely that the most dramatic and sustained increases in average height occurred during the course of the twentieth century, and probably after the end of the First World War. Harris's (1993) study of the average heights of children in different parts of England and Wales found little evidence of any sustained improvement in the average heights of either infants (aged 4–6), intermediates (aged 7–9), or school-leavers (aged 12–14) in the majority of areas before 1918 (Harris 1993, pp. 361–363). However, the average heights of children in the more prosperous parts of the country did increase during the 1920s, and even children attending schools in depressed areas such as Rhondda and Glasgow experienced some improvement in average heights during the 1930s (Harris 1994, pp. 32–35; Floud and Harris 1997, pp. 107–109). There is little continuous information about changes in the average heights of children after 1945, but it is clear that progress continued. Between 1939 and 1958, the average heights of 6-year-old boys in the northern town of Wakefield increased by two inches (5 cm), and the average heights of 12-year-old boys in London increased by a similar amount between 1938 and 1966 (Cameron 1979, p. 514; Harris 1997b). The average heights of 6-year-old children in different parts of Sheffield increased by

---

[2] This figure is based on the average values of the heights of men who were born in 1822.5 and 1827.5, and in 1842.5 and 1847.5, and were aged between 21 and 23 years at the time of measurement.

between 0.17 inches (0.4 cm) and 0.40 inches (1 cm) between 1951 and 1968 (Floud and Harris 1997, p. 114).

Anthropometric historians have recently begun to pay more attention to changes in weight and the body mass index (BMI). Horrell, Meredith, and Oxley (2009) have recently compared the heights and weights of men and women who were incarcerated in the Surrey House of Correction in Wandsworth, South London, between 1858 and 1878. Both male and female convicts were both shorter and lighter than their modern counterparts, but the BMIs of female convicts also appeared to decline with age. Horrell, Meredith, and Oxley (2009, p. 116) argued that this divergence reflected the impact of anti-female discrimination in adulthood, but they also acknowledged that "far more work needs to be done" before any final conclusions can be reached.

Floud (1998) has also attempted to examine changes in BMIs. His work was based on the analysis of a small number of published surveys but has the advantage of covering a wider population and a longer period. Although the surveys were based on very small numbers of individuals, the height data were broadly (though not entirely) consistent with the results which Floud, Wachter, and Gregory had published, on the basis of a much larger study, eight years earlier. However, although there was a small increase in the average heights of the men in these surveys from the birth cohorts of the 1860s onwards (a decade after the initial improvement in the heights of army recruits), there was no comparable improvement in weight, with the result that BMI values actually declined. Floud (1998, p. 28) speculated that the data might be consistent with the view that "as populations move from a state of relative deprivation and under-nutrition, the mean height ... of infants and children ... increases first, with mean weight and body mass increases lagging behind," but the statistics may also reflect the impact of differences in the ages at which the different birth cohorts were weighed and measured (see Figure 4.1).

We possess rather more information about the weights of people in the twentieth century, and much of this is related to schoolchildren. During the 1980s, Harris collected data on both the heights and weights of children in many different parts of the country, and this information can be supplemented with Noel Cameron's account of changes in the heights and weights of children attending schools run by the London County Council between 1905 and 1966. The results, which are summarized in Appendix D (see Table D.1) and Table 4.1, show that although there were

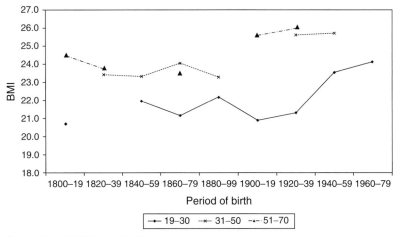

Source: Floud 1998, pp. 34–36.

Figure 4.1 Average BMI, by age and birth cohort, 1800–1979

substantial changes in both height and weight during the course of the twentieth century, there was relatively little change in the average value of the body mass index, or BMI, of children below the age of eight. However, there is rather more evidence of changes in the average BMIs of older children. This may be partly attributable to the effects of earlier maturation, but is also consistent with increases in levels of childhood obesity (see also Rona 1998, pp. 340–341).

It is possible to supplement these data with additional information drawn from the analysis of changes in the average height and weight of army recruits at various points in time between 1860 and 1974. These data show how adult BMIs have changed within cohorts and over time. The table suggests that there was little change in the average BMI of men who joined the Army between 1860 and 1913, but there was a consistent upward trend in BMIs between the 1950s and the first half of the 1970s. The data support the view that there has been an increase in the average weight of the adult population over the last fifty years, and that this increase exceeds the level which might have been expected to occur as a result of increases in stature and rates of maturation (Table 4.2).

Although this section has been primarily concerned with changes in the height and weight of the British population, it also has important implications for the study of mortality. The average height of a

Table 4.1 *Changes in the body mass index of British schoolchildren, 1905–2007*

Period	Mid year	BOYS	5	7–9	8	8–9	10–11	11	12	12–13	14	14–15	16
1905	1905	London	15.72		16.18				16.89				
1910–11	1910.5	Harris dataset	16.43	16.08						16.93			
1920–22	1921	Harris dataset	16.48			16.15				17.18			
1929–31	1930	Harris dataset	16.47			16.47				17.65			
1938	1938	London	16.30		16.49				17.93				
1938–41	1939.5	Harris dataset	16.38			16.34				17.78			
1944–50	1947	Harris dataset	16.47			16.65	17.03			17.98			
1949	1949	London	16.05		16.42				17.85				
1950	1950	Harris dataset										19.01	
1954	1954	London	16.12		16.56				18.25				
1959	1959	London	16.18		16.75				18.58				
1965	1965	Britain											
1966	1966	London	16.36		16.55				18.58				
1990	1990	United Kingdom	15.99					17.30					20.65
1996	1996	England	16.24		16.65			18.11	18.93		20.39		
2003	2003	England	16.44		16.85			19.30	19.38		21.62		
2007	2007	England	16.32		17.18			18.78	19.99		21.01		

Table 4.1 (*cont.*)

Period	Mid year	GIRLS	5	7–9	8	8–9	10–11	11	12	12–13	14	14–15	16
1905	1905	London	15.84		15.85				16.85				
1910–11	1910.5	Harris dataset	16.35	15.93									
1920–22	1921	Harris dataset	16.43			15.84				16.97			
1929–31	1930	Harris dataset	15.92			16.06				17.10			
1938	1938	London	16.08		16.31				18.17	17.57			
1938–41	1939.5	Harris dataset	16.11			16.03				17.88			
1944–50	1947	Harris dataset	16.22			16.41	17.09			18.37			
1949	1949	London	15.84		16.26				18.34				
1950	1950	Harris dataset										19.75	
1954	1954	London	15.97		16.50				18.48				
1959	1959	London	15.97		16.58				18.98				
1965	1965	Britain											
1966	1966	London	16.13		16.65				19.41				
1990	1990	United Kingdom	15.87					17.73					21.14
1996	1996	England	16.82		16.73			18.75	20.06		21.21		
2003	2003	England	16.60		16.81			19.31	20.12		22.29		
2007	2007	England	16.36		17.52			19.73	20.46		21.72		

Sources: See Table D.1.

Table 4.2 *Changes in the height, weight, and body mass index of regular army recruits, 1860/4–1970/4*

		1860–4	1880–4	1885–9	1890–4	1895–9	1900–4	1905–9	1910–13	1951–4	1955–9	1960–4	1965–9	1970–4
20–24	Height (cm)	168.8	167.3	167.3	167.9	168.1	167.5	168.7	168.4	172.6	172.7	173.0	173.5	174.1
	Weight (kg)	61.4	61.3	61.3	61.3	61.4	60.3	61.3	60.8	63.8	64.8	65.4	67.1	68.2
	BMI (kg/m²)	21.6	21.9	21.9	21.8	21.7	21.5	21.5	21.5	21.4	21.7	21.9	22.3	22.5
≥25	Height (cm)	170.7	168.9	168.9	169.7	169.9	168.4	168.9	168.9					
	Weight (kg)	62.5	63.1	63.0	64.1	63.9	63.7	63.5	62.6					
	BMI (kg/m²)	21.5	22.1	22.1	22.3	22.1	22.5	22.3	22.0					
25–29	Height (cm)									171.8	172.0	172.5	173.3	173.9
	Weight (kg)									64.2	65.4	66.7	68.7	69.9
	BMI (kg/m²)									21.8	22.1	22.4	22.9	23.1
30–34	Height (cm)									171.6	171.7	173.0	173.9	174.4
	Weight (kg)									65.2	66.2	68.4	71.3	72.4
	BMI (kg/m²)									22.1	22.5	22.9	23.6	23.8
35–39	Height (cm)									171.0	171.8			
	Weight (kg)									65.8	67.3			
	BMI (kg/m²)									22.5	22.8			
≥40	Height (cm)									171.0				
	Weight (kg)									66.4				
	BMI (kg/m²)									22.7				

Source: Rosenbaum 1988, pp. 278–279, 282–284, 293.
Notes: Figures for 1860/4–1910/13 are based on the estimated mean heights and weights of the populations from which army recruits were drawn as truncated distributions. Figures for 1951/4–1970/4 are actual measurements.

population is largely determined by the conditions experienced in childhood, and there is now growing evidence to support the view that child health also has a direct bearing on adult mortality (Kermack, McKendrick, and McKinlay 1934; Floud, Wachter, and Gregory 1990; Harris 2001). During the last thirty years, economic and demographic historians have made enormous progress in charting the history of mortality in Britain since the beginning of the eighteenth century, and it is to this evidence that we shall now turn.

4.2 Mortality

During the last twenty years, historians have devoted a lot of effort to the search for an accurate depiction of eighteenth-century mortality trends. Razzell (1994, pp. 185–195; 1998, pp. 485–500) has argued that mortality rates declined significantly during the first half of the century, but Wrigley, Davies, Oeppen, and Schofield (1997, pp. 282–284) rejected this view on the grounds that it attached too much weight to changes in adult mortality rates, and failed to pay sufficient attention to countervailing trends at younger ages. Although Wrigley and his co-authors now accept that mortality changes exerted a stronger influence on eighteenth-century population change than they had previously thought, they have continued to argue that the secular decline in English mortality began during the second half of the eighteenth century and continued into the first two decades of the nineteenth century. There was then an arrest of progress between circa 1820 and 1850, followed by a resumption of mortality decline from the 1850s onwards (Figure 4.2).

Although few historians have challenged this view, a considerable amount of effort has been devoted to the attempt to break this "arrest of progress" down into its component parts. Woods (1985) suggested that aggregate mortality rates leveled off because an increasing proportion of the population was living under urban conditions, even though mortality rates within both urban and rural areas continued to decline, but Szreter and Mooney (1998) claimed that the increasing pace of urbanization also led to a decline in the average level of life expectancy within urban areas. The precise details of these changes continue to be the subject of debate, but Woods (2000, pp. 362, 369) now appears to concede that urban mortality rates may have increased, even though the scale of that increase may have been less dramatic than Szreter and Mooney's figures led them to suggest (see also Harris 2004b, pp. 394–396).

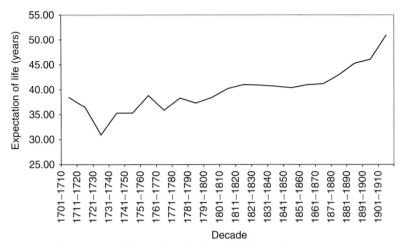

Sources: Wrigley *et al.* 1997, pp. 614–15; Woods 2000, p. 365.

Figure 4.2 Expectation of life at birth in England and Wales, 1701–1910

It is also important to consider differences in the timing of mortality changes at different ages. As we can see from Figure 4.3, the earliest improvements in aggregate mortality rates were registered among those aged 5–9, in the 1850s, followed by those aged 10–14 and 15–19, and then by young adults in the age groups 20–24, 25–34, and 35–44. There was little evidence of any significant improvement in the mortality rates of older adults before the end of the nineteenth century while, at the opposite end of the age spectrum, infant mortality rates remained stubbornly high until the beginning of the twentieth century, and both neonatal mortality and maternal mortality rates only began to fall during the 1930s (Mitchell 1988, pp. 57–59; Loudon 1992, pp. 542–545; Office for National Statistics 2004a).

The decline of mortality after circa 1850 was primarily associated with a decline in the death rate from infectious diseases. McKeown (1976, pp. 54–62) argued that these diseases accounted for 91.8 percent of the overall decline in mortality in England and Wales between 1848/54 and 1901, and that the most important contributions were made by respiratory tuberculosis; scarlet fever and diphtheria; cholera, diarrhea, and dysentery; and typhoid and typhus. Woods (2000) conducted a more exhaustive analysis of the main changes in mortality between 1861/70 and 1891/1900, and even though his analysis revealed some

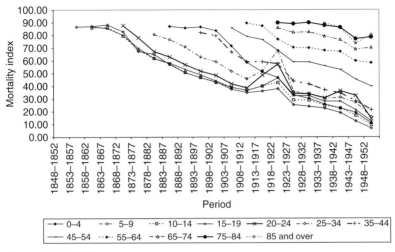

Source: Harris 2001.

Figure 4.3 Age-specific mortality in England and Wales, 1848/52–1948/52 (1838/42 = 100)

differences of emphasis, the broad outlines remained the same. Tuberculosis still appeared as the most important single contributor to the overall decline of mortality, but the relative importance of cholera, diarrhea, and dysentery declined, while that of scarlet fever and diphtheria increased (Harris 2004b, pp. 400–401).

As we have already seen, the decline of mortality in the second half of the nineteenth century was concentrated in the age groups 5–44, and was strongly associated with deaths from infectious diseases, but the twentieth century also witnessed substantial declines in death rates at other ages and from other causes. The infant mortality rate declined from a peak of 163 deaths per thousand births in 1899 to 4.8 in 2008, and significant reductions were also experienced at older ages (Mitchell 1988, pp. 57–59; Office for National Statistics 2009b). These changes are reflected in the statistics of life expectancy. During the period between 1901/10 and 2000/02, the average life expectancy of new-born children increased by 27.4 years (for boys) and 28.2 years (for girls), but significant improvements were also observed at older ages. In 1901/10, the average 65-year-old man had a life expectancy of 10.8 years, while the average woman could expect to live for a further 12 years, but by the beginning of the twenty-first century these figures had

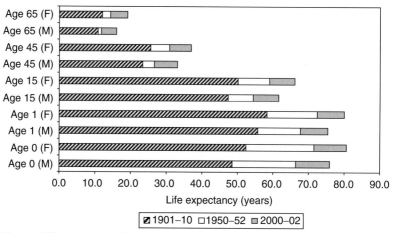

Source: Office for National Statistics 2004b, p. 82.

Figure 4.4 Average life expectancy at different ages, 1901/10–2000/02

risen to 16 years and 19.1 years respectively, with much of this increase occurring since the 1950s (see Figure 4.4).

These changes have also been reflected in the cause structure of mortality. At the beginning of the twentieth century, infectious diseases still accounted for between 25 and 30 percent of all deaths, but this figure fell sharply between 1901 and 1951, with the result that (after allowing for diagnostic changes and changes in the system of classification) a much larger proportion of all deaths was associated with cancer and diseases of the circulatory system. However, although the death rates from these diseases increased in both absolute and relative terms between the 1920s and the 1970s, they also began to decline from the 1970s onwards (Figure 4.5). Nevertheless, there are also some diseases whose incidence continued to increase, such as ovarian cancer (for women) and cancer of the prostate (for men). Certain other diseases have also become more prevalent as causes of death since the 1970s, such as esophageal cancer and malignant melanoma (Fitzpatrick and Chandola 2000, pp. 101–104).

Despite the changes which have undoubtedly occurred, there is still room for further improvement. During the twentieth century, mortality rates have declined for both sexes and among all social classes, but differences between the mortality rates of different social classes have

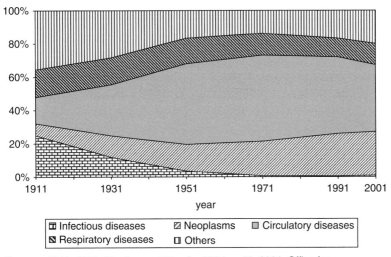

Sources: 1911–1991: Charlton and Murphy 1997: p. 43. 2001: Office for National Statistics 2002, pp. 2–213.

Figure 4.5 Causes of death in England and Wales, 1911–2001

persisted. As we can see from Tables 4.3 and 4.4, the gap has narrowed in absolute terms but remains significant in relative terms. These differences are still apparent even after allowances have been made for the effects of changes in the occupational structure of the British population and selection effects (Harding *et al.* 1997, p. 154; Fitzpatrick and Chandola 2000, pp. 120–123).

There are many different explanations for the persistence of health inequalities, and these are often interrelated. During the 1970s, the Black Committee on Inequalities in Health argued that health inequalities were directly related to patterns of social deprivation (Townsend, Davidson, and Whitehead 1988), but the mechanisms which underpin this relationship remain unclear (Mackenbach *et al.* 2002, p. 13). In the meantime, a growing number of researchers have argued that material deprivation is not only responsible for poor health among those who are directly affected by it, but that inequality itself has a damaging effect on the health of the population as a whole. This may be partly related to deficiencies in welfare provision, but also to the psychosocial effects of high levels of inequality on subjective well-being (Wilkinson 1996; Marmot 2004; Wilkinson and Pickett 2009).

Table 4.3 *Infant mortality rates, both sexes, by father's social class, in England and Wales, 1930/2–2001*

Social Class	1930–32	1949–53	1970–72	1993–95	2001
I	32	19	12	4.5	3.8
II	46	22	14	4.8	3.7
IIIN				5.5	4.8
IIIM				5.9	5.4
III	59	28	16		
IV	63	35	20	6.6	6.4
V	80	42	31	7.7	7.4

Sources: 1930–32, 1949–53, 1970–72: Townsend, Davidson, and Whitehead 1988, pp. 40, 63. 1993–95: Botting 1997, p. 86. 2001: Rowan 2003, p. 38.
Notes: Social Class I: Professional; II: Intermediate; IIIN: Skilled non-manual; IIIM: Skilled manual; IV: Partly-skilled manual; V: Unskilled manual.

One of the most important dilemmas facing health policy-makers concerns the dissemination of health advice. During the last three decades, successive UK governments have emphasized the role of health education, but this policy tends to exacerbate health inequalities (while improving average standards of health) because of differences in the rate at which beneficial advice is adopted by different groups (Marmot 2004, p. 251). This tendency has been reflected in a series of surveys, all of which have shown that people in the "higher" social classes are more likely to eat healthy foods and engage in voluntary physical activity, and less likely to smoke, than people in Social Classes IV and V (Acheson 1998; Fitzpatrick and Chandola 2000, pp. 120–121; Mackenbach *et al.* 2002, pp. 14–15).

Although many of the explanations for the persistence of health inequalities focus on current differences in social status, income, and behavior, today's inequalities may also be the result of earlier differences. During the last twenty years, there has been an enormous increase in the volume of research devoted to the "early-life" origins of adult disease, and this has led to a strong focus on the need for improvements in the health of today's children (see, e.g., Acheson 1998). However, many of today's adults experienced conditions of considerable deprivation in their own childhoods, and these experiences may be continuing to exercise a significant impact on the social patterning of health today. This may also help to explain the persistence of

Table 4.4 *Social class variations in expectation of life at different ages, 1972–1991*

	Male				Female			
	1972–76	1977–81	1982–86	1987–91	1972–76	1977–81	1982–86	1987–91
Class	Expectation of life at birth				Expectation of life at birth			
I/II	71.7	72.8	74.1	74.9	77.1	78.2	78.7	80.2
IIIN	69.5	70.8	72.2	73.5	78.0	78.1	78.6	79.4
IIIM	69.8	70.0	71.4	72.4	75.1	76.1	77.1	77.6
IV/V	67.8	68.3	69.8	69.7	74.7	75.7	76.8	76.8
Class	Expectation of life at age 15				Expectation of life at age 15			
I/II	57.9	58.8	59.9	60.5	63.0	64.1	64.3	65.8
IIIN	56.5	56.9	58.2	59.8	63.8	64.1	64.3	65.3
IIIM	56.4	56.8	57.3	58.1	61.6	62.2	62.9	63.2
IV/V	54.9	55.1	55.9	55.8	61.9	62.0	62.7	62.5
Class	Expectation of life at age 65				Expectation of life at age 65			
I/II	13.4	14.3	14.5	15.0	17.3	17.9	18.0	18.7
IIIN	12.6	13.3	13.6	14.1	17.8	17.7	18.0	18.3
IIIM	12.2	12.6	13.0	13.4	16.3	16.9	16.8	16.8
IV/V	12.0	12.0	12.3	12.4	16.7	16.6	17.0	16.7

Source: Hattersley 1997, pp. 75–78.
Notes: See Table 4.3.

social class inequalities in health among adults who can no longer be said to be living in poverty (Wadsworth 1997; Elstad 2005).

4.3 Wages, nutrition, and the standard of living

McKeown (1976) attributed the decline of mortality in England and Wales to four possible sets of causes: changes in the biological relationship between infective organisms and their hosts; therapeutic and medical intervention; measures to control exposure to disease; and improvements in "nutritional state." He attached particular importance to improvements in nutritional state, and this led to a fierce debate concentrating, particularly, on the relative importance of the contributions made by public health reforms and improvements in the "standard of living" (e.g., Szreter 1988). However, although McKeown's work has been widely criticized, it still provides a useful starting point for investigations into the different factors which have contributed to the decline of mortality and the improvement of human health in Britain over the last three hundred years.

As the introduction to this book has already shown, few topics have received more attention in the long-running debate over the standard of living during the Industrial Revolution than the question of real wages. Although it is important to recognize the importance of regional variations in both prices and wages (see e.g. Crafts 1982; Clark 2001), by the early 1990s there was a broad consensus that real wages rose during the first half of the eighteenth century and either stagnated or declined after 1750, with little evidence of any sustained improvement before 1800 or even 1820 (e.g., Wrigley and Schofield 1981, pp. 642–644; Lindert and Williamson 1983b; Crafts 1985a; Lindert and Williamson 1985; Schwarz 1985; Floud and Harris 1997, p. 95). However, more recent estimates have given grounds to modify this picture. Charles Feinstein (Feinstein 1998, p. 648) suggested that average real earnings rose by 12.5 percent in Great Britain between 1770/2 and 1818/22, and by 23.1 percent between 1818/22 and 1848/52. These figures have since been modified by Clark (2001; 2005) and, more recently, by Allen (2007). However, even though Allen believes that Feinstein may have overestimated the improvement in real wages between circa 1815 and 1830, his figures are still significantly less "pessimistic" than those produced by earlier researchers (see Figure 4.6).

Although McKeown was unable to produce any direct evidence of changes in diet, other writers have attempted to estimate the nutritional value of the food consumed by working-class families in different parts of Britain from the late eighteenth century onwards. As we have already seen (see Section 3.1), two of the essential starting points for any study of household diets in the late eighteenth century are the studies published by David Davies and Frederick Morton Eden in 1795 and 1797 respectively. Shammas (1984, pp. 256–258; 1990, p. 134) examined the diets of seven northern and fifteen southern families from these surveys and concluded that the average number of calories consumed by each individual was equal to 1,734 calories per day in the south of England and 2,352 calories per day in the north. Clark, Huberman, and Lindert (1995, pp. 222–223) used the same sources to examine a broader range of household budgets, and concluded that average calorie consumption was equal to just 1,508

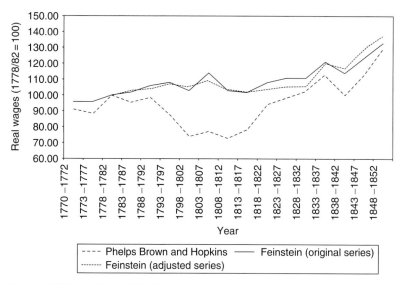

Figure 4.6 Real wages (1770/2–1848/52)

Source: Wrigley and Schofield 1981, pp. 642–4; Feinstein 1998, p. 648; Allen 2007, p. 36.
Notes: The data for "Feinstein (original series)" are his estimates for real earnings adjusted for unemployment in Great Britain. These figures have been modified in the light of Allen's revised consumer price index to produce the estimates in "Feinstein (adjusted series)".

calories per day, while Oddy (1990, p. 274) suggested that average consumption among these families may have been as high as 2,028 calories per day.

As these figures indicate, there is a wide range of variation in the estimates constructed by different authors even when using the same sources, and these differences are compounded by the different assumptions which these authors make about the social status of the households they studied. Oddy (1990, p. 269) argued that the Davies–Eden surveys "provide a cross-section of rural life in England, since the majority of Davies' families were from southern England and the largest group in Eden's were from the northern counties," but Clark, Huberman, and Lindert (1995, p. 222, note 16) claimed that the Davies–Eden households were drawn from the poorest decile of the population, whereas Shammas (1984, pp. 255–256; 1990, p. 134) implied that they were representative of the working class as a whole. However, both Oddy and Clark, Huberman, and Lindert thought that diets did improve during the first half of the nineteenth century. Clark, Huberman, and Lindert estimated that the nutritional value of the diets consumed by working-class families between 1837 and 1863 ranged between 1,974 calories per head per day and 2,395 calories, whereas Oddy (using a very similar set of sources) calculated that energy values ranged between 2,300 calories in 1841 and 2,600 in 1863 (Oddy 1990, p. 274).

Although these figures provide a useful starting point for the study of dietary trends, it is important to remember that they are merely snap-shots, based on the household budgets of a small number of families living at different points in time in different parts of the country. However, it is possible to supplement this information by using the available evidence on food production and the import and export of different foodstuffs to construct an alternative picture of changes in the amount and nature of the food available to the population as a whole (see Chapter 2). We can then combine this information with information from other sources to provide new estimates of the amount of energy available to the British population between the end of the seventeenth century and the outbreak of the First World War.

Since the 1980s, there have been a number of attempts to estimate British agricultural output in the eighteenth and nineteenth centuries. King ([1696] 1973, p. 53) published figures showing the annual output of wheat, rye, barley, oats, beans, and peas and these figures were reproduced by Chartres (1985, p. 444) in his contribution to the *Agrarian History of England and Wales*. Holderness (1989, p. 145) published comparable estimates of the output of cereals and pulses for 1750, 1800, and 1850, and Allen (1994, p. 112) combined both sets of figures in his contribution to the second edition of *The Economic History of Britain* in 1994. However, in 2001, Turner, Beckett, and Afton produced new estimates, based on the actual records of farm inventories. Their calculations suggest that the previous authors underestimated the level of output (on average) in 1750 and 1850, and overestimated output in 1800 (see Table 4.5).

Although these figures enable us to estimate the total output of these crops, it is important to remember that only a proportion of the total crop was made available for human consumption, since some was retained as seed and some was used to feed livestock. We do not have precise figures for these ratios for England and Wales, but we have attempted to com-pensate for this using the estimates made by Gallman (1960, p. 52) and Towne and Rasmussen (1960, pp. 294–304) to calculate the value of the crops entering gross product in the United States in the first half of the

Table 4.5 *Agricultural output, in millions of bushels, in England and Wales, 1700–1850*

	Allen 1994				Turner, Beckett, and Afton 2001			
	1700	1750	1800	1850	1700	1750	1800	1850
Wheat	21.8	32.4	53.8	100.8	n.a.	39.6	52.7	104.0
Rye	15.1	9.0	7.8	2.8	n.a.	n.a.	7.0	2.8
Barley	43.7	35.0	39.0	54.8	n.a.	34.7	38.0	54.6
Oats	29.4	56.0	56.0	80.0	n.a.	73.5	74.9	94.8
Beans and peas	26.0	28.0	28.0	30.0	n.a.	21.8	26.4	29.6

Sources: See Tables D.2 and D.3.
Notes: (1) Output figures are based on the acreages used by Allen 1994, p. 112.
(2) Crop yields for individual years from Turner, Beckett, and Afton (2001) were calculated as follows: Wheat, barley, and oats: 1750: weighted average of results for 1740s and 1750s; 1800: weighted average of results for 1790s and 1800s; 1850: weighted average of results for 1840s and 1850s; Rye, beans, and peas: 1750 (beans and peas only): weighted average of results for 1725/49 and 1750/74; 1800: weighted average of results for 1775/79 and 1800/24; 1850: weighted average of results for 1825/49 and 1850/74.

nineteenth century. We have also used US data to make allowances for milling losses (US Department of Agriculture 1939, p. 39) and included an additional allowance of 10 percent for distribution losses. We have used information from John (1989, pp. 1124–1125) and the US Department of Agriculture (1952, p. 40; 1992, pp. 11, 14) to convert bushels into imperial pounds, and we have used McCance and Widdowson's (1960, pp. 116–117, 138–139) data to calculate energy values. The final stage was to divide the total number of calories available for human consumption by the population to estimate the daily consumption of calories by the average person in each year.

The results of this analysis are summarized in Tables 4.6 and 4.7, and set out in more detail in Appendix D (see Tables D.2 and D.3). We have decided to include separate estimates based on the initial output figures supplied by Allen (1994) and Turner, Beckett, and Afton (2001) for two reasons. In the first place, Turner and his co-authors do not have figures for any crops in 1700, or for rye in 1750, and it may therefore be misleading to compare Allen's figures for 1700 with their figures for the later periods. Secondly, it is also important to recognize that even though their figures are based on the direct observation of farm

Table 4.6 *Average number of calories per head per day derived from domestically produced cereals and pulses in England and Wales, 1700–1850*

	Allen 1994				Turner, Beckett, and Afton 2001			
	1700	1750	1800	1850	1700	1750	1800	1850
Wheat	502	430	732	706	502	526	717	729
Rye	251	131	76	14	251	131	69	14
Barley	598	421	315	227	598	418	307	227
Oats	122	205	172	101	122	269	184	120
Beans and peas	93	88	71	33	93	68	56	32
Total	1,566	1,275	1,366	1,082	1,566	1,412	1,333	1,122

Sources: See Tables D.2 and D.3.
Notes: We have used Allen's estimates for rye to fill the gap in Turner, Beckett, and Afton's in 1750.

Table 4.7 *Average number of calories available for consumption per capita per day from domestically produced food sources in England and Wales, 1700–1909/13*

Source of kcal	1700	1750	1800	1850	1909–13
Cereals and pulses (1A)	1,566	1,275	1,366	1,082	217
Cereals and pulses (1B)	*1,566*	*1,412*	*1,333*	*1,122*	*217*
Meat and lard (2)	307	507	456	348	325
Dairy (3)	231	279	236	219	286
Fish (4)	24	24	24	24	24
Garden vegetables (5)	12	12	12	12	12
Fruits and nuts (6)	10	10	10	10	10
Potatoes (7)	53	79	154	255	196
Cottage produce (8)					135
Farm produce (9)					26
Poultry, game and rabbits (10)					28
Total (11A)	2,202	2,185	2,257	1,949	1,259
Total (11B)	*2,202*	*2,323*	*2,224*	*1,990*	*1,259*

Sources: 1700, 1750, 1800, and 1850: Row 1A: See Table D.2; Row 1B: See Table D.3; Row 2: See Table D.4; Row 3: See Table D.5; Row 4: See Table D.11; Row 5: See Table D.12; Row 6: See Table D.14; Row 7: See Table D.15. 1909–13: See Table D.16.

inventories, the number of records is quite small and may not always be representative of the entire country (see Thirsk 2002). As a result, it may be more prudent to regard the two sets of figures as upper- and lower-bound estimates of the number of calories derived from domestically produced cereals and pulses in the years under review. Although the differences are not great in terms of the overall trend of calorie consumption, they are not insignificant. Allen's figures suggest that the number of calories obtained from these sources rose between 1750 and 1800 and fell between 1800 and 1850, whereas Turner, Beckett, and Afton's figures imply that average daily consumption levels declined during both periods.

The following two rows of Table 4.7 include calculations showing the number of calories obtained from domestically produced meat and dairy products. We have estimated the calorific value of the food consumed in the form of mutton, lamb, beef, veal, pork, and ham using information obtained from King ([1696] 1973, p. 545) and Holderness (1989, p. 155). We do not have direct information about the consumption of lard, but have estimated this using figures showing the consumption of bacon, lard, and pork in the United States at the end of the 1870s (Bennett and Pierce 1961, pp. 114–115). We have used Holderness's (1989, p. 170) data to estimate the number of calories derived from cheese, butter, and milk in 1750, 1800, and 1850, and extrapolated from the data on meat and dairy products in 1750 to estimate the number of calories which might have been obtained from dairy products fifty years earlier.

Table 4.7 also includes estimates showing the number of calories obtained from domestically obtained fish, garden vegetables, fruit, nuts, and potatoes. The figures for fish, garden vegetables, fruit, and nuts are derived from the Royal Society's investigation into the food supply of the United Kingdom before the First World War, and we have assumed – in the absence of any other information – that these figures remained constant over the whole of the period (Parliamentary Papers 1917). The figures for potatoes are extrapolated from Salaman's (1949, pp. 434, 539, 613) figures for 1600, 1775, 1795, 1814, 1838, and 1851, but we have assumed that the figure provided by Salaman for the last of these years should have been 0.70, rather than 0.07. The results illustrate the growing importance of the potato in the average British diet, as consumption rose from 53 calories per head per day at the start of our period to 255 calories per head at the beginning of the 1850s, but the total amount of energy derived from domestically produced foodstuffs declined by between 212 and 253 calories over the same period.

The apparent inability of domestic agriculture to keep pace with the needs of an expanding population meant that Britain became increasingly reliant on imported foodstuffs. We have used information from Mitchell (1988, pp. 221–222) and from the *Annual Accounts* (Parliamentary Papers 1849a; 1849b; 1851; 1853) to calculate the amount of energy derived from imported cereals between 1700 and 1850, after making similar allowances for losses due to milling and distribution to those made when calculating the energy derived from domestically produced cereals. Our estimates suggest that Britain moved from being a net exporter of cereals to a net importer during the first half of the nineteenth century. Throughout the period, the main form of cereal involved in these transactions was wheat, but after 1800 Britain began to import increasing quantities of oats, barley, and especially maize, which provided about one-fifth of the energy derived from imported cereals during the middle years of the nineteenth century.

The first half of the nineteenth century also saw the importation of small quantities of meat, dairy products, wines and spirits, and fruit and nuts, but the most striking development was the dramatic increase in the volume of imported sugar. According to Schumpeter (1960, pp. 52–55), Britain imported just under 10 pounds of sugar per head at the start of the eighteenth century, but this figure increased by more than 150 percent between 1700 and 1850, and even after allowing for re-exports, the number of calories obtained from sugar rose from 28 calories per head per day at the start of the period to 136 calories in 1850. However, the rate of increase accelerated dramatically after this date. The figures provided by the Royal Society in 1917 suggest that the average consumer derived the equivalent of 395 calories per day from sugar in the years immediately preceding the First World War (Table 4.8).

When the figures for domestically produced and imported food are taken together, they present an intriguing picture of the main trends in food consumption in Britain between 1700 and 1914. As we have already seen, a number of authors have suggested that UK food production failed to keep pace with the growth of population during the second half of the eighteenth century, leading to claims that the country was facing a "Malthusian crisis" before the outbreak of the Napoleonic Wars, but our figures suggest that the amount of energy derived from domestically produced food remained roughly constant during the course of the eighteenth century, and only began to decline consistently

Table 4.8 *Average number of calories available for consumption per capita per day from imported food sources in England and Wales, 1700–1909/13*

Source of kcal	1700	1750	1800	1850	1909–13
Cereals and pulses (1)	–13	–168	86	366	788
Meat (2)				12	262
Dairy (3)			16	20	166
Fish (4)					8
Garden vegetables (5)					31
Fruit and nuts (6)				9	55
Potatoes (7)					13
Sugar (8)	28	72	95	136	395
Wine and spirits (9)	12	11	17	12	
Total (10)	26	–85	215	555	1,718

Sources: 1700, 1750, 1800 and 1850: Row 1: See Table D.6; Row 2: See Table D.7; Row 3: See Table D.8; Row 4: See Tables D.11 and D.16; Row 5: See Table D.12; Row 6: D.13; Row 7: Table D.16; Row 8: See Table D.9; Row 9: See Table D.10. 1909–13: See Table D.16.

after 1800. However, the most important change was the increase in the amount of energy derived from imported foods. The combined effect of these changes was that even though energy values either fell or remained broadly constant during the first half of the eighteenth century, they rose between 1750 and 1800 and between 1800 and 1850. They then rose much more rapidly between 1850 and 1914 (Table 4.9).

Our estimates also enable us to calculate the ways in which the composition of the average diet changed over the course of the period. At the start of the eighteenth century, it seems likely that the average person obtained more than 60 percent of their total calories from cereals. This figure declined during the course of the century but the British population still obtained more than half their calories from these sources in 1850. The proportion of calories derived from meat and dairy products increased during the first half of the eighteenth century but declined between 1750 and 1850, and only regained its earlier level between 1909 and 1913. There were also small increases in the proportion of calories obtained from fruit and vegetables and a much larger increase in the proportion derived from imported sugar, but the

Table 4.9 *Average number of calories available for consumption per capita per day in England and Wales, 1700–1909/13*

Source of kcal	1700	1750	1800	1850	1909–13
Domestically produced foods (A)	2,202	2,185	2,257	1,949	1,259
Domestically produced foods (B)	*2,202*	*2,323*	*2,224*	*1,990*	*1,259*
Imported foods	26	–85	215	555	1,718
Grand total (A)	2,229	2,100	2,472	2,504	2,977
Grand total (B)	*2,229*	*2,237*	*2,439*	*2,544*	*2,977*

Sources: See Tables 4.7 and 4.8.
Notes: A: Based on crop yields estimated by Chartres (Chartres 1985), Holderness (Holderness 1989), and Allen (Allen 1994); B: Based on crop yields estimated by Turner, Beckett, and Afton (2001).

proportion of calories derived from fish remained very low throughout the period (see Table 4.10).

What do these calculations tell us about the adequacy of the diets available to the British population at the start of the eighteenth century, and about the relationship between nutrition and mortality between 1700 and 1914? Livi-Bacci (1991, p. 27) has claimed that "a population which could rely on a normal consumption of 2,000 calories per head would have been, in centuries past, an adequately-fed population, at least from the point of view of energy," and this figure is lower than any of the figures which we have calculated for the British population in either 1700 or 1750. However, this argument fails to take account of the impact of inequalities in the distribution of food within the population (see also Fogel 1993a, p. 12; Fogel 1994, pp. 373–374). Even though the new figures on food consumption are higher than some of our earlier figures, a significant proportion of the population might still have experienced a diet which fell below Livi-Bacci's measure of sufficiency.

It is also important to consider the ways in which food was distributed within the household. It is now widely acknowledged that women received less pay than men during the second half of the eighteenth century, and a number of authors have argued that this imbalance was reflected in the allocation of food (e.g., Eden 1797, p. 47; Oren 1974, p. 221; Nicholas and Oxley 1993, p. 737). Several nineteenth- and twentieth-century commentators also noted that women in poorer families tended to receive smaller amounts of food (Harris 1998, p. 418). These "customs" had a damaging effect on the health of the

A. Crop yields from Chartres, Holderness, and Allen

Source of kcal	Calories					%				
	1700	1750	1800	1850	1909–13	1700	1750	1800	1850	1909–13
Cereals	1,461	1,019	1,382	1,396	999	65.54	48.51	55.88	55.74	33.55
Fish	24	24	24	24	32	1.07	1.13	0.96	0.95	1.08
Fruit and vegetables	167	189	247	338	476	7.50	8.98	9.97	13.50	15.98
Meat and dairy products	538	786	708	599	1,075	24.13	37.42	28.63	23.92	36.12
Other	39	83	113	147	395	1.77	3.95	4.56	5.89	13.27
Total	2,229	2,100	2,472	2,504	2,977	100.00	100.00	100.00	100.00	100.00

B. Crop yields from Turner, Beckett, and Afton

Source of kcal	Calories					%				
	1700	1750	1800	1850	1909–13	1700	1750	1800	1850	1909–13
Cereals	1,461	1,176	1,363	1,437	999	65.54	52.55	55.90	56.46	33.55
Fish	24	24	24	24	32	1.07	1.06	0.97	0.93	1.08
Fruit and vegetables	167	169	231	338	476	7.50	7.55	9.49	13.27	15.98
Meat and dairy products	538	786	708	599	1,075	24.13	35.13	29.02	23.54	36.12
Other	39	83	113	147	395	1.77	3.71	4.62	5.80	13.27
Total	2,229	2,237	2,439	2,544	2,977	100.00	100.00	100.00	100.00	100.00

Sources: See Tables 4.7 and 4.8.

Notes: We have calculated that the average daily consumption of "cottage produce" in 1909–13 was equal to 135 calories per head. The Royal Society estimated that the total number of calories from this source was equivalent to one-half of the calories obtained from home-produced poultry, eggs, and vegetables, and one-third of the calories obtained from home-produced fruit. We have used these figures to estimate the proportion of the calories derived from "cottage produce" which may be allocated to each of the other categories. For further information, see Parliamentary Papers 1917, p. 7.

women themselves and may also have impaired the health of their children if their mothers continued to receive inadequate diets during pregnancy (Osmani and Sen 2003, pp. 114–118).

Recent research has also cast doubt on the extent to which it is possible to judge the adequacy of historical diets using the standards applied to well-nourished populations living under modern industrial conditions. When McKeown examined the relationship between nutrition and mortality, he was primarily concerned with the ways in which inadequate nutrition impaired resistance to infection, and he failed to consider the ways in which exposure to infection might damage "nutrition." It is well known that many infections can lead to a loss of appetite and that infection increases the body's need for nutritional resources (Eveleth and Tanner 1976, p. 246), but infection can also have a dramatic effect on the body's ability to digest the nutrients which are consumed. Uauy (1985) found that people living in less-developed countries showed signs of sub-clinical nutrient malabsorption which meant that they were unlikely to digest more than ninety percent of the nutrients they consumed, while a second study showed that undernourished individuals and individuals who had recently experienced episodes of acute diarrhea absorbed less than eighty percent of nutrients (Dasgupta and Ray 1990, p. 215).

The absorption of nutrients can also be influenced by the composition of the diet. As we have already seen, people living in preindustrial and early-industrial Britain derived a high proportion of their energy from cereals, but Dasgupta and Ray (1990, pp. 215–216) have argued that the consumption of a high-fiber diet also leads to a significant reduction in nutrient retention. Their overall conclusion is that individuals living under preindustrial conditions in the modern world may need to increase their total consumption by more than 35 percent to derive the same nutritional benefit from the food they consume as people living under more favorable conditions.

In view of these arguments, it is particularly intriguing to compare our new estimates of the main trends in food consumption with the chronology of changes in height and mortality. As we have already seen, those data suggested that the average height of the population and average levels of life expectancy rose between circa 1750 and 1820, followed by a period of stagnation or decline, and then further improvement from the 1850s onwards. These trends are broadly consistent with our new estimates of food availability (certainly for the periods 1750–1800 and 1850–1914), and help to reinforce the link between nutrition

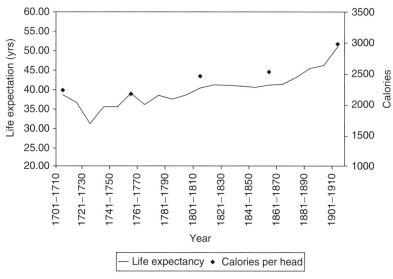

Sources: See text.
Notes: Estimates for "calories per head" are based on the mean of the totals in Table 4.9.

Figure 4.7 Food availability and life expectation at birth, 1700–1910

and mortality which McKeown could only infer when he attempted to account for the modern rise of population in the 1970s (see also Figure 4.7). However, one of the main themes of our argument has been to emphasize the *synergistic* nature of the relationship between nutrition and infection, and it would certainly not be correct to conclude that dietary change was the only reason for improvements in either height or life expectancy.

It is also important to recognize that even though there were significant improvements in both the quality and quantity of the average diet in Britain before 1914, many people continued to be inadequately fed. At the beginning of the twentieth century, a series of nutritional surveys conducted among working-class families in different parts of the country suggested that not only the urban poor, but also "the bulk of the semi-skilled workers, the routine clerical workers, and even those of the skilled artisan class" were likely to be undernourished (Oddy 2003, p. 65). Orr (1937, pp. 23–42) estimated that ten percent of the population consumed a diet which was inadequate in all respects, while a further forty percent consumed a diet which was deficient in proteins, vitamins, and minerals; only one person in ten enjoyed a diet which was adequate in all respects. However, there have been further improvements in the nutritional adequacy of the average diet since the Second World War, partly as a result of improvements in living standards, partly as a result of changes in food policy, and partly as a result of improvements in technology (such as refrigeration), which have enabled even the poorest sections of the population to enjoy a much more varied diet than that which was available to their grandparents and great-grandparents at the start of the previous century (Oddy 2003, pp. 133–235) (Table 4.11).

4.4 Diet, nutrition, and work intensity

In recent years, arguments about diet and nutrition have played an increasingly important part in debates about the origins and nature of Britain's Industrial Revolution. Voth (2000) has examined changes in the length of the working year over the course of the eighteenth century and de Vries (2008) has incorporated these arguments into his account of an

Table 4.11 *Changes in the composition of working-class diets, 1899–2000*

Period	1899–1904	2000
Number of households/families	2,234	2,000
Milk and cream (ml)	1,022	2,289
Cheese (g)	82	102
Eggs (no.)	2	2
Fruit (g)	152	937
Potatoes (g)	1,396	1,063
Other vegetables (g)	794	1,033
Bread and cereal products (g)	3,148	1,621
Sugar and preserves (g)	553	173
Fish and fish products (g)	206	137
Fats (g)	218	211
Meat and meat products (g)	569	993

Sources: Oddy 2003, p. 237; Department of Environment, Food and Rural Affairs 2001.
Notes: Figures for 1899–1904 are based on surveys conducted in a variety of areas at the beginning of the twentieth century. Figures for 2000 are based on the food consumed by all households in which there was no earner, and average current income was less than £180 per week, or in which there was at least one earner, and the gross income of the head of household was less than £180 per week.

"industrious revolution" in Britain and other parts of Europe and North America over the same period. Although these arguments are not directly concerned with either diet or nutrition, they do make important assumptions about the amount of food available to support the work involved.

Arguments about diet and nutrition have also played an important part in Allen's (2009) attempt to answer the question of why Britain became "the first industrial nation" (Mathias 2001). He argued that the high cost of labor in Britain provided manufacturers with the necessary incentive to invest in the new technologies which defined the new industrial era. Although this argument was based primarily on comparisons of national wage rates, he also drew on nutritional data to support his claim that British workers and their families enjoyed a much higher standard of living before industrialization than their continental counterparts.

As Allen (2009, p. 38) has pointed out, actual food requirements vary according to age, gender, and body size. He therefore argued that it was appropriate to assume that the nutritional needs of "a family with a father, a mother and some children" were equivalent to those of three adult males. He then used this formula to estimate the number of calories available per adult male at different income levels in 1843 (Allen 2009, p. 47).

Allen acknowledged that these estimates had been framed "rather loosely" (Allen 2009, p. 38). However, it is possible to make the frame somewhat tighter by using current information on the dietary requirements of men and women at different ages and combining this information with data on the age- and sex-structure of the British population between 1700 and 1914. We can then use the results of this exercise to calculate the factors which should be used to convert our estimates of the number of calories available per head into new estimates of the number of calories available per adult male equivalent.

The relevant data are shown in Table 4.12. The figures in Columns 1–3 show the number of calories required by males and females in each group as a fraction of the calories required by an average male between the ages of 20 and 39. These figures have then been multiplied by the percentage of the population in each age group to estimate the total food requirements of all the individuals in that age group in each period, and these figures have been added together to estimate the conversion factors for the population as a whole. We can then use these figures to estimate the number of calories available per adult male equivalent in each period (Table 4.13). The results suggest that this figure increased from just under 3,000 calories per adult male equivalent (or per consuming unit) at the

Table 4.12 *Conversion factors for estimating calories per consuming unit in England and Wales, 1700–1909/13*

Age	Calories required as proportion of adult male (20–39) requirements			1700		1750		1800		1850		1909–13	
	Male	Female	Persons	Persons in each group as % of total population	Calories required by persons in each age group	Persons in each group as % of total population	Calories required by persons in each age group	Persons in each group as % of total population	Calories required by persons in each age group	Persons in each group as % of total population	Calories required by persons in each age group	Persons in each group as % of total population	Calories required by persons in each age group
	(1)	(2)	(3)	(4)	(3) * (4) (5)	(6)	(3) * (6) (7)	(8)	(3) * (8) (9)	(10)	(3) * (10) (11)	(12)	(3) * (12) (13)
0–4	0.4413	0.4367	0.4390	12.28	0.0539	12.61	0.0554	14.32	0.0629	13.10	0.0575	10.69	0.0469
5–14	0.8050	0.7334	0.7692	19.81	0.1524	20.30	0.1561	23.09	0.1776	22.34	0.1719	19.95	0.1535
15–24	1.0084	0.7583	0.8833	16.35	0.1444	17.47	0.1543	17.73	0.1566	19.10	0.1687	18.05	0.1595
25–59	0.9400	0.6893	0.8147	42.18	0.3436	41.39	0.3372	37.60	0.3063	38.14	0.3108	43.27	0.3525
≥60	0.7500	0.5500	0.6500	9.38	0.0610	8.22	0.0534	7.26	0.0472	7.32	0.0476	8.04	0.0522
Total				100.00	0.7553	99.99	0.7564	100.00	0.7506	100.00	0.7564	100.00	0.7646

Sources: Calorie requirements: Derived from Fogel 1993, p. 7; Population figures: 1700, 1750, and 1800: Wrigley and Schofield 1981, pp. 528–529; 1850 and 1909–13 (1911): Mitchell 1988, pp. 15–16.

start of the eighteenth century to nearly 4,000 calories on the eve of the First World War. Since it is unreasonable to assume that all individuals consumed the same amounts of food (in relation to their physiological needs) regardless of their personal or household circumstances, we can also use the calculations described in Chapter 2 to estimate the size distribution of calories in different periods. The details of these

Table 4.13 *Calories per consuming unit in England and Wales, 1700–1909/13*

A. Crop yields from Chartres, Holderness, and Allen					
	Calories				
Source of kcal	1700	1750	1800	1850	1909–13
Cereals	1,461	1,019	1,382	1,396	999
Fish	24	24	24	24	32
Fruit and vegetables	167	189	247	338	476
Meat and dairy products	538	786	708	599	1,075
Other	39	83	113	147	395
Total	2,229	2,100	2,472	2,504	2,977
Conversion factor	0.7553	0.7564	0.7506	0.7564	0.7646
Calories per consuming unit	2,951	2,776	3,293	3,311	3,893

B. Crop yields from Turner, Beckett, and Afton					
	Calories				
Source of kcal	1700	1750	1800	1850	1909–13
Cereals	1,461	1,176	1,363	1,437	999
Fish	24	24	24	24	32
Fruit and vegetables	167	169	231	338	476
Meat and dairy products	538	786	708	599	1,075
Other	39	83	113	147	395
Total	2,229	2,237	2,439	2,544	2,977
Conversion factor	0.7553	0.7564	0.7506	0.7564	0.7646
Calories per consuming unit	2,951	2,957	3,249	3,363	3,893

Sources: See Tables 4.9 and 4.12.

calculations have already been described, and they suggest that approximately 20 percent of the British population is likely to have received fewer than 2,500 calories per consuming unit at the start of the nineteenth century.

What do these figures imply about the relationship between diet and working capacity in the eighteenth and nineteenth centuries? The World Health Organization, in association with the Food and Agriculture Organization of the United Nations and the United Nations University, has estimated the number of calories required by men and women of different sizes and at different ages engaged in different levels of physical activity, and we can combine this information with our existing knowledge of the heights and weights of British men in the nineteenth and early twentieth centuries to estimate the calorific needs of such individuals during this period. The results are shown in Table 4.14. They imply that the number of calories required to enable an adult male to satisfy his basic metabolic requirements and perform a full day's work is likely to have ranged from approximately 2,400 calories per day for light work to 3,500 calories per day for heavy work. However, our figures suggest that the number of calories available for consumption is unlikely to have reached the latter figure before the second half of the nineteenth century.

These figures imply that a significant proportion of the British population may not have had access to the number of calories which they needed to undertake physically demanding work on a regular basis at the start of the nineteenth century. The increase in the amount of food which was available for human consumption therefore helped to improve the working capacity of the population as a whole by enabling a larger proportion of the potential workforce to contribute in this way. However, there is also evidence to suggest that many families responded to this situation by transferring resources from women and children to male breadwinners. Many contemporary observers, such as the mid nineteenth century medical officer, Dr. Edward Smith, saw this as a rational response, because it enabled the male breadwinner to remain in work and therefore contribute to the well-being of the family as a whole (Parliamentary Papers 1864, p. 249). However, it also contributed to the undernutrition of other household members, and the effects of this were likely to have been reflected not only in the poor nutritional status of working-class children, but also in the premature mortality of their mothers (Harris 1998; Harris 2008).

Table 4.14 *Calories required for different types of work, 1800–1914*

Year of birth	Age at measurement	Year of measurement	Height (cm)	Weight (kg)	BMI	BMR (kcal/hr)	Light work	Moderate work	Heavy work
1777.5	23	1800.5	168.83	59.08	20.73	65.95	2,435.93	2,816.27	3,376.89
1827.5	23	1850.5	172.87	61.94	20.73	67.78	2,503.30	2,894.16	3,470.28
1886–1893	20–24	1910–13	168.80	61.40	21.55	67.05	2,476.44	2,863.11	3,433.05

Sources: Floud, Wachter, and Gregory 1990, pp. 140–149; Floud 1998, pp. 34–36; Rosenbaum 1988, pp. 278–279, 282–284, 293; FAO/WHO/UNU 1985, pp. 71, 76–77.

Notes: (1) The height data are based on the heights of military recruits in 1800, 1850, and 1910–14.

(2) The average weights of recruits in 1800 and 1850 have been estimated using the BMIs of men who were born in the first two decades of the nineteenth century and measured between 1826 and 1849, when they were between the ages of 26 and 30.

(3) The numbers of calories required for basal metabolism have been estimated using the formula described in Chapter 2, Appendix A (Equation [A.7]). The FAO/WHO/UNU Expert Consultation (1985: 178) also recommends an alternative formula, using both height and weight, but the results are almost identical when the alternative formula is applied to these data.

4.5 The contribution of other factors to the decline of mortality

When McKeown outlined his analysis of the causes of mortality decline, he argued that some part of this decline could be attributed to changes in the relationship between infective organisms and their hosts if the organisms themselves became less virulent, or if the human population became more resistant to infection as a result of genetic selection. He acknowledged that "scarlet fever is the outstanding example of an infection in which the relation between host and parasite is unstable, and the decline of mortality since the mid-nineteenth century can be attributed confidently to a change in the character of the disease" (McKeown 1976, p. 82), but he was unwilling to concede that similar factors might have contributed to declines in mortality from other diseases. Nevertheless, it is certainly possible to argue that he under-estimated the overall significance of this effect in his overall schema, given the extent of the contribution made by this disease to the decline of mortality as a whole in England and Wales between 1861/70 and 1891/1900 (Harris 2004b, pp. 398–400).

Although few historians would deny that the decline of mortality from scarlet fever was associated with changes in the virulence of the disease itself, the role played by disease virulence in the decline of tuberculosis has recently become rather more controversial. Woods (2000, pp. 336, 340, 359) argued that mortality from phthisis, or respiratory tuberculosis, "appears to have declined in nearly all districts regardless of the initial rate or whether the place had urban or rural characteristics," and that "the simplest explanation is that the disease became less virulent and . . . this was the principal reason for a reduction in the risk of disease developing and leading to early death" (see also Woods and Shelton 1997, pp. 143–144). However, Woods was unable to provide any direct evidence for this assertion, and his interpretation has been challenged by a number of leading authorities (e.g., Landers 2000, p. 468; Szreter 2001, p. 563).[3] In 1976, when McKeown himself discussed this issue, he concluded that "there is no evidence that the virulence of the organism has changed significantly; the disease

---

[3] Stephen Kunitz (2007, p. 196) has suggested that virulence may have declined as a result of reduced exposure. However, although he regarded this proposal as "conceivable," he also acknowledged that it was "highly speculative."

continues to have devastating effects in populations not previously exposed to it; and the virulence of the bacillus appears not to have diminished when it has been possible to assess it in the laboratory" (McKeown 1976, p. 83).

Although it seems unlikely that the decline in tuberculosis mortality can be attributed either to changes in the virulence of the tubercle bacillus or to any changes in the genetic susceptibility of the human population (see McKeown 1976, pp. 83–84), it is possible that changes in the nature of infectious disease have affected patterns of mortality in other ways. As Kunitz and Engerman have argued, the main causes of premature death from infectious diseases in the sixteenth and seventeenth centuries were associated with epidemic or pandemic diseases, but these either became less important (in the case of plague) or more endemic (in the case of smallpox) in the eighteenth century. They argued that the transition from epidemic and pandemic diseases to endemic diseases meant that social factors, such as personal hygiene, domestic sanitary arrangements, and nutritional status, played an increasingly important part in the determination of death rates as the century progressed, and this was one of the main reasons for the emergence of a "social gradient" in health and mortality from the 1750s onwards (Kunitz and Engerman 1992, p. 33).

Historians of mortality change have often tended to pay particular attention to the relationship between real wages and diet, but it is also important to consider their impact on other items of consumption, including housing. During the early stages of the Industrial Revolution, it is widely accepted that housing conditions deteriorated in both urban and rural areas, but conditions began to improve from the 1850s onwards. These improvements were caused partly by the introduction of new bylaws which established higher standards for the construction of new housing, but also by the increase in the value of real wages, which enabled more households to afford a higher standard of accommodation. However, it was not until 1919 that the state began to make a concerted attempt to provide subsidized housing for working-class tenants and even then it decided to concentrate on the construction of new housing at the upper end of the working-class market. The government only began to launch a direct assault on the problem of the slums following the introduction of the Greenwood Housing Act of 1930, which offered a more generous form of subsidy to local authorities that linked the construction of new housing to the demolition of slum properties and formed the basis of public housing policy for the remainder of the decade (Harris 2004a, pp. 125–135, 245–254).

As we have already seen, the debate over the causes of mortality decline has often appeared to be polarized between those who apportion a dominant role to "living standards" (and, by implication, diet) and those who prefer to emphasize the role of public action and, especially, sanitary intervention, but it is clear that, even during the eighteenth century, there were a number of ways in which individual communities could act collectively to reduce mortality risk. Dobson (1997) has shown how the marshland communities of Essex, Kent, and Sussex were able to reduce mortality from malaria by instituting drainage schemes, and Razzell (1965; 1977, pp. 140–158) and Mercer (1985; 1990, pp. 46–73) have provided strong grounds for believing that the introduction of inoculation and vaccination played a major role in the decline of smallpox mortality from the 1750s onwards. These efforts were complemented by the measures taken by local bodies in the market towns of southern England and London to improve the quality of the urban environment during the same period (Jones and Falkus 1990; Porter 1991; Landers 1993). However, it is difficult to reach any categorical conclusions about the overall impact of these measures, particularly in the poorest and most rapidly growing areas. Hennock (1957, p. 117) argued that the Improvement Commissioners who were primarily responsible for urban government in the late eighteenth century "were primarily concerned with the comfort of the wealthier citizens … . As measures of sanitary reform, their value was marginal. For the same reason, they are not conclusive evidence that there existed an effective local public opinion in favor of sanitary reform."

Despite the best intentions of late-eighteenth and early-nineteenth-century reformers, there seems little doubt that their efforts were insufficient to cope with the rapidly expanding pace of urban growth during the first half of the nineteenth century. As Wohl (1984, p. 4) has shown, the period between 1800 and 1850 saw a dramatic increase in the proportion of the population who lived in towns and in the size of the towns in which they lived, and both Szreter and Mooney (1998, p. 104) and Woods (2000, pp. 360–380) have argued that this led to an absolute deterioration in the standard of public health in many urban areas. Szreter (1997, p. 64) suggested that the rapidity of urban growth gave rise to the "four Ds" of disruption, deprivation, disease, and death, and that these features continued to blight the lives of Britain's urban citizens for much of the nineteenth century.

One of the most important aspects of early-nineteenth-century urban growth was the deterioration in the quality and quantity of the water supply. As Hassan (Hassan 1985, pp. 533, 538, 543) has shown, it was already apparent by the end of the eighteenth century that many local authorities lacked the resources to maintain an adequate water supply. During the first half of the nineteenth century Parliament had encouraged them to transfer responsibility for water provision to private companies, but by 1850 "significant sections of Victorian public opinion" had come to the conclusion that it was inefficient "to leave the profitable activities of water, gas, electricity and urban transport to unregulated private enterprise" and there was widespread support for the view that these utilities should be restored to municipal ownership. However, although there was a rapid increase in the number of municipally owned water companies after 1850, it is difficult to say how far this may have contributed to any immediate improvement in urban health standards. This was partly because a substantial proportion of the increased supply of water was reserved for industrial use, and partly because "the direct environmental benefits of increased water deliveries for sanitary purposes were probably limited before the whole range of water services, including sewage treatment and river conservancy, were modernized."

In view of the close association between the improvement of water supplies and the broader concerns of sanitary engineering, it is clearly important to pay close attention to the chronology of nineteenth-century sanitary reform. As Michael Flinn and others have demonstrated, there was a significant growth of interest in the need for sanitary reform in the 1830s and 1840s, and this culminated in the passage of the Public Health Act of 1848, but this was a largely permissive piece of legislation which had relatively little impact, at least in the short term, on the largest urban centers (Flinn 1965, pp. 18–43; Harris 2004a, p. 110). Szreter (1988, p. 22) argued that the real beginning of sanitary reform occurred in the 1870s, when local authorities began to borrow much larger sums of money from central government funds for public health purposes, but Millward and his co-authors have demonstrated that they only began to invest substantial amounts of money in sewerage systems during the 1890s and early 1900s (Millward and Sheard 1995; Bell and Millward 1998; Millward and Bell 1998; Millward 2000). Their conclusions are reinforced by our own analysis of the Local Government Board's loan

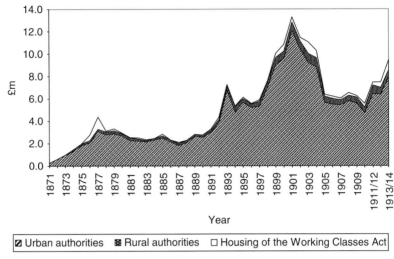

Year

| ☑ Urban authorities   ⊞ Rural authorities   □ Housing of the Working Classes Act |

Sources: Annual Reports of the Local Government Board, 1871–1914.
Notes: The graph shows the value of the loans sanctioned by the Local Government Board for public health purposes to urban and rural sanitary authorities between 1871 and 1914. The figures for 1871 refer to the period between August 19 and December 31 only, and neither these figures, nor the figures for 1872, differentiate between loans to urban authorities and loans to rural authorities. Full details of the authorities in receipt of loans and the purposes to which they were put were given in the appendices to the Local Government Board's reports.

Figure 4.8 Loans for public health purposes in England and Wales, 1871–1914

figures, which shows that the value of the loans provided to local sanitary authorities rose from £2.56 million in 1890 to a peak of just over £12 million eleven years later (Figure 4.8).

These findings have important implications for the debate about the causes and timing of the decline of mortality in England and Wales in the late nineteenth and early twentieth centuries. They suggest that, even though sanitary reform may have made a significant contribution to the decline of mortality before 1900, it is likely to have played an even more decisive role after that date, as the scale of public health investment increased. Recent historians of public health have tended to concentrate the bulk of their attention on the second half of the nineteenth century, but these figures reinforce the case for believing that more attention should now be paid to the early years of the twentieth century (see also Harris 2004b, p. 405).

As we have already seen, the most dramatic improvements in mortality in the nineteenth century were concentrated among those between the ages of 5 and 44, whereas the twentieth century also witnessed substantial improvements in the survival prospects of infants and older adults. It is tempting to assume that these developments must have reflected the impact of other changes which also occurred after 1900 but there is an impressive body of evidence which suggests that they should also be seen in the context of the more long-term improvement in health status which began around 1850.

In recent years, a growing number of researchers have paid increasing attention to the impact of cohort, or life course, approaches to the study of mortality change, and such cohort factors may have played an important role in the decline of both infant mortality and older-age mortality. Baird (1974, pp. 330, 334–335, 340; 1975, p. 139) suggested that women who were born during the economic recession of the late 1920s and early 1930s were more likely to give birth to low-birth-weight infants at the end of their own pregnancies, and Kramer (1987, p. 718) argued that "maternal height and pre-pregnancy weight, though listed as direct determinants [of birth weight] may themselves be affected by the mother's intrauterine and postnatal growth which depend, in part, on *her* mother's pregnancy and on subsequent nutritional and environmental influences during childhood." However, while most authorities seem to agree that there is some relationship between a mother's fetal environment and the health of her own offspring, the precise nature of this relationship remains unclear. Lumey (1998, p. 132) argued that undernutrition of the grandmother and thus of the mother during the first trimester of her own gestation had no effect on the mother's own birth weight but did affect the birth weight of her children, while undernutrition in the third trimester of gestation had an effect on the mother's birth weight but not that of her infants.

In view of these arguments, it is important to consider the extent to which changes in the health of adult females during the last thirty years of the nineteenth century may have contributed to the decline of infant mortality in the twentieth century, but the evidence for such a relationship is far from clear. Floud (1998, p. 11) found that there were "insufficient observations" to draw any conclusions about trends in the heights and weights of women born during the second half of the nineteenth century, but Millward and Bell (2001) have suggested that it might be possible to infer levels of maternal nutrition from the death rate from tuberculosis among women of childbearing age. However, even though they found that there was a close relationship between the tuberculosis mortality rate and infant mortality *before* 1900, there is little evidence to suggest that this factor can also account for the acceleration in the rate of infant mortality decline after this date.

Although it is difficult, on the basis of current knowledge, to attach too much importance to the impact of life-course effects on the decline of infant mortality, that does not mean we should ignore their effect on the decline of mortality at older ages. Since the mid 1980s, a great deal of attention has been focused on the possible impact of developments before and immediately after the time of birth on health in later life (e.g., Barker *et al.* 2002), but this research has not been accepted uncritically (see e.g. Lancet 2001) and it is also important to recognize the extent to which developments at older ages can also influence susceptibility to disease. Davey Smith, Gunnell, and Ben-Shlomo (2001, p. 113) found that "two . . . conditions – stroke and stomach cancer – appear to be particularly responsive to early-life influences while others – coronary heart disease, chronic obstructive respiratory disease, breast cancer and suicide – appear to be influenced by socially-patterned exposures acting right across life," and a third set of conditions, such as lung cancer, "appear to be mostly determined by . . . factors . . . in adulthood." They concluded that "there is no single answer to the question . . . on whether deprivation in childhood or adulthood is a more important determinant of adult mortality risk."

One of the main problems in evaluating the impact of life-course factors on historical changes in adult mortality is the difficulty of finding an appropriate proxy for health in early life. If improvements in fetal and infant health were the main reason for the decline of adult mortality in the first half of the twentieth century, one might expect to find stronger evidence of a relationship between changes in infant mortality and subsequent changes in adult mortality but, as we have already seen, the infant mortality rate did not begin to decline in Britain until the decline in death rates among older children and young adults was already under way. However, there does appear to be a much more obvious relationship between changes in *child* mortality and the decline of adult mortality. In 1934, Kermack, McKendrick, and McKinlay showed that when the death rate experienced by each age group was expressed as a percentage of the death rate for that age group in the 1840s, "each generation after the age of five years seems to carry along with it the same relative mortality throughout adult life, and even into old age," and this led them to conclude that the "care of children during their first 10–15 years of life is of supreme importance.

It is at this period ... that improved environment exercises its effects most promptly, and ... the improved physique built up during this period would seem to be of decisive effect at all later ages" (Kermack, McKendrick, and McKinlay 1934, pp. 699, 702).

These arguments are reinforced by evidence of changes in human stature. As we have already seen, the average height of the population from which army recruits were drawn increased, albeit inconsistently, between the birth cohorts of the 1740s and the 1820s and declined between the birth cohorts of the 1820s and the early 1850s, before resuming its upward path from the early 1850s onwards. The increase in the average height of men born after circa 1850 coincided with the onset of the decline in child mortality, and the cohorts that experienced these improvements also experienced lower rates of age-specific mortality throughout the life course. Although these findings do not necessarily provide unequivocal support for McKeown's view that the decline of mortality was caused by improvements in diet, they do provide further evidence of the link between improvements in child health and the subsequent decline of adult mortality (Floud, Wachter, and Gregory 1990, pp. 313–314; Harris 1994, p. 312; Harris 2001, p. 693).

Although these findings continue to provide strong support for a life-course approach to the understanding of mortality change, they also suggest that researchers need to look beyond a straightforward focus on the health and nutrition of the future child in the womb. Bengtsson and Lindström (2000) found that there was a close relationship between infant mortality in four Swedish parishes and the mortality rates experienced by the survivors of these cohorts between the ages of 55 and 80, and suggested that this was a consequence not so much of access to nutrients (either in the womb or during infancy), but exposure to infection. There are obvious problems in applying this directly to England and Wales in the absence of any similar relationship between infant mortality and mortality at older ages, but their emphasis on the relationship between childhood infection and later-life mortality may still have an important part to play in enhancing our understanding of the relationship between the decline of child mortality and the decline of adult mortality during the first half of the twentieth century (see also Finch and Crimmins 2004) (Table 4.15).

The preceding paragraphs have shown that improvements in the health of children and young adults in the second half of the nineteenth century may have made a significant contribution to the decline of

Technophysio evolution and human health

Table 4.15 *England and Wales: relative mortalities (the figures in the zero row refer to deaths under one year per 1,000 births)*

YEAR	1845	1855	1865	1875	1885	1895	1905	1915	1925	
0	100	101	101	98	93	101	83	65	46	
10	100	94	87	72	59	48	39	41	28	
20	100	93	87	75	60	50	41	45	35	30
30	100	95	95	87	74	62	50	53	36	
40	100	95	99	99	90	81	64	57	43	40
50	100	97	102	105	101	99	84	74	59	50
60	100	97	102	106	105	105	94	64	71	60
70	100	97	99	102	102	102	92	82	82	80
										90
OVER 75	100	99	99	101	97	97	90	89	87	

(AGE on vertical axis)

Source: Kermack, McKendrick, and McKinlay 1934, p. 699 (reprinted in *International Journal of Epidemiology,* Vol. 30, p. 678).

mortality among older adults in the first half of the twentieth century. However, this century also witnessed major developments in medical science which made their own contribution to the improvement of health and the decline of mortality at all ages.

As McKeown (1976, pp. 91–110) showed more than a third of a century ago, it would be easy to exaggerate the importance of scientific medicine when one considers that much of the decline in the mortality associated with infectious diseases predated the introduction of effective medical measures to deal with it, but this does not mean that its contribution should be discounted altogether. In the late nineteenth and early twentieth centuries, researchers such as Robert Koch, Albert

Calmette, and Jean-Marie Guérin pioneered the development of bacteriological tests for diseases such as tuberculosis and diphtheria which led to the introduction of mass immunization campaigns in many parts of Europe and America (Porter 1997, pp. 436–442). In Britain, the onset of mass immunization was delayed until after the Second World War, but it had a significant and substantial impact on the morbidity associated with many common diseases, including diphtheria, tetanus, tuberculosis, poliomyelitis, whooping cough, measles, mumps, rubella, and, more recently, chicken pox. Despite some concerns, the vast majority of commentators and health professionals believe that mass immunization has led to major improvements in the health of both children and adults (Fraser *et al.* 1997, pp. 65–66; British Medical Association 2003).

The twentieth century also witnessed some important developments in the treatment of disease, beginning with the use of Prontosil as a treatment for puerperal fever in the 1930s. This condition had been a major cause of maternal mortality, and the introduction of Prontosil (the first of the sulfonamide drugs) led to an immediate and dramatic reduction in its incidence (Loudon 1992, pp. 258–261). The decline of mortality was also accelerated by the introduction of penicillin and other antibiotics after 1945. Penicillin was used to treat a range of conditions, including anthrax, tetanus, syphilis, diphtheria, and pneumonia, and streptomycin and isoniazid were highly effective agents in the battle against tuberculosis. The impact of these innovations was reinforced by the use of insulin therapy in the treatment of diabetes. This "proved to be one of the century's most valuable life-savers, not least because diabetes is spreading and remains incurable" (Porter 1997, pp. 448–461, 567–568).

The "therapeutic revolution" (Hardy 2001, p. 152) also achieved some important successes in the fight against the two leading causes of premature death in modern Britain, namely heart disease and cancer. It is now more than half a century since Doll and Hill (1950, p. 746) demonstrated that "smoking is a factor, and an important factor, in the production of carcinoma of the lung," and this led to a concerted and ongoing campaign to alert smokers to the risks they incurred, but there have also been some significant breakthroughs in the management and treatment of many of these diseases. In the period between 1971 and 1990, major reductions were achieved in the death rates associated with a range of cancers, including the majority of childhood cancers, leukemia, and cancer of the breast, colon, cervix, and testes, and the proportions of sufferers who survived for more than five years after their initial diagnosis rose accordingly. However, many of the most common forms of cancer remained stubbornly resistant to therapeutic efforts. By the end of the 1990s, only 2.5 percent of patients with pancreatic cancer, and 6.1 percent of patients with lung cancer, survived for more than five years (Coleman and Salt 1992, p. 279; Office for National Statistics 1999, Table 4.4; Office for National Statistics 2005).

Medical science has achieved rather more success in the battle against heart disease. Since the end of the Second World War, a considerable amount of attention has been paid to the role of diet in the etiology of heart disease, and this has led to a growing emphasis on the consumption of low fat foods, but there have also been significant developments in the management and treatment of heart disease. These have included the use of beta-blockers (for reducing blood pressure and steadying the heartbeat), streptokinase and aspirin (for blood thinning and clot dissolving), defibrillators (to regulate the heartbeat) and pacemakers. Since the end of the 1960s, there has also been a dramatic increase in the incidence of heart transplants. This remains a "technique of last resort" but its benefits should not be underestimated. As Anne Hardy has noted, "there were by the 1990s many hundreds of patients whose lives had been prolonged for many years in a condition of much greater comfort and fitness than they could have hoped to achieve before 1970" (Porter 1997, pp. 580–586; Hardy 2001, p. 160).

4.6 Morbidity

As many historians have pointed out, it is extremely difficult to reconstruct the morbidity of past generations. Measures of height and weight can provide an indirect indication of the impact of sickness on children's growth, and cause-specific mortality rates can shed new light on the illnesses which caused death, but it is much more difficult to find unambiguous evidence of non-fatal diseases. As a result, historians have often been forced to infer the extent of these conditions from other sources, such as the health insurance statistics compiled by friendly societies, trade unions, and the statutory national health insurance scheme. However, the interpretation of these data is complicated by disagreements over the definition of sickness, the impact of contextual and institutional factors on claiming behavior, and the relationship between sickness and age.

One of the main reasons why historians have often been mistrustful of health insurance statistics is the extent to which the "sickness threshold" may have changed over time. As Johansson (1991, p. 43) has argued, the distinction between "sickness" and "health" is intrinsically fuzzy, and this means that trends in sickness behavior may owe as much, if not more, to cultural changes as they do to changes in biological conditions. Variations in sickness rates are also likely to be influenced by differences in the operation of different benefit societies, the financial health of these societies, and the incentives to claim provided by different economic circumstances (Whiteside 1987; Murray 2003). The interpretation of sickness statistics is also complicated by differences in the age structures of the populations at risk. This is not simply a question of calculating the average age of friendly society members, but also of working out the proportion of members belonging to the age groups at which the incidence and duration of sickness episodes tend to be greater (Emery 1998).

Although these are important considerations, they do not mean that the effort to derive information about sickness from health insurance records should be abandoned altogether. Southall and Garrett (1991, pp. 249–252) published a pioneering analysis of the individual sickness records of an early-nineteenth-century engineering trade union, the Steam Engine Makers' Society. Although they did not attempt to examine changes in sickness rates over time, they were able to investigate the relationship between sickness and age, the seasonality of sickness claims, and their relationship to mortality. Their results showed that older members were much more likely to be sick than younger members, mainly because the duration of sickness episodes increased rapidly at higher ages, and that the seasonal distribution of sickness episodes was closely related to the seasonality of mortality. Both morbidity and mortality peaked during the first quarter of the year, before declining during the spring and summer months, and rising once more between September and December.

Other work has proved more controversial. Riley (1997, p. 198) examined the incidence and duration of sickness episodes among members of one of the largest English friendly societies, the Ancient Order of Foresters. After controlling for the effects of both age and region, he concluded that even though the incidence of sickness episodes may have declined between 1870 and 1914, their duration increased, with the result that the overall prevalence of morbidity increased, even though mortality rates were declining. He also put forward a number of hypotheses to explain these somewhat surprising findings. These included (a) insult accumulation; (b) differential frailty; and (c) the beneficial impact of medical attendance on the survival prospects of men who were suffering from fatal diseases (see also Alter and Riley 1989, pp. 26, 31; Riley 1989, pp. 44, 47; Riley and Alter 1989, p. 208).

Riley's findings have continued to spark considerable debate (e.g., Murray 2003), but they have also encouraged other researchers to investigate alternative sources for the study of nineteenth- and twentieth-century morbidity patterns. Edwards *et al.* (2003, pp. 114–160) presented the initial results of a study of sickness rates among members of the Hampshire Friendly Society, a small "county" society serving a predominantly agricultural population in the south of England.[4] By following through the experience of nearly four hundred men who joined the Society in 1871 and between 1895 and 1899, they were able to show how both the incidence and the duration of sickness episodes increased with age, and they claimed that this was largely responsible for the changes in annual sickness rates which the Society itself reported between 1868 and 1921. They were also able to shed new light on the nature of the conditions which gave rise to these claims. In 1910, the leading causes of sickness claims were injuries and accidents (17.74 percent of all episodes), influenza (13.96 percent), and colds (8.74 percent), followed by rheumatism (6.29 percent) and bronchitis (5.17 percent).[5]

Despite the wealth of information held by organizations such as friendly societies, it took many years for the state to add the collection of sickness data to the tasks which public health authorities routinely undertook as part of their strategy for monitoring health conditions, and the earliest attempts to measure the incidence of non-fatal diseases were more concerned with the health of children than with that of adults. In 1907, the Education (Administrative Provisions) Act instructed every local education authority in England and Wales to make arrangements for the medical inspection of children "immediately before, or at the time of, or as soon as possible after their admission to a public elementary school, and on such other occasions as the Board of Education direct" (Harris 1995, p. 2). However, even though the Board issued a series of Circulars telling school doctors what conditions to examine, most commentators believed that the results of these

---

[4] For more information on the occupational details of the men who joined the Hampshire Friendly Society, see Edwards *et al.* 2003, p. 138.
[5] Gorsky *et al.* have recently extended this analysis, using the records of a much larger number of individuals. For an initial summary, see Harris, Hinde, and Gorsky 2009.

inspections were too unreliable to be used for statistical purposes, and little use was ever made of them. In 1927, the Medical Officer of Health and School Medical Officer for Stockton-on-Tees, Dr. G. C. M. M'Gonigle, concluded that "the absence of standards has seriously limited the usefulness of the huge mass of clinical data accumulated by the numerous School Medical Officers scattered throughout the country," and there is little evidence to suggest that there had been any improvement on this front before the end of the 1930s (Harris 1995, p. 108).

Although little effort was made to improve the quality of the school medical statistics during the Second World War, the government began to pay more attention to surveys of adult health, partly as a way of monitoring the impact of war conditions, and partly to monitor the civilian demand for medical services (General Register Office 1953, p. 8; Logan and Brooke 1957, p. 12). The researchers interviewed a representative sample of the population aged sixteen and over, and obtained information about sickness (the number of persons reporting an illness in a given month), incapacity (the number of days away from work), prevalence (the number of illnesses per 100 persons), and consultation rates (the number of respondents consulting a general practitioner). Although the results were not strictly comparable with the statistics derived from friendly society records, they provided further evidence of the relationship between sickness and age, and revealed similar patterns of seasonal morbidity to those experienced by members of the Hampshire Friendly Society and in other surveys (Gorsky, Harris, and Hinde 2004). The most common causes of sickness were ill-defined symptoms, colds and influenza, rheumatism, and "other respiratory diseases." Injuries and accidents accounted for a high proportion of the sickness episodes experienced by men between the ages of sixteen and sixty-four, but were less prevalent among other groups (General Register Office 1953, pp. 16–23, 41–46; Logan and Brooke 1957, pp. 42–47, 52–26, 59–62).

It is possible to obtain further evidence of changes in recorded levels of morbidity since 1951 by examining the statistics collected by general practitioners and the General Household Survey (GHS). The GHS was initiated at the beginning of the 1970s, and respondents were invited to state whether they had experienced any long-standing illness (including limiting long-standing illness) over the previous twelve months, or any acute illness, leading to restricted activity, over the previous two weeks. The results, which are shown in Figure 4.9, suggest that there was a definite increase in all three gauges of recorded morbidity during the

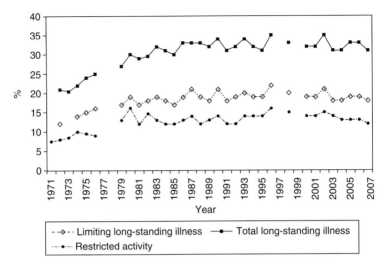

Source: General Household Survey, 1971–2007.

Figure 4.9 Percentage of persons reporting acute or chronic illnesses, 1971–2007

1970s, with relatively little change thereafter. However, a rather different picture emerges when one looks at the number of respondents who consulted a doctor over this period. The responses to these questions (see Figure 4.10) suggest that the proportion of patients who consulted their doctor in the two weeks before they were interviewed, and the average number of consultations per patient over the course of the year, rose consistently between the mid 1970s and the early 1990s.

It is also possible to compare the information obtained from the General Household Survey with the patient-consultation data provided by general practitioners at various points in time between 1955/6 and 1991/2. One of the main disadvantages of the GHS data is that it is not possible to say whether the increase in the number of patient consultations was caused by an increase in the number of patients who consulted their doctor over the course of a year, or by an increase in the number of occasions on which the same patient consulted their doctor, but the GP statistics show that although there was little change in the percentage of patients who consulted their doctor over the course of a year between 1955/6 and 1970/2, this figure rose substantially between the beginning of the 1970s and the start of the 1990s. The GP statistics tend to show lower numbers of consultations per patient (in 1991/2, the GP statistics showed an average of 348 consultations per 100 patients, whereas the

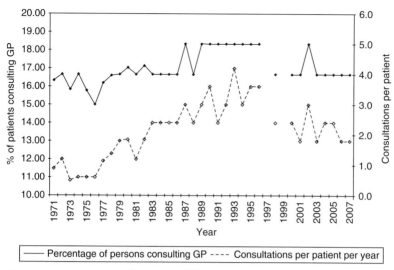

Sources: *General Household Survey*, 1971–2007.

Figure 4.10 Percentage of patients consulting an NHS GP over a two-week period and average number of consultations per patient per year, 1971–2007

GHS data suggest approximately five consultations per patient), but the overall trends, from the early 1970s onwards, are very similar, and although there was a sharp fall in the number of consultations per sick patient between the mid 1950s and the early 1970s, it remained relatively constant over the next two decades (Table 4.16).

Although it is tempting to regard these statistics as evidence of increased morbidity among the population as a whole, it is probably more appropriate to regard them as a measure of increases in health awareness and in the provision of preventive services, such as screening for breast cancer (see Murray and Chen 1992; Murray and Chen 1993; Riley 1993). Even though it may be possible to ask survey respondents the same question, their answers are almost certain to reflect changes in the ways in which "illness" is defined, the seriousness with which they view different degrees of discomfort (or "dis-ease"), and the actions they will take in the light of this, and this will in turn reflect changes in the quality and availability of medical services, and the capabilities of medical science. This does not mean that information on morbidity should be discounted altogether, but it does show that this information needs to be interpreted with considerable care (Grundy 1994, pp. 199–200).

4.7 Cohort factors and mortality change

As the preceding section has shown, there are many different reasons for the improvement of health and life expectancy since 1700, including improvements in diet and nutrition, sanitation and the environment, and medical science. Some of these changes have led to immediate improvements in the health and survival prospects of those affected by them, while others also led to improvements in later life. It is also clear that many of the most dramatic improvements in health and life expectancy have occurred over the course of the last century. What are the implications of these changes for the health of the British population in the future?

One of the most important starting points for this particular strand of anthropometric history was Barker and Osmond's (1986) investigation into the links between fetal and infant development and health in later life, but the precise nature of this relationship remains unclear. In one recent review, Barker *et al.* (2002) suggested that when undernutrition during early development is followed by improved nutrition, many animals and plants experience a period of compensatory or

Table 4.16 *Percentage of patients who consulted their general practitioners, 1995/6–1991/2*

		1955–6	1970–2	1981–2	1991–2
Percentage of patients who consulted a general practitioner					
0–14	male	74	71	73	81
	female	74	71	74	84
	total	74	71	73	82
15–44	male	58	58	58	61
	female	70	74	78	87
	total	64	66	67	74
45–64	male	60	60	63	69
	female	67	67	72	83
	total	64	64	67	76
65 and over	male	68	66	74	85
	female	73	67	77	87
	total	71	66	76	86
Total	male	63	63	65	70
	female	70	71	77	86
	total	67	67	71	78

Table 4.16 (*cont.*)

		1955–6	1970–2	1981–2	1991–2
Number of consultations per year, per one hundred patients at risk					
0–14	male	320	252	266	304
	female	309	241	264	313
	total	315	247	265	308
15–44	male	247	206	190	187
	female	370	392	419	429
	total	312	301	309	308
45–64	male	395	311	305	306
	female	412	339	393	433
	total	404	325	350	369
65 and over	male	586	401	447	467
	female	641	413	498	509
	total	619	409	477	492
Total	male	339	261	271	272
	female	408	350	402	421
	total	375	307	340	348
Number of consultations per year, per patient who consulted their doctor					
0–14	male	4.32	3.53	3.66	3.75
	female	4.18	3.42	3.58	3.75
	total	4.26	3.48	3.62	3.75
15–44	male	4.26	3.54	3.27	3.06
	female	5.29	5.28	5.35	4.92
	total	4.88	4.53	4.61	4.15
45–64	male	6.58	5.16	4.83	4.42
	female	6.15	5.07	5.48	5.21
	total	6.31	5.12	5.18	4.85
65 and over	male	8.62	6.11	6.05	5.52
	female	8.78	6.21	6.45	5.82
	total	8.72	6.17	6.30	5.70
Total	male	5.38	4.16	4.16	3.89
	female	5.83	4.97	5.25	4.91
	total	5.60	4.60	4.77	4.46

Source: Morbidity Statistics from General Practice, 1955/6–1991/2.

accelerated growth which may impose a penalty in later life. However, whatever the precise mechanisms, there appears to be a general consensus that early-life developments do have an effect on subsequent health, even if the reasons for this have still to be established (Leon 2001, p. 62).

The debate over the relationship between fetal and infant health and adult mortality is closely related to the ongoing debate over the relationship between height and mortality. Waaler (1984) showed that shorter men and women were more likely to die at younger ages than taller men and women, and Costa (1993) identified a very similar relationship in her analysis of height and mortality among men who joined the Union Army in the United States a century earlier. However, the interpretation of this relationship remains controversial. Both Waaler and Costa argued that, since height is a marker for health in childhood, the relationship between height and mortality is likely to reflect the impact of early-life conditions on health in later life, but both Riley (1994) and Alter (2004) have suggested that the relationship may be a purely genetic one, in that individuals who have "tall genes" are also less vulnerable to premature mortality.

Alter (2004) argued that a person's height is determined by a combination of genetic and environmental factors, but that the relationship between height and mortality may be either genetic or environmental in origin. In the past, environmental factors (including diet and nutrition) are likely to have exerted a much stronger influence on variations in stature than they do today, so one would expect the relationship between height and mortality to have been stronger in the past, if this was a purely environmental relationship, and weaker if the relationship was primarily genetic. However, it is difficult to design a straightforward empirical test of this hypothesis using current data, because of the impact of environmental and nutritional inequalities in the first half of the twentieth century on the heights of those who are at the greatest risk of mortality today.

Despite these arguments, there are a number of reasons for thinking that the relationship between height and mortality is not a purely genetic one. As we have already seen, Costa and Waaler believe that there was a strong relationship between height and mortality among two very different populations, but this in itself does not really help to resolve the dilemma which Alter proposes. However, it is noteworthy that both of these authors found that the relationship between height and mortality appeared to break down above a certain cutoff point (men with a height of 73 inches, or 185 centimeters). If the relationship between height and mortality was purely genetic, one might expect this cutoff point to increase as the average height of the population increased. The fact that this change does not appear to have occurred may therefore reflect the fact that the relationship is environmental in origin (Harris 1994, p. 503).

This is not the only reason why one might expect the relationship between height and mortality to be a reflection of environmental circumstances. Tanner *et al.* (1982) showed that most of the increase in the average heights of Japanese people since the Second World War was associated with an increase in leg-length, and this led them to conclude that leg-length was the component of height which was most susceptible to environmental effects. This finding is important because it also appears that leg-length is the component of height which is most closely associated with the reduced risk of mortality from both cancer and coronary heart disease (1998). This is therefore a strong indication that the relationship between height and mortality is associated with variations in childhood living conditions (see also Gunnell *et al.* 2003).

Although height is inversely associated with many of the leading causes of premature mortality, it would be wrong to assume that this will continue to be the case indefinitely. If environmental factors are largely responsible for the relationship between height and mortality, then it is likely that improvements in environmental and nutritional conditions will lead to a reduction in the association between these factors and later-life mortality (see also Su 2009). It is also important to recognize that the second half of the twentieth century has witnessed a decline in the relative importance of those diseases which are inversely associated with stature and an increase in the importance of diseases which are positively associated (Davey Smith *et al.* 2000, p. 102; Samaras, Elrick, and Storms 2003). However, despite this, diseases such as stomach cancer and coronary heart disease are still important causes of death in contemporary Britain (Office for National Statistics 2009a, pp. 28, 98), and even though living conditions have improved since the Second World War, the association between height and all-cause mortality has persisted across the generations (Galobardes, Lynch, and Davey Smith 2004; Galobardes, Lynch, and Davey Smith 2008; Batty *et al.* 2009). In the short term, therefore, one might reasonably expect to find that the changes which have led to improvements in childhood conditions over the course of the last century will continue to lead to improvements in adult mortality in the current century, even though these relationships may not continue indefinitely.

Although students of "life-course" factors have paid particular attention to the importance of factors which influence health during the fetal and infant stages, and in childhood, considerable attention has also been paid to factors which operate across the life course, including cigarette smoking. Although there are strong grounds for believing that exposure to cigarette smoke in the womb and in early childhood has deleterious effects on the health of the child (e.g., Cook and Strachan 1999), most smokers only take up the habit for themselves in their early teens (Peterson and Peto 2004, p. 21). However, there is evidence which shows that the consumption of tobacco has declined considerably during the last thirty years. Wald and Nicolaides-Bouman (Wald and Nicolaides-Bouman 1991) showed that there was a dramatic increase in the average annual number of cigarettes consumed by men between 1905 and the early 1940s, and by women between 1920 and the beginning of the 1970s, but consumption levels have fallen for both sexes since the 1970s. These figures are reinforced by data from the General Household Survey, which show that there were reductions in the proportions of men and women in all social classes who smoked between 1974 and 2007 (Fitzpatrick and Chandola 2000; Peterson and Peto 2004, p. 25; Robinson and Lader 2007, pp. 6–9).

While there have been many improvements in the factors which influence health over the last one hundred years, some changes have tended in the opposite direction. The British Nutrition Foundation (British Nutrition Foundation 2003) argues that "a healthy diet is a diet based on breads, potatoes and other cereals, and is rich in fruits and vegetables. [It] will include moderate amounts of milk and dairy products, meat, fish or meat/milk alternatives, and limited amounts of foods containing fat or sugar," but the evidence regarding dietary trends is mixed. Charlton and Quaife (1997) showed that average per capita consumption of sugar, meat, and meat products increased between 1950 and 1980 and fell between 1980 and 1994, but consumption of fruits increased consistently over the whole of the period and consumption of vegetables declined. Average consumption of butter and lard, and total fat consumption, rose between 1950 and 1970, before falling significantly. However, although Britons now appear to consume a "healthier" diet, levels of obesity have continued to rise. In 1980, approximately 33 percent of men and 24 percent of women were described as "overweight," while 6 percent of men and 8 percent of women were described as "obese," but in 2007, 41 percent of men and

32 percent of women were "overweight," and 24 percent of men and 24 percent of women were officially "obese" (Knight and Eldridge 1984, p. 33; Fitzpatrick and Chandola 2000, pp. 116–118; National Health Service Information Centre 2008).[6]

A number of commentators have also expressed concern about increasing levels of alcohol consumption. In 2002, the authors of the General Household Survey (Rickards *et al.* 2002, p. 157) reported that there had been "a slight increase in overall weekly alcohol consumption among men and a much more marked one among women" since the late 1980s, but they also found "some indication of a slight decline" since 2000, and there is evidence to suggest that this trend continued subsequently. The later statistics are not directly comparable with those for earlier periods but the authors of the 2007 report concluded that "there has been a slight fall in the proportions of men and women who say that they had an alcoholic drink in the previous week compared to four years ago" and there was also a fall "in the proportions of both men and women exceeding the daily benchmarks between 2003 and 2005," although there was little further change in 2006 and 2007. There was also little change "in the proportions of men and women drinking heavily (more than 8 units and 6 units respectively) on at least one day in the previous week" (Robinson and Lader 2007, p. 42).[7]

As these figures indicate, it can be difficult to make any definite predictions about the impact of recent trends on the factors which affect health and their impact on standards of health in coming years, but there are clear indications that most of the factors which influence health have improved over the last hundred years, and that these changes are likely to continue to influence the health of those who lived through them for many years to come. As a result, it does not seem unreasonable to assume that standards of health and longevity will continue to rise for a significant part of the current century.

We have already seen that it can be particularly difficult to obtain objective evidence regarding levels of morbidity. However, there is evidence from the United States which suggests, contrary to the impression which might be obtained from the General Household Survey, that

---

[6] The Department of Health defines individuals with a body mass index of 25–30 as "overweight," while individuals with BMIs in excess of 30 are regarded as "obese" (Department of Health 2006).

[7] For statistics on alcohol consumption in 2008, see Lader 2009.

significant progress has been achieved in the fight against morbidity. Costa (2000; 2002) compared disability rates among the Union Army veterans with those observed among men who were examined as part of the National Health Examination Surveys (1959–62) and the National Health and Nutritional Examination Surveys (1971–5, 1976–80, and 1988–94), and found that in almost every case the Union Army veterans showed higher rates of disability than their successors. Among those aged 60–74, the proportion suffering from respiratory complaints declined from 37.8 percent in 1910 to 10.8 percent in 1988–94, and the proportion displaying signs of an irregular heartbeat fell from 42 percent in 1910 to 8.5 percent toward the end of the century (Costa 2000, p. 58; Costa 2002, p. 126; Manton, Corder, and Stallard 1997; Cutler 2001; Manton and Gu 2001; Manton, Gu, and Lamb 2006; Schoeni, Freedman, and Martin 2008).

It is also possible to examine changes in morbidity using estimates of "healthy life expectancy," or HLE. These indicators seek to measure the number of years which an individual can expect to live while enjoying either "good" or "fairly good" health, or without experiencing limiting long-standing illness or disability (Breakwell and Bajekal 2005). As we have already seen, evidence from the General Household Survey suggests that an increasing proportion of respondents reported higher levels of limiting long-standing illness at all ages, and this has led some commentators to conclude that "the extra years of life gained by the elderly may be extra years with a disability, not extra years of healthy life" (Dunnell 1997, p. 175). However, more recent research suggests that health-expectancy levels may be increasing. Smith, Edgar, and Groom (2008) have recently published new estimates of HLE for males and females in the UK for 2000/02 and 2004/06. Their figures show that male HLE rose from 66.8 years to 68.2 years, while female HLE rose from 69.9 years to 70.4 years. They have also estimated that the health-expectancy of females at the age of 65 rose from 14.0 to 14.5 years, while that of males rose from 11.9 to 12.8 years.

Despite the difficulties involved in measuring changes in morbidity, there is little doubt over the extent of changes in longevity. As we have already seen, most of the increase in life expectancy before 1950 was associated with reductions in mortality at younger ages (see Figure 4.4), but the period since 1950 has also seen significant increases in life expectancy at older ages, and this has been the main reason for the recent increase in the proportion of the population surviving to very old ages and for increases in the ages at which the oldest individuals have finally expired (see also Wilmoth *et al.* 2000). The extent of these changes can be illustrated by looking at trends in the numbers of people who have survived to the age of eighty and above since the end of the Second World War. In 1992, Roger Thatcher estimated that the number of people aged eighty and over in England and Wales increased from 563,000 in 1946 to just under 1.7 million forty years later, while the number of centenarians increased from just 210 to more than 3,200 (Thatcher 1992, p. 416; Thatcher 1997, pp. 205–206; Rau *et al.* 2008).

The increase in the proportion of the population surviving to very high ages has, inevitably, raised questions about the concept of a "natural" human life span. In one recent study, Oeppen and Vaupel (2002) examined the trend in maximum age at death in a range of different countries, and showed that this had increased at a steady rate of about three months per year for the last 160 years, with no evidence yet of any deceleration (see also Christensen *et al.* 2009). If their account is correct, there is every reason to expect that average life expectancy will continue to increase for many years to come, with profound implications for current assumptions about the limits to human longevity and the proportion of individuals surviving to very high ages throughout the developed world (see also Carey 2001).

New research into trends in morbidity and ageing has also raised important questions about the quality of the lives "saved" at older ages. In 1980, James Fries argued that delays in the onset of chronic diseases, allied to the concept of a fixed human life span, would lead to the "compression" of morbidity at older age, but other writers have argued that the addition of extra years of life at ages at which morbidity rates are highest means that standards of health are more likely to deteriorate as longevity increases (Verbrugge 1984; Riley 1989, p. 246). However, there is now a growing body of evidence from a variety of countries which suggests that both health expectancy and life expectancy are increasing (Robine, Romieu, and Cambois 1999, p. 183; see also Brønnum-Hansen 2005). In the UK, Smith, Edgar, and Groom (2008) estimate that the ratio of "disability-free" years to total years rose from 79.7 percent to 81.2 percent, in the case of men, and from 78.1 percent to 78.6 percent for women, between 2000/02 and 2004/06. They also calculated that the proportion of disability-free years for women over the age of 65 increased from 53.7 percent to 53.9 percent, and for men from 55.3 percent to 59.7 percent.

During the last twenty years, British governments have become increasingly exercised by issues relating to the age of retirement and the provision of financial support for people in old age. Over the course of the twentieth century, falling birth rates and declining death rates led to a reduction in the ratio of people of "working" age (conventionally assumed to be between the ages of 15 or 16 and 65) and pensionable age – or, alternatively, an increase in the "pensioner" or "old age" dependency ratio. At the same time, although there has been a substantial increase in female labor force participation rates, changes in the school-leaving age and increases in the length of time spent in post-school education have meant that people enter the workforce at later stages in their lives, and the number of years lived beyond retirement has also increased (Warnes 2006). As a result of these changes, there have been growing calls for changes in the statutory retirement age, and this is now expected to rise to 68, for both men and women, before 2050 (Department for Work and Pensions 2006, paragraph 39).

Although this development has generated considerable controversy, it is important to remember that when UK governments first began to discuss the introduction of old-age pensions, the concept of "retirement" was linked, in part, to observations about the age at which older workers were already being excluded from the workforce on grounds of declining physical ability (Macnicol 1998, pp. 125–131), but the nature of the working environment has changed and the physical and mental health of older workers has improved considerably. There is therefore considerable scope for increasing the current age of retirement and this may well be necessary if the United Kingdom to finance extended periods of retirement, either individually or collectively, in the future. In 2002, the Department for Work and Pensions (2002, p. 16) estimated that the proportion of the population aged 65 and over, expressed as a proportion of the population between the ages of 15 and 64, was likely to rise from 24.4 percent in 2000 to 39.2 percent in 2050, but this figure only allowed for relatively limited improvements in life-expectancy and may need to be revised again if current expectations regarding the maximum length of the human life span are realized.[8]

---

[8] The Department for Work and Pensions assumes that life expectancy at age 65 will rise by 3 years for men, and by 2.7 years for women, between 2000 and 2050. However, if the rate of increase which has been identified by Oeppen and Vaupel continues for the next fifty years, average life expectancy could increase by more than 12 years for both sexes.

Appendix D

Table D.1 *Changes in the average height, weight, and body mass index of British schoolchildren, 1905–2007*

Place	Year	Age last birthday	Boys			Girls		
			Height (m)[a]	Weight (kg)[a]	BMI (kg/m²)[b]	Height (m)[a]	Weight (kg)[a]	BMI (kg/m²)[b]
Bradford	1910	5	1.03	17.10	16.02	1.02	16.80	16.08
		13	1.42	34.00	16.91	1.45	35.60	17.05
	1920	5	1.04	17.70	16.49	1.02	17.30	16.69
		8	1.21	23.90	16.24	1.21	23.30	15.83
		12	1.39	33.70	17.42	1.39	33.50	17.22
	1930	5	1.06	18.50	16.47	1.07	17.80	15.69
		8	1.22	24.70	16.49	1.22	23.90	16.09
		12	1.39	34.20	17.70	1.42	34.90	17.84
	1938	5	1.07	18.90	16.42	1.07	18.30	16.07
		8	1.25	25.50	16.45	1.23	24.60	16.13
		12	1.42	36.10	17.86	1.44	37.20	17.92
Cambridge	1910	5	1.03	17.41	16.37	1.02	17.09	16.31
		12	1.38	32.00	16.82	1.41	34.00	17.05
	1920	5	1.05	18.14	16.31	1.04	17.20	15.98
		8	1.21	23.47	16.12	1.20	22.83	15.75
		12	1.40	33.48	17.03	1.42	31.90	15.85
	1930	5	1.08	18.72	16.15	1.07	18.22	15.77
		8	1.25	25.76	16.50	1.23	24.62	16.14
		12	1.43	36.46	17.84	1.45	37.08	17.63

Table D.1 (cont.)

Place	Year	Age last birthday	Boys			Girls		
			Height (m)[a]	Weight (kg)[a]	BMI (kg/m²)[b]	Height (m)[a]	Weight (kg)[a]	BMI (kg/m²)[b]
	1940	5	1.09	19.11	16.14	1.09	18.47	15.46
		8	1.26	26.73	16.86	1.25	25.71	16.37
		12	1.45	36.85	17.52	1.48	38.88	17.85
	1950	5	1.09	19.39	16.25	1.10	19.14	15.83
		10	1.38	32.14	16.83	1.38	32.93	17.31
		14	1.59	48.46	19.29	1.59	50.29	19.88
Croydon	1910	5	1.05	17.73	15.95	1.04	17.50	16.14
		12	1.41	33.27	16.68	1.44	34.77	16.82
	1920	5	1.08	18.41	15.80	1.07	17.73	15.50
		8	1.23	23.23	15.37	1.21	23.05	15.77
		12	1.43	35.09	17.16	1.47	39.23	18.14
	1930	5	1.08	18.82	16.07	1.07	18.32	15.87
		8	1.22	23.91	16.15	1.23	22.91	15.16
		12	1.42	34.36	16.92	1.42	34.82	17.15
	1938	5	1.09	19.27	16.08	1.09	18.82	15.92
		8	1.25	25.45	16.17	1.24	24.27	15.73
		12	1.46	38.45	17.97	1.49	39.00	17.66
	1950	5	1.10	19.86	16.35	1.09	19.23	16.04

Edinburgh	1910	8	1.27	26.45	16.40	1.26	25.45	16.10
		11	1.40	34.27	17.43	1.41	34.82	17.46
		15	1.62	51.68	19.68	1.59	51.50	20.37
	1920	5	1.04	18.40	16.85	1.04	17.96	16.64
		9	1.24	25.64	16.57	1.24	24.36	15.72
		13	1.43	35.96	17.52	1.44	36.90	17.77
	1931	5	1.05	18.50	16.81	1.02	17.77	17.22
		9	1.26	26.36	16.68	1.25	25.36	16.24
		13	1.42	34.73	17.23	1.45	35.95	17.21
	1941	5	1.06	18.36	16.37	1.05	17.64	15.95
		9	1.24	25.09	16.40	1.24	24.93	15.83
		13	1.48	39.91	18.26	1.50	41.55	18.37
	1950	5	1.09	19.47	16.33	1.08	18.83	16.07
		9	1.31	27.80	16.16	1.30	27.70	16.34
		13	1.50	41.57	18.39	1.52	43.20	18.67
Glasgow	1920	5	1.08	19.34	16.62	1.07	18.73	16.35
		9	1.31	29.11	16.95	1.30	28.52	16.83
		13	1.50	41.89	18.56	1.52	44.32	19.15
	1930	5	1.04	17.82	16.51	1.03	17.55	16.42
		9	1.22	24.41	16.29	1.21	23.45	16.11
		13	1.41	34.55	17.45	1.42	36.32	17.95
	1939	5	1.04	17.91	16.51	1.04	17.27	16.08
		9	1.24	26.00	16.78	1.24	25.00	16.14
		13	1.43	36.36	17.72	1.45	37.77	17.89
		5	1.06	18.50	16.49	1.05	17.91	16.12
		9	1.28	27.05	16.63	1.26	26.33	16.39

Table D.1 (*cont.*)

Place	Year	Age last birthday	Boys			Girls		
			Height (m)[a]	Weight (kg)[a]	BMI (kg/m²)[b]	Height (m)[a]	Weight (kg)[a]	BMI (kg/m²)[b]
	1949	13	1.46	38.64	18.05	1.49	40.86	18.51
		5	1.08	19.13	16.50	1.07	18.40	16.15
		9	1.30	28.29	16.66	1.29	27.35	16.44
		13	1.49	40.41	18.14	1.50	42.28	18.72
Huddersfield	1920	5	1.07	18.76	16.39	1.01	17.32	17.01
		8	1.20	23.46	16.20	1.21	23.02	15.70
		12	1.38	32.90	17.24	1.41	33.66	17.01
	1930	5	1.08	18.79	15.99	1.13	18.18	14.25
		8	1.25	24.89	16.03	1.24	24.35	15.82
		12	1.42	35.80	17.81	1.44	35.30	17.11
	1940	5	1.10	19.20	15.76	1.08	18.24	15.54
		8	1.25	24.87	15.89	1.25	24.14	15.52
		12	1.43	35.30	17.30	1.45	36.07	17.08
	1950	5	1.12	20.38	16.27	1.14	21.30	16.51
		8	1.28	26.81	16.44	1.26	25.75	16.26
		14	1.57	46.74	18.91	1.57	47.68	19.43
Leeds	1910	5	1.01	16.95	16.59	1.00	16.45	16.43
		12	1.37	31.77	16.95	1.39	32.32	16.80

Place	Year	Group						
	1920	5	1.03	17.64	16.58	1.02	17.05	16.35
		8	1.19	23.14	16.44	1.19	22.36	15.89
		12	1.36	32.14	17.27	1.38	32.18	16.92
	1930	5	1.06	18.27	16.37	1.05	17.68	15.99
		8	1.21	24.45	16.73	1.22	23.64	15.97
		12	1.39	33.73	17.41	1.41	34.50	17.30
	1940	5	1.08	19.00	16.23	1.07	18.36	16.14
		8	1.24	25.36	16.44	1.23	24.64	16.17
		12	1.42	36.00	17.73	1.45	37.00	17.71
	1946	5	1.07	19.18	16.62	1.07	18.59	16.18
		8	1.24	25.64	16.75	1.23	24.68	16.20
		12	1.42	35.73	17.60	1.44	37.05	17.86
Reading	1922	5	1.05	18.60	17.00	1.03	17.30	16.21
		8	1.22	23.90	16.14	1.20	23.40	16.20
		12	1.39	33.90	17.67	1.40	33.50	16.97
	1930	5	1.04	18.52	17.08	1.04	18.18	16.97
		8	1.21	25.11	17.07	1.19	23.98	16.82
		12	1.40	35.68	18.28	1.41	35.45	17.84
	1938	5	1.05	18.64	16.98	1.07	18.30	15.89
		8	1.24	25.23	16.29	1.24	24.55	16.01
		12	1.43	35.80	17.54	1.45	37.16	17.57
Rhondda	1911	5	1.01	16.77	16.50	1.02	16.77	16.25
		12	1.37	32.09	17.12	1.38	32.73	17.08
	1922	5	1.04	17.24	16.09	1.01	17.04	16.54
		8	1.18	22.65	16.16	1.18	21.25	15.34
		12	1.37	31.71	16.92	1.36	31.80	17.20

Table D.1 (*cont.*)

Place	Year	Age last birthday	Boys			Girls		
			Height (m)[a]	Weight (kg)[a]	BMI (kg/m^2)[b]	Height (m)[a]	Weight (kg)[a]	BMI (kg/m^2)[b]
	1931	5	1.04	17.49	16.24	1.03	17.10	15.99
		8	1.21	23.73	16.31	1.19	22.77	15.98
		12	1.37	33.04	17.56	1.40	34.35	17.59
	1940	5	1.04	18.74	17.42	1.03	19.28	18.03
		8	1.24	24.89	16.19	1.23	23.72	15.73
		12	1.43	35.10	17.25	1.40	36.67	17.61
	1950	5	1.08	19.38	16.48	1.07	18.21	15.97
		10	1.34	31.25	17.34	1.35	31.39	17.32
		14	1.60	45.91	17.90	1.52	45.55	19.69
Sheffield	1910	5	1.02	17.00	16.24	1.01	16.40	15.98
		12	1.37	31.90	16.92	1.39	32.80	16.86
	1920	5	1.03	17.55	16.58	1.04	17.68	16.50
		8	1.19	22.80	16.06	1.19	22.30	15.71
		12	1.37	32.00	16.98	1.38	32.30	16.85
	1928	5	1.05	19.39	17.62	1.05	17.64	15.87
		8	1.23	24.23	16.10	1.22	23.55	15.94
		12	1.40	34.07	17.39	1.44	35.23	17.10
	1933	5	1.07	18.30	15.85	1.06	17.33	15.67
		8	1.23	24.84	16.38	1.23	23.81	15.83
		12	1.41	34.74	17.36	1.44	36.04	17.33

Year	Place	n						
1940		5	1.08	18.98	16.15	1.08	18.46	15.89
		8	1.26	25.77	16.36	1.25	24.97	16.01
		12	1.44	36.60	17.70	1.46	38.40	17.94
1948		5	1.11	20.56	16.58	1.10	19.73	16.30
		8	1.26	26.38	16.69	1.25	25.47	16.31
		12	1.45	37.50	17.95	1.46	38.64	18.10
1929	Wakefield	5	1.03	17.45	16.49	1.02	17.30	16.55
		8	1.18	23.72	17.01	1.17	22.79	16.51
		12	1.37	33.24	17.83	1.38	33.41	17.43
1940		5	1.05	17.87	16.08	1.05	17.79	16.20
		8	1.23	24.55	16.17	1.24	24.29	15.84
		12	1.39	35.51	18.36	1.38	34.63	18.07
1950		5	1.05	18.13	16.31	1.05	18.35	16.72
		10	1.31	28.24	16.50	1.31	28.13	16.28
		14	1.50	43.70	19.29	1.50	43.55	19.39
1958		5	1.10	19.55	16.20	1.09	18.52	15.53
		10	1.37	32.61	17.50	1.37	32.39	17.22
		14	1.57	47.73	19.24	1.57	47.61	19.35
1910	Warrington	5	1.00	16.97	16.95	0.98	16.23	16.97
		7	1.11	19.30	15.59	1.08	18.81	16.14
		12	1.36	30.55	16.48	1.38	31.23	16.30
1920		5	1.03	17.76	16.70	1.02	16.98	16.36
		8	1.15	21.10	15.94	1.15	20.74	15.74
		12	1.38	31.63	16.63	1.38	31.98	16.75

Table D.1 (*cont.*)

Place	Year	Age last birthday	Boys			Girls		
			Height (m)[a]	Weight (kg)[a]	BMI (kg/m²)[b]	Height (m)[a]	Weight (kg)[a]	BMI (kg/m²)[b]
	1930	5	1.04	17.61	16.27	1.03	17.00	16.00
		8	1.22	23.86	16.04	1.21	23.93	16.34
		12	1.39	33.15	17.10	1.40	34.68	17.58
	1940	5	1.05	18.06	16.49	1.04	17.37	15.94
		8	1.23	24.95	16.44	1.23	24.20	16.08
		12	1.40	34.96	17.72	1.43	36.59	17.95
	1944	5	1.05	18.32	16.73	1.04	17.59	16.14
		8	1.23	25.37	16.65	1.23	25.25	16.75
		12	1.43	35.97	17.65	1.44	37.25	18.02
London	1905	5	1.04	17.00	15.72	1.03	16.80	15.84
		8	1.21	23.50	16.18	1.20	22.90	15.85
		12	1.39	32.50	16.89	1.41	33.30	16.85
	1938	5	1.09	19.40	16.30	1.08	18.90	16.08
		8	1.26	26.10	16.49	1.25	25.40	16.31
		12	1.45	37.60	17.93	1.47	39.10	18.17
	1949	5	1.11	19.60	16.05	1.10	19.10	15.84
		8	1.28	26.70	16.42	1.27	26.10	16.26
		12	1.47	38.30	17.85	1.49	40.60	18.34
	1954	5	1.11	19.90	16.12	1.10	19.40	15.97

Survey	Age						
	8	1.29	27.60	16.56	1.28	26.90	16.50
	12	1.49	40.40	18.25	1.50	41.70	18.48
1959[c]	5	1.11	19.90	16.18	1.10	19.40	15.97
	8	1.29	28.00	16.75	1.28	27.20	16.58
	12	1.50	41.70	18.58	1.52	43.80	18.98
1966[c]	5	1.11	20.30	16.36	1.11	19.70	16.13
	8	1.29	27.50	16.55	1.28	27.20	16.65
	12	1.50	41.70	18.58	1.52	44.60	19.41
Britain[c] 1965	5	1.12	20.14	16.20	1.10	19.85	16.32
	8	1.29	26.96	16.23	1.28	27.02	16.54
	11	1.45	36.48	17.42	1.46	38.50	18.04
	12	1.50	41.17	18.22	1.53	43.86	18.86
	14	1.61	53.49	20.71	1.61	53.77	20.72
United Kingdom[c, d] 1990	5	1.10	19.24	15.99	1.09	18.75	15.87
	11	1.43	35.48	17.30	1.44	36.66	17.73
	16	1.73	61.79	20.65	1.63	56.17	21.14
England[d] 1996	5	1.09	19.29	16.24	1.09	19.97	16.82
	8	1.28	27.37	16.65	1.28	27.28	16.73
	11	1.44	37.61	18.11	1.45	39.25	18.75
	12	1.50	42.31	18.93	1.51	45.92	20.06
	14	1.62	53.60	20.39	1.60	54.01	21.21
2003	5	1.10	19.73	16.44	1.09	19.77	16.60
	8	1.29	27.99	16.85	1.27	27.14	16.81
	11	1.44	40.21	19.30	1.45	40.89	19.31
	12	1.49	42.87	19.38	1.52	46.66	20.12

Table D.1 (*cont.*)

Place	Year	Age last birthday	Boys			Girls		
			Height (m)[a]	Weight (kg)[a]	BMI (kg/m²)[b]	Height (m)[a]	Weight (kg)[a]	BMI (kg/m²)[b]
	2007	14	1.64	58.55	21.62	1.60	57.01	22.29
		5	1.13	21.02	16.32	1.12	20.66	16.36
		8	1.31	29.62	17.18	1.31	29.85	17.52
		11	1.47	40.84	18.78	1.49	43.90	19.73
		12	1.53	46.90	19.99	1.55	48.93	20.46
		14	1.68	58.96	21.01	1.62	56.93	21.72

Sources: Unless otherwise stated, height and weight data are taken from Harris 1997b. Data for other areas were obtained from the following sources: London (all years): Cameron 1979, pp. 514–515; Britain: Tanner, Whitehouse, and Takaishi 1966, pp. 626–628; United Kingdom: Freeman *et al.* 1995, pp. 20, 22; England (all years): National Health Service Information Centre 2008.

Notes: [a] Children were normally weighed and measured without footwear and in their ordinary indoor clothing.
[b] The heights and weights of children in Bradford, Cambridge, Croydon, Edinburgh, Glasgow, Huddersfield, Leeds, Reading, Rhondda, Sheffield, Wakefield, and Warrington were originally recorded in inches and pounds, and these figures have been used to calculate the BMI values in Columns 6 and 9.
[c] Children who were weighed and measured in London in 1959 and 1966, in Britain in 1965, and in the United Kingdom in 1990 were weighed and measured in their underclothes and without footwear, and the weight of their underclothes was subtracted from the recorded weight to give a "nude weight." These figures have been adjusted to take account of the clothing allowances suggested by Noel Cameron (Cameron 1979, p. 510).
[d] The figures for England in 1990, 1996, 2003, and 2007 show the average heights and weights of children at their exact ages; these children will therefore be approximately six months younger than children whose heights and weights are given according to their age at last birthday.

Table D.2 *Energy derived from domestically produced cereals and pulses, 1700–1850 (based on crop yields estimated by Chartres, Holderness, and Allen)*

	Millions of acres	Yields per acre (mil. bu.)	Gross output (mil. bu.)	% entering gross product	Millions of bushels as food	lbs per bushel	Ounces of food (000,000s)	kcal per ounce	Proportion net of milling and distribution losses	Total kcal net of milling and distribution losses (000,000s)	Population (England and Wales)	kcal per cap. available for consumption per day
	(1)	(2)	(3) (1)*(2)	(4)	(5)	(6)	(7) (5)*(6)*16	(8)	(9)	(10) (7)*(8)*(9)	(11)	(12) (10)/(11)*365
1700 Wheat	1.361	16.0	21.8	0.855	18.6	57	16,980	95	0.6189	998,427	5,444,426	502.43
Rye	0.890	17.0	15.1	0.737	11.2	55	9,813	95	0.5345	498,307	5,444,426	250.76
Barley	1.901	23.0	43.7	0.850	37.2	49	29,137	102	0.4000	1,188,790	5,444,426	598.22
Oats	1.223	24.0	29.4	0.280	8.2	38	4,997	114	0.4263	242,824	5,444,426	122.19
Beans & peas	1.300	20.0	26.0	0.600	15.6	60	14,976	30	0.4050	184,371	5,444,426	92.78
Total												1,566.37
1750 Wheat	1.8	18.0	32.4	0.855	27.7	57	25,264	95	0.6189	972,041	6,192,091	430.09
Rye	0.5	18.0	9.0	0.737	6.6	55	5,837	95	0.5345	296,416	6,192,091	131.15

Table D.2 (*cont.*)

	Millions of acres (1)	Yields per acre (mil. bu.) (2)	Gross output (mil. bu.) (3) = (1)*(2)	% entering gross product (4)	Millions of bushels as food (5)	lbs per bushel (6)	Ounces of food (000,000s) (7) = (5)*(6)*16	kcal per ounce (8)	Proportion net of milling and distribution losses (9)	Total kcal net of milling and distribution losses (000,000s) (10) = (7)*(8)*(9)	Population (England and Wales) (11)	kcal per cap. available for consumption per day (12) = (10)/(11)*365
Barley	1.4	25.0	35.0	0.850	29.8	49	23,324	102	0.4000	951,619	6,192,091	421.05
Oats	2.0	28.0	56.0	0.280	15.7	38	9,533	114	0.4263	463,278	6,192,091	204.98
Beans & peas	1.0	28.0	28.0	0.600	16.8	60	16,128	30	0.4050	198,553	6,192,091	87.85
Total												1,275.12
1800 Wheat	2.5	21.5	53.8	0.855	46.0	57	41,912	95	0.6189	2,464,431	9,223,320	732.04
Rye	0.3	26.0	7.8	0.737	5.7	55	5,059	95	0.5345	256,893	9,223,320	76.31
Barley	1.3	30.0	39.0	0.850	33.2	49	25,990	102	0.4000	1,060,376	9,223,320	314.98
Oats	2.0	35.0	70.0	0.280	19.6	38	11,917	114	0.4263	579,097	9,223,320	172.02
Beans & peas	1.2	28.0	33.6	0.600	20.2	60	19,354	30	0.4050	238,264	9,223,320	70.77
Total												1,366.12

1850													
Wheat	3.6	28.0	100.8	0.855	86.2	57	78,600	95	0.6189	4,621,669	17,928,000	706.28
Rye	0.1	28.0	2.8	0.737	2.1	55	1,816	95	0.5345	92,218	17,928,000	14.09
Barley	1.5	36.5	54.8	0.850	46.5	49	36,485	102	0.4000	1,488,604	17,928,000	227.49
Oats	2.0	40.0	80.0	0.280	22.4	38	13,619	114	0.4263	661,826	17,928,000	101.14
Beans & peas	1.0	30.0	30.0	0.600	18.0	60	17,280	30	0.4050	212,735	17,928,000	32.51
Total												1,081.50

Sources: Col. 1. 1700: Figures for wheat, rye, barley, and oats from Chartres 1985, p. 444; figures for beans and peas from Allen 1994, p. 112; 1750–1850: Holderness 1989, p. 145.

Col. 2. As for Column 1.

Col. 4. Figures for wheat, oats, barley, and beans and peas from Towne and Rasmussen 1960, pp. 294, 298, 304; for rye, see Gallman 1960, p. 52.

Col. 6. Conversion rates for wheat, barley, rye and oats from John 1989, pp. 1124–1125. Figures for beans and peas from US Department of Agriculture 1992, pp. 11, 14.

Col. 8. Energy values for wheat, rye, barley, and oats from McCance and Widdowson 1960, pp. 116–117; and for beans and peas from Parliamentary Papers 1917, Appendix 1A.

Col. 10. Allowances for milling losses derived from US Department of Agriculture 1939, p. 8. An additional 10 percent has been allowed for losses associated with distribution.

Col. 11. 1700–1800: England (figures for 1701, 1751, and 1801): Wrigley and Schofield 1981, pp. 533–534; Wales (1701, 1751, and 1801): Deane and Cole 1967, p. 103; 1850 (1851): Mitchell 1988, p. 9.

Table D.3 *Energy derived from domestically produced cereals and pulses, 1700–1850 (based on crop yields estimated by Turner, Beckett, and Afton)*

	Millions of acres	Yields per acre	Gross output	% entering gross product	Millions of bushels as food	lbs per bushel	Ounces of food (000,000s)	kcal per ounce	Proportion net of milling and distribution losses	Total kcal net of milling and distribution losses (000,000s)	Population (England and Wales)	kcal per cap. available for consumption per day
	(1)	(2)	(3)	(4)	(5)	(6)	(7) (5)*(6)*16	(8)	(9)	(10) (7)*(8)*(9)	(11)	(12) (10)/(11)
1700 Wheat	1.361	16.0	21.8	0.855	18.6	57	16,980	95	0.6189	998,427	5,444,426	502.43
Rye	0.890	17.0	15.1	0.737	11.2	55	9,813	95	0.5345	498,307	5,444,426	250.76
Barley	1.901	23.0	43.7	0.850	37.2	49	29,137	102	0.4000	1,188,790	5,444,426	598.22
Oats	1.223	24.0	29.4	0.280	8.2	38	4,997	114	0.4263	242,824	5,444,426	122.19
Beans & peas	1.300	20.0	26.0	0.600	15.6	60	14,976	30	0.4050	184,371	5,444,426	92.78
Total												1,566.37
1750 Wheat	1.8	22.0	39.6	0.855	33.9	57	30,915	95	0.6189	1,189,448	6,192,091	526.28
Rye	0.5	18.0	9.0	0.737	6.6	55	5,837	95	0.5345	296,416	6,192,091	131.15
Barley	1.4	24.8	34.7	0.850	29.5	49	23,137	102	0.4000	943,980	6,192,091	417.67
Oats	2.0	36.7	73.5	0.280	20.6	38	12,511	114	0.4263	607,968	6,192,091	269.00
Beans & peas	1.0	21.8	21.8	0.600	13.1	60	12,551	30	0.4050	154,519	6,192,091	68.37
Total												1,412.46
1800 Wheat	2.5	21.1	52.7	0.855	45.1	57	41,095	95	0.6189	2,416,388	9,223,320	717.77
Rye	0.3	23.4	7.0	0.737	5.2	55	4,558	95	0.5345	231,451	9,223,320	68.75

Barley	1.3	29.2	38.0	0.850	32.3	49	25,311	102	0.4000	1,032,676	9,223,320	306.75
Oats	2.0	37.4	74.9	0.280	21.0	38	12,742	114	0.4263	619,221	9,223,320	183.94
Beans & peas	1.2	22.0	26.4	0.600	15.9	60	15,225	30	0.4050	187,442	9,223,320	55.68
Total												1,332.89
1850 Wheat	3.6	28.9	104.0	0.855	89.0	57	81,132	95	0.6189	4,770,543	17,928,000	729.03
Rye	0.1	27.8	2.8	0.737	2.1	55	1,805	95	0.5345	91,674	17,928,000	14.01
Barley	1.5	36.4	54.6	0.850	46.4	49	36,376	102	0.4000	1,484,143	17,928,000	226.80
Oats	2.0	47.4	94.8	0.280	26.6	38	16,143	114	0.4263	784,473	17,928,000	119.88
Beans & peas	1.0	29.6	29.6	0.600	17.7	60	17,037	30	0.4050	209,742	17,928,000	32.05
Total												1,121.77

Sources: Col. 1. See Table D.2.

Col. 2. 1700 (all crops): see Table D.2; 1750 (rye): see Table D.2; 1750 (all other crops): Turner, Beckett, and Afton 2001, pp. 129, 153, 158, 163–164; 1800 and 1850 (all crops): Turner, Beckett, and Afton 2001, pp. 129, 153, 158, 163–164.

Cols. 4, 6, 10, and 11. See Table D.2.

Table D.4 *Energy derived from domestically farmed animals*

1700	oz (000,000)	Population	oz/head/ day	kcal/oz	kcal/head
Mutton and lamb	1,638.40	5,444,426	0.82	92.01	75.86
Beef and veal	3,328.00	5,444,426	1.67	82.39	137.97
Pork and ham	956.80	5,444,426	0.48	127.56	61.42
Others	446.24	5,444,426	0.22	42.96	9.65
Lard	173.42	5,444,426	0.09	252.53	21.99
Total					306.88
1750					
Mutton and lamb	3,476.48	6,192,091	1.54	92.01	141.53
Beef and veal	4,569.60	6,192,091	2.02	82.39	166.57
Pork and ham	2,598.40	6,192,091	1.15	127.56	146.65
Lard	470.96	6,192,091	0.21	252.53	52.50
Total					507.25
1800					
Mutton and lamb	5,017.60	9,223,320	1.49	92.01	137.90
Beef and veal	5,824.00	9,223,320	1.73	82.39	143.32
Pork and ham	3,368.96	9,223,320	1.00	127.56	128.37
Lard	610.62	9,223,320	0.18	252.53	45.70
Total					453.01
1850					
Mutton and lamb	7,490.56	17,928,000	1.14	92.01	105.32
Beef and veal	9,640.96	17,928,000	1.47	82.39	121.38
Pork and ham	4,569.60	17,928,000	0.70	127.56	89.08
Lard	828.24	17,928,000	0.13	252.53	31.89
Total					347.67

Sources: Meat production
1700: King (1696) 1973, pp. 54–55
1750–1850: Holderness 1989, p. 155.
Lard
Derived from the ratio of lard to bacon and pork production in Bennett and Pierce
1961, pp. 114–115.
Energy values
Parliamentary Papers 1917, Appendix 1A.

Table D.5 *Energy derived from domestically produced dairy products*

	Consumption per head per week		oz/day	kcal/oz	kcal/day
	oz	Pints			
1700					
Cheese					
Butter					
Milk					
Total					230.75
1750					
Cheese	5.00		0.71	109.85	78.46
Butter	3.50		0.50	225.78	112.89
Milk	30.00	1.50	4.29	20.35	87.23
Total					278.58
1800					
Cheese	4.50		0.64	109.85	70.62
Butter	3.50		0.50	225.78	112.89
Milk	18.00	0.90	2.57	20.35	52.34
Total					235.84
1850					
Cheese	3.30		0.47	109.85	51.79
Butter	2.40		0.34	225.78	77.41
Milk	31.00	1.55	4.43	20.35	90.14
Total					219.33

Sources: Holderness 1989, p. 170. Energy values derived from Parliamentary Papers 1917, Appendix 1A.
Notes: Figure for total consumption of energy from dairy products in 1700 derived from the ratio of beef and cattle production in 1700 to beef and cattle production in 1750 (roughly 1.67:2.02). For sources, see Table D.4.

Table D.6 *Energy derived from imported cereals and pulses*

	Net imports (cwt., 000s)	Quantity as food (ozs, 000s)	kcal/oz	Net of milling losses (35% of grain) (kcal)	Net of distribution losses (10% of grain and flour/meal) (kcal)	kcal/head/day for consumption (constant losses)
1700 (GB)						
Wheat	-157.94	-283,028	95	-17,476,975	-15,729,278	-6.59
Wheat flour	-41.56	-74,476	95	-7,075,225	-6,367,703	-2.67
Total	-199.50	-357,504	95	-24,552,201	-22,096,981	-9.25
Barley	-115.50	-206,968	102	-13,721,995	-12,349,795	-5.17
Barley meal	0.00	-8	102	-791	-712	0.00
Total	-115.50	-206,976	102	-13,722,786	-12,350,507	-5.17
Oats	29.99	53,742	114	3,982,259	3,584,033	1.50
Oatmeal	0.11	195	114	22,282	20,053	0.01
Total	30.10	53,937	114	4,004,541	3,604,087	1.51
Maize	0.00	0	104	0	0	0.00
Cornmeal	0.00	0	104	0	0	0.00
Total	0.00	0	104	0	0	0.00
Grand total	-284.90	-510,543		-34,270,446	-30,843,401	-12.91

1750 (GB)						
Wheat	−3,062.10	−5,487,276	95	−338,839,321	−304,955,389	−111.52
Wheat flour	−805.76	−1,443,924	95	−137,172,737	−123,455,463	−45.15
Total	−3,867.86	−6,931,200	95	−476,012,058	−428,410,852	−156.66
Barley	−335.99	−602,089	102	−39,918,530	−35,926,677	−13.14
Barley meal	−0.01	−23	102	−2,300	−2,070	0.00
Total	−336.00	−602,112	102	−39,920,831	−35,928,748	−13.14
Oats	29.75	53,310	114	3,950,280	3,555,252	1.30
Oatmeal	0.11	194	114	22,103	19,892	0.01
Total	29.86	53,504	114	3,972,382	3,575,144	1.31
Maize	0.00	0	104	0	0	0.00
Cornmeal	0.00	0	104	0	0	0.00
Total	0.00	0	104	0	0	0.00
Grand total	−4,174.00	−7,479,808		−511,960,506	−460,764,456	−168.50
1798–1802 (UK)						
Wheat	2,532.38	4,538,033	95	280,223,542	252,201,188	43.01
Wheat flour	666.37	1,194,139	95	113,443,240	102,098,916	17.41
Total	3,198.76	5,732,172	95	393,666,782	354,300,104	60.43

Table D.6 (*cont.*)

	Net imports (cwt., 000s)	Quantity as food (ozs, 000s)	kcal/oz	Net of milling losses (35% of grain) (kcal)	Net of distribution losses (10% of grain and flour/meal) (kcal)	kcal/head/day for consumption (constant losses)
Barley	234.48	420,188	102	27,858,477	25,072,629	4.28
Barley meal	0.01	16	102	1,605	1,445	0.00
Total	234.49	420,204	102	27,860,082	25,074,074	4.29
Oats	1,046.73	1,875,741	114	138,992,386	125,093,147	21.33
Oatmeal	3.81	6,822	114	777,692	699,923	0.12
Total	1,050.54	1,882,563	114	139,770,078	125,793,070	21.45
Maize	0.00	0	104	0	0	0.00
Cornmeal	0.00	0	104	0	0	0.00
Total	0.00	0	104	0	0	0.00
Grand total	4,483.78	8,034,939		561,296,943	505,167,248	86.17
1848–1852 (UK)						
Wheat	13,892.78	24,895,853	95	1,537,318,944	1,383,587,049	138.66
Wheat flour	3,655.75	6,551,102	95	622,354,710	560,119,239	56.13
Total	17,548.52	31,446,956	95	2,159,673,653	1,943,706,288	194.79

Barley	3,406.84	6,105,054	102	404,765,108	364,288,597	36.51
Barley meal	0.13	229	102	23,323	20,991	0.00
Total	3,406.97	6,105,283	102	404,788,431	364,309,588	36.51
Oats	3,052.88	5,470,767	114	405,383,869	364,845,482	36.56
Oatmeal	11.10	19,897	114	2,268,210	2,041,389	0.20
Total	3,063.99	5,490,664	114	407,652,079	366,886,871	36.77
Maize	6,732.28	12,064,250	104	815,543,304	733,988,974	73.56
Cornmeal	71.50	128,129	104	13,325,387	11,992,848	1.20
Total	6,803.78	12,192,379	104	828,868,691	745,981,822	74.76
Rye	340.80	610,710	104	41,284,006	37,155,605	3.72
Ryemeal	12.56	22,515	104	2,341,528	2,107,375	0.21
Total	353.36	633,225	104	43,625,533	39,262,980	3.93
Peas	722.63	1,294,949	78	65,653,933	59,088,540	5.92
Pea meal	0.16	279	78	21,777	19,599	0.00
Total	722.78	1,295,229	78	65,675,710	59,108,139	5.92
Beans	1,783.76	3,196,493	73	151,673,583	136,506,225	13.68
Bean meal	0.01	11	73	785	706	0.00
Total	1,783.76	3,196,504	73	151,674,368	136,506,931	13.68
Buckwheat	7.11	12,743	97	805,402	724,862	0.07
Buckwheat meal	0.29	528	97	51,300	46,170	0.00
Total	7.41	13,270	97	856,702	771,032	0.08

Table D.6 (*cont.*)

	Net imports (cwt., 000s)	Quantity as food (ozs, 000s)	kcal/oz	Net of milling losses (35% of grain) (kcal)	Net of distribution losses (10% of grain and flour/meal) (kcal)	kcal/head/day for consumption (constant losses)
Beer or bigg	2.56	4,579	102	303,606	273,245	0.03
Malt	0.01	15	102	984	886	0.00
Grand total	33,693.13	60,378,103		4,063,119,758	3,657,807,782	366.47

Sources: Grain imports

1700 and 1750: Mitchell 1988, pp. 221–222.

1798–1802: Parliamentary Papers 1849b.

1848–52: Parliamentary Papers 1849a; Parliamentary Papers 1851; Parliamentary Papers 1853.

Quarters were converted into hundredweights using the conversion factors in Table D.2. Conversion factors for maize were derived from US Department of Agriculture 1952, p. 40, and for buckwheat, beer, bigg, and malt from US Department of Agriculture 1992, pp. 12, 14.

Energy values

Wheat, barley (including beer or bigg), oats, rye, peas, and beans: McCance and Widdowson 1960, pp. 116–117.

Maize (yellow corn), buckwheat, and malt: US Department of Agriculture, National Nutrient Database (www.nal.usda.gov/fnic/foodcomp/search/).

Losses due to milling and distribution

See Table D.2.

Population

1700–1800: England (figures for 1701, 1751, and 1801): Wrigley and Schofield 1981, pp. 533–534; Wales (1701, 1751, and 1801): Deane and Cole 1967, p. 103; 1850 (1851): England and Wales 1851: Mitchell 1988, p. 9; Scotland: 1700 and 1750: Schofield 1994, p. 93; Scotland and Ireland (1801 and 1851): Mitchell 1988, pp. 11–12.

Table D.7 *Energy derived from imported meat*

	cwt (000s)	oz/head/day	kcal/oz	kcal/head/day
1850	699	0.13	93.48	11.74

Sources: Meat imports: Mitchell 1988, p. 233. Energy values derived from estimates of total meat consumption and total calories derived from consumption of meat products in Table D.4.

Table D.8 *Energy derived from imported dairy products*

	1800	1850
Butter (oz)	206,312,960	593,393,920
Cheese (oz)	222,510,848	623,209,216
kcal per ounce (butter)	225.96	225.96
kcal per ounce (cheese)	110.97	110.97
Population (Great Britain)	10,686,000	
Population (United Kingdom)		27,524,000
kcal per day (butter)	11.94	13.33
kcal per day (cheese)	4.25	6.88
kcal per day (total)	16.20	20.22

Sources: Imports of dairy products
1800 (1801): John 1989, pp. 1027–1029; Parliamentary Papers 1851, p. 2.
Population
Mitchell 1988, p. 11.
Energy values
Parliamentary Papers 1917, Appendix 1A.

Table D.9 *Energy derived from retained sugar imports*

	cwt	Population	lbs/head/year	oz/head/year	cal/oz	cal/head/day
1700	442,800	5,444,426	5.68	90.84	112	27.87
1750	913,080	6,192,091	14.72	235.55	112	72.28
1800			19.45	311.12	112	95.47
1850			27.69	442.96	112	135.92

Sources: Sugar: 1700 and 1750: Sheridan 1973, p. 22; 1800 and 1850: Mokyr 1988, p. 75.
Energy values: McCance and Widdowson 1960, p. 142.
Population: 1700 and 1750: Deane and Cole 1967, p. 103; Wrigley and Schofield 1981, pp. 533–534.

Table D.10 *Wine and spirits*

	1700	1750	1800	1850
Total wine (oz)	914,739,840	621,532,800	1,225,042,560	1,482,811,680
Total spirits (oz)	380,480	138,317,120	577,401,280	1,242,124,640
kcal per oz of wine	25	25	25	25
kcal per oz of spirits	63	63	63	63
Population	5,444,426	6,192,091	10,686,000	27,393,000
kcal/oz/head/day (wine)	11.51	6.88	7.85	3.71
kcal/oz/head/day (spirits)	0.01	3.86	9.33	7.83
kcal/oz/head/day (total)	11.52	10.73	17.18	11.53

Sources: Imported wines and spirits: 1700–1800: Schumpeter 1960, pp. 52–59; 1850: Parliamentary Papers 1851.
Population: England and Wales 1700 (1701) and 1750 (1751): Wrigley and Schofield 1981, pp. 533–534; Deane and Cole 1967, p. 103; Great Britain: 1800 (1801): Mitchell 1988, p. 11; United Kingdom: 1850 (1851), p. 12.
Notes: Imported wine was normally measured in tuns, and imported spirits in tuns and/or gallons. These figures have been converted into ounces on the basis that each tun contained 252 gallons, and that each gallon contains 160 fluid ounces.

Table D.11 *Energy derived from fish*

		Herrings	Other fish, fresh	Shellfish (without shell)	Canned and salted fish	Total
Metric tons (000s)	Home	99.00	606.00	10.50	0.00	715.50
	Imported	63.00	30.00	1.90	38.00	132.90
	Total	162.00	636.00	12.40	38.00	848.40
Calories (000,000,000s)	Home	82.00	306.00	4.00	0.00	392.00
	Imported	57.00	12.00		70.00	139.00
	Total	139.00	318.00	4.00	70.00	531.00
Calories per head per day	Home	4.97	18.55	0.24	0.00	23.76
	Imported	3.45	0.73	0.00	4.24	8.43
	Total	8.43	19.28	0.24	4.24	32.19

Sources: Parliamentary Papers 1917, Appendix 1A. The population was taken as 45.2 million.

Table D.12 *Energy derived from garden vegetables*

		Beans, peas and lentils	Other vegetables (including tomatoes)	Preserved vegetables	Total
Metric tons	Home	0.00	700.00	0.00	700.00
(000s)	Imported	116.00	295.00	21.00	432.00
	Total	116.00	995.00	21.00	1,132.00
Calories	Home	0.00	191.00	0.00	191.00
(000,000,000s)	Imported	421.00	83.00	8.00	512.00
	Total	421.00	274.00	8.00	703.00
Calories per	Home	0.00	11.58	0.00	11.58
head per day	Imported	25.52	5.03	0.48	31.03
	Total	25.52	16.61	0.48	42.61

Source: Parliamentary Papers 1917, Appendix 1A. The population was taken as 45.2 million.

Table D.13 *Energy derived from imported fruit and nuts, 1850*

	cwt	oz	kcal/oz	Population (UK)	kcal/ head/day
Currants	405,388	726,455,296	69	27,524,000	4.99
Figs	33,499	60,030,208	61	27,524,000	0.36
Lemons and oranges	537,960	964,024,927	7	27,524,000	0.67
Raisins	218,982	392,415,744	70	27,524,000	2.73
Total					8.76

Source: Parliamentary Papers 1851, p. 3.
Note: The figure for lemons and oranges has been estimated using the ratio of the amount of duty paid to the volume of fruit imported for currants, figs, and raisins. The energy obtained from these fruits has been calculated on the assumption that equal quantities of lemons and oranges were imported.

Table D.14 *Energy derived from fruit and nuts, 1909–1913*

		Apples	Bananas	Nuts	Fresh fruit	Preserved fruit (without sugar)	Calories per head per day
Metric tons (000s)	Home	127.00	0.00	0.00	214.00	0.00	341.00
	Imported	163.00	150.00	38.00	430.00	149.00	930.00
	Total	290.00	150.00	38.00	627.00	149.00	1,271.00
Calories (000,000,000s)	Home	57.00	0.00	0.00	111.00	0.00	168.00
	Imported	74.00	99.00	100.00	231.00	405.00	909.00
	Total	131.00	99.00	100.00	442.00	405.00	1,077.00
Total	Home	3.45	0.00	0.00	6.73	0.00	10.18
	Imported	4.49	6.00	6.06	14.00	24.55	55.10
	Total	7.94	6.00	6.06	20.73	24.55	65.28

Source: Parliamentary Papers 1917, Appendix 1A. The population was taken as 45.2 million.

Table D.15 *Energy derived from potatoes*

	lbs/head/day	oz/head/day	kcal/oz	kcal/person/day
1700	0.14	2.29	23	52.57
1750	0.21	3.43	23	78.86
1800	0.42	6.69	23	153.98
1850	0.69	11.10	23	255.34

Sources: Potatoes
Figures for 1700, 1750, 1800, and 1850 derived from Salaman 1949, pp. 434, 539, 613, assuming that consumption was zero before 1600, and grew at a linear rate between 1600 and 1775, 1795 and 1814, and 1838 and 1851, and that the figure quoted in the text for 1851 (0.07 lbs per head per day) should be 0.70.
Energy value
McCance and Widdowson 1960, p. 140.

Table D.16 *Energy derived from domestically produced and imported foods, 1909–1913*

	Metric tons (000s)			Calories per ounce			Calories per head per day		
	Home	Imported	Total	Home	Imported	Total	Home	Imported	Total
Wheat flour, shredded wheat, etc.	840.00	3,485.00	4,325.00	95.00	95.00	95.00	170.26	706.38	876.64
Oatmeal	145.00	55.00	200.00	114.00	114.00	114.00	35.27	13.38	48.65
Barley meal	25.00	25.00	50.00	102.00	102.00	102.00	5.44	5.44	10.88
Tapioca, sago, arrowroot, etc.		100.00	100.00		100.28	100.28		21.40	21.40
Maize meal		50.00	50.00	104.00	104.00	104.00		11.09	11.09
Rice		140.00	140.00		100.65	100.65		30.06	30.06
Cereals	1,010.00	3,855.00	4,865.00	104.21	103.22	103.43	210.97	787.75	998.72
Beef and veal	820.00	491.00	1,311.00	82.39	64.92	75.84	144.14	68.01	212.15
Mutton	294.80	182.20	477.00	95.02	79.21	88.98	59.76	30.79	90.56
Lamb	36.20	83.80	120.00	67.49	67.12	67.23	5.21	12.00	17.21
Bacon	80.00	228.00	308.00	170.10	169.96	169.99	29.03	82.68	111.71
Hams	20.00	44.00	64.00	109.38	105.89	106.98	4.67	9.94	14.61
Other pig meat	304.00	41.00	345.00	117.56	114.33	117.18	76.25	10.00	86.25
Meat offals	60.00		60.00	49.72		49.72	6.36	0.00	6.36
Meat	1,615.00	1,070.00	2,685.00	94.44	93.48	94.06	325.43	213.42	538.85

Poultry (and game)	41.00	14.00	55.00	42.96	36.53	41.32	3.76	1.09	4.85
Eggs (at 2 oz)	129.00	129.00	258.00	38.10	38.10	38.10	10.49	10.49	20.97
Rabbits (excl. skins)		18.00	18.00	55.24	55.24	55.24		2.12	2.12
Poultry, eggs, etc.	170.00	161.00	331.00	39.27	39.88	39.57	14.24	13.70	27.94
Herrings	99.00	63.00	162.00	23.53	25.70	24.38	4.97	3.45	8.43
Other fish, fresh	606.00	30.00	636.00	14.35	11.36	14.20	18.55	0.73	19.28
Shellfish (without shell)	10.50	1.90	12.40	10.82		9.16	0.24		0.24
Canned and salted fish		38.00	38.00		52.33	52.33		4.24	4.24
Fish	715.50	132.90	848.40	15.56	29.71	17.78	23.76	8.43	32.19
Milk (incl. cream)	4,500.00		4,500.00	20.35	20.35	20.35	195.42	195.42	195.42
Butter	114.00	207.00	321.00	225.78	225.76	225.77	54.92	99.71	154.62
Cheese	30.00	117.00	147.00	109.85	110.97	110.74	7.03	27.70	34.73
Condensed milk		2.20	2.20						
Sweetened condensed milk		53.00	53.00		94.34	94.34		10.67	10.67
Margarine	60.00	58.60	118.60	222.06	223.01	222.53	28.43	27.88	56.31
Lard		90.00	90.00		252.53	252.53		48.49	48.49
Dairy produce	4,704.00	527.80	5,231.80	28.48	190.43	44.81	285.79	214.45	500.24
Apples	127.00	163.00	290.00	12.75	12.90	12.83	3.45	4.49	7.94
Bananas		150.00	150.00	18.75	18.75	18.75		6.00	6.00
Nuts		38.00	38.00	74.76	74.76	74.76		6.06	6.06
Fruits, fresh	214.00	430.00	644.00	14.74	15.26	15.09	6.73	14.00	20.73

Table D.16 (*cont.*)

	Metric tons (000s)			Calories per ounce			Calories per head per day		
	Home	Imported	Total	Home	Imported	Total	Home	Imported	Total
Fruits, preserved (without sugar)		149.00	149.00		77.22	77.22		24.55	24.55
Fruit	341.00	930.00	1,271.00	14.00	27.77	24.07	10.18	55.10	65.28
Potatoes	3,988.00	262.00	4,250.00	23.00	23.00	23.00	195.70	12.86	208.56
Beans, peas, and lentils		116.00	116.00		103.11	103.11		25.52	25.52
Green peas and broad beans (shelled)	100.00		100.00	30.40		30.40	6.49		6.49
Other vegetables (incl. tomatoes)	700.00	295.00	995.00	7.75	7.99	7.82	11.58	5.03	16.61
Preserved vegetables		21.00	21.00		10.82	10.82		0.48	0.48
Vegetables	4,788.00	694.00	5,482.00	24.05	31.03	24.94	213.76	43.89	257.66
Cocoa and chocolate		36.00	36.00		177.56	177.56		13.64	13.64
Sugar taken as refined		1,525.00	1,525.00		112.00	112.00		364.42	364.42
Molasses		33.00	33.00		63.71	63.71		4.49	4.49

Glucose, solid	18.00	18.00		96.28	96.28		3.70	3.70
Glucose, liquid	45.00	45.00		90.28	90.28		8.67	8.67
Sugar, cocoa, etc.	1,657.00	1,657.00		113.72	113.72		394.91	394.91
Cottage produce						134.99		134.99
Farm produce (consumed by producers)						25.94		25.94
Totals	13,343.50	9,027.70	22,371.20	43.73	89.90	62.36	1,245.08	1,731.64	2,976.72

Sources: Parliamentary Papers 1917, Appendix 1A. For alternative energy values, see Tables D.2, D.6, D.9 and D.15.

Notes: Energy values have been calculated using the original figures, with the following exceptions: wheat: 95 calories per ounce (rather than 103 calories); oats: 114 calories per ounce (rather than 109); maize: 104 calories per ounce (rather than 97); sugar: 112 calories per ounce (rather than 114); potatoes: 23 calories per ounce (rather than 27). The population has been taken to be 45.2 million (in accordance with the original estimates).

5 | Height, health, and mortality in continental Europe, 1700–2100

The previous chapter examined long-term changes in health and welfare in England and Wales since circa 1700 and explored their implications for the future. The present chapter extends these ideas to different parts of continental Europe. Section 5.1 looks at long-term trends in height, weight, and (where possible) BMI, and Section 5.2 examines the main changes in mortality rates. Section 5.3 presents a brief overview of the main changes in environmental and nutritional conditions in different parts of Europe since the beginning of the eighteenth century, and Section 5.4 examines the relationship between improvements in health and economic growth. The final section assesses the implications of these changes for health in later life and future trends in life expectancy.

5.1 The anthropometric history of continental Europe

Although anthropometric historians have recently begun to examine very long-run changes in human stature from skeletal remains (Steckel 2003), we possess very little information about the heights of Europeans who were measured while they were still alive before the early eighteenth century. However, Komlos (2003) has unearthed data relating to the heights of French army recruits who were born during the second half of the seventeenth century. These men were extremely short by modern European standards and the height data confirm the traditional view that the seventeenth century was a time of considerable and sustained hardship in many parts of Europe (de Vries 1976). However, some of Komlos's other results are rather more surprising. He argued that there was a sharp increase in the average heights of men born in the late seventeenth and early eighteenth centuries, followed by a decline between circa 1716 and the mid 1720s and a further increase between the 1720s and 1740s. He then argued that average heights declined again between the 1740s and 1760s. These results run counter to what might have been expected, given the evidence which we have already presented with regard to changes in food production in Chapter 3, and other evidence reflecting trends in both welfare standards (Allen 2001b) and mortality rates (Blayo 1975; pp. 128–131; Dupâquier 1979, p. 99; Van de Walle 1979, p. 142).

Komlos and other writers have also examined the heights of men born in other parts of Europe from the mid eighteenth century onwards. Baten (1999, pp. 52–87; 2000b, pp. 68–70; 2001) has argued that the average heights of Bavarian-born men declined by more than three centimeters between the birth cohorts of the early 1750s and the early 1770s, but these results are obtained from data derived from two different sources and may also have been affected by variations in the average ages of the soldiers being measured.[1] On the other hand, they do correlate quite closely with information relating to grain and potato production in southern Germany and mean winter temperatures elsewhere in Europe.

Despite the questions raised by some of these findings, other writers have also concluded that there was a significant reduction in the average heights of different European populations during this period. Sandberg and Steckel (1987, p. 109; see also Sandberg 1989) have argued that the average heights of Swedish men declined by nearly 2.5 centimeters between the birth cohorts of the 1740s and 1760s and did not regain their former level until the second decade of the nineteenth century, and Komlos (1989, pp. 57, 242) has shown that the average heights of men in five separate provinces of the Habsburg Empire also declined between the 1730s and the 1790s. A'Hearn (2003, p. 364, 371) has produced new evidence of a decline in heights in northern Italy. His calculations suggest that average heights declined by almost five centimeters between the early 1740s and the 1770s, and did not begin to rise consistently before the 1830s.

It is important for anthropometric historians to place their findings in the context of other indicators of biological well-being, where such

---

[1] Baten compared the heights of men who volunteered for the Bavarian army between 1760 and 1787 with those conscripted between 1805 and 1811, and the results which he obtained for the birth cohorts of 1760–64 and 1765–69 included an increasing proportion of younger recruits who may not have attained their maximum height at the time of measurement (see Baten 1999, pp. 53–65; Baten 2001, pp. 12–24).

data are available. Breschi's analysis suggests that there was an overall decline in infant mortality rates in Tuscany during the course of the eighteenth century, but in northern Italy (the area studied by A'Hearn), infant mortality rates rose from the 1670s onwards, with particular peaks in the 1740s and 1760s (Del Panta 1997). However, this was not the case in other parts of Europe. Lee (1979, p. 182, 186) found that infant mortality rates in the Bavarian village of Massenhausen rose sharply between the 1750s and 1760s, but fell by nearly 40 percent between the 1760s and 1780s, and there was little change in the crude death rate in Landsberg between 1750 and 1800. In Sweden, Hofsten and Lundström (1976, pp. 48–49, 54) found that there was a small reduction in infant and child mortality rates from the 1750s onwards, together with a slight increase in life expectancy at birth, and in France, Blayo (1975, pp. 128–131) showed that there were small improvements in both infant and child mortality between the 1740s and the 1780s (see also Dupâquier 1979, p. 99; Van de Walle 1979, p. 142).

Although the archive of data relating to the heights of men born during the eighteenth century is still relatively small, we know rather more about changes in the heights of men in a number of continental European countries from the early nineteenth century onwards, but the evidence from these surveys is mixed. Despite some regional variations (Heyberger 2007, p. 244), average heights in France appear to have increased slowly but consistently throughout the century, but the heights of Dutch soldiers rose during the first two decades of the nineteenth century and then fell, and only resumed their upward path from the 1840s onwards. There is also some evidence of a dip in heights in Sweden during the 1840s, but the extent of this decline has been questioned (Heintel, Sandberg, and Steckel 1998) and heights rose consistently from the mid century onwards (see Figure 5.1). We possess rather less evidence about changes in the heights of men in other parts of Europe before 1850, but the evidence which is available suggests that average heights were increasing in several countries after this date, and this is reflected in the data for Spain, Italy, Poland, Russia, and Germany (see Figure 5.2).[2]

---

[2] Average heights also increased in the different territories of the Habsburg Empire between 1850 and 1910 (birth cohorts) (Komlos 2007).

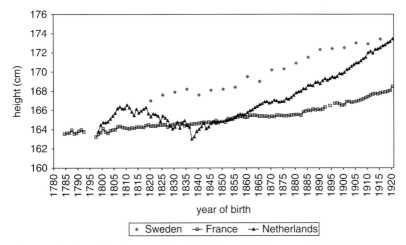

Sources: Sweden: Sandberg and Steckel 1997, p. 129; France: 1784–1902:
Weir 1997, p. 191; 1903–1920: Drukker and Tassenaar 1997, pp. 358–60;
Netherlands: Drukker and Tassenaar 1997, pp. 358–60.

Figure 5.1 Adult male heights in Sweden, France, and the Netherlands,
1780–1920

It is also possible to look more closely at variations both within and
between countries. At the beginning of the nineteenth century, the
average heights of French and Dutch recruits appear to have been
very similar, but the Dutch recruits who were born at the end of the
nineteenth century were more than three centimeters taller than their
French counterparts, and the gap was increasing. The data also suggest
that there was something of a "north–south divide" in European
heights during the second half of the nineteenth century, with the tallest
populations residing in Sweden and the Netherlands, and the shortest in
Spain and Italy. The average height of Russian recruits was also greater
than that of Spanish or Italian recruits, although it is important to note
that the Russian recruits were also slightly older than the Italian recruits
at the time of measurement.

Several writers have noted the relationship between height and
social status. Floud and Wachter (1982, pp. 424–426) and Floud,
Wachter, and Gregory (1990, pp. 196–198, 216–224) showed that
there were substantial variations in stature within the working class
and between the working and upper classes in nineteenth-century

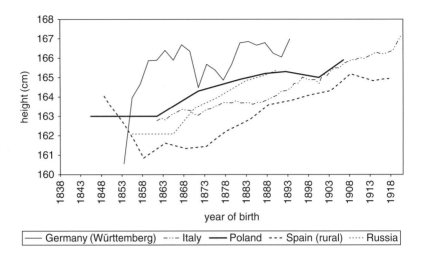

year of birth

| — Germany (Württemberg) --·- Italy — Poland - - - Spain (rural) ····· Russia |

Notes: Spanish figures are averages based on the proportions of day-laborers and peasant farmers included in the sample population over the whole period. Recruits born in 1866–70 and 1871–75 are assumed to have been aged nineteen (rather than twenty) at the time of measurement, and 0.3 cm has been added to their heights to allow for additional growth (see Drukker and Tassenaar 1997, p. 357). Recruits born from 1886 onwards are assumed to have been aged twenty-one at the time of measurement, but no further adjustments have been attempted.

Figure 5.2 Adult male heights in Germany, Italy, Poland, Russia, and Spain

Britain, and these results have been paralleled by continental studies. In France, Komlos (1994, p. 895) found that students attending the École Polytechnique were four centimeters taller than the men who were conscripted into the national army between 1819 and 1826, and Le Roy Ladurie (1979a, p. 59) showed that recruits who were able to afford the cost of a replacement were significantly taller than those who were "not replaced" in the draft of 1868 (see also Berlanstein 1998, pp. 303–304). In the Netherlands, De Beer (2004, p. 52) has shown that the sons of elite families in nineteenth-century Utrecht were ten centimeters taller than children from unskilled working-class families when they were measured at the age of 18 years and 9 months, and Alter, Neven, and Oris (2004, p. 242) have reported "very large differences in height by occupation" among men born in Belgium before 1850. Martinez-Carrión and Perez-Castejón (2002, p. 447) have examined social class variations in stature among Spanish army recruits between 1837 and 1948. Their results show that there was a difference of between 0.5 and 2.81 centimeters in the average heights of successive cohorts of landless laborers (*jornaleros*) and peasant farmers (*labradores*) who were born during the second half of the nineteenth century.

Baten (2000a) has examined the extent to which increases in income inequality can explain the declines in average stature which have been observed in some parts of Europe during the second quarter of the nineteenth century. Focusing on Bavaria, he argued that there was a close relationship between the extent of nutritional inequality (as measured by height) and the level of industrialization, and that nutritional inequality increased between 1815 and 1839. He also argued that both the enhanced degree of inequality in the more economically developed areas and the increase in inequality over time were directly related to variations in stature between social classes, and this led him to conclude that "[the] height decline of industrial lower classes probably influenced the average height stagnation or decline in Bavaria and other European countries in the early-nineteenth century" (p. 104).

Although Baten and other authors have emphasized the influence of income and diet on stature, urbanization and the epidemiological environment may also have affected children's growth. In both Sweden and the Netherlands, as well as in the United Kingdom, there is evidence to suggest that men who grew up in urban areas were shorter than men from rural areas (Floud, Wachter, and Gregory 1990, pp. 200–206; Riggs 1994, pp. 65–68; Drukker and Tassenaar 1997, pp. 351–353; Sandberg and Steckel 1997, p. 145), but this was not true across the continent as a whole. Rural-born men were shorter than urban-born men in Belgium (Alter, Neven, and Oris 2004, pp. 237–239) and Spain (Martinez-Carrión 1994, p. 80; Martinez-Carrión and Moreno-Lázaro 2007), and they also appear to have been shorter in France, even though life expectancy was higher (Weir 1997, p. 182).[3] Twarog (1997, p. 302) found that urban-born men were also taller than rural-born men in

---

[3] Heyberger (2007, p. 237) has recently compared the heights of men in the industrial town of Mulhouse, in Alsace, with those of men who were born in the rural areas of Sélestat and Melun. Although he found that men who were born in Mulhouse in the second half of the nineteenth century were shorter than their rural-born neighbors, the differences were smaller than those reported in other urban–rural studies.

Württemberg, but she also pointed out that most "urban" settlements were quite small, and that men who grew up in the largest center (Stuttgart) were shorter than men who grew up in smaller population centers.

These findings suggest that it is difficult to reach any categorical conclusions about the impact of urbanization on stature in the nineteenth century, but Twarog's comments also illustrate the need to treat the concept of urbanization itself with considerable care. In many cases, men who moved from the countryside to the towns traded poorer environmental conditions for increased earning power, and in some cases this may have been sufficient to offset the disadvantages associated with urban living (Williamson 1981). However, many of the areas identified as "urban" were still quite small, and may therefore have been less susceptible to the combinations of factors which caused health standards to deteriorate in more rapidly growing areas. Szreter and Mooney (1998, pp. 89, 107; see also Szreter 1997, pp. 702–707) warned "against any simplistic thesis that mere size and speed of urban growth alone were the principal factors accounting for the relative unhealthiness of Britain's largest cities," but their results did tend to suggest that it was the pace of urban growth, rather than sheer size, which was likely to provoke the greatest hazards.

Although the vast majority of the data relating to the heights of nineteenth-century Europeans are derived from military records and relate solely to adult males, some writers have also looked at the heights of prisoners, and these included both males and females. Nicholas and his co-authors argued that there was a disproportionate decline in the average heights of rural-born female convicts who were born between 1790 and 1820 and transported from Britain to Australia between 1826 and 1840, even though they found no significant differences in the movements of male and female heights among habitual criminals who were born between 1812 and 1857, and incarcerated in Newgate Gaol in 1877 (Nicholas and Steckel 1991; Nicholas and Oxley 1993; Johnson and Nicholas 1995; Johnson and Nicholas 1997). However, Riggs (1994, pp. 70–73) argued that there were significant differences in the heights of men and women who were born between 1800 and 1850 and imprisoned in Glasgow between 1840 and 1880. He calculated that the heights of successive birth cohorts of both men and women declined between the 1810s and the 1830s, but female heights continued to decline during the 1840s, even though male heights increased.

Baten and Murray (1997; 2000) have attempted to extend this discussion by examining the heights of women who were born between 1819 and 1886 and incarcerated in Wasserburg prison in Bavaria. In 1997, they showed that there were no significant differences between the heights of women who were born illegitimately in cities or to middle-class families, but there was a significant difference between the heights of legitimately and illegitimately born women from peasant families, especially among those born in the 1840s. In 2000, they extended this analysis by looking more closely at trends in the heights of both male and female prisoners across the whole century. Their most striking finding was that "economic factors in early childhood had more systematic influence on girls' than boys' heights, and were more important than disease factors for both sexes" (Baten and Murray 2000, p. 351).

These findings are suggestive rather than conclusive. It is difficult to find any direct evidence of discrimination against female children in the distribution of household resources in eighteenth- or nineteenth-century Europe at younger ages, and much of the evidence which does exist relates to the relative deprivation of adult women, rather than their daughters (Imhof 1981; Henry 1987; Humphries 1991; Harris 1998; Klasen 1998; McNay, Humphries, and Klasen 1998; McNay, Humphries, and Klasen 2005; Harris 2008).[4] Some of the differences in male and female heights may reflect physiological differences, in the sense that girls may have been more susceptible to certain diseases which are more likely to have affected their final stature (Harris 1998, pp. 437–439). However, it is difficult to rule out the possibility that at least some of the differences revealed by these authors are a consequence of selection biases in the populations they studied. This has certainly been proposed as an explanation for the appearance of sex-specific differences in height trends in England and Wales, and may also be true in both Scotland and Bavaria (Riggs 1994; Jackson 1996; Harris 2009).

We possess much more information about a range of anthropometric measurements, affecting individuals of different ages and both sexes in a larger range of countries, during the twentieth century, including, in a

---

[4] There is some evidence which suggests that fathers were more likely to sacrifice some of their resources in favor of their sons, but mothers were more likely to share their resources with their daughters (see Klasen 1998, pp. 455–456).

small number of cases, information on often-neglected variables such as length- and weight-at-birth and age-at-menarche. A number of authors, including Antonov (1947) and Stein *et al.* (1975), have shown that children who were born during conditions of extreme deprivation at the height of the Second World War were both shorter and lighter than children born before or after that period, and Vlastovsky (1966) obtained similar results in a study of the weight and length at birth of new-born infants in Kursk between 1930 and 1959. This study showed that the average weight and length at birth of new-born infants rose between 1930 and 1939, and fell between 1939 and 1944, but the average weight of new-born infants had recovered its prewar level by 1948, whereas average birth length only surpassed prewar levels during the mid 1950s.[5]

These data are especially interesting in the light of more recent arguments about the relationship between weight- and length-at-birth and subsequent longevity (Kajantie *et al.* 2005). The majority of countries lack information about long-term changes in either birth weight or birth length but, where such data are available, there is little evidence of a secular trend over a long period (Cole 2000b, pp. 320–323; Cole 2003, p. 165). Rosenberg (1988) found that the mean birth weight of children born to married mothers in three Norwegian cities fell slightly between 1860 and 1900, rose between 1900 and 1940, and then leveled off again, and Fredriks *et al.* (2000) found that there was little change in the length of one-year-old children in the Netherlands between 1955 and 1997. These findings raise important questions about the relationship between fetal and maternal nutrition, postnatal growth, and growth in later childhood.

One possible explanation for this puzzle may lie in the relationship between maternal nutrition and the scale and timing of the expression of growth hormone receptors in infancy. Cole (2000b, p. 322) argued that stunting only starts to become apparent at the age of 4–6 months, and this is also the age at which growth hormone receptors start to be expressed. He also suggested that although both the scale and the timing of this event are influenced by the size of the child's parents, they also reflect the impact of the child's current environment and the environment which he or she experienced *in utero* (see also Karlberg 1989;

---

[5] For additional data on weight and length at birth in Moscow and St Petersburg, see Mironov 2007.

Waterlow 1994). This would certainly help to explain why cross-sectional differences in infant stature and secular changes in height only start to become apparent toward the end of the first year, even if it does not provide a full explanation for the lack of change which has recently been observed among Dutch children between the ages of one and five years (Fredriks *et al.* 2000, p. 318).

Toward the end of the nineteenth century, a growing number of European countries began to investigate the development of school health services (Harris 1995, pp. 27–32), and many medical officers advocated the weighing and measuring of schoolchildren as part of a routine program of health surveillance. These statistics represent a significant addition to the armory of anthropometric data because they shed new light on the health of children of both sexes at ages when growth was still occurring. In the Netherlands, Van Wieringen (1978, pp. 454–457; 1986, pp. 314–316) used data from a variety of locations to show that there had been a general increase in the average heights of both boys and girls between 1865 and 1965, and Fredriks *et al.* (2000) have shown that the rate of increase continued among older children between 1965 and 1997. They found that much of the recent increase in the average values of both boys' and girls' heights had occurred between the ages of five and ten, and by the end of the twentieth century, the average ten-year-old boy was more than twenty centimeters taller than the Dutch schoolboys who were measured in the mid 1860s.

Changes in the average heights of children in a range of European countries are shown in Figures 5.3–5.10. The results suggest that the average heights of many European children were well below modern standards on the eve of the First World War, but there were substantial increases in the average heights of children in parts of Germany, Greece, and Norway during the interwar period (despite the economic depression), and in other countries after 1945. By the end of the twentieth century, there were signs that the international gradient in height between children in different parts of Europe was beginning to decline, but there was still a significant gap between children in the "tallest" countries, such as Croatia, the Czech Republic, Greece, and the Netherlands, and those in "shorter" countries such as Poland and Italy. The average height of children in almost all these countries is now well above the fiftieth percentile of the NCHS height standards (Steckel 1995a; see also Harris 2009).

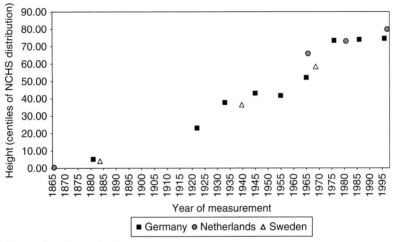

Source: See Appendix E.

Figure 5.3 Heights of boys in Germany, Sweden, and the Netherlands, 1865–1997

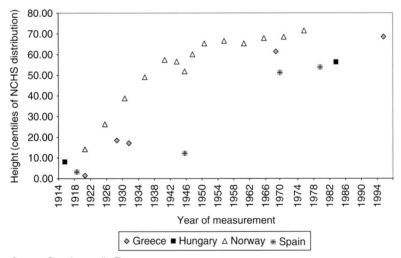

Source: See Appendix E.

Figure 5.4 Heights of boys in Greece, Hungary, Norway, and Spain, 1914–1997

Tanner (1962, p. 127) argued that girls are "less easily thrown off their growth curves by adverse circumstances than are boys," and show "more power of homeorrhesis." This argument is reinforced by the data in Figures 5.3–5.10 and Appendix E, which suggest that girls growing

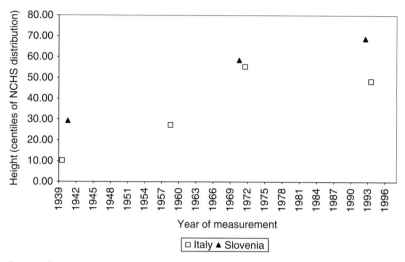

Source: See Appendix E.

Figure 5.5 Heights of boys in Italy and Slovenia, 1939–1997

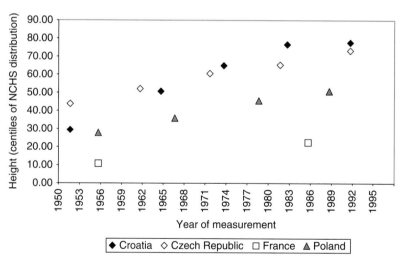

Source: See Appendix E.

Figure 5.6 Heights of boys in Croatia, the Czech Republic, France, and Poland, 1950–1997

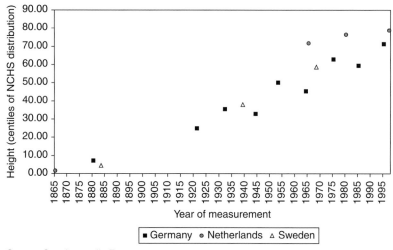

Source: See Appendix E.

Figure 5.7 Heights of girls in Germany, Sweden, and the Netherlands, 1865–1997

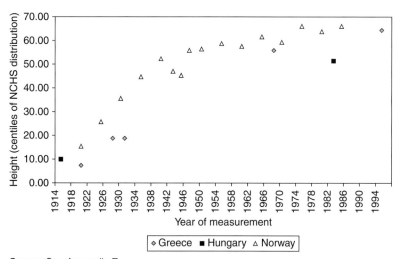

Source: See Appendix E.

Figure 5.8 Heights of girls in Greece, Hungary, and Norway, 1914–1997

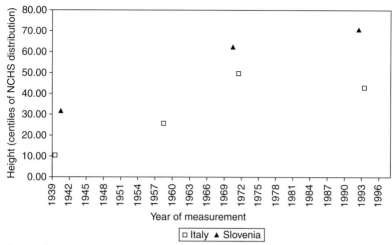

Source: See Appendix E.

Figure 5.9 Heights of girls in Italy and Slovenia, 1939–1997

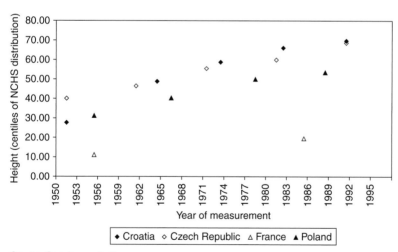

Source: See Appendix E.

Figure 5.10 Heights of girls in Croatia, the Czech Republic, France, and Poland, 1950–1997

up under the harshest circumstances in the late nineteenth and early twentieth centuries were taller, in comparison with modern height standards, than past generations of boys. However, Brundtland, Liestøl and Walløe (1980, pp. 311–312) found that the average heights of 11-13-year-old girls fell in Oslo between 1940 and 1945 even though the average heights of 11–13-year-old boys were largely unchanged (see also Angell-Andersen *et al.* 2004). It is not entirely clear why the deprivations of war should have affected older girls more than boys, but the explanation may be related to differences in the timing of the adolescent growth spurt. As Eveleth and Tanner (Eveleth and Tanner 1990, pp. 194–196) have pointed out, children are most sensitive to the effects of malnutrition and infection during the periods in their lives when they should be growing more rapidly, and a significant proportion of 12- and 13-year-old boys may not have reached this stage before they were measured (see also Hermanussen, Burmeister, and Burkhardt 1995, p. 514).

The data in Appendix E provide further evidence of changes in children's weights and body mass indices, or BMIs. Chapter 4 showed that even though there was little change in the average BMIs of younger children in Britain during the course of the twentieth century, there was evidence of increases in BMIs at older ages. The data in Appendix E suggest that the average value of children's BMIs also increased in some other European countries, but not in others. There was relatively little change in the Czech Republic, the Netherlands, Norway (Oslo), or Sweden, but increases did occur in Croatia (Zagreb), France, Italy, and Slovenia (Ljubljana). In Jena, in eastern Germany, Zellner, Ulbricht, and Kromeyer-Hauschild (2007) argued that there was a long-term increase in the average BMIs of 7–14-year-olds but this may also reflect the impact of earlier maturation. The data in Appendix E suggest that there was little change in the average BMIs of either nine-year-old boys or girls before 1985, although their BMIs rose sharply over the next decade.[6]

The factors which contributed to changes in the average heights of children in the twentieth century also contributed to changes in the ages

---

[6] BMI levels also rose in Cracow (Poland) between 1971 and 2000 (Chrzanowska, Koziel, and Ulijaszek 2007). Vignerová *et al.* (2007) have argued that even though there was little change in average BMIs between 1951 and 2001, the proportion of overweight and obese children has increased.

at which they achieved their peak-height-velocity and in the age at which girls reached menarche, but changes in the age of menarche are much better documented (Hauspie, Vercauteren, and Susanne 1997, pp. 22–23; Susanne *et al.* 2001, pp. 72–74). Although menarcheal age increased in some countries during the Second World War and during other periods of economic stress, the average age of menarche declined in most parts of Europe over the twentieth century as a whole. Tanner (Tanner 1962, pp. 152–155) reported that menarcheal age declined by four years in Norway between 1840 and 1950; by 1.7 years in Sweden between 1890 and 1950; by 2.3 years in Finland between 1860 and 1940; and by 3.0 years in Germany over the same period; and other studies have shown that menarcheal age continued to decline in Austria, Belgium, Bulgaria, Denmark, Finland, France, Germany, Greece, Hungary, Italy, the Netherlands, Poland, Romania, Spain, Sweden, and the countries of the former Yugoslavia and the Soviet Union after the Second World War (Harris 2000, p. 1429; Onland-Moret *et al.* 2005). Hauspie, Vercauteren, and Susanne (1997, pp. 22–3) have suggested that the reduction in *average* menarcheal age is likely to have been caused by a reduction in the proportion of girls who reach menarche at later ages. In Belgium, there was little change in the value of the tenth centile of menarcheal age after 1940 or in the value of the fiftieth centile of menarcheal age after 1950, but the age of those who reached menarche in the ninetieth centile fell by approximately one year between 1950 and 1970.

These increases in the average heights and rates of growth of children have also been reflected in the heights of European adults. The average height of army recruits in Bavaria, Belgium, Denmark, France, Italy, the Netherlands, Norway, Spain, and Sweden increased by between 3.1 and 11.1 centimeters during the first seventy-five years of the twentieth century (Floud 1994, pp. 16–19), and Susanne *et al.* (2001, p. 72) reported similar increases in Germany, Greece, Hungary, and Poland between 1930 and the mid 1990s (see also Harris 1997a, p. 499; Heirmeyer 2009).[7] The average height of women who were born between the mid 1940s and the early 1970s and admitted to the St Petersburg Maternity Hospital between 1980 and 2005 increased by nearly six centimeters (Mironov 2007, p. 124). Susanne *et al.* summarized changes in the

---

[7] The average height of Italian army recruits increased by 12.19 cm between the birth cohorts of 1854 and 1980 (Arcaleni 2006, p. 27).

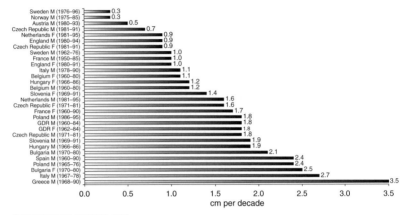

Source: Susanne *et al.* 2001, p. 73.

Figure 5.11 Increases in the average heights of European adults (cm per decade)

average heights of both men and women in sixteen countries from 1950 onwards. Their results (reproduced in Figure 5.11) show that average height increased throughout Europe, with some of the most rapid changes taking place in Spain, Bulgaria, Italy, and Greece (see also Garcia and Quintana-Domeque 2007; Costa-Font and Gil 2008; and Webb *et al.* 2008). These changes support the view that there is now a general "leveling-up" of heights both within countries and across Europe. Susanne *et al.* (2001, p. 79) found that socioeconomic differences in height and other anthropometric indicators were diminishing and that the most rapid improvements had occurred within the most disadvantaged groups, and this tendency has also been reflected in international comparisons. However, the persistence of both socioeconomic and international variations in stature suggests that the scope for further improvement has not yet been eliminated.

5.2 The decline of mortality in continental Europe

One of the main arguments which has been used to justify the use of anthropometric data is the relative paucity of comparable information on mortality rates for many European countries before circa 1850 (e.g., Komlos 1991, p. 99). However, this book has argued that height is not merely a proxy for other health indicators but that increases in average height reflect improvements in the health and well-being of children which have lasting consequences for their health at all ages. It is therefore particularly important to examine the extent to which the changes in stature and other anthropometric indicators described in the previous section have been accompanied by similar changes in mortality and life expectancy.

Caselli (1991, pp. 68–9) identified three broad patterns of mortality change during the eighteenth and nineteenth centuries. In Scandinavia, mortality rates began to fall during the late eighteenth and early nineteenth centuries and continued to decline throughout the nineteenth century, but in central and other parts of northern Europe mortality rates remained roughly constant between 1820 and 1870, and this led to a "second phase" of mortality decline from 1870 onwards. However, there was little evidence of any concerted decline in mortality in the Mediterranean countries before the 1880s, when the average level of life expectancy in Italy rose from 33 to 38 years between 1881 and 1891.

The data presented in Table 5.1 and in Figures 5.12 and 5.13 enable us to put some more flesh on the bare bones of this initial outline. The available evidence suggests that the average level of life expectancy in France rose from around 25 years in the 1740s to 27 in the 1790s, and then rose more rapidly between the 1790s and the 1840s. There was a small reduction in life-expectancy levels in the 1850s but life expectancy continued to increase thereafter. However, life expectancy in France was still quite low, in comparison with the more northern countries, at the end of the nineteenth century.

Figure 5.12 also illustrates the different experiences of the Scandinavian countries in this period. In Sweden, there was little change in average life expectancy during the second half of the eighteenth century, but life expectancy rose by nearly five years between the 1800s and the 1820s. This was followed (as Caselli suggests) by a further period of stagnation before life expectancy rose again between the 1850s and the 1890s. In Denmark, life expectancy seems to have improved more rapidly during the closing decades of the eighteenth century, but there was a sharp decline between the 1810s and the 1830s, and a substantial increase in the 1840s. We do not possess information about trends in life expectancy in Norway before the 1820s, but crude death rates appear to have declined substantially from the 1730s onwards (Drake 1969, p. 49; Saugstard 1979, p. 84) and life expectancy had already reached 46 years by the end of the 1820s. In Iceland, the average level of life expectancy remained below forty for much of the

Table 5.1 *Average life expectancy at birth, for both sexes, in selected European countries, 1741–2000*

	Austria	Belgium	Bulgaria	Czech Republic	Denmark	Finland	France	Germany	Hungary	Iceland	Italy	Latvia	Lithuania	Netherlands	Norway	Russia	Slovak Republic	Spain	Sweden	Switzerland
1741–1750							25.04	37.41												
1751–1760							27.86	35.99											36.80	
1761–1770							27.79	35.68											35.54	
1771–1780							28.77	38.15											34.33	
1781–1790					35.49		28.18	38.04											35.27	
1791–1800					40.50		31.99	36.58											38.71	
1801–1810					41.83		34.74	39.91											36.21	
1811–1820					41.98		35.46	39.27											38.44	
1821–1830					40.49		38.61	41.36							46.50				41.69	
1831–1840					37.89		38.77	39.78							43.70				41.65	
1841–1850					42.10		40.52	40.95		35.64					46.20				43.73	
1851–1860					43.60		39.39	39.51		36.81				36.56	50.03				42.41	
1861–1870					44.87		40.45	36.06		32.40				37.55	48.15				44.53	
1871–1880					46.39		41.45	37.14		38.13				39.40	49.83				47.08	
1881–1890					48.15	42.63	43.30	39.01		39.29	36.26			43.36	50.08				50.14	44.48
1891–1900					50.25	44.75	45.14	41.20		49.25	40.83			47.23	52.09				52.49	47.36
1901–1910					55.57	46.64	48.66	44.22		50.87	44.32			52.30	56.24				55.90	50.69
1911–1920					57.61	46.40	48.14	42.49		55.37	45.00			55.35	57.11			40.91	57.23	53.95
1921–1930					61.60	52.56	54.83	50.66		58.26	51.73			62.42	62.50			46.80	62.18	59.87
1931–1940		59.24			63.99	55.13	58.09			63.20	56.26			66.33	65.85			49.83	64.93	62.80
1941–1950		61.61			67.95	57.08	60.88			67.74	59.02			66.22	68.53			56.97	69.25	66.34
1951–1960	67.53	68.89	64.99	68.55	71.67	67.57	68.57		65.80	72.91	67.68			72.55	73.25			66.65	72.48	70.29

Period																				
1961–1970	69.99	70.64	70.71	70.17	72.74	69.48	71.24	70.47	69.21	73.60	70.46	70.63	71.18	73.56	73.73	69.15		70.86	73.92	72.28
1971–1980	71.62	72.24	71.11	70.45	73.99	72.02	73.25	71.96	69.52	75.46	73.05	69.67	71.21	74.73	74.93	68.40		73.76	75.16	74.73
1981–1990	74.34	74.82	71.33	71.26	74.68	74.67	75.74	74.59	69.36	77.35	75.86	70.05	71.33	76.53	76.06	68.94	70.84	76.53	76.96	76.91
1991–2000	77.02	77.12	71.06	73.61	75.87	76.71	78.18	76.95	70.13	78.96	78.36	68.47	70.41	77.77	77.97	66.22	72.31	78.25	78.95	78.94

Sources: Denmark: 1781–1840: Andersen 1979: 19; France: 1741–1810: Ministère du Travail 1977: 40; 1811–1898: Vallin and Meslé 2001: Table II-A-I; Germany: 1741–1930: Imhof 1990, pp. 462–464; Norway: 1821–1850: Drake 1969, p. 47. All other information was obtained from the Human Mortality Database (www.mortality.org).

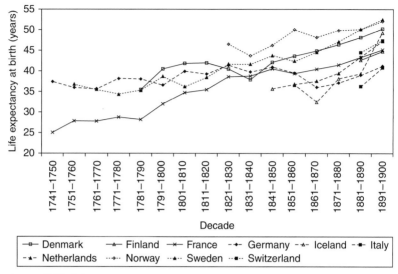

Source: Table 5.1.

Figure 5.12 Life expectancy in western Europe, 1741–1900

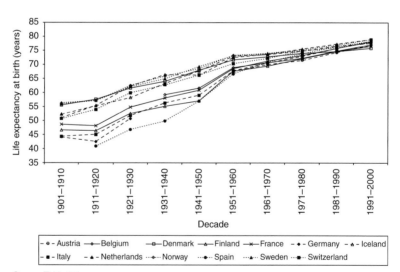

Source: Table 5.1.

Figure 5.13 Life expectancy in western Europe, 1901–2000

1840s, 1850s, and 1860s, but there was a substantial increase in life expectancy from the 1870s onwards.

Figure 5.12 also presents information about the average level of life expectancy in Italy and Switzerland at the end of the nineteenth century. Schofield and Reher (1991, p. 4) argued that life expectancy in southern and eastern Europe "was only very modest by the middle part of the nineteenth century ... and any improvement over the conditions which applied a century earlier must have been marginal at best," but the average level of life expectancy in Italy in 1880 was still significantly greater than the generally accepted estimates of life expectancy in France before 1800. Nevertheless, Italian life expectancy was still significantly lower than that found in Switzerland during the same period, and this may be a reflection of the comparative healthiness of Alpine districts at this time (Viazzo 1997).

The mortality experience of these countries can also be compared with that of Germany and the Netherlands. In Germany, life expectancy appears to have increased very slowly between the 1740s and the 1820s, before falling substantially between the 1820s and the 1870s, and life expectancy was still lower at the end of the nineteenth century than it had been eighty years earlier. We possess very little continuous information about life expectancy in the Netherlands before the second half of the 1850s,[8] but there was a substantial reduction in mortality and an improvement in life expectancy from the 1850s onwards.

There have been several attempts to explain these changes on both a national and an international basis. Schofield and Reher (1991, p. 10) identified a battery of factors which are likely to have contributed to the long-term decline in mortality including nutrition, living standards, public health, sanitation, changing disease patterns, living and working conditions, education, medical attendance, infant-feeding practices, and personal hygiene, and some of these will also be discussed in more detail in the next section of this chapter. They also highlighted the extent to which urbanization and industrialization may have retarded the pace of improvement during the middle years of the nineteenth century. This certainly seems to have been the case in England and Wales and may also have been true of Germany (Steckel

---

[8] Flora, Kraus, and Pfenning (1987, p. 104) include estimates for life expectancy at various ages for the periods 1816–25 and 1840–51; the Human Mortality Database contains annual data from 1850.

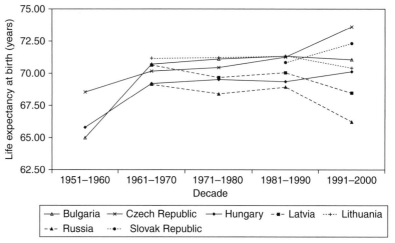

Source: Table 5.1.

Figure 5.14 Life expectancy in central and eastern Europe, 1951–2000

and Floud 1997a, p. 430). However, the onset of industrialization in other countries appears to have been associated with an acceleration in the rate of mortality decline, highlighting the need for further research into the different responses to industrialization, and the strategies for dealing with urban growth, in different European countries.

The main changes in life expectancy in different parts of western Europe in the twentieth century are shown in Figure 5.13. This graph illustrates the extent of the international gradient in mortality which had emerged in Europe before the start of the First World War. The average level of life expectancy in Norway, Denmark, and Sweden exceeded 55 years in the first decade of the twentieth century, whereas life expectancy in Italy, Spain, and Germany was less than 45 years. Although life expectancy improved in all these countries during the interwar period, there is little evidence to suggest that the gap was diminishing. However, mortality rates converged rapidly after the end of the Second World War and the average level of life expectancy ranged from 75.87 years in Denmark to 78.96 years in Iceland at the end of the century.

Although Figure 5.13 suggests that mortality rates in western Europe converged rapidly after the Second World War, the gap between these countries and those of eastern Europe appears to have widened. Figure 5.14 shows that although life expectancy rates improved in

Bulgaria, Hungary, and within the territory of what is now the Czech Republic during the 1950s, this was followed by a period of stagnation during the next three decades. However, life expectancy rates followed very different paths in the countries of eastern Europe following the collapse of the Soviet Union at the beginning of the 1990s. Figure 5.14 shows that life expectancy rose in Hungary and in both parts of the former Czechoslovakia, but declined in Bulgaria, Lithuania, and Russia. By the end of the decade, the lowest mortality rates were found in the Czech and Slovak Republics, but their life expectancy rates were still between 3.74 and 5.61 years lower than an unweighted average of life expectancy rates in the thirteen countries represented in Figure 5.13, while life expectancy rates in Latvia, Lithuania, and Russia were lower than the rates reported in the 1960s.[9]

It is also possible to distinguish between male and female life expectancy. Table 5.2 shows that the gap between the two sexes has increased in the majority of countries since records became available, partly as a result of changes in the status and entitlements of women, but also because of the reduction in the number of pregnancy-related deaths and sex-specific differences in the consumption of alcohol and, especially, tobacco (e.g., Harris 1998; 2008). However, in recent years the gap between male life expectancy and female life expectancy has grown much larger in certain parts of eastern Europe than elsewhere, and this was one of the main reasons for the overall decline in life expectancy in Bulgaria, Latvia, Lithuania, and Russia and for the growing divide between the two halves of Europe during this period.

When Kermack, McKendrick, and McKinlay published their initial analysis of the impact of cohort-related factors on the decline of mortality in England, Scotland, and Wales, they also compared their findings with the pattern of mortality decline in Sweden, and concluded that "corresponding regularities seem to exist," even though they were "partly obscured by some influence the nature of which we are not in a position to identify" (Kermack, McKendrick, McKinlay 1934, p. 698). Fridlizius (1989, p. 17) extended Kermack, McKendrick,

---

[9] In 2000, average life expectancy at birth was 73.17 years in the Slovak Republic and 75.04 years in the Czech Republic. The unweighted average of the life expectancy rates in Austria, Belgium, Denmark, Finland, France, Germany, Iceland, Italy, the Netherlands, Norway, Spain, Sweden, and Switzerland was 78.78 years. Estimates of life expectancy in Latvia and Russia for the period 1959–69 should be treated with particular caution (see www.mortality.org).

Table 5.2 *Differences between life expectancy rates for males and females in selected European countries, 1751–2000*

	Austria	Belgium	Bulgaria	Czech Republic	Denmark	Finland	France	Germany	Hungary	Iceland	Italy	Latvia	Lithuania	Netherlands	Norway	Russia	Slovak Republic	Spain	Sweden	Switzerland
1751–1760																			3.01	
1761–1770																			2.89	
1771–1780																			2.35	
1781–1790																			3.37	
1791–1800																			2.77	
1801–1810																			3.12	
1811–1820							6.03												3.44	
1821–1830							1.46												4.36	
1831–1840							1.53												4.21	
1841–1850					2.72		1.57				4.89								4.48	
1851–1860					2.38		1.64				5.52			1.58	3.07				3.94	
1861–1870					1.90		1.77				6.08			1.87	2.95				3.67	
1871–1880					1.85		2.48				5.69			2.46	2.95				3.35	
1881–1890					2.04	2.79	2.71				5.15	0.05		2.69	2.53				2.88	2.49
1891–1900					2.86	2.79	3.23				5.49	0.26		2.85	3.63				2.64	2.89
1901–1910					3.12	2.93	3.69				5.06	0.61		2.57	2.85				2.45	2.94
1911–1920					2.61	5.05	7.39				5.39	0.94		1.85	3.23			1.86	2.70	3.31
1921–1930					1.67	4.92	4.38				4.73	1.68		1.47	2.69			2.93	2.17	3.31
1931–1940	4.65				2.02	6.99	5.69				4.64	2.65		1.67	3.32			6.11	2.40	3.93

Period																				
1941–1950		5.60			2.21	11.68	6.80			4.20	3.83			3.77	4.33			5.77	2.63	4.24
1951–1960	5.77	5.27	3.35	5.24	3.08	6.59	6.27		4.31	4.26	4.27			3.09	3.96			4.66	3.21	5.00
1961–1970	6.52	6.10	3.89	6.49	4.50	7.46	7.25	5.71	4.95	5.45	5.63	7.97	7.18	5.07	5.36	9.27		5.33	4.43	5.84
1971–1980	7.06	6.55	4.93	7.05	5.78	8.67	7.93	6.37	6.27	5.97	6.39	9.86	9.21	6.23	6.35	10.93	7.54	5.90	5.84	6.44
1981–1990	6.93	6.67	6.15	7.29	5.91	8.19	8.19	6.45	8.01	5.42	6.57	9.86	9.53	6.54	6.67	10.54	8.10	6.61	5.92	6.75
1991–2000	6.49	6.56	7.11	7.09	5.09	7.40	7.95	6.37	9.05	4.37	6.39	11.84	11.18	5.65	5.79	12.52	8.28	7.20	5.15	6.29

Sources: See Table 5.1.

Note: The figures in each cell represent the difference in years between female life expectancy at birth and male life expectancy at birth (i.e. life expectancy at birth [female] – life expectancy at birth [male]).

and McKinlay's analysis by identifying four occasions on which the underlying pattern of cohort-related mortality change was overlain, or "deformed," by period effects. These included an alcohol-induced increase in the mortality of working-age males between 1820 and 1850; an increase in tuberculosis-related mortality among men and women between the ages of ten and thirty in the late nineteenth and early twentieth centuries; an improvement in social conditions in Stockholm during the second half of the nineteenth century; and "a remarkable mortality change in the initial group of the cohort of the 1850s and 1860s."

Although both Kermack *et al.* and Fridlizius recognized the importance of period factors in understanding the course of Sweden's mortality decline, they did not believe that this undermined their basic contention that "the mortality decline during the nineteenth century contained a marked cohort element and that interpretations of the causes and consequences of this decline might well be oversimplified unless this aspect is taken into account" (Fridlizius 1989, p. 3). This conclusion has been echoed by students of mortality decline in both France and Italy. Preston and van de Walle (1978, p. 284) compiled mortality statistics for the three largest urban areas of France during the nineteenth century and concluded that "the most striking tendency . . . is for the improvement in mortality that began around mid-century to proceed in a cohort-specific fashion ... the first ages to experience improved mortality were those below age fifteen or twenty (except infancy) and the cohorts so benefiting tended to retain their favored position relative to earlier cohorts as they passed through life." In Italy, Caselli and Capocaccia (Caselli and Capocaccia 1989, pp. 152–153) found that there was a close association between childhood mortality and adult mortality among men below the age of forty-five and among women at all ages. Although they were unable to offer a full explanation for the absence of a similar relationship between childhood mortality and adult mortality among older men, they suggested that this may have reflected the debilitating effects of the Second World War, industrial employment, and the "stresses of changing lifestyles" on the generations concerned.

Figures 5.15–5.21 help to place these results in a broader international context. All the data have been obtained from the Human Mortality Database, with the exception of the German data, which are derived from Arthur Imhof's study of mortality changes in Germany, Norway, and Sweden in the nineteenth and twentieth

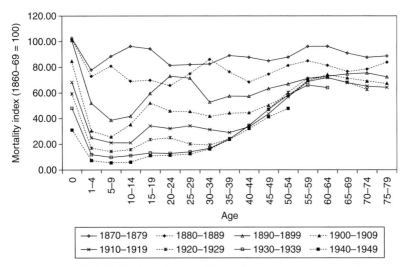

Source: Human Mortality Database (www.mortality.org).

Figure 5.15 Cohort-specific mortality in Denmark, 1870–1949

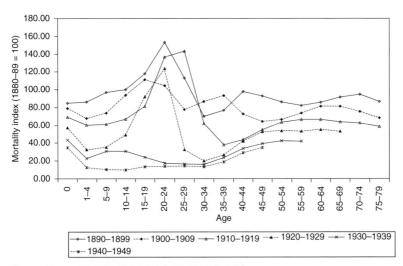

Source: Human Mortality Database (www.mortality.org).

Figure 5.16 Cohort-specific mortality in Finland, 1890–1949

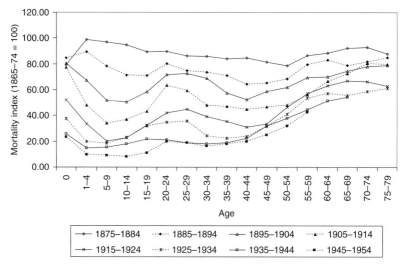

Source: Imhof 1994, p. 396 (Table 1.3.1.3.1).

Figure 5.17 Cohort-specific mortality in Germany (West), 1875–1954

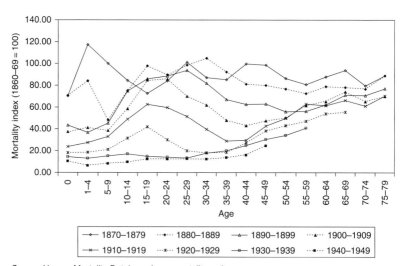

Source: Human Mortality Database (www.mortality.org).

Figure 5.18 Cohort-specific mortality in Iceland, 1870–1949

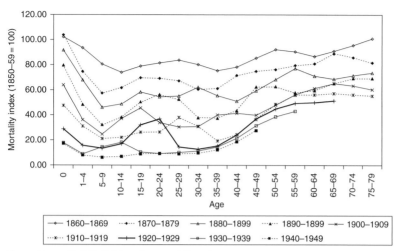

Source: Human Mortality Database (www.mortality.org).

Figure 5.19 Cohort-specific mortality in the Netherlands, 1860–1949

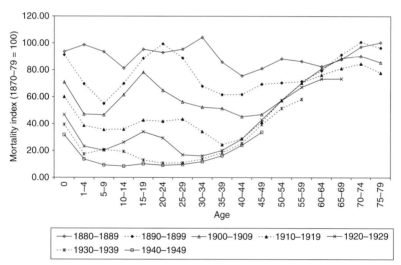

Source: Human Mortality Database (www.mortality.org).

Figure 5.20 Cohort-specific mortality in Norway, 1880–1949

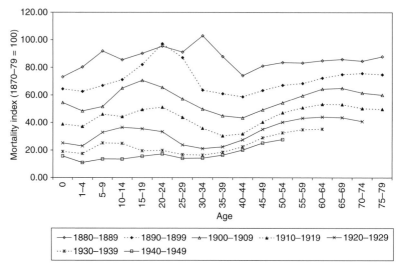

Source: Human Mortality Database (www.mortality.org).

Figure 5.21 Cohort-specific mortality in Switzerland, 1880–1949

centuries, and cover the whole of the territory encompassed by the German Reich, including the areas which subsequently formed part of both East and West Germany (Imhof 1994, p. 10). The graphs show the mortality rates experienced by successive birth cohorts at different ages, expressed as a percentage of the mortality rate experienced by an earlier cohort. In the case of the Netherlands, the data have been compared with the cohort born between 1850 and 1859; the Danish and Icelandic data have been compared with the birth cohorts of the 1860s; the German data have been compared with the birth cohort of men and women born between 1865 and 1874; the Norwegian and Swiss data have been compared with the birth cohorts of the 1870s; and the Finnish data have been compared with the birth cohorts of the 1880s.[10]

The results provide further evidence of the "regularities" in cohort-specific mortality which Kermack and his colleagues identified for England, Scotland, and Wales in the 1930s, but there are some differences. In the majority of cases there is clear evidence of the impact of

---

[10] Janssen and Kunst (2005) have conducted a similar analysis of cohort patterns in mortality trends in seven European countries (Denmark, England and Wales, Finland, France, Netherlands, Norway, and Sweden) since 1950.

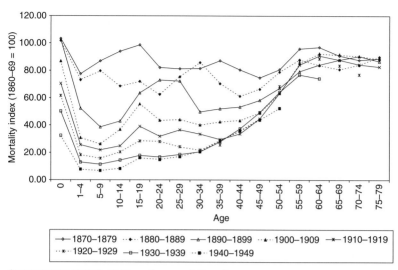

Source: Human Mortality Database (www.mortality.org).

Figure 5.22 Cohort-specific mortality among Danish males, 1870–1949

period-specific factors during the influenza pandemic of 1918–1919 and the two world wars. In three cases – Finland, Iceland, and Switzerland – the relationship between childhood mortality and adult mortality appears to have been established during infancy, whereas both the French data and the Anglo-Welsh data suggest that it only really became apparent later on in childhood (see Kermack *et al.* 1934, p. 700; Preston and van de Walle 1978, p. 284). Finally, there is also some evidence to suggest that the beneficial effects of reductions in childhood mortality may have been less apparent at older ages. This is particularly true in Denmark, where there is very little difference between the relative mortality rates among those born after 1900 beyond the age of forty.

The attenuation of the relationship between childhood mortality and adult mortality in Denmark is particularly interesting because of its implications for future changes in old-age mortality, but it may simply reflect the impact of period-specific factors on the health of those who reached early middle age during the 1930s and 1940s. Fridlizius (1989, p. 16) argued that during the twentieth century the pattern of mortality change in Sweden had been subject to a fifth "deformation," which was nicotine-induced and particularly apparent among the male population. The sex-specific nature of this fifth "deformation" is also reflected in

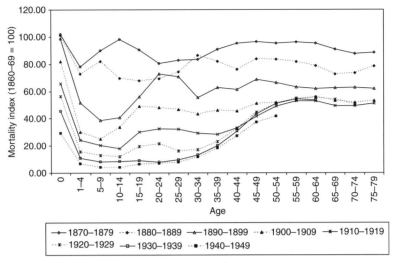

Source: Human Mortality Database (www.mortality.org).

Figure 5.23 Cohort-specific mortality among Danish females, 1870–1949

the Danish statistics (Figures 5.22 and 5.23), which show that the relationship between childhood mortality and adult mortality was much weaker among males than among females. If this pattern also reflects sex-specific differences in cigarette use, the decline of tobacco consumption in Denmark (and other countries) since the 1970s may help to re-establish the connection between child mortality and adult mortality which is clearly apparent in the earlier data.[11]

5.3 Economic and social change in continental Europe since 1700

The previous chapter examined the impact of a variety of factors, including improvements in real wages, nutrition, housing, public health provision and medical care, on the improvement in height and life expectancy in England and Wales since 1700. This section summarizes evidence of similar changes in other parts of Europe over the same period.

---

[11] Information concerning international changes in tobacco consumption can be found in OECD 2005 (Chart 4.3).

Allen (2001a) examined movements in wages and prices in eighteen European cities over a period of 650 years. During the fifteenth century, building workers in Antwerp, Amsterdam, and London enjoyed somewhat higher real wages than building workers in other European cities but the differences were relatively small. However, over the next three centuries the gap widened significantly because real wages remained roughly constant in north-western Europe and fell sharply elsewhere. Allen concluded that "it was only between 1870 and 1913 that the standard of living in the industrialized world rose noticeably above early-modern levels. For many Europeans, the escape from mass poverty waited until the twentieth century" (p. 413).

Allen also estimated the cost of a basket of essential goods, based on prices in the French city of Strasbourg between 1745 and 1754. The basket included sufficient food to provide a daily allowance of 1,941 calories and 80 grams of protein, together with additional allowances for fuel, clothing, and lighting.[12] After making a further allowance for rent, he then compared the cost of supporting a standard-sized household with the wages which different groups of workers might expect to earn if they worked for 250 days in each calendar year, and used this figure to calculate a "welfare ratio." If the average worker earned enough money to meet the basic needs of his household, the welfare ratio would be 1.00; a value of less than 1.00 would imply that wages fell below the level needed to meet basic needs (Allen 2001a, pp. 419–431).

The results of this exercise for the period 1701–1913 are summarized in Table 5.3. During the eighteenth century, a significant proportion of craft workers and the majority of building laborers were unlikely to earn enough money to meet their basic needs, and this continued to be true of the majority of unskilled workers during the greater part of the nineteenth century. Although wage levels improved during the second half of the nineteenth century, the only building laborers whose wages were consistently above the poverty line were those in Amsterdam, Antwerp, London, Paris, and Warsaw. The wages earned by building laborers in Madrid only rose above Allen's poverty line at the very end

---

[12] Allen (2009, p. 35) has recently provided an alternative set of estimates, based on what he calls the "respectability basket." The respectability basket includes a more generous allowance of bread and is designed to raise the daily consumption of calories from 1,941 calories (the figure of 1,914 calories cited in Allen's footnote is presumably a misprint) to 2,500 calories.

Table 5.3 Construction workers' welfare ratios, 1701–1913

	1701–1710	1711–1720	1721–1730	1731–1740	1741–1750	1751–1760	1761–1770	1771–1780	1781–1790	1791–1800	1801–1810	1811–1820	1821–1830	1831–1840	1841–1850	1851–1860	1861–1870	1871–1880	1881–1890	1891–1900	1901–1910	1911–1913
Building craftsmen																						
Antwerp	2.09	2.20	2.27	2.37	2.23	2.31	2.24	2.19	2.04	1.82	1.53	1.60	2.53	2.29	2.18	2.00	1.99	2.24	2.45	2.72	2.95	3.48
Amsterdam	2.02	1.91	2.07	2.20	1.94	2.02	1.92	1.77	1.73	1.63	1.51	1.38	1.66	1.51	1.40	1.28	1.23	1.46	1.91	2.48	2.89	
London	2.07	2.08	2.06	2.32	2.56	2.38	2.24	2.08	2.24	1.98	2.05	2.12	2.45	2.53	2.49	2.62	2.83	3.35	3.85	4.23	4.26	4.00
Paris	1.50	1.39	1.16	1.15	1.18	1.25	1.21	1.16							1.78	1.84	1.85	1.69	2.68	2.67	2.70	
Strasbourg	0.77	0.85	0.95	0.89	0.84	0.92	0.88	0.88	0.99	0.84	1.27	1.11	1.11	1.11	1.02	0.94	1.01					
Florence	1.24	1.34	1.60	1.29	1.17	1.23	1.14	0.89	0.84	0.67	0.68	0.59	0.91	0.90	0.83	0.65	0.79	0.74	1.09	1.34	1.67	1.79
Naples						1.31	1.23	1.09	1.03	0.81												
Valencia	1.09	1.12	1.18	1.06	1.12	1.02	0.88	0.82														
Madrid	1.88	2.05	2.08	1.73	1.79	1.49	1.27	1.30	1.23	1.10	1.32	1.36	2.21	1.75	2.07	2.00	1.74	1.97	1.74	1.81	1.65	2.19
Augsburg	1.06	1.13	1.27	1.19	1.08	1.08	0.90	0.90	0.86	0.75												
Leipzig	1.34	1.26	1.33	1.26	1.17	1.10	1.01	1.15	1.03				1.37	1.30	1.25	1.16	1.42	1.61	2.19	2.51	2.66	2.70
Munich	0.85	0.76	0.81	0.77	0.70	0.67					1.01											
Vienna	1.23	1.19	1.51	1.44	1.30	1.23	1.13	1.10	1.03	1.13												
Gdansk	1.90	1.81	1.98	1.88	1.82	1.64	1.18	1.10	1.04	1.17												
Kraków	1.31	1.11	1.42	1.15	1.23	1.24	1.20	1.11	1.12			1.19	1.35	1.41	1.19	1.30	1.67	1.92	2.41	2.32	1.99	
Warsaw	1.97	1.58	2.01	1.95	1.74	1.99	2.09	2.03	2.00			2.07	2.96	2.74	3.35	3.52	3.17	2.58	2.50	3.43	3.47	3.83
Lwow	1.02	0.98	1.10	0.91	0.82	0.82	0.78	0.73	0.81													
Hamburg																		2.46	3.02	3.30	3.33	3.27
Building laborers																						
Antwerp	1.25	1.32	1.36	1.42	1.34	1.38	1.35	1.31	1.22	1.09	0.92	0.96	1.52	1.38	1.31	1.20	1.19	1.40	1.49	1.72	1.83	2.01
Amsterdam	1.54	1.48	1.61	1.66	1.47	1.54	1.50	1.38	1.35	1.25	1.15	1.05	1.26	1.14	1.06	0.97	0.93	1.10	1.45	1.88	2.19	

The following is a price/welfare-ratio matrix (rows = cities). The first row (London) gives the reference values that also head the columns. Empty cells indicate no value.

City	1.53	1.53	1.51	1.63	1.71	1.59	1.49	1.31	1.34	1.32	1.30	1.33	1.47	1.52	1.50	1.65	1.69	2.14	2.56	2.80	2.82	2.86
London	1.53	1.53	1.51	1.63	1.71	1.59	1.49	1.31	1.34	1.32	1.30	1.33	1.47	1.52	1.50	1.65	1.69	2.14	2.56	2.80	2.82	2.86
Paris	0.94	0.87	0.73	0.72	0.75	0.76	0.73	0.70				0.85	0.90	0.79	0.77	1.12	1.01	1.12	1.14	1.49	1.83	1.88
Strasbourg	0.50	0.57	0.63	0.59	0.56	0.61	0.73	0.56		0.96			0.77	0.81	0.80		0.67	0.74	0.79	0.92		
Florence									0.61						0.76	0.45	0.45	0.59	0.74	0.82	0.92	1.01
Milan	0.66	0.70	0.83	0.67	0.61	0.64	0.60	0.47	0.45	0.36	0.34	0.30	0.45	0.45	0.33							0.91
Naples						0.89	0.82	0.73	0.72	0.54												
Valencia	0.73	0.75	0.79	0.71	0.89	0.68	0.59	0.55														
Madrid						0.74	0.63	0.65	0.61	0.55		0.61	1.04	0.87	1.02	0.96	0.93	0.87	0.91	0.98		1.29
Augsburg	0.81	0.87	0.85	0.77	0.69	0.71	0.61	0.69	0.62													
Leipzig	0.77	0.76	0.80	0.75	0.70	0.66	0.71	0.69	0.65													
Vienna	0.88	0.80	0.95	0.90	0.81	0.77			0.71	0.71												
Gdansk	1.11	1.01	1.06	1.07	0.99	0.94	0.96	0.87	0.89	0.74	0.60											
Kraków	0.90	0.80	0.83	0.83	0.86	0.87	0.86	0.92	0.90		0.63	0.64	0.60	0.54	0.63	0.88	0.91	0.97	0.99	1.38	1.84	1.38
Warsaw	0.72	0.63	0.67	0.64	0.67	0.87	0.99	1.09	0.85		0.87	1.28	1.07	1.35	1.34	1.29	1.26	1.31	1.62	1.84	1.99	1.99

Source: Allen 2007b. For explanation, see text.

of the century, and wage levels in Florence and Milan remained extremely low on the eve of the First World War.

Although these figures are based on purely urban experiences and take little account of the possible impact of regional variations in either prices or wages, they nevertheless have important implications for debates about the extent of hunger in the European past. Livi-Bacci (Livi-Bacci 1991, p. 27; Livi-Bacci 2000, p. 43) has argued that "a population which could rely on a normal consumption of 2000 calories per head would have been, in centuries past, an adequately-fed population, at least from the point of view of energy" and that "an average daily consumption of 2000 calories per person ... should provide sufficient nourishment, at least in terms of energy." However, he has also acknowledged that these arguments "[do] not take into account either the quality or variety of food, or its distribution" (Livi-Bacci 1991, p. 27; Livi-Bacci 2000, p. 43), and Allen's figures underline the significance of this proviso. If his figures are correct, they imply that a significant proportion of the working-class population of many of Europe's largest cities lacked the resources needed to obtain a nutritionally adequate diet before the final decades of the nineteenth century.

We can also compare Allen's data with the biomedical evidence assembled in the preceding sections of this chapter. These sections showed that there was relatively little improvement in either height or life expectancy in the majority of European countries during the first half of the nineteenth century and that a significant disparity had emerged by the end of the century between the health of people living in northern and western Europe and those in the south and east. Even though it would be wrong to assume that there is a straightforward relationship between real wages and either height or life expectancy, these findings are broadly consistent with the pattern which Allen's welfare ratios suggest.

Although these figures suggest that improvements in real wages may have exercised a significant influence on the timing of changes in both height and life expectancy in different parts of Europe during the nineteenth century, the evidence for the twentieth century is more complex. In Chapter 3, we argued that it was important to take account of the long-term nature of the relationship between sanitary investments and health improvements, and that this might help to explain why mortality rates continued to decline in the United States, despite high levels of unemployment, between 1929 and 1939. The evidence presented in Figure 5.24 suggests that a similar mechanism may also have been at

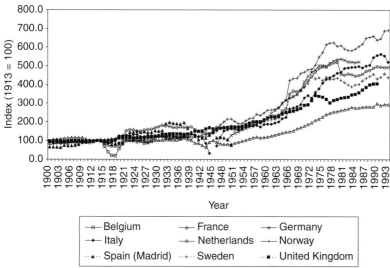

Year

—□— Belgium	—▲— France	—×— Germany
—◆— Italy	—○— Netherlands	—+— Norway
··▲·· Spain (Madrid)	··+·· Sweden	··■·· United Kingdom

Sources: Belgium: Scholliers 1995, pp. 130–134. France: Sicsic 1995, pp. 206–209 (Table A.2, cols. 1–2); Mitchell 2003, pp. 186–201, 863–868. Germany: Hohls 1995, pp. 221–230 (Table A.4, col. 12, Table A.5, col. 4). Italy: Zamagni 1995, pp. 231–233 (Table A. 6); Mitchell 2003, pp. 153, 186–201, 863–868. Netherlands: Vermaas 1995, pp. 234–237 (Tables A.8, A.10); Mitchell 2003, pp. 186–201, 863–868. Norway: Hodne, Grytte, and Alme 1995, pp. 238–248 (Tables A.12–A.13, A.15); Mitchell 2003, pp. 154, 186–201, 863–868. Spain (Madrid): Simpson 1995, pp. 250–252 (Tables A.18–A.19). Sweden: Björklund and Stenlund 1995, pp. 253–257 (Table A.20–A.22); Mitchell 2003, pp. 186–201, 863–868. United Kingdom: Feinstein 1995, pp. 264–266 (Table A.24).

Figure 5.24 Real wages in selected European countries, 1900–1993

work in several European countries, because there is little evidence of any substantial improvement in real wages in these countries before 1939. However, real wages increased much more rapidly after that date. In France, real wages increased by 192 percent between 1945 and 1993, and real wages in Norway increased by 359 percent over the same period. Despite these variations, all these countries enjoyed substantially greater increases in real wages than they had done previously.

These statistics are broadly consistent with the evidence provided by Maddison's (2003) estimates of changes in the value of each country's gross domestic product. He estimated that the average GDP per capita of 29 western European countries increased by 58 percent between 1900 and 1950, and by 315 percent between 1950 and the end of the century (see Table 5.4). His data also reveal the extent of the disparity

Table 5.4 Gross domestic product per capita (1990 international Geary–Khamis dollars)

	1900	1910	1920	1930	1940	1950	1960	1970	1980	1990	2000
Western Europe											
Austria	2,882	3,290	2,412	3,586	3,959	3,706	6,519	9,747	13,759	16,905	20,097
Belgium	3,731	4,064	3,962	4,979	4,562	5,462	6,952	10,611	14,467	17,197	20,742
Denmark	3,017	3,705	3,992	5,341	5,116	6,943	8,812	12,686	15,227	18,452	23,010
Finland	1,668	1,906	1,846	2,666	3,220	4,253	6,230	9,577	12,949	16,866	20,235
France	2,876	2,965	3,227	4,532	4,042	5,271	7,546	11,664	15,106	18,093	20,808
Germany	2,985	3,348	2,796	3,973	5,403	3,881	7,705	10,839	14,114	15,929	18,596
Italy	1,785	2,332	2,587	2,918	3,505	3,502	5,916	9,719	13,149	16,313	18,740
Netherlands	3,424	3,789	4,220	5,603	4,831	5,996	8,287	11,967	14,705	17,262	21,591
Norway	1,937	2,256	2,780	3,712	4,088	5,463	7,208	10,033	15,129	18,466	24,364
Sweden	2,561	2,980	2,802	3,937	4,857	6,739	8,688	12,716	14,937	17,695	20,321
Switzerland	3,833	4,331	4,314	6,246	6,397	9,064	12,457	16,904	18,779	21,482	22,025
United Kingdom	4,492	4,611	4,548	5,441	6,856	6,939	8,645	10,767	12,931	16,430	19,817
Ireland				2,897	3,052	3,453	4,282	6,199	8,541	11,818	22,015
Greece	1,351			2,258	2,223	1,915	3,146	6,211	8,971	9,988	12,044
Portugal	1,302	1,228	1,229	1,571	1,615	2,086	2,956	5,473	8,044	10,826	14,022
Spain	1,786	1,895	2,177	2,620	2,080	2,189	3,072	6,319	9,203	12,055	15,269
Total 29 western European countries	2,893			4,014	4,548	4,579	6,896	10,195	13,197	15,966	19,002

Eastern Europe

Albania	685	780				1,001	1,451	2,004	2,347	2,494	2,651
Bulgaria	1,223	1,456		1,284	1,548	1,651	2,912	4,773	6,044	5,597	5,365
Czechoslovakia	1,729	1,991	1,933	2,926		3,501	5,108	6,466	7,982	8,513	8,630
Hungary	1,682	2,000	1,709	2,404	2,626	2,480	3,649	5,028	6,306	6,459	7,138
Poland	1,536	1,690		1,994		2,447	3,215	4,428	5,740	5,113	7,215
Romania	1,415	1,660		1,219		1,182	1,844	2,853	4,135	3,511	3,002
Yugoslavia	902	1,057	1,031	1,318		1,551	2,437	3,755	6,063	5,779	4,258
Total 7 eastern European countries	1,438	1,636		1,448		2,111	3,070	4,315	5,786	5,450	5,804
USSR	1,237				2,144	2,841	3,945	5,575	6,426	6,878	4,351

Source: Maddison 2003.

between the continent's two halves. In 1900, the average GDP of seven eastern European countries (excluding the territories which subsequently became part of the Soviet Union) was equal to just 36 percent of the western European average, but the gap widened between 1900 and 1950 and widened still further between 1950 and 2000. Over the century as a whole, the average GDP per capita of the non-Soviet territories of eastern Europe increased by 304 percent, while GDP in western Europe increased by 557 percent.

It is also possible to compare these results with estimates of changes in food consumption in different European countries. There is relatively little evidence on the composition of European diets in the eighteenth and early nineteenth centuries but Grigg (1995, p. 248) has argued that "the starchy staples – cereals and potatoes – accounted for 65–75 percent of total calories." This reflects the fact that the majority of the population was poor, and these foods represented the cheapest source of calories.

Grigg has also attempted to summarize the available evidence on calorie consumption in a number of western European countries since 1800, and Segers (2004) has added new data for Belgium, Iceland, and the Netherlands (see Table 5.5). It appears that energy consumption rose in most parts of western Europe during the nineteenth century, although there may have been little improvement in Italy before the start of the twentieth century (see also Federico 2003, pp. 297–298, 302–304). However, these statistics have been drawn from a variety of sources and may not always be strictly comparable, and the estimates for individual countries reveal a high level of volatility.

It is probably easier to estimate changes in both the quality and the quantity of European diets in the twentieth century. The most important change, as shown in Table 5.6, was the decline in the proportion of calories derived from starchy foods and the increase in the consumption of meat and dairy products. However, this did not lead to an increase in the proportion of protein in the diet as a whole. This was because there was also an increase in the proportion of calories derived from sugars and fats, which had a lower nutritional value than the foods they replaced (Grigg 1995, p. 254).

There can be little doubt that the changes which have taken place over the last two centuries have led to an improvement in the diets consumed by large sections of the population. The expansion of social welfare programs and the improvements in real wages have ensured that even the poorest sections of the population are likely to have access to

Table 5.5 *Daily calorie consumption per head in western Europe, 1800–1960*

	1800	1810	1820	1830	1840	1850	1860	1870	1880	1890	1900	1910	1920	1930	1940	1950	1960
Belgium	2,840					2,423	2,426	2,553	2,663	2,851	2,987	3,278		2,940			3,040
England	2,436					2,512			2,773			2,977		2,810	3,060	3,120	3,280
Finland							1,900					3,000		2,950			3,110
France	1,846		1,984	2,118	2,377	2,840	2,854	3,085	3,085	3,220	3,192	3,323	3,133				
Germany	2,210						2,120										3,050
Iceland			2,887		3,080	3,381		2,573	3,002	3,106	3,316	3,499					2,960
Italy								2,647	2,197	2,119		2,617		2,627			2,730
Netherlands							2,227		2,493		2,721						
Norway		1,800			2,250		3,300										2930

Sources: Grigg 1995, p. 249; Segers 2004, p. 166. For England between 1800 and 1910, we have substituted our own figures, based on the estimates presented in Table 4.9 of the previous chapter.

Table 5.6 *The starchy staples as a percentage of all calories per capita per day*

	1810	1820	1830	1840	1850	1860	1870	1880	1890	1900	1910	1920	1930	1940	1950	1960
Belgium	70												50			37
Finland													53			37
France	77	77	77	77	75	74	72	71	71	67	64	57	54			37
Italy				72		60							63			47
Portugal													60			50
Spain													57			48
United Kingdom								56			44		39			30

Source: Grigg 1995, p. 253.

enough food to meet their basic needs, and improvements in technology, together with the growth of international trade, mean that Europeans now enjoy a much wider range of foods than previously. However, the increased availability of food, combined with lower levels of physical activity, has also promoted the spread of a different range of nutritional hazards, and these have been reflected in the growth of a range of obesity-related diseases (Grigg 1995, pp. 257–258).

Although housing may have only accounted for a small proportion of total expenditure in the past,[13] the increase in real wages also contributed to the improvement of housing conditions. This development was reinforced by falling birth rates, and by changes in social policy which led to the introduction of new bylaws governing the construction of new properties and the creation of subsidized housing programs in many European countries from the late nineteenth century onwards (Pooley 1992; Power 1993). One way of illustrating the effects of this is by looking at changes in the rate of overcrowding in different parts of western Europe between 1900 and 1975. Although some of the figures in Table 5.7 are not directly comparable with each other, it is clear that there has been a substantial reduction in the number of persons per room, and the number of persons per dwelling, since the end of the nineteenth century, and this is likely to have made a significant contribution to the reduction in the extent to which both children and adults were exposed to different types of infectious disease, including tuberculosis, during the course of the period.

In recent years, considerable attention has been paid to the relationship between urbanization and public health in the nineteenth century. Several writers have used the term "urban penalty" (Kearns 1988) to describe the disadvantages of urban living and Szreter (1988) has argued that sanitary reform, rather than improvements in diet and nutrition, was primarily responsible for the decline of mortality between 1870 and 1914. However, this conclusion rests very strongly on the experience of England and Wales, and it is interesting to compare their experience with that of other European countries.

Our understanding of the relationship between urbanization and health is complicated by the variety of ways in which the statistics of

---

[13] Allen (2001a, pp. 422, 426–427) estimated that housing costs accounted for between 5 and 10 percent of total working-class expenditure in Europe before 1914.

Table 5.7 *Housing conditions in Europe, 1900–1975*

Austria	Occupied dwellings (000s)	Persons (000s)	Rooms (000s)	Persons per dwelling	Rooms per dwelling	Persons per room	Comments
1910	847	3,509	2,591	4.14	3.06	1.35	Major cities of the Austrian monarchy
1951	2,138	6,923		3.24			
1961	2,153	6,805	5,458	3.16	2.54	1.25	1961 housing census

Belgium	Occupied dwellings (000s)	Persons (000s)	Rooms (000s)	Persons per dwelling	Rooms per dwelling	Persons per room	Comments
1910	832	2,979	3,310	3.58	3.98	0.90	Cities of ≥ 10k inhabitants
1920	953	3,080	3,492	3.23	3.66	0.88	Cities of ≥ 10k inhabitants
1930	1,113	3,507	4,669	3.15	4.19	0.75	Cities of ≥ 10k inhabitants
1947a	1,435	3,833	5,322	2.67	3.71	0.72	Cities of ≥ 10k inhabitants
1947b	2,816	8,338	10,890	2.96	3.87	0.77	Total population
1961	3,016	8,998	14,444	2.98	4.79	0.62	Total population
1970	3,135	9,493	15,865	3.03	5.06	0.60	Occupied dwellings = private households

Denmark	Occupied dwellings (000s)	Persons (000s)	Rooms (000s)	Persons per dwelling	Rooms per dwelling	Persons per room	Comments
1901	119	456	361	3.83	3.03	1.26	Copenhagen
1916	165	569	494	3.45	2.99	1.15	Copenhagen
1930	238	767	735	3.22	3.09	1.04	Copenhagen
1960	1,463	4,466	4,941	3.05	3.38	0.90	Copenhagen

	Private households (000s)	Persons (000s)	Rooms (000s)	Persons per dwelling	Rooms per dwelling	Persons per room	Comments
1965	1,578	4,629	5,510	2.93	3.49	0.84	Whole country
1970	1,743	4,780	6,251	2.74	3.59	0.76	Whole country

England and Wales	Private households (000s)	Persons (000s)	Rooms (000s)	Persons per dwelling	Rooms per dwelling	Persons per room	Comments
1911	7,943	34,606	37,800	4.36	4.76	0.92	
1921	8,739	36,180	39,786	4.14	4.55	0.91	
1931	10,233	38,042	46,036	3.72	4.50	0.83	
1961	14,641	44,543	67,009	3.04	4.58	0.66	
1971	16,434	47,119	80,692	2.87	4.91	0.58	

Finland	Occupied dwellings (000s)	Persons (000s)	Rooms (000s)	Persons per dwelling	Rooms per dwelling	Persons per room	Comments
1900	43	197	97	4.58	2.26	2.03	Helsinki, Turku, Tampere, Uleåborg; dwellings
1910	62	273	141	4.40	2.27	1.94	Helsinki, Turku, Tampere, Uleåborg; dwellings
1930	58	209	139	3.60	2.40	1.50	Helsinki; dwellings
1950	998	3,954	2,607	3.96	2.61	1.52	Whole country; dwellings
1960a	1,204	4,352	3,297	3.61	2.74	1.32	Whole country; dwellings
1960b	1,276	4,352	3,299	3.41	2.59	1.32	Whole country; households
1970	1,495	4,516	4,340	3.02	2.90	1.04	Whole country; households

Table 5.7 (*cont.*)

France	Occupied dwellings (000s)	Persons (000s)	Rooms (000s)	Persons per dwelling	Rooms per dwelling	Persons per room	Comments
1901a	1,915	5,689	5,564	2.97	2.91	1.02	Cities of ≥ 50k inhabitants
1901b	9,690	33,480	29,133	3.46	3.01	1.15	Whole country
1911	2,299	6,706	6,873	2.92	2.99	0.98	Cities of ≥ 50k inhabitants
1946	12,672	38,742	33,951	3.06	2.68	1.14	Whole country
1954	13,402	41,109	45,785	3.07	3.42	0.90	Whole country
1962	14,565	45,169	45,111	3.10	3.10	1.00	Whole country
1968	15,778	48,255	52,206	3.06	3.31	0.92	Whole country
1975	17,744	51,214	61,828	2.89	3.48	0.83	Whole country

Germany	Occupied dwellings (000s)	Persons (000s)	Rooms (000s)	Persons per dwelling	Rooms per dwelling	Persons per room	Comments
1927	8,709	33,192		3.81			Occupied dwellings; municipalities of ≥ 50k inhabitants
1950a	10,082	47,060	41,057	4.67	4.07	1.15	Including West Berlin; all dwellings
1950b	15,534	47,060	41,057	3.03	2.64	1.15	Including West Berlin; private households
1956	13,483	52,723	50,965	3.91	3.78	1.03	Including West Berlin; all dwellings; population derived from figures for 1950 and 1961 (Flora *et al.* 1987, p. 262).
1968a	19,154	58,613	81,013	3.06	4.23	0.72	Housing census; occupied dwellings

	Occupied dwellings (000s)	Persons (000s)	Rooms (000s)	Persons per dwelling	Rooms per dwelling	Persons per room	Comments
1968b	19,640	58,613	81,013	2.98	4.12	0.72	Housing census; all dwellings
1968c	20,664	58,613	81,013	2.84	3.92	0.72	Housing census; private households

Italy	Occupied dwellings (000s)	Persons (000s)	Rooms (000s)	Persons per dwelling	Rooms per dwelling	Persons per room	Comments
1911	430	2,142		4.98			Florence, Milan, Rome, Turin, Venice; population from Flora et al. 1987, p. 268.
1931a	1,263	5,220	4,161	4.13	3.29	1.25	Bologna, Catania, Florence, Genova, Milan, Naples, Palermo, Rome, Trieste, Turin, Venice
1931b	9,070	42,230	30,078	4.66	3.32	1.40	Whole country; population from Flora et al. 1987, p. 267.
1961	13,032	49,314	43,424	3.78	3.33	1.14	Whole country
1971	15,301	53,157	56,242	3.47	3.68	0.95	Whole country

Netherlands	Occupied dwellings (000s)	Persons (000s)	Rooms (000s)	Persons per dwelling	Rooms per dwelling	Persons per room	Comments
1899	1,089	5,105		4.69			Population from Flora et al. 1987, p. 270.
1909	1,267	5,859		4.62			Population from Flora et al. 1987, p. 270.
1930	1,886	7,935	8,079	4.21	4.28	0.98	Population from Flora et al. 1987, p. 270.
1947	2,050	9,138	10,120	4.46	4.94	0.90	
1971	3,894	12,589	18,847	3.23	4.84	0.67	Private households

Table 5.7 (*cont.*)

Norway	Occupied dwellings (000s)	Persons (000s)	Rooms (000s)	Persons per dwelling	Rooms per dwelling	Persons per room	Comments
1910	53	242		4.56			Oslo; population from Flora *et al.* 1987, p. 273.
1920	57	259		4.54			Oslo; population from Flora *et al.* 1987, p. 273.
1930	201	772	713	3.84	3.55	1.08	All cities
1933	64	245	165	3.83	2.58	1.48	Oslo
1946	244	815	825	3.34	3.38	0.99	All cities
1960	1,075	3,521	4,551	3.28	4.23	0.77	Whole country
1970	1,297	3,819	5,674	2.94	4.37	0.67	Whole country

Sweden	Private households (000s)	Persons (000s)	Rooms (000s)	Persons per dwelling	Rooms per dwelling	Persons per room	Comments
1930	143	473	412	3.31	2.88	1.15	Stockholm; dwellings
1945	2,082	6,707		3.22			Whole country; private households; population derived from figures for 1940 and 1950 (Flora *et al.* 1987, p. 274).
1960	2,582	7,495		2.90			Whole country; private households; population from Flora *et al.* 1987, p. 274.
1965	2,778	7,624	10,015	2.74	3.61	0.76	Whole country; 'dwelling households'

Switzerland	Private households (000s)	Persons (000s)	Rooms (000s)	Persons per dwelling	Rooms per dwelling	Persons per room	Comments
1920	883	3,743		4.24			Whole country; households
1930a	36	497	519	3.65	3.82	0.96	Basle, Berne, Zurich; dwellings
1930b	995	3,904		3.92			Whole country; households
1960	1,581	5,162	5,987	3.27	3.79	0.86	Whole country; households
1970	2,052	6,009	7,603	2.93	3.71	0.79	Whole country; households
1970	3,050	7,915	11,731	2.60	3.85	0.67	Whole country; 'dwelling households'
1975	3,325	8,016	13,263	2.41	3.99	0.60	Whole country; 'dwelling households'

Source: Flora, Kraus, and Pfenning 1987, pp. 285–333.

urban growth can be constructed. This is partly because of the different thresholds which can be used to distinguish between "urban" and "rural" areas, and partly because of differences in the ways in which different countries have defined the administrative units on which such figures might be based (e.g., Weber 1899, pp. 1–19). However, if these caveats are borne in mind, it is possible to construct a rough picture of the pattern of urban growth in different parts of western Europe since the early nineteenth century.

At the start of the nineteenth century, there were only two countries – England and Wales, and the Netherlands – in which more than a fifth of the population resided in administrative units containing more than 10,000 inhabitants (de Vries 1984, p. 45). However, although the increase in the size of the urban population in the Netherlands barely kept pace with the increase in the size of the population as a whole during the first half of the nineteenth century, the proportion of the population who lived in towns and cities containing more than 10,000 inhabitants in England and Wales almost doubled. By contrast, the majority of other western European countries only began to experience a significant level of urban growth during the second half of the nineteenth century, and these countries continued to lag well behind Britain, in terms of the level of urbanization, for much of the twentieth century (see Figure 5.25).

These statistics have important implications for the debate about the impact of urbanization on public health during this period. It is clear that urbanization occurred much later in many parts of Europe than in Britain, and this meant that they were in a rather better position to deal with its consequences. This is reflected in the measures which were introduced in many European countries during the final third of the nineteenth century and which helped to ensure that average life expectancy rates improved despite the accelerating rate of urban growth.

We can illustrate this point by examining the history of public health reform in Sweden and Norway. Sweden enjoyed a long history of interest in public health dating back to the mid eighteenth century, but this was prompted by fears of population decline and tended to emphasize the importance of personal responsibility for health improvement. However, a Public Health Act was passed in 1857 and this encouraged several towns, including Uppsala and Gävle, to establish health committees (Widding 2006). The pace of reform accelerated in line with the rate of urbanization during the 1870s and 1880s, when a further Public Health Act was passed and local Boards of Health took responsibility

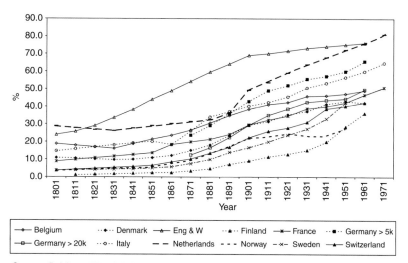

Sources: Belgium: 1800: de Vries 1984, p. 45; England and Wales: 1801–1911: Law 1967, p. 141; 1931, 1961: Wood and Carter 2000, pp. 416–417; France: 1800: de Vries 1984, p. 45; Italy: 1800, 1850: de Vries 1984, p. 45; Netherlands: 1800–1889: Weber 1899, p. 115; Switzerland: 1800: de Vries 1984, p. 45. All other data from Flora, Kraus, and Pfenning 1987, pp. 247–281.

Figure 5.25 Percentage of the population of selected European countries residing in towns and cities containing more than 10,000 inhabitants

for the control of pollution and the improvement of water supplies (Johannisson 1994, pp. 172–173; Nelson and Rogers 1994, pp. 21–26). A similar pattern emerged in Norway, following the introduction of a permissive Health Law in 1860. The country's two largest cities, Kristiania (Oslo) and Bergen, both took steps to introduce clean water supplies, although only Bergen linked this to an efficient system of waste removal. Further measures were introduced during the 1890s, including the isolation of suspected disease carriers, the regulation of food quality, and the introduction of new housing regulations (Hubbard 2000, pp. 345–346).

The expansion of sanitary activity was particularly noticeable in Germany. According to Hennock (Hennock 2000, pp. 273–280), the Prussian authorities showed little interest in sanitary reform during the 1850s and 1860s, even though urban death rates were significantly higher than those found in more rural areas. However, during the 1870s municipal investment in public health increased rapidly, and the proportion of the urban population which was served with waterworks increased from just 3 percent in 1867 to 86 percent in 1895. This investment helped to ensure that the crude death rate in Prussian cities fell from 30.7 deaths per thousand during the cholera epidemic of 1865–1867 to 19.2 in 1905 (Brown 1988; Brown 2000, pp. 307–308; Vögele 1998; Vögele *et al.* 2000; Lee and Vögele 2001).

Although this section has emphasized the importance of environmental and nutritional improvements, it is also important to recognize the significance of developments in the provision of health care, especially during the twentieth century. During the late nineteenth and early twentieth centuries, several countries introduced voluntary or compulsory health insurance schemes, beginning with Germany in 1884. The earliest schemes were limited to the provision of cash benefits, but they were gradually extended to include the provision of medical care, initially to insured workers, but subsequently (in many cases) to their dependants (Flora and Alber 1982, pp. 52–59). The provision of medical services continued to expand after 1945. According to Carine Boonen (Boonen 2004, p. 46), public health expenditure accounted for approximately 75 percent of the European Union's total health expenditure between 1960 and 2000, and the member states of the EU devoted 8.69 percent of their GDP to health services at the start of the new millennium (World Health Organisation 2006). Much of this increase was fueled by the development of new techniques and forms of treatment which had a significant impact on the survival prospects of people of all ages (see Chapter 4).

5.4 Health and economic development

During the last decade, economists and economic historians have devoted increasing attention to the ways in which health improvement can be a cause of economic development as well as a (possible) consequence of development. There is now a very substantial literature which emphasizes the role which health can play in improving the economic well-being of individuals and nations. Much of this literature has focused on the role played by health in low-income countries and in cross-sectional comparisons between low-income countries and high-income countries, but there is also growing interest in the ways in which investment in health can continue to generate economic benefits in countries which are already economically advanced (Suhrcke *et al.* 2005).

It is easy to see why improvement in health should promote economic development. One of the most frequently cited arguments emphasizes the impact of child health on education and schooling. It has often been argued that parents are more likely to invest in their children's education if they are confident that the children will survive into adulthood, and that healthier children attend school more regularly. There is also considerable evidence to show that the premature death of a parent can have an adverse impact on school attendance, even though the extent of this can be mitigated by family and community support, and the effect of variations in child health on school learning is less conclusive (Miguel 2005, pp. 163–164).

Improvements in health can also promote economic improvement in other ways. A number of authors have argued that improvements in adult health can help to reduce the amount of time taken off work due to illness, although the extent of this may be limited by what Johansson (Johansson 1991; Johansson 1992) has called "the cultural inflation of morbidity." However, there is considerable evidence to show that poor health does affect labor productivity in poor countries. As Strauss and Thomas (Strauss and Thomas 1998, pp. 811–812) concluded: "several studies indicate that poor health reduces labor force participation ... [and] there is abundant evidence that a range of dimensions of health do reap a reward in the labor market."

Much of the literature on health and development has tended to focus on the immediate impact of health variations on variables such as education and labor productivity, but it is also important to consider the impact of health improvements in a longitudinal and intergenerational perspective. We can illustrate this at a very basic level by considering the impact of improved survival rates on the reproductive capacity of successive generations in Sweden between 1751 and 1909. In the decade between 1751 and 1760, 324,966 female children were born, and 200,544 of these children survived until their fifteenth birthday; the total number of years lived by these children between the ages of 15 and 44 was (324,966 × 15.76834) = 5,124,174. In the first decade of the twentieth century, the total number of female births was 666,249, and the total number of years lived between the ages of 15 and 44 was (666,249 × 23.570085) = 15,703,546. The total number of births increased by a factor of 2.05, and the total number of years lived between the ages of 15 and 44 (the "childbearing years") increased by a factor of 3.06 (Table 5.8).

Table 5.8 *Number of years lived between the age of 15 and 44 in three Swedish birth cohorts*

	1751–60	1830–39	1900–09
Number of female births in decade	324,966	461,507	666,249
Proportion surviving to age 15 (per 100,000 births)	61,712	72,439	85,727
Years lived between the ages of 15 and 44 (per 100,000 births)	1,576,834	1,927,649	2,357,009
Number surviving to age 15	200,544	334,311	571,155
Person-years lived between the ages of 15 and 44	5,124,174	8,896,233	15,703,546

Source: Human Mortality Database (www.mortality.org).

Improvements in the survival rates of both children and adults also had implications for the size of the workforce and for the productive capacity of each generation. This can also be illustrated with the aid of the Swedish data. In the decade between 1751 and 1760, 664,211 people were born, of whom 401,400 survived to the age of 15. The total number of "working years" for this cohort, including both the male and female populations, was 15,034,630. By contrast, the total number of working years for those born between 1830 and 1839 was 27,609,398 and the total for those born between 1900 and 1909 was 52,739,033 (see Table 5.9). The improvement in survival rates contributed to the increase directly, by increasing the number of people who survived to each age and, indirectly, as a result of increases in reproductive capacity.

Although these figures tell a largely optimistic story about the relationship between health and economic growth, they also help to highlight one of the major challenges facing western (and non-western) countries in the future. As we have already seen, the improvement in child and adult survival rates has led to a substantial increase in the working capacity of each generation, but the figures also show the increase in the proportion of individuals who have survived beyond what is normally regarded as "working age," and in the number of additional years they can expect to live (see also Figure 5.26). This underlines the need for new thinking to consider the ways in which older members of the population can maintain their living standards in the future.

Table 5.9 *Number of years lived at each age for both sexes, Sweden, 1751–1912*

Period	Number of births	Years lived at each age, per 100,000 births			Years lived at each age, per cohort			% of years lived at each age		
		0–14	15–64	≥65	0–14	15–64	≥65	0–14	15–64	≥65
1751–1759	595,827	1,006,491	2,264,088	237,773	5,996,945	13,490,048	1,416,716	28.7	64.5	6.8
1760–1769	678,545	977,826	2,203,407	235,016	6,634,989	14,951,105	1,594,686	28.6	64.5	6.9
1770–1779	666,308	994,285	2,269,502	252,185	6,624,997	15,121,870	1,680,329	28.3	64.5	7.2
1780–1789	698,220	1,026,609	2,379,068	277,183	7,167,986	16,611,129	1,935,344	27.9	64.6	7.5
1790–1799	759,482	1,042,191	2,429,678	309,869	7,915,253	18,452,967	2,353,399	27.6	64.2	8.2
1800–1809	729,472	1,027,993	2,450,918	345,155	7,498,917	17,878,761	2,517,805	26.9	64.1	9.0
1810–1819	819,383	1,073,363	2,671,433	426,857	8,794,950	21,889,268	3,497,590	25.7	64.0	10.2
1820–1829	943,478	1,123,261	2,863,736	503,365	10,597,720	27,018,714	4,749,133	25.0	63.8	11.2
1830–1839	944,826	1,129,667	2,922,168	548,904	10,673,388	27,609,398	5,186,183	24.6	63.5	11.9
1840–1849	1,016,087	1,141,336	2,956,112	571,522	11,596,962	30,036,665	5,807,161	24.4	63.3	12.2
1850–1859	1,171,430	1,129,434	2,956,184	584,918	13,230,529	34,629,620	6,851,899	24.2	63.3	12.5
1860–1869	1,294,397	1,153,912	3,061,582	621,391	14,936,196	39,629,026	8,043,260	23.9	63.3	12.8
1870–1879	1,322,877	1,171,492	3,131,251	670,927	15,497,392	41,422,599	8,875,532	23.6	63.0	13.5
1880–1889	1,358,865	1,224,043	3,337,505	770,437	16,633,085	45,352,187	10,469,199	23.0	62.6	14.4
1890–1899	1,334,184	1,262,953	3,536,535	893,634	16,850,117	47,183,884	11,922,715	22.2	62.1	15.7
1900–1909	1,370,922	1,312,095	3,846,976	1,064,416	17,987,799	52,739,033	14,592,313	21.1	61.8	17.1
1910–1912	401,470	1,340,736	4,024,262	1,172,116	5,382,653	16,156,203	4,705,692	20.5	61.6	17.9

Source: Human Mortality Database (www.mortality.org).

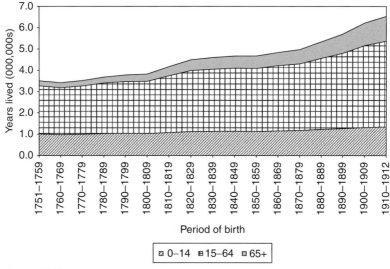

Source: Table 5.9.

Figure 5.26 Number of person-years in each age group, by birth cohort: Sweden, 1751–1912

A number of authors have attempted to measure the impact of differences in health status on levels of economic growth on an international basis. Barro (1996, p. 14) found that "the relation between health status and subsequent growth is clearly positive, roughly linear (in the log of life expectancy) and . . . not driven by outliers," and Jamison, Lau, and Wiang (2004, p. ii; 2005, p. 81) concluded that changes in adult ($_{45}q_{15}$) mortality rates accounted for approximately 11 percent of the total growth in income in 53 countries between 1965 and 1990. Bloom, Canning, and Sevilla (2001, p. 18) concluded that each extra year of life expectancy was associated with an increase of 4 percent in output in an international analysis of changes in growth rates between 1960 and 1990. Sala-i-Martin, Doppelhofer, and Miller (2004) found that health ranked eighth out of 18 variables that were significantly related to growth when they examined the impact of 68 separate variables on growth rates in 88 countries between 1960 and 2000. However, while these results are highly instructive, they are also limited to what is, in historical terms, a relatively short time span (see also Arora 2001; Arora 2005). It is therefore worth making the effort to investigate the impact of health changes on changes in GDP over a longer period.

Table 5.10 *The impact of changes in health on changes in GDP per capita*

Country	e_0 period	GDP period	Constant	$\Delta e_{0fem(-40)}$	R^2	Sig
Denmark	1841–1960	1881–2000	719.378	351.031	0.136	0.264
England and Wales	1841–1960	1881–2000	107.067	408.055	0.490	0.016
France	1811–1960	1851–2000	360.283	372.956	0.320	0.035
Norway	1841–1960	1881–2000	795.269	508.728	0.389	0.054
Netherlands	1851–1960	1891–2000	536.247	284.116	0.121	0.325
Sweden	1781–1960	1821–2000	386.320	276.149	0.237	0.047

Sources: e_0: Human Mortality Database (www.mortality.org); GDP per capita: Maddison 2003.

Table 5.10 attempts to do this by examining the relationship between changes in health (measured by female life expectancy at birth) and changes in GDP per capita in six western European countries. Here, Δe_{0fem} = changes in health between consecutive decades, and ΔGDP = changes in GDP per capita between consecutive decades. We have chosen female life expectancy at birth as the health indicator in order to reduce the impact of war-related deaths on the male population during the Franco-Prussian War and the two World Wars, and the impact of changes in life expectancy on changes in GDP per capita is shown with a lag of forty years.[14] Although not all the results are statistically significant, they support the view that improvements in health (as indicated by changes in female life expectancy) have been associated with increases in economic performance. The signs on the independent variable are consistently positive, and changes in the health indicator appear to explain between 12 and 49 percent of the variation in changes in GDP per capita.

This conclusion is also supported by Suchit Arora's analysis of the relationship between health and economic performance in ten countries, including all the countries listed in Table 5.10, together with two additional European countries (Finland and Italy) and two non-European countries (Japan and Australia). Arora examined a wider range of health indicators (he included life expectancy at birth and at the ages of five, ten, fifteen, and twenty, together with estimates of adult

---

[14] The lag period is derived from Sala-i-Martin, Doppelhofer, and Miller's (2004) finding that life expectancy in 1960 was closely related to the growth rate in GDP per capita between 1960 and 2000.

stature), and used a cointegration method to assess their impact on the rate of economic growth. He concluded that improvements in health helped to raise the annual average rate of growth in all ten countries from 1.25 percent per annum to 1.95 percent per annum over a period of 120 years. If health standards had not improved, average output per capita would have been reduced by 56 percent at the end of this period (Arora 2001, p. 717; see also Arora 2005).

Some authors have argued that the returns to health are likely to vary with the level of economic development. Strauss and Thomas (1998, p. 813) found that "a small number of studies suggest that health has a large return at very low levels of health and (perhaps) in jobs requiring more strength. With economic development, these types of jobs will shrink, and one might expect the labor market impact of improved health to decline, especially relative to the impact of education and skill acquisition." However, although there has been rather less research into the effect of health on the performance of more advanced economies, there are a number of ways in which health improvements can continue to promote economic growth in the future. As López-Casasnovas, Rivera, and Currais (2005, p. 6) have argued, "even under decreasing marginal returns, fighting obesity, alcohol abuse, smoking, drug addiction, and lack of exercise improves industrial output, lowers absenteeism, and reduces losses of human capital (and social investment opportunities) for the economy."

One of the most controversial ways in which poor health affects overall economic performance is through its influence on the decision to retire. As Suhrcke *et al.* (2005, pp. 49–51, 87–88) have pointed out, there are a number of studies from Europe and America which suggest that ill-health plays "a significant and robust role . . . in anticipating the decision to retire from the labor force" and their findings suggest that improvements in the health of older people may play an important part in helping them to remain in the workforce for longer. This is therefore an issue of major importance, not only for the welfare of older people themselves, but also for the relationship between health and economic performance more generally.

5.5 Future prospects

During the last fifty years, there has been a significant increase in the life expectancy of European populations at higher ages. In 1950, average

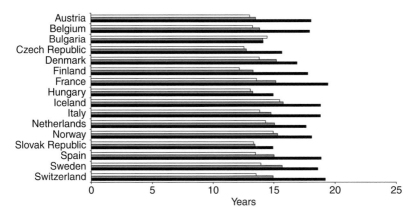

Source: Human Mortality Database (www.mortality.org).

| □ 1950 ▪ 1970 ▪ 2000 |

Figure 5.27 Life expectancy at age 65 in selected European countries, 1950–2000

life expectancy at the age of 65 in sixteen predominantly western European countries was 13.69; by 2000 this figure had risen to 17.50 (see Figure 5.27). These figures reflect the fact that mortality rates have declined at all ages since the end of the Second World War. However, some writers have questioned the extent to which these improvements have been accompanied by an increase in *healthy* life expectancy. In some cases, it has been claimed that the majority of the years which have been added to life are years of disability (Gruenberg 1977; Olshansky *et al.* 1991).

In Chapter 4, we reviewed some of this evidence in relation, particularly, to Britain and the United States. We showed that, despite initial fears, there is now growing evidence to suggest that the incidence of chronic disability has declined at each age and that the extent of "healthy life expectancy" has increased. Although it is difficult to find evidence from European countries which is directly comparable with some of the US evidence, the majority of the evidence which does exist suggests that healthy life expectancy in Europe has increased since the early 1980s.

One of the main difficulties in assessing the extent of "healthy" or "disease-free" life expectancy is the choice of indicator. In one recent study, Perenboom *et al.* (2005) found that morbidity-free life expectancy in the Netherlands had decreased by 0.8 years (in the case of men) and by 4.3 years (in the case of women) between 1989 and 2000, but they also suggested that "part of this decrease could be attributed to earlier diagnosis of chronic diseases. Although their findings suggested that the number of morbidity-free years had declined, other investigators found that the number of disability-free years and the extent of "life expectancy in well-being" had increased.

In the view of possible impact of diagnostic factors on the recording of chronic disease rates, the majority of authors have preferred to focus on alternative measures of "healthy life expectancy." These studies normally rely on data from health surveys in which respondents are asked to state whether they are suffering from any functional impairment or disability (Mutafova *et al.* 1996; Gutiérrez-Fisac, Gispert, and Solà 2000; Cambois, Robine, and Hayward 2001; Winblad *et al.* 2001; Michel 2002; Otero *et al.* 2004), or to describe their current health status according to whether it is "very good," "good," "fair," "poor," or "very poor" (Van Oyen, Tafforeau, and Roelands 1996; Regidor *et al.* 1999; Doblhammer and Kytir 2001; Van Oers 2002; Groenewegen, Westert, and Boshuizen 2003; Bossuyt *et al.* 2004; Kalèdienè and Petrauskienè 2004; Brønnum-Hansen 2005; Treurniet *et al.* 2005), or a combination of the two (Valkonen, Sihvonen, and Lahelma 1997; Sihvonen *et al.* 1998; Dalstra *et al.* 2002). The subjective nature of these assessments means that one needs to be particularly cautious when attempting to compare the results across time or space, but some broad patterns are beginning to emerge.

A number of writers have attempted to compare regional variations in life expectancy with similar variations in healthy life expectancy within national populations. In the Netherlands, Groenewegen, Westert, and Boshuizen (2003) found that "the correlation between life expectancy and healthy life expectancy for each region is moderately strong for men ... [but] much weaker for women," and that for women, "regional life expectancy and healthy life expectancy are nearly independent of each other." However, Van Oyen, Tafforeau, and Roelands (1996) observed no such discrepancy in their analysis of regional inequities in health expectancy in Belgium. Their results showed that men and women in the Flemish region lived longer and healthier lives than men and women in the Walloon region. Walloon-speakers experienced a greater number of unhealthy years, in both absolute and relative terms.

Other studies have suggested that there is also a close association between educational qualifications, life expectancy and healthy life expectancy. Bossuyt *et al.* (2004) found that people with a low level of education "have fewer years in good perceived health and can expect more years in poor health in their shorter lives," and Valkonen and his colleagues obtained similar results when they investigated the extent of health inequalities in Finland and Norway. In both countries, the more highly educated segment of the population enjoyed longer and healthier lives, and could expect to spend a higher proportion of their lives in good health (Valkonen, Sihvonen, and Lahelma 1997; Sihvonen *et al.* 1998).

These results suggest that sections of the population with the lowest mortality rates also enjoy the highest levels of healthy life expectancy, but life expectancy and healthy life expectancy may not show the same relationship over time. Winblad *et al.* (2001) investigated the incidence of disability among three Finnish cohorts who were examined by a trained nurse in 1979, 1989, and 1999 when they were aged 75 or over. They concluded that "as far as the whole aged populations were concerned, longer life was not accompanied by improving health" (p. 1019). However, the age- and sex-compositions of the three groups were not identical and an analysis of the results for separate groups of men and women between the ages of 75 and 79 yields a rather more complicated picture. The figures shown in Table 5.11 suggest that disability rates rose among men and women between 1979 and 1989, but they fell between 1989 and 1999, and were lower at the end of the period than they had been at the beginning.

Although Winblad *et al.* were largely, though not entirely, pessimistic about the relationship between health and life expectancy, other authors have argued that improvements in health expectancy and life expectancy are related.[15] In Denmark, Brønnum-Hansen (2005) found

---

[15] Although Winblad *et al.* argued that "longer life was not accompanied by improving health," they also concluded that "the third cohort, born in 1923 or earlier, has enjoyed relatively good health and social care services and a higher standard of living for 20 years longer than the cohort born in 1903 or earlier. This has not, so far, led to a decreasing rate of disability in the total population. There may be, however, a promising trend among the female cohorts entering old age. Further research may show whether this predicts improving functional abilities even among men or the older age groups" (2001, p. 1023).

Table 5.11 *Prevalence of disability in three birth cohorts aged 75–79 over twenty years*

	1979 (born ≤ 1903)			1989 (born ≤ 1913)			1999 (born ≤ 1923)		
	Disabled	All	Disabled as % of total	Disabled	All	Disabled as % of total	Disabled	All	Disabled as % of total
Male	8	59	13.6	21	93	22.6	17	132	12.9
Female	24	100	24.0	47	174	27.0	32	209	15.3
All	32	159	20.1	68	267	25.5	49	341	14.4

Source: Winblad *et al.* 2001.

that the time spent with long-term illness had increased, but people aged 65 and over spent less time with long-term disabilities and could expect to enjoy a greater number of years in self-rated "good health." Similar results have also been reported by investigators in Austria (Doblhammer and Kytir 2001), France (Cambois, Robine, and Hayward 2001), Lithuania (Kalėdienė and Petrauskienė 2004), the Netherlands (Van Oers 2002), Spain (Otero *et al.* 2004), and Switzerland (Michel 2002). In Austria, Doblhammer and Kytir (2001, pp. 389–390) examined changes in life expectancy and healthy life expectancy among men and women aged sixty and above between 1978 and 1998 and found that "not only life expectancy but also healthy life expectancy significantly rose over the study period ... The positive trend in healthy life expectancy and in the health ratio (i.e. the ratio of 'healthy years' to total years) is present in all age groups above age sixty."

Although these results are broadly positive, they are not unequivocally so. Robine and his co-authors have examined data from a range of countries and obtained somewhat mixed results. They found that the number of years lived with minor disabilities had increased but there was little or no change in the number of years lived with severe disabilities, despite increases in life expectancy. However, they rejected suggestions that these results indicated an "expansion of morbidity" (Olshansky *et al.* 1991). They concluded that the evidence was more consistent with Manton's concept of a "dynamic equilibrium," in which improvements in life expectancy were accompanied by a deceleration in the rate at which chronic diseases progressed (Manton 1982; Robine, Cambois, and Romieu 1999; Robine, Romieu, and Cambois 1999, p. 183).

The results of these surveys also raise questions about future trends in life expectancy. The last century witnessed dramatic reductions in childhood mortality and improvements in other child health indicators. In view of the impressive body of evidence which has been assembled by a growing army of medical and epidemiological researchers, there are good reasons for believing that these improvements will continue to influence developments at older ages for many years to come. This is in addition to any further changes which may affect survival rates at older ages as a result of improvements in social and economic conditions, systems of social support, and medical technology.

Although there are many indications that life expectancy at older ages is increasing, some observers may feel that these conclusions underestimate the capacity of European populations to engage in activities which are deleterious to health, such as cigarette smoking, and excessive food consumption. However, although cigarette smoking has undoubtedly acted as a barrier to health improvement over the course of the last century, there is considerable evidence to suggest that its incidence has declined, particularly in western Europe, over the last twenty years. In 2005, the OECD found that the proportion of smokers in ten European countries, including the United Kingdom, had declined from an average of 36.8 percent in 1980 to 25.4 percent in 2003 (OECD 2005, table 4.3).[16]

The decline in the incidence of cigarette smoking has meant that an increasing amount of attention has been devoted to the problem of obesity (e.g., International Obesity Taskforce 2002). Even though some of the concerns about obesity levels among younger children may have been exaggerated, it is clear that obesity has increased among older children and adults, and this condition is known to be closely associated with diabetes, hypertension, coronary heart disease, asthma, and poor health status (Mokdad *et al.* 2003; Centers for Disease Control 2006). This evidence suggests that the rise in obesity represents one of the major challenges which need to be faced if European populations are to build on the advantages which a century of economic and social progress has bequeathed (see also James 2008).

---

[16] The other countries were Belgium, Denmark, Finland, France, Germany, Italy, the Netherlands, Norway, and Sweden.

Appendix E

Table E.1 *Height, weight, and BMI of children in selected European countries, 1865–1997*

| | Year of measurement | Boys | | | | Girls | | | Percentiles of NCHS height standards | |
		Age	Height (m)	Weight (kg)	BMI (w/h²)	Height (m)	Weight (kg)	BMI (w/h²)	Boys Percentile	Girls Percentile
Croatia (Zagreb)	1951	9.0	1.292	26.4	15.82	1.282	26.0	15.82	30.06	27.73
	1964	9.0	1.324	28.6	16.32	1.320	28.5	16.36	51.39	48.82
	1973	9.0	1.345	30.6	16.92	1.337	30.7	17.17	65.57	58.77
	1982	9.0	1.365	31.6	16.96	1.350	30.4	16.68	77.31	66.09
	1991	9.0	1.367	32.7	17.50	1.357	32.1	17.43	78.35	69.74
Czech Republic	1951	9.0	1.314	28.2	16.33	1.305	27.9	16.38	44.46	40.09
	1961	9.0	1.326	29.1	16.55	1.316	28.8	16.63	52.78	46.47
	1971	9.0	1.338	29.8	16.62	1.331	29.6	16.69	61.24	55.46
	1981	9.0	1.346	30.2	16.70	1.339	29.9	16.65	65.95	59.97
	1991	9.0	1.359	30.7	16.62	1.355	30.4	16.54	73.93	68.70
France	1955	8.0	1.253	24.7	15.73	1.239	23.8	15.50	11.47	11.07
	1985	8.0	1.280	27.0	16.48	1.264	25.7	16.09	23.22	19.58

Germany (Jena)	1880	9.0	1.232	24.1	15.85	1.223	23.0	15.34	5.85	7.18
	1921	9.0	1.281	26.5	16.12	1.276	25.4	15.60	23.75	24.84
	1932	9.0	1.305	26.5	15.56	1.297	26.3	15.65	38.35	35.32
	1944	9.0	1.313	27.2	15.78	1.292	25.9	15.52	43.77	32.88
	1954	9.0	1.311	27.5	16.00	1.322	26.9	15.39	42.40	50.00
	1964	9.0	1.326	27.5	15.64	1.314	27.5	15.93	52.78	45.30
	1975	9.0	1.359	30.0	16.24	1.344	28.8	15.94	74.04	62.74
	1985	9.0	1.360	29.5	15.95	1.338	28.2	15.75	74.60	59.34
	1995	9.0	1.361	30.7	16.57	1.360	31.0	16.76	75.16	71.27
Greece (Athens)	1920	9.0	1.200			1.224			1.68	7.39
	1928	9.0	1.271			1.262			18.71	18.77
	1931	9.0	1.268			1.262			17.34	18.77
	1968	9.0	1.339			1.332			61.65	55.87
	1995	9.0	1.350			1.347			68.72	64.40
Hungary	1910–20	9.0	1.242			1.235			8.28	9.96
	1981–84	9.0	1.332			1.324			56.57	51.42
Italy	<1939	9.0	1.247	25.8	16.58	1.238	24.7	16.12	9.51	10.44
	1951–65	9.0	1.288	27.2	16.38	1.278	26.7	16.38	27.51	25.74
	1970–71	9.0	1.330	30.4	17.19	1.322	30.1	17.21	55.54	49.70
	1993?	9.0	1.320	30.7	17.62	1.310	30.2	17.60	48.61	42.96
Netherlands	1865 (Orphans)	6.5	1.020			1.029			0.05	0.34
	1865 (Schoolchildren)	6.5	1.060			1.059			0.60	1.56

Table E.1 (*cont.*)

Year of measurement	Age	Boys			Girls			Percentiles of NCHS height standards	
		Height (m)	Weight (kg)	BMI (w/h²)	Height (m)	Weight (kg)	BMI (w/h²)	Boys Percentile	Girls Percentile
1965 (Lower SES)	6.5	1.199			1.194			56.91	62.99
1965 (Higher SES)	6.5	1.224			1.220			74.46	79.11
1965 (Mean)	6.5	*1.212*			*1.207*			66.13	71.60
1965 (National)	6.5	120.8	22.3	15.28	1.204	22.0	15.18	63.62	69.70
1980 (Lower SES)	6.5	1.217			1.211			69.92	74.04
1980 (Higher SES)	6.5	1.227			1.219			76.29	78.58
1980 (Mean)	6.5	*1.222*			*1.215*			73.20	76.37
1997 (National)	6.5	1.234	23.8	15.61	1.220	23.3	15.63	79.99	78.85
Norway (Oslo) 1920	9.0	1.261	25.3	15.91	1.253	24.6	15.67	14.40	15.41
1925	9.0	1.286	26.2	15.84	1.278	25.7	15.74	26.53	25.79
1930	9.0	1.306	27.2	15.95	1.297	27.0	16.05	39.02	35.60
1935	9.0	1.321	28.1	16.10	1.313	28.0	16.24	49.31	44.71
1940	9.0	1.333	28.9	16.26	1.326	28.8	16.38	57.60	52.36
1943	9.0	1.329	27.7	15.68	1.317	27.3	15.74	56.86	47.05
1945	9.0	1.325	27.9	15.89	1.314	27.5	15.93	52.09	45.30
1947	9.0	1.337	29.6	16.56	1.332	29.6	16.68	60.31	55.87

1950	9.0	1.345	30.1	16.64	1.333	29.6	16.66	65.57	56.45
1955	9.0	1.347	29.8	16.42	1.337	29.6	16.56	66.84	58.77
1960	9.0	1.345	30.0	16.58	1.335	29.6	16.61	65.57	57.61
1965	9.0	1.349	29.8	16.38	1.342	29.3	16.27	68.10	61.62
1970	9.0	1.350	29.6	16.24	1.338	29.6	16.53	68.72	59.34
1975	9.0	1.355	29.5	16.07	1.350	29.2	16.02	71.73	66.04
1980	9.0				1.346	29.5	16.28		63.85
1985	9.0				1.350	30.3	16.63		66.04
Poland									
1955 (Cities)	7.0	1.198			1.176			35.92	30.00
1955 (Towns)	7.0	1.187			1.178			28.46	31.22
1955 (Villages)	7.0	1.177			1.166			22.39	24.22
1966 (Cities)	7.0	1.207			1.192			42.47	40.33
1966 (Towns)	7.0	1.199			1.192			36.63	40.33
1966 (Villages)	7.0	1.180			1.168			24.13	25.32
1978 (Cities)	7.0	1.241			1.223			67.56	61.68
1978 (Towns)	7.0	1.212			1.206			46.22	50.00
1978 (Villages)	7.0	1.200			1.191			37.35	39.66
1988 (Cities)	7.0	1.239			1.233			66.18	68.15
1988 (Towns)	7.0	1.219			1.211			51.52	53.48
1988 (Villages)	7.0	1.212			1.203			46.22	47.91
Slovenia									
(Ljubljana)									
1939/40	11.0	1.396	32.5	16.68	1.413	33.1	16.58	29.48	31.63
1969/70	11.0	1.448	37.2	17.74	147.1	39.1	18.07	58.66	62.33
1991/92	11.0	1.467	39.4	18.31	148.8	40.0	18.07	68.99	70.76

Table E.1 (cont.)

	Year of measurement	Age	Boys Height (m)	Weight (kg)	BMI (w/h²)	Girls Height (m)	Weight (kg)	BMI (w/h²)	Percentiles of NCHS height standards Boys Percentile	Girls Percentile
Spain (Barcelona)	<1918	13.0	1.410						3.41	
	1944/45 (Lower class)	13.0	1.426						5.12	
	1944/45 (Upper class)	13.0	1.508						24.97	
	1944/45 (Mean)	13.0	1.467						12.42	
	1969 (Urban)	13.0	1.568						51.50	
	1978/79 (Urban)	13.0	1.574						54.08	
Spain (Madrid)	<1896	13.0	1.378						1.39	
	<1954 (Urban)	13.0	1.501						22.58	
	<1985 (Alcalá de Henares)	13.0	1.587						60.30	
	<1988 (Rural)	13.0	1.542						39.38	

Sweden	1883	13.0	1.420	36.1	17.90	1.455	37.8	17.86	4.40	4.57
	1938/39	13.0	1.536	42.7	18.10	1.550	44.3	18.44	36.65	37.99
	1965/71	13.0	1.562	43.6	17.87	1.586	46.0	18.29	48.59	58.64

Sources: Croatia (Zagreb): Prebeg, Jureša, Kujundžič 1995, p. 101; Czech Republic: Vignerová and Bláha 1998, pp. 97–100; France: Demoulin 1998, p. 127; Germany (Jena): Jaeger 1998, pp. 140–141; Greece (Athens): Papadimtriou 1998, p. 165; Hungary: Bodzsár 1998, p. 177; Italy: Floris and Sanna 1998, pp. 210–213; Netherlands: Burgmeijer and Wieringen 1998, p. 246; Van Wieringen *et al.* 1971, pp. 18–19, 24; Fredriks *et al.* 2000, p. 319; Norway (Oslo): Brundtland, Liestøl, and Walløe 1980, pp. 311–312; Liestøl and Rosenberg 1995, p. 201; Poland: Bielicki and Hulanicka 1998, pp. 270–272; Slovenia (Ljubljana): Štefančič and Tomoazo-Favnik 1998, p. 284; Spain (Barcelona): Rebato 1998, pp. 307–308; Spain (Madrid): Rebato 1998, pp. 307–308; Sweden: Ljung, Bergsten-Brucefors, and Dindgren 1974, pp. 247–249; NCHS height standards: Steckel 1995a, pp. 14–15, 18–19.

Notes: NCHS = National Center for Health Statistics.

SES = socioeconomic status. In the Dutch studies whose results are reported in this table, it was defined by father's occupational status (Burgmeijer and Van Wieringen 1998, pp. 233, 246).

6 | *The American experience of technophysio evolution*

In the preceding chapters, we have explored how the health indicators of British and European populations – stature, mortality, and morbidity – have evolved over the past three centuries. That evolution was a process of adapting to the long-term changes in social, environmental, and nutritional factors that have been substantially influenced by techno-logical progress in various fields. One lesson from the preceding chap-ters is that the experience of technophysio evolution varied across countries, mainly depending on country-specific trends of diet and environment. During the course of the past three centuries, America shared the experiences of urbanization, industrialization, and agricul-tural progress with Britain and European countries, but there existed differences as well as similarities. America uniquely observed dynamic demographic, social, and economic features such as mass migration from Europe, slavery, the opening up of unexploited land, overcoming the variety of disease environments, and so on. America also developed institutions and technologies that are peculiar to those unique experi-ences. Thus, the study of American experiences and its comparison with British and European experiences deepens our understanding of technophysio evolution.

Since the eighteenth century, changes in human development in Europe have been tied, to a large extent, to the acceleration of economic change. As we have already seen, economic historians now believe that the pace of economic change during the eighteenth century was some-what slower than an earlier generation of historians may have supposed but the cumulative effect of the changes which did occur was never-theless dramatic. Although there is a continuing debate over the impact of industrialization on the standard of living in the short to medium term, it nevertheless laid the foundations for the long-term improve-ment in both health and living standards of the population since the end of the eighteenth century (Deane and Cole 1967; Crafts and Harley 1992; Floud and Harris 1997; Clark 2007).

The same period was a time of challenge for the American colonies. Compared to Europe, colonial America was primitive in the sense that it did not have advanced markets for exchange. The settlers of this new world faced rough frontiers to explore for self-sufficiency. Thus, the early experience of technophysio evolution in America was a course of adapting to new land and environments.

Fortunately, the harshness of colonial life was tempered by the profusion of natural resources and favorable epidemiological environments. The climate and soil were suitable for more productive harvests, even though agricultural tools were wretched, and the small population living in a vast expanse of land prevented the contagion of infectious diseases (Carr 1992; McWilliams 2005).[1] This ecological environment was so beneficial that Americans of the period were relatively better nourished and healthier than European populations throughout the colonial era even though the sophistication of American agricultural technology and medicine was far behind that of England and western European countries. In terms of stature and life expectancy, which have been widely used to measure the standard of living of a population, American white males were taller than European males and had achieved longer life expectancy toward the start of the nineteenth century.[2]

---

[1] Richard Hakluyt, an active promoter of English colonization of North America, looked at the colonial landscape and predicted that the colonies, once established, would "yelde unto all the commodities of Europe, Affrica, and Asia . . . and supply the wants of all our decayed trades" (McWilliams 2005).

[2] Even though we need to control for genetic and biological factors to compare two populations' heights, many sources suggest that colonial Americans were taller than populations in the United Kingdom and other European countries throughout the second half of the eighteenth century. During those periods, the average height of native-born American adult males is estimated to be around 172–173 cm, and that of United Kingdom – estimated from adult recruits – is 165–169 cm (Fogel 1986b; Floud, Wachter, and Gregory 1990). Figure 5.1 in Chapter 5 also shows that the average height of adult males in continental Europe was 163–167 cm at the beginning of the nineteenth century.

In addition, the estimated life expectancy at age 10 for American native-born white males who were born in the fourth quarter of the eighteenth century is about 52 years, which is greater than the 46 years for the British peerage in the same period (Fogel 1986b). Moreover, even though the life expectancy at birth (e_0) in colonial America is not available, some statistics for selected European countries make it feasible to conjecture that Americans in the late eighteenth century lived longer than populations in those countries: e_0 for both sexes as of 1800, England: 40 years, Denmark: 41 years, France: 32 years, Germany: 37 years, and Sweden 39 years (Wrigley *et al.* 1997; Table 5.1 in Chapter 5).

However, the average height of native-born American males shrank by about 4.4 cm between 1830 and 1890; the life expectancy at age 10 of American males followed a pattern similar to that of heights, but began to decline earlier, during the 1790s, and continued to do so for about half a century (Figure 6.1).[3] During this period, the overall change in stature and longevity was contrary to the expectation for a period of rapid economic growth.[4] This trend has been a much-studied issue in the fields of economic history and historical demography. Many studies have looked for its fundamental cause within demographic change over the nineteenth century. With burgeoning agricultural technologies, Americans were able to produce more foodstuffs throughout this puzzling period, but the increase in agricultural productivity did not keep up with the rapid growth of the population and its food demands. Migration and urbanization led to sanitary problems and accelerated disease contagions. People required calories for combating diseases and intensive labor, but per capita food intake was

---

[3] It is well known that genetic, social, and environmental factors influence height in adulthood. A large number of researchers have examined the height–mortality relation. They found that height has inverse relations with all-cause, cardiovascular, and respiratory mortality, but conflicting association is found for some specific causes of death (Marmot, Shipley, and Rose 1984; Leon *et al.* 1995; Jousilahti *et al.* 2000; Samaras, Elrick, and Storms 2004; Silventoinen *et al.* 2006). So far various mechanisms have been explored: poor childhood nutrition (Ruel *et al.* 1995), social backgrounds (Silventoinen, Lahelma, and Rahkonen 1999), biological process during fetal life (Barker 1995), postnatal environmental factors (Wadsworth *et al.* 2002), and health behaviors in early life. However, it is still unclear whether this inverse relation is because of genetic factors, socioeconomic background or other environmental conditions; those early life conditions work as confounding factors affecting both height and mortality risk. It is thus reasonable to consider height not a causal factor that directly influences health and mortality in later life, but a marker of genotype, *in utero* and childhood exposures to health insults, and the age of puberty.

Figure 6.1 shows that the decline of life expectancy precedes that of height by several decades. However, this finding should be interpreted carefully in the light of previous studies on the height-mortality association. Although a population's average height is considered a revealed status of the population's socioeconomic and environmental conditions, the trend of height does not always directly determine that of mortality. It should also be noted that adult height is measured for those who survived various health insults in early life.

[4] While this trend is not widely observed in European countries, the English experience is notable. In particular, special attention was paid to the decline in stature among those born in the second quarter of the nineteenth century (Floud, Wachter, and Gregory 1990).

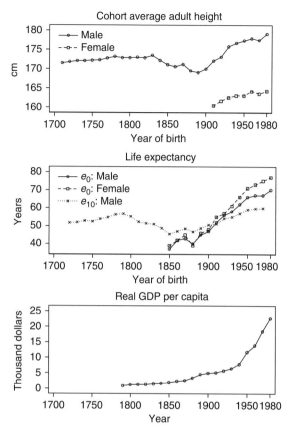

Figure 6.1 Trends in adult height, life expectancy, and real GDP per capita since 1700

limited. Consequently, the elimination of chronic malnutrition and secular improvements in population health – death and sickness – would not be realized until the beginning of the twentieth century, when modern technologies in food production, work conditions, and disease controls began to be established.

This chapter explores the American experience of technophysio evolution. Section 6.1 examines the long-term changes of various components that determine nutritional status and human development in America, including changes in population and in agricultural, medical, and environmental technologies. Section 6.2 looks into how the dynamic changes of food availability, disease controls, and work conditions shaped the trends in American levels of stature, sickness, longevity, and economic productivity. In Section 6.3, recent experiences of technological and physiological changes and future implications are discussed.

6.1 Elimination of chronic malnutrition

In economic and demographic history, large numbers of deaths have been observed during periods of famine and prolonged starvation. For a long time, many studies have examined the relationship between food availability and mortality, with more attention paid to the periods of famines that caused mortality crises. Some contemporaries believed that people could escape from high mortality and hunger by eliminating the sort of famines that were prevalent throughout, at least, the first half of the eighteenth century.[5] But subsequent studies have revealed that the elimination of famines and mortality crises explains only about 6 percent of the decline in annual mortality between the third quarter of the eighteenth century and the second quarter of the nineteenth century, and that over 90 percent of the initial decline was due to the reduction in "normal" mortality (Fogel 1991).

Once it was determined that famines and famine-related mortality had only a small impact on aggregate mortality in the early modern period, the research began to examine the issue of chronic malnutrition and its relevance to the secular decline in mortality. *Malnutrition* puts stress on the importance of the balance between the caloric intake

[5] In 1798, Thomas Malthus described famine as the positive check on population growth and argued that the rapid growth of populations would outpace food resources (Malthus 1993). Coinciding with his belief, historians discovered that an increase in mortality in pre-industrial Europe followed harvest failure and a sharp increase in food prices. Several subsistence crises in England happened in the first half of the eighteenth century: 1709–1710, 1723–1730, and 1740. The famines in those periods were directly related to severe weather and food shortages, and the combination of a succession of infections and deficient harvests considerably worsened the nutritional status of the English population, causing the substantial increases in crisis mortality rate (Clarkson 1975; Walter and Schofield 1989).

(*diet*) and the claims on that intake (*work* and *disease*). The concept of "chronic" malnutrition emphasizes the long-term trend of this balance. Thus, studies of American histories of *diet, work,* and *disease* are necessary for understanding the secular trends of life expectancy and physical development from colonial to modern America.

6.1.1 Technological breakthroughs in food production

"Free land" has been considered one of the main influences on the development of the American economy. Abundant farmland in favorable climates was a foundation of early American economic growth, and America's location, close to the English market, was another economic advantage (Temin 1991). Compared with European populations, early Americans who settled in the colonial period benefited from favorable conditions for food production (Carr 1992).

Compared to the modern era, however, this period (the mid seventeenth century) of early settlement in New England was characterized by a scarcity of livestock and food supplies. Because of the lack of capital and insufficient agricultural technology, farming tools and implements, such as the plow, were scarce and of poor quality. Inadequate knowledge of crop rotation and cultivation techniques was also a major cause of low productivity in agriculture. To make up for the scarcity, New England and the Middle Colonies in the seventeenth century imported crops from western Europe and purchased more corn from the natives.[6] But trades generally occurred in limited areas, depending on the accessibility of water transportation and trails, and the amount that could be traded was limited by storage technology. People frequently suffered from food shortages and sudden drops in food supply, mainly due to climate shock (Bidwell and Falconer 1941).

The situation did not significantly improve throughout the eighteenth century. Eighteenth-century farming was similar to that of the previous century. Farmers sowed by hand, cultivated by hoe, cut grains with a sickle, and threshed with a flail. Although the plow had been introduced several millennia before, colonial Americans still used crude wooden plows, which required more human energy than the use of iron plows.

---

[6] The term *maize* is more frequently used in scientific references than *corn*, which was the English term for some cereal crops in many regions. However, *corn* has commonly referred to *maize* in North America, so we have used it in this chapter.

Loss due to poor agricultural technology was particularly substantial during harvest season. In most areas, harvesting had to be completed in a short period to prevent crops and grains from being harmed by wind, rain, and frost, but using crude sickles caused farmers to lose considerable amounts of crops while consuming much energy (Carrier 1923; Bidwell and Falconer 1941; Rasmussen 1960; Fogel 2000).

During these periods based on the labor-intensive agricultural technology, food supply was no more than self-sufficient because agricultural production was limited by the amount of farming labor. Over 90 percent of the working population was engaged in agriculture, but farm families were barely able to produce enough for their own consumption, and food supplies per capita were very limited. Since a majority of the population was engaged in farming, little in the way of time and resources was invested in the production of manufacturing, clothing, and housing. This situation also deterred the development of urban areas, migration into cities, and industrialization.

The diet in the colonial period was less diverse than in the modern period. Breads and cereals were prominent, and the major source of calories was grain. The first colonists planted wheat and rye in New England, but they soon realized that the Indian corn (maize) was a better fit to the soil and climate. An example of allowances of grains and meat for widows in Middlesex County, Massachusetts shows that corn, wheat, and rye were the major crops in New England until the mid eighteenth century (Table 6.1). Various livestock were also raised for meat, as well as for milk and wool, but meat was of limited use because of problems with spoilage.[7]

Raising livestock was further made difficult because farmers could not produce sufficient crops to feed livestock, and meadow grazing for cattle was available only in temperate seasons. Consequently, meat produced in that period was not a full year's food supply. Dairy products were less affected by spoilage problems than fresh meat. Although feeding cattle during winter was an obstacle, the production of dairy products did increase during the period (Bidwell and Falconer 1941).

---

[7] Fresh meat was difficult to store, particularly during the summer, and all meat had to be consumed quickly before it rotted. Although some fowl could be consumed in one meal, most families did not have enough fowl for regular meals. Salt meat was not used widely until the early eighteenth century, and its use was limited to rich families (Bidwell and Falconer 1941).

Table 6.1 *Average annual allowances of grains and meat for widows in Middlesex County, Massachusetts, 1654–1799*

Item	1654–98	1705–18	1721–39	1740–59	1760–78	1781–99
	(a) Allowances of grains (bushels)					
Indian corn	9.4	10.6	9.5	11.8	10.6	10.9
Wheat	4.3	1.6	1.6	1.4	1.3	1.5
Rye	4.7	2.9	3.7	4.4	5.3	6.3
	(b) Allowances of meat (pounds)					
Salt pork	80.0	100.0	103.4	122.9	128.0	118.5
Salt beef		61.4	64.4	72.8	82.0	75.3

Source: McMahon 1985, pp. 54, 56.

Summing up the situation in the colonial period, its technology of food production was very primitive, even by contemporary European standards. However, the early American settlers could overcome this disadvantage because of environmental and epidemiological conditions favorable to agriculture and public health.

Changes that increased agricultural productivity began in the late eighteenth century, although they originated from the Second Agricultural Revolution in western Europe, beginning early in the seventeenth century (Rasmussen 1960; Fogel 2000). The introduction of crop rotation replenished soil nutrients, and in so doing, increased soil fertility. Developed by the British agriculturist Charles Townshend in the eighteenth century, a four-field rotation system (wheat, barley, turnips, and clover) increased the availability of fodder and grazing crops, and made it possible to feed cattle year-round. The spread of high-yield crops such as corn and potatoes also played a key role in enhancing agricultural productivity. Farmers also planted other crops (including pumpkins, beans, peanuts, and maple trees) that were better adapted to the American soil and climate, following the example of Native Americans (Carrier 1923).[8]

---

[8] Although this chapter is primarily concerned with the non-indigenous population, some anthropometric studies on American Indians provide another aspect of adapting the ways of life to ecological conditions. Using the anthropometric and demographic data of about several thousand Native Americans who lived on reservation in 1888–1903, Prince and Steckel (2003) show that Great Plains Native American men were taller than almost all populations in the world during

Grain production was mainly improved by the introduction of various agricultural tools. In 1794, Thomas Jefferson tested the moldboard plow, and in 1797, Charles Newbold patented the first cast-iron plow. Although the plows still relied on oxen, horses, or men for power, these new plows allowed farmers to cut through tough ground more easily and thus reduce labor and save energy. The use of the cradle and scythe significantly increased the harvest of grain, and these tools were commonly used until the early twentieth century. With the benefit of improvements in technology and the grain-to-seed ratio, farmers began to produce more grains than their own consumption required; this opened up the possibility of population increase and the movement of the labor force from agriculture to other industries in urban areas (Johnson 2000).

Around the period of the American Revolutionary War (1775–1783), the number of European immigrants to the New England colonies was decreasing, yet population size was increasing (Table 6.2).[9] The rapid growth of the colonies' population in the eighteenth century resulted from high birth rates and low death rates. Abundant farmland in favorable climates resulted in growing agricultural output, while settlement over a widespread area prevented the contagion of diseases.[10] The colonial era's annual natural growth of population increased from 1.27 percent in the 1710s to 3.23 percent in the 1780s.[11]

the mid nineteenth century. The study suggests that the nutritional success of American natives can be attributed to a rich and varied diet, a modest disease load other than epidemics, a remarkable facility at reorganization following demographic disasters, and egalitarian principles of cooperation.

[9] For the colonies, immigrants were the solution to a chronic labor shortage and the means of promoting land settlement and developing resources, and they made contributions to frontier defense and internal security. Therefore, every colony offered numerous inducements to immigrants, such as the granting of land. From the 1770s, the number of immigrants began to decrease because restrictions imposed by European governments made it extremely difficult to leave, and the war conditions prevailing after 1793 in Europe – the French Revolutionary Wars – added greatly to the normal hazards of the Atlantic crossing (Jones 1992).

[10] It is also known that European and African diseases brought by European and slave immigration decimated the aboriginal inhabitants of America (McCusker and Menard 1985).

[11] According to Table 6.2, the decadal natural growth rate of population between 1710 and 1720 is 0.135 or equivalently 13.5 percent. Then, the annual growth rate in the 1710s is calculated by $(1.135)^{1/10} - 1 = 0.0127$ or 1.27 percent. Similarly, the annual natural growth rate of population in the 1780s is calculated from the decadal growth rate between 1780 and 1790. The estimated annual rate of natural increase in England was 0.33 percent in the 1710s and 0.82 percent in the 1780s (source: Wrigley and Schofield 1981).

Table 6.2 *American trends of population, migration, and urbanization,*
1710–1980

Year	Population (millions)	Net migration (millions)	Import of slaves (thousands)	Population increase from previous census (%)	Natural population growth rate (%)	% of urban population
1710	0.3	0.04	16			
1720	0.5	0.07	23	42.8	13.5	
1730	0.6	0.08	20	36.1	14.7	
1740	0.9	0.12	45	43.5	16.9	
1750	1.2	0.06	64	30.0	16.3	
1760	1.6	0.09	55	34.3	22.4	
1770	2.2	0.08	73	35.9	26.0	
1780	2.8	0.00	33	29.2	27.8	
1790	3.9	0.01	77	40.4	37.4	5.1
1800	5.3	0.04	71	35.1	32.3	6.1
1810	7.2	0.08	143	36.4	32.1	7.3
1820	9.6	0.13		33.1	31.4	7.2
1830	12.9	0.14		33.5	32.0	8.8
1840	17.1	0.61		32.7	28.0	10.8
1850	23.2	1.71		35.9	25.8	15.4
1860	31.4	2.60		35.6	24.4	19.8
1870	38.6	2.31		22.6	15.3	25.7
1880	50.2	2.81		30.1	22.8	28.2
1890	62.9	5.25		25.5	15.0	35.1
1900	76.0	3.69		20.7	14.9	39.8
1910	92.0	7.97		21.0	10.5	45.7
1920	105.7	3.59		14.9	11.0	51.3
1930	122.8	3.06		16.1	13.2	56.3
1940	131.7	0.07		7.2	7.2	56.7
1950	150.7	0.88		14.5	13.8	59.0
1960	179.3	2.33		19.0	17.4	64.0
1970	203.2	3.32		13.3	11.5	65.7
1980	226.5	4.49		11.5	9.3	67.6

Sources: (Population) 1710–1780: US Bureau of Census 1975, Part 2, Series Z1; 1790–1980: Carter *et al.* 2006, Vol. 1, Series Aa2. (Net Migration) 171–1780: Galenson 2000, pp. 178, 180; 1790–1800: Blodget 1964, p. 58; 1810–1820: McClelland and Zeckhauser 1982, pp. 30–49; 1830–1980: Carter *et al.* 2006, Vol. 1, Series Ad1–Ad2. (Slaves) Fogel, Galantine, and Manning 1992, p. 55. (Urban Population) Carter *et al.* 2006, Vol. 1, Series Aa700.
Notes: The figures in net migration and import of slaves cover the decade ending in the year shown. Natural population growth rate was calculated as (population – net migration – import of slaves/1,000 – population in previous census) ÷ population in previous census × 100. Urban areas are defined as towns or cities with populations of 2,500 or more.

With natural population growth, the expansion of settlements to the western frontiers continued throughout the mid eighteenth century. Because of its victory in the French and Indian Wars of the 1760s, Britain took over the French colonial areas west of the Appalachians to the Mississippi River. Americans began to move to Pennsylvania and Ohio across the Appalachians. After the American Revolutionary War, those frontiers were areas of significant migration, which then expanded further west. On the other hand, the development of the southern frontiers was closely associated with plantation growing (cotton, rice, tobacco, and indigo). For the trade of these plantation crops, major cities like Richmond, Virginia, began to grow in the south. About 650,000 Africans were imported to the American colonies for labor starting in 1654, when a black man was first legally recognized as a slave, until a bill abolishing the British slave trade was passed in 1807 (Ballagh 1902; Franklin 1969).

As the expansion of frontiers provided more opportunities for cultivation and exploitation of new land, the number of immigrants from other countries gradually increased from the first decade of the nineteenth century and more rapidly from the 1830s. Mobility from abroad in the 1840s exploded because of the great famine in Europe. Due to blight, the Irish potato famine, which began in 1845 and lasted six years, killed approximately one million people through starvation and diseases (Mokyr 1983). About 781,000 Irish migrated into the United States to escape hunger and death during the period. In addition, 435,000 Germans, 267,000 British, and 77,000 French immigrants entered America in search of land, freedom, opportunity, and jobs during the 1840s (Jones 1992). By 1850, many major eastern cities like New York, Boston, and Baltimore, which were full of those immigrants, suffered from high population density and sanitary problems.

As new agricultural techniques were introduced and new frontiers were populated, early-nineteenth-century America saw a great increase in domestic crop production (Table 6.3). Between 1800 and 1850, gross wheat and corn production increased by 285 percent and 259 percent, respectively. But the higher population growth rate – 338 percent over the same period – eroded the benefit of this achievement. In particular, food output did not keep pace with the demands of the urban-industrial sectors whose population increased approximately ten times during the first half of the nineteenth century. By 1860, per capita crop production had stagnated or weakly decreased. Since the US net export of major crops had been positive and slightly increased during the period,

Table 6.3 *Annual production and price of major crops in the United States, 1800–1920*

	Food grains												Feed crop		
	Wheat			Rye			Rice			Buckwheat			Corn		
Year	Production (mil. bu.)	Per capita (bushels)	Price ($/bu.)	Production (mil. bu.)	Per capita (bushels)	Price ($/bu.)	Production (mil. cwt.)	Per capita (cwt.)	Price ($/cwt.)	Production (mil. bu.)	Per capita (bushels)	Price ($/bu.)	Production (mil. bu.)	Per capita (bushels)	Price ($/bu.)
1800	26	4.87	0.52	5.27	0.99	0.28	0.76	0.14	1.36	2.03	0.38	0.30	165	31.11	0.27
1810	35	4.85	0.65	7.30	1.01	0.42	0.92	0.13	1.11	2.90	0.40	0.33	219	30.21	0.29
1820	47	4.85	0.26	9.59	1.00	0.28	0.63	0.07	1.13	3.91	0.41	0.20	279	28.98	0.17
1830	61	4.74	0.48	12.84	1.00	0.44	0.84	0.07	1.20	5.07	0.39	0.31	372	28.93	0.27
1840	85	4.98	0.48	18.65	1.09	0.50	0.83	0.05	1.51	7.25	0.42	0.32	378	22.14	0.28
1850	100	4.31	0.80	14.19	0.61	0.70	1.48	0.06	1.82	8.99	0.39	0.46	592	25.53	0.40
1860	173	5.50	0.94	21.10	0.67	0.71	1.38	0.04	2.15	17.54	0.56	0.48	839	26.68	0.43
1870	288	7.47	0.61	16.92	0.44	0.56	1.01	0.03	1.48	10.44	0.27	0.51	761	19.74	0.45
1880	459	9.15	0.84	19.83	0.40	0.71	1.80	0.04	2.16	11.74	0.23	0.55	1755	34.99	0.42
1890	468	7.43	0.72	28.42	0.45	0.49	2.12	0.03	1.69	11.65	0.19	0.47	2122	33.71	0.42
1900	659	8.67	0.63	25.57	0.34	0.56	4.03	0.07	1.64	11.20	0.15	0.52	2666	35.08	0.36
1910	683	7.43	0.92	29.52	0.32	0.64	10.61	0.11	1.55	14.76	0.16	0.58	2552	27.75	0.52
1920	945	8.94	1.04	75.99	0.72	0.74	19.31	0.15	2.94	12.71	0.12	0.75	2346	22.19	0.72

Sources: To get the values of production and price, we used data from the US agricultural census found in Carter *et al.* 2006, Vol. 4, Series Da668–Da669 for rice, Series Da709–Da710 for corn, Series Da731–Da732 for wheat, Series Da750–Da751 for rye, and Series Da753–Da754 for buckwheat. When data were not available from the census, the estimates by Towne and Rasmussen (1960) were employed. Note that no US censuses of agriculture were taken for 1800–1830. Towne and Rasmussen (1960) estimated output by extrapolating 1840 estimates back to 1800 by assuming per capita rates of production in these earlier years to be about the same as in the benchmark year of 1840; they suggest that although per capita production implies more or less static agricultural technology and productivity during this period, it does not necessarily imply a lack of consistency (p. 257). Per capita production was calculated using population in Table 6.2. Price was converted to 1899 constant dollars using consumer price indexes (BLS) in US Bureau of the Census 1975a, Part 1, Series E135.

per capita crop consumption may have declined throughout the antebellum period. Excess demand had increased grain prices by 1860, and the change in food availability contributed to the decline in the population's nutritional status in the first half of the nineteenth century.[12]

The great increases in gross and per capita crop production had been followed by the mechanical revolution and the invention and improvement of more advanced technologies for food production. The changes in plow technology during the nineteenth century were dramatic. In 1837, the first steel plow was manufactured by John Deere. The advent of the modern steam engine in 1850 allowed for plows to be pulled by steam tractors. In the 1860s, gang plows using up to fourteen blades were introduced. Other harvesting tools underwent improvements: a reaper invented by Cyrus McCormick in 1834 revolutionized the harvesting of grain, although it was drawn by horses and could only cut short grain. With continuous developments, the reaper was replaced by the binder, which was invented by Charles Withington in 1872. Drawn by steam tractors, it could cut and gather crops mechanically. A crude version of the threshing machine was invented by Scottish mechanical engineer Andrew Meikle around 1786 to separate grains from stalks and husks. Its function was added to the reaper, and the devices were combined by the late nineteenth century.

Additionally, late-nineteenth-century America observed a rapid change in the geographical pattern of crop production. Technological adaptations to unfavorable environments and to climate shock were at the center of the change. The early frontier settlements faced many environmental obstacles. Many undeveloped lands in the Old Northwestern states were filled with wetlands and swamps that plagued dwellers and travelers with malignant fevers. Major agricultural drainage began during the 1870s. The drainage effort increased available farmland, and was also effective in preventing malarial fevers (Boyd 1941). Settlement in the further west

---

[12] Grain prices have been considered a key indicator of food availability. In general, a high price of grain means the lack of consumption, given demand and inventories. For low-income workers, high price directly meant a low consumption of food and could lead to chronic malnutrition if the high price was prolonged. In particular, food consumption by price depended on the demand elasticity of food price. Using the data from England, earlier studies estimated the elasticity to be around 0.4. It has been more recently corrected to 0.18 by considering the exceedingly inelastic demand for inventories in the early modern period. This number implies that a reduction in the supply of grain by about 5 percent would result in a large increase in prices that would cut the consumption of the laboring classes by a third (Fogel 1992c and see Chapter 3 for detailed discussion).

was initially interrupted by climate shock, mainly droughts. Those areas began to be equipped with irrigation systems and methods of managing water sources to adapt to the seasonal fluctuation of precipitation. From the 1880s, each state began to establish experimental agricultural stations that conducted scientific investigations into agricultural problems. Due to improvements that made seeds more able to endure drought and low temperature, the Corn Belt and wheat areas extended west and north throughout the late nineteenth century (Olmstead and Rhode 2008).

As the Frontier Era came to an end, more people migrated into urban areas. At the beginning of the nineteenth century, 5 percent of the US population lived in towns or cities with populations of more than 2,500, and the proportion increased to 39.8 percent in 1900 (Table 6.2). The national food supply was no longer self-sufficient: urban communities now required increasing amounts of food from rural ones. Consequently, the volume of agricultural commodities transported between regions increased over the period, especially with the advent of cheap, fast, and capacious railroad transportation.[13] The surplus of the Midwest was first concentrated in the great primary markets of the region such as Chicago, Minneapolis, Duluth, Milwaukee, Peoria, Kansas City, St. Louis, Cincinnati, Toledo, and Detroit. Then, food was shipped from the primary markets to about ninety secondary markets in deficit areas, and finally distributed within the territory. In the mid nineteenth century, water transportation such as boats and barges dominated the inter- and intra-regional transportation of these goods. But in the late nineteenth century, food was carried mainly by railroad, as the rate and overall cost fell to less than the cost of water transportation. By 1890, the total quantity of corn, wheat, pork, and beef shipped inter-regionally was approximately equal to the local deficits of the trading areas of the east and south, plus net exports (Fogel 1964).

Although national and regional grain deficits were stabilized by redistribution, the meat industry did not make much progress during the nineteenth century (Table 6.4). The shipment of fresh meat was still constrained by spoilage problems, and shipping livestock was expensive. Although

---

[13] By 1890, 60 percent of the population lived in areas with foodstuff deficits. The greatest shortages were incurred in the North Atlantic regions including New York, New Jersey, and Pennsylvania. Those states produced about 36 percent of the wheat and 45 percent of the corn required to feed the local population. The south produced a greater share of its local needs, but it still required food from elsewhere. Only the North Central region produced a surplus of agricultural goods (Fogel 1964).

Table 6.4 *Annual production and price of meat products in the United States, 1800–1920*

	Pork			Beef and veal			Mutton			Chicken		
Year	Production (mil. lbs.)	Per capita (lbs.)	Price ($/cwt.)	Production (mil. lbs.)	Per capita (lbs.)	Price ($/cwt.)	Production (mil. lbs.)	Per capita (lbs.)	Price ($/cwt.)	Production (mil. lbs.)	Per capita (lbs.)	Price (¢/lbs.)
1800	651	122.58	2.50	393	74.02	1.83	5	1.03	0.90	80	15.07	3.92
1810	868	119.84	3.39	533	73.57	1.99	7	1.03	0.97	108	14.92	3.56
1820	1,139	118.15	2.26	711	73.75	1.83	10	1.03	0.90	144	14.94	2.93
1830	1,518	118.02	3.24	955	74.21	2.54	14	1.12	1.25	194	15.08	5.23
1840	2,223	130.25	3.61	1,343	78.70	3.47	20	1.17	1.71	256	15.00	6.25
1850	2,711	116.91	3.25	1,649	71.09	2.87	33	1.42	2.39	348	15.01	9.40
1860	3,362	106.93	4.53	2,298	73.07	3.56	57	1.82	3.89	471	14.98	5.93
1870	5,038	130.65	4.25	2,384	61.84	3.56	123	3.19	2.98	661	17.14	6.06
1880	5,864	116.92	5.42	3,713	74.03	3.45	184	3.67	3.27	920	18.34	5.63
1890	6,196	98.42	3.33	5,558	88.29	3.04	279	4.43	3.87	1,270	20.18	6.76
1900	6,310	83.03	4.75	5,909	77.76	4.08	487	6.41	4.44	1,680	22.11	7.30
1910	6,557	71.29	6.81	7,575	82.36	5.88	608	6.61	6.85	1,803	20.05	11.81
1920	8,477	80.19	8.61	7,575	71.66	7.48	590	5.58	7.72	1,908	18.46	12.80

Sources: In the table, we estimated the production of pork, beef, and mutton in terms of dressed weight. Data on dressed weight are available after 1900; more detailed sources are available from Carter *et al.* 2006, Vol. 4, pp. 172–178 (Series Da997, Da1003, Da1009, and Da1016). Each production estimated in live weight is available for 1800–1900 in Towne and Rasmussen 1960, pp. 283–285. We estimated dressed-weight production before 1900 by extrapolating the 1900 rate of dressed weight to live weight – calculated from two data sources – back to earlier years in Towne and Rasmussen 1960. The production of chicken is estimated in terms of live weight. 1800–1900: Towne and Rasmussen 1960, p. 287; 1910–1920: US agricultural censuses report only the number of chickens produced. This was converted into live-weight production based on the converting rate between the number of production and live-weight production in 1929 (see Carter *et al.* 2006, Vol. 4, p. 187, Series Da1041–Da1042). Per capita production was calculated using population information from Table 6.2. Price of each meat product was obtained from Towne and Rasmussen 1960, pp. 283–285 for 1800–1900 and Carter *et al.* 2006, Vol. 4, pp. 172–178 and 187 for 1910–1920; price was converted to 1899 constant dollars using consumer price indexes (BLS) in US Bureau of the Census 1975a, Part 1, Series E135.

mechanical advances in agricultural tools made it possible to produce enough grain to support the rapidly increasing population throughout the late nineteenth century, per capita meat production was considerably lacking, especially the per capita production of pork (in terms of dressed weight), which declined by about 35 percent between 1800 and 1900.

The market for perishable commodities, including dairy products, increased at the turn of the twentieth century with the introduction of refrigeration technology (Table 6.5). Although most people relied on melting ice to cool their food even in the early twentieth century, the mechanical refrigerator system, first sold in 1911 by General Electric, made it feasible to store perishable commodities while maintaining high hygienic standards, which promoted its market growth. Railroads adopted this technology in the form of the refrigerator car and could then ship dressed meat to urban areas which had meat deficits, promoting integration into the market. According to a recent study, the adoption of refrigeration increased dairy consumption by 1.7 percent and overall protein intake by 1.25 percent annually after the 1890s (Craig, Goodwin, and Grennes 2004). The canning industry was another factor in increasing meat and vegetable consumption and enhancing the level of protein intake. Food packing technology that had been developed in the 1860s to meet the demand of the Civil War soldiers was, by the late nineteenth century, sophisticated enough to support the high demand from urban populations.

6.1.2 Food consumption and diet

Advances in agricultural technologies have changed the American diet pattern over the centuries. In order to estimate historical daily consumption of calories, researchers have calculated daily consumption of crops, meat, and other foodstuffs in units of weight and then converted them to calorie units. As the principal sources in diet studies, researchers have used national food balance sheets, household consumption surveys, food entitlements to widows in wills, and so on (Fogel 1993b).[14]

---

[14] The studies using national food balance sheets estimated the national supply of food by subtracting allowances for seed and feed, losses and wastes from processing, changes in inventories, and net exports from the annual production of crops to obtain the amount available for consumption. The estimation results depend on how losses were defined from production to consumption. In the case of using household survey reports, the estimation depended on the level of household income and the interviewee's memories.

Table 6.5 *Annual production and price of eggs, dairy products, vegetables, and fruits in the United States, 1800–1920*

	Eggs			Dairy Products			Irish Potatoes			Sweet Potatoes			Fruits		
Year	Production (mil. doz.)	Per capita (doz.)	Price (¢/lbs.)	Production (mil. lbs.)	Per capita (lbs.)	Price ($/bu.)	Production (mil. bu.)	Per capita (bushels)	Price ($/cwt.)	Production (mil. bu.)	Per capita (bushels)	Price ($/bu.)	Production (mil. bu.)	Per capita (bushels)	Price ($/bu.)
1800	32	6.03	4.41	1,769	333.26	0.41	17	3.16	0.19	12	2.28	0.25	11	2.00	0.10
1810	43	5.94	5.85	2,424	334.86	0.39	23	3.15	0.21	17	2.28	0.27	15	2.00	0.10
1820	58	6.02	5.43	3,276	339.90	0.25	30	3.15	0.18	22	2.27	0.24	19	2.00	0.15
1830	77	5.98	6.25	4,390	341.21	0.53	41	3.16	0.24	29	2.28	0.31	26	2.00	0.14
1840	103	6.03	7.03	5,766	337.79	0.67	54	3.16	0.23	39	2.31	0.30	45	2.66	0.12
1850	139	5.99	9.00	7,636	329.25	0.74	55	2.35	0.37	35	1.50	0.48	37	1.59	0.24
1860	188	5.98	10.19	10,690	339.98	0.77	92	2.93	0.34	38	1.22	0.44	56	1.77	0.26
1870	329	8.53	12.50	12,484	323.77	0.96	105	2.71	0.37	26	0.67	0.59	70	1.82	0.27
1880	588	11.72	10.71	19,402	386.83	0.94	138	2.75	0.39	35	0.70	0.46	231	4.61	0.27
1890	1,038	16.49	12.96	30,260	480.72	0.81	161	2.56	0.50	41	0.65	0.50	129	2.05	0.58
1900	1,615	21.25	13.00	34,806	458.01	0.93	221	2.91	0.43	41	0.54	0.52	417	5.49	0.29
1910	2,108	22.92		38,715	420.94		301	3.27		55	0.60		429	4.66	
1920	2,542	24.04		45,388	429.36		229	2.17		73	0.69		536	5.07	

Sources: Source for 1800–1900: Towne and Rasmussen 1960, pp. 288–289, 303, and 303. Source for 1910–1920: Carter *et al.* 2006, Vol. 4, Series Da775 and Da778 (Irish and sweet potatoes), Series Da1029 (dairy products), and Series Da1048 (eggs). The unit of production in each source was adjusted for consistent comparison over time. Fruit production in 1910–1920 was extrapolated using the linear trend in 1800–1900. Weight of dairy products is milk-equivalent weight based on the equation: 10 pounds butter = 21 pounds cheese = 100 pounds fluid milk (see Towne and Rasmussen 1960, p. 288). Per capita production was calculated using population in Table 6.2. Price was converted to 1899 constant dollars using consumer price indexes (BLS) in US Bureau of the Census 1975a, Part 1, Series E 135.

Table 4.9 of Chapter 4 reports that the estimated daily caloric supplies at the beginning of the eighteenth century were 2,229 kcal per capita for England and Wales or equivalently 2,951 kcal per consuming unit, and slightly decreased to 2,169 kcal per capita or equivalently 2,867 kcal per consuming unit in circa 1750.[15] Little data for America in this period exist, but some suggest that Americans in the colonial period consumed more calories than the English populations did in the same period. For example, members of the Massachusetts militia in the first half of the eighteenth century were known to have consumed about 3,100 kcal daily (US Bureau of the Census 1975a). Because a member of the militia is considered a consuming unit which denotes an adult male aged 20–39, this partly suggests that American adult males in the colonial period consumed more calories than the English adult males did in the same period. Carr (1992) argues that early colonists could be better nourished by adopting Indian corn as the main source of nourishment, and that they were provided with enough meat from wild animals and livestock herds under favorable climate and environments.

Although consistent comparisons of American diet over the centuries are impractical mainly due to lack of reliable data in the colonial period, the use of the US agricultural censuses makes the comparison feasible for the post-colonial period. Using the per capita production of crops, meat, dairy products, eggs, vegetables, and fruits reported in Tables 6.3, 6.4, and 6.5, we estimated per capita daily caloric intake between 1800 and 1920 (Table 6.6).[16] According to this estimate, Americans consumed about 2,952 kcal daily in 1800 on average, which was about 20.2 percent higher than that which the average English person consumed daily at the same time. Using the conversion factor calculated in Appendix F, the per-consuming-unit caloric intake is estimated 3,934 kcal, which is the daily caloric consumption of average adult males aged 20–39. This level

---

[15] The estimates are the averaged value of grand total (A) and (B) in Table 4.9 of Chapter 4.

[16] We converted crops into domestic production levels using the ratios in Towne and Rasmussen (1960). It was assumed that 12 percent of total corn production was consumed as food, based on the ratio estimated for 1880, following Komlos (1987). Fruit production in 1909 and 1919 – which is not available in census records – was imputed using its time trend: in terms of gross production, 428.6 (million bushels) for 1909 and 536.4 (million bushels) for 1919. The calorie unit of each food item was taken from Watt and Merrill (1950). Finally, 10 percent of total available calories were considered as waste. Also see footnote 20 below for the issues in estimating caloric consumption from meat products.

Table 6.6 *Estimated daily caloric intake per capita, 1800–2004*

Year	Calories	Distribution of calories by food type (%)			
		Grains	Meat	Dairy/Eggs	Others
1800	2,952[a]	46.7	30.8	9.0	13.5
1810	2,935	46.9	30.5	9.1	13.5
1820	2,904	46.5	30.5	9.3	13.7
1830	2,888	46.1	30.7	9.4	13.7
1840	3,013	44.7	32.1	8.9	14.3
1850	2,585	45.0	33.8	10.2	11.1
1860	2,826	50.3	29.4	9.6	10.7
1870	3,029	52.4	30.4	8.7	8.5
1880	3,237	50.3	27.7	9.8	12.1
1890	3,134	51.6	27.3	12.8	8.3
1900	3,212	51.1	23.4	12.2	13.3
1910	3,068	51.6	23.0	12.0	13.4
1920	3,259	54.7	21.8	11.6	11.9
1930	3,400[b]				
1940	3,300				
1952	3,200	23.0[c]	22.0	19.0	36.0
1960	3,100				
1970	3,200	19.7	18.1	13.3	48.9
1980	3,200				
1990	3,500				
2000	3,900				
2004	3,900	23.5	13.4	10.0	53.1

Sources: [a] The values for 1800–1920 were calculated from food production statistics reported in Tables 6.3, 6.4, and 6.5. See the text for detailed calculations.
[b] The values for 1930–2004 were obtained from the USDA Daily Caloric Intake in 1909–2004 Database (US Department of Agriculture 2009).
[c] The distribution of calories in 1952 was obtained from the US Department of Agriculture 1953.

of daily food intake was enough for conducting heavy work in the period that demanded more intensive labor. According to a report by FAO/ WHO/UNU (1985), the energy use for modern workers who daily conduct ten-hour heavy work is 3,937 kcal. Similarly, Gallman (1971) estimated that the typical colonial adult – who was shorter than modern adults – required 3,750 kcal for daily life and work.

What was the daily life and work of the typical colonial adult male who required 3,750 kcals per day? Assuming that average height was 173.5 cm and average BMI was 22, the corresponding BMR is 1,631 kcal, and the physical activity level (PAL) – a person's daily physical activity level as a multiple of BMR – is estimated at 2.3 BMR (= 3,750 ÷ 1,631). This average PAL amounts to the bottom level of the third highest decile among British adult males in the same period (see Table 2.6 of Chapter 2). A plausible scenario of caloric use for an individual with this level of physical activity is as follows: sleeping (8 hrs), taking a rest (2 hrs), cooking (1 hr), eating (2 hrs), strolling (1 hr), making a fence (2 hrs), milking a cow by hand (2 hrs), weeding (1 hr), uprooting sweet potatoes (1 hr), digging holes for posts (1 hr), and plowing (3 hrs).[17] It is likely that he had sufficient caloric intake to conduct ten hours of heavy work on a farm while sustaining body maintenance at the relevant height and BMI level. In the appendix to this chapter, we have estimated the size distribution of caloric consumption per consuming unit in the United States at the beginning of the nineteenth century and calculated the distribution of PAL among American adult males. The estimated distributions suggest that about half of the male population was below the level of caloric intake required to conduct ten hours of heavy work. But the American situation was much better than that of Britain and France, where about 70 percent and 90 percent, respectively, of male populations are estimated to be below the level.[18]

The level of estimated dietary intake in the early nineteenth century was steady around 2,900–3,000 kcal per capita until 1840, implying that the increase in gross food production was keeping up with population growth until that time. This also suggests that the level of per capita food production in the early nineteenth century is insufficient for explaining the decline in life expectancy after 1790, and that other explanations therefore need to be invoked later.

---

[17] According to Table 2.1 of Chapter 2, the energy requirement of each activity (ratio relative to BMR) is as follows: sleeping (1.0), taking a rest (1.4), cooking (1.8), eating (1.4), strolling (1.5), making fence (2.7), milking cow by hand (2.9), weeding (3.8), uprooting sweet potatoes (3.5), digging holes for post (5.0), and plowing (4.6). Then, the above scenario is estimated by the following calculation: 2.3 PAL = (8 × 1.0 + 2 × 1.4 + 1 × 1.8 + 2 × 1.4 + 1 × 1.5 + 2 × 2.7 + 2 × 2.9 + 1 × 3.8 + 1 × 3.5 + 1 × 5.0 + 3 × 4.6) ÷ 24. For more explanations for the estimation, see Section 2.4 in Chapter 2.

[18] We estimated the proportion of consuming units whose PAL is less than 2.3 using the size distribution of caloric consumption and the assumption of body size for Britain in circa 1800 and for France in circa 1785 as discussed in Chapter 2.

The estimates in Table 6.6 then indicate a considerable decline in diet after 1840; the 1840 level was not recovered until 1870.[19] A large decline in per capita production of wheat, rye, pork, and beef accounts for this big deficit in American dietary history. The lack of nutrients was demonstrated by the soaring prices of those foodstuffs, another downside indicator of food consumption (Tables 6.3 and 6.4). The downward trend resulted mainly from the rapid growth of immigration and population relative to domestic food production.[20] With the end of the Civil War, American per capita food production and diet rose again. The average level of the population's diet around 1880 reached the level it would be in the 1970s and 1980s.

In addition to the cyclical trend in the level of food consumption, Americans have experienced big changes in diet patterns. In the seventeenth century, Native Americans in New England depended largely on grains as their energy source. It is estimated that 65 percent of their food

---

[19] A similar pattern is also found in Komlos (1987). He employed a full set of foodstuffs available in the 1840–1880 US agricultural censuses. According to the upper bound of his estimates, daily consumption of calories per capita was 3,021 in 1840, 2,754 in 1850, 2,989 in 1860, 2,962 in 1870, and 3,130 in 1880 (unit: kcal).

[20] The estimation of daily pork consumption has been particularly controversial. Calculation depends on the data source and the rate at which live weight is converted into dressed weight. In 1987, Komlos estimated the trend of per capita daily caloric intake in mid-nineteenth-century America and argued that American consumption of meat declined and deprived Americans of an adequate supply of protein. For Komlos's calculation, Gallman (1996) argued that the census figures that Komlos used refer to June 1, while the figures in the Bureau of Agricultural Economics that other researchers have used refer to January 1. Thus, Komlos's slaughter-weight assumptions yield smaller outputs per animal in inventory than have been studied by other researchers. But another study by Towne and Rasmussen (1960), which estimates farm gross product throughout the nineteenth century, says that Gallman's estimates and those of Strauss and Bean (1940) on pork production are too high for the years before 1900. The question has not yet been resolved.

In Table 6.6, we estimate per capita daily caloric intake in 1800–1920. Besides the above issue on calculation methods, we had difficulty locating a data source that reports meat output and consumption using consistent criteria. Two useful sources are Towne and Rasmussen (1960) for 1800–1900, US agricultural censuses for the twentieth century (see the notes of Table 6.4 for detailed sources). Although there are discrepancies between the two sources, we combined them using the difference in the figures in 1900. Then, we applied Komlos's rate (0.76 for pork and 0.54 for beef) to convert live weight into dressed weight. The estimation result in Table 6.6 should be considered in the light of this calculation and the data issues.

consumption came from grain products and 10 percent came from meat products (Bennett 1955). This pattern did not change in the eighteenth century. Although the direct comparison to the experience of American Indians above requires careful interpretation, Philadelphian laborers consumed 62 percent of their calories from grains and 17 percent from meat products (Smith 1981). Throughout the nineteenth century, grains were still the main source of nutrients, but their share declined to less than 60 percent as presented in Table 6.6. The share of meat products was 20–30 percent, but decreased throughout the nineteenth century because of reductions in per capita meat production.

This trend of diverting away from grain dependence accelerated toward the mid twentieth century. Grains account for around 20 percent of the American diet today, but this does not mean that there has been a proportionate increase in the share of meat products, which was 13.4 percent in 2004. Instead, modern Americans increasingly get their energy from foodstuffs that consist of fat, oil, and sugar. This change in diet pattern is related to income elasticities for the different types of food. As some studies suggest, people's proportionate expenditure on grains, meat, dairy products, and other foodstuffs depends on their level of wealth and income. As people got richer, they spent extra income on non-grain products. Urban populations particularly became wealthier with industrialization and demanded more non-grain foodstuffs (Walter and Schofield 1989).

6.1.3 Hours at work and labor intensity

In addition to dramatically increasing available agricultural output, technological advances led to changes in work hours and labor productivity in farming and manufacturing. In the colonial period, when farming depended entirely on less-advanced farming tools and human or animal power, the farm's productivity was primarily determined by the number of hours devoted to farming. The average colonial farmer needed about eight to ten hours of heavy labor every day during the farming seasons (Carr 1992). Considering the other tasks necessary for running a farm, weekly work hours were easily over 70 hours.

Although it is possible, or even likely, that the introduction of new farming tools reduced the early-nineteenth-century farmers' working hours, there are some studies documenting the working hours of farmers that show that working hours did not decline or increase until the end of the Civil War.[21] The main arguments include the shift of farming into time-intensive dairy and livestock, the shift of labor away from agriculture, a decline in the seasonality of labor demand, and reductions in annual periods of unemployment (Fogel and Engerman 1974b; Weiss and Craig 1993; Margo 2000).

African-American slaves on southern plantations labored under heavy work conditions. They worked approximately 70–75 hours per week during the peak labor periods of farming – roughly 265–275 days, and the intensity of labor per hour was very high (Fogel and Engerman 1974b). To sustain such heavy levels of activity, they were comparatively well fed. According to the estimate by Fogel and Engerman (1974b), the average slave's daily caloric intake in 1860 exceeded the average daily food consumption of the entire population in 1879 by more than 10 percent. The adequacy of the adult slave diet was supported by Margo and Steckel (1982), who found that slaves were taller than English adults on average. With the end of slavery, which also caused a significant reduction of 26–35 percent in the working hours of African-Americans, southern labor changed from slave to free labor. As the amount of labor supply decreased, southern states' agricultural production became depressed (Ransom and Sutch 1977; Ng and Virts 1989). By 1900, about 90 percent of the black population still lived in former slave states. By around 1910, a great number of blacks had migrated from the south to the north, Midwest, and west (particularly industrial areas) to seek better economic and social opportunities.

The increase in agricultural labor productivity during the nineteenth century was remarkable (Table 6.7). The number of person-hours required to produce 100 bushels of corn fell by 57 percent between 1800 and 1900. A farmer could produce four times more wheat in 1900 than he did in 1800, within the unit of a working hour. But after 1900, the increase in labor productivity slowed. By contrast, the productivity

---

[21] Some statistics suggest that agricultural factors in the early nineteenth century were moving to the direction in which the level of agricultural output was increasing. As presented in Table 6.7, the average working hours for producing 100 bushels of corn or wheat substantially reduced from 1800 to 1840. The ratio of male workforce in agricultural sector relative to total population increased from 15.4 percent in 1800 to 17.5 percent in 1840. Female workforce in agriculture relative to male during that period increased from 1.9 percent in 1800 to 3.9 percent in 1840. (Note: The figures of agricultural workforce were calculated from the online database, "The Rural Agricultural Workforce by County, 1800 to 1900," gathered by Lee Craig [http://eh.net/databases/agriculture].)

Table 6.7 **Work level and productivity in the United States, 1800–2000**

	Agriculture				Manufacturing	
	Working hours for producing 100 bushels		Average yield (bushels per acre)		Weekly hours worked	Wage ($/hour)
Year	Corn	Wheat	Corn	Wheat		
1800	344	373	25.0	15.0		
1830					69.1	
1840	276	233	25.0	15.0	67.1	
1850					65.5	
1860					62.0	
1870					61.1	
1880	180	152	25.6	13.2	60.7	
1890					60.0	
1900	147	108	25.9	13.9	58.5	
1910	135	106	26.0	14.4	55.7	0.85
1920	122	90	26.8	13.8	50.0	1.71
1930	123	70	23.0	13.5	48.7	1.42
1940	79	44	32.2	17.1	42.5	1.20
1950	34	27	39.4	17.3	41.1	2.05
1960	11	12	62.2	25.2	41.0	2.52
1970	7	11	72.4	31.0	41.1	3.31
1980	3	8	91.0	33.5	39.9	7.03
1990			118.5	39.5	40.2	10.94
2000					41.4	14.32

Sources: Carter *et al.* 2006, Vol. 4, Series Da1143–Da1144 for working hours for producing 100 bushels; Carter *et al.* 2006, Vol. 4, Series Da1095–Da1096 for average yield; US Department of Interior 1883, US Senate 1893, Owen 1976 and 1988, and US Bureau of the Census 2007 for weekly hours worked; and US Bureau of the Census 1975a and 2007 for wage, which is adjusted in 2000-constant dollars.

of the soil measured by the yield per acre did not improve until the late 1930s, when new biotechnology like hybrid corn began to be widely used.[22] This implies that crop rotation – a low level of agricultural

[22] While hybrid corn was developed in the late nineteenth century with the help of modern genetics (of Charles Darwin and Gregor Mendel), corn heterosis (crossing one pure strain with another) was demonstrated in the first decade of the

improvement – helped to provide more food supplies in the eighteenth century, but that its impact did not last.

Compared to farming, manufacturing depended less on seasonality or climate changes and more on technology and the quality of machines, tools, and operating power. Thus, industrial technological advances led to a continuing decrease in hours worked in manufacturing throughout the nineteenth century (a reduction of 10.6 hours in weekly working hours between 1830 and 1900, as presented in Table 6.7).[23] But this level was still much higher than the standard of the twentieth century. The improvement of work conditions was more substantial during the twentieth century. Between 1900 and 2000, weekly hours worked in manufacturing declined by 17 hours. Reflecting the improvement in labor productivity, the real wage in manufacturing increased more than 14 times during the same period.

In summary, Americans became better nourished over the course of the late nineteenth century. The level of their diet reached that of twentieth-century Americans. Because of mechanical advances, they could work more productively than they had been able to in previous periods. Gradually, they had more available energy for body maintenance and physical development. They began to escape from chronic malnutrition. However, their activities still demanded intense labor, and prevailing diseases and infectious environments still plagued populations until the early twentieth century, claiming more energy and causing nutritional loss. The elimination of chronic malnutrition could therefore be achieved only after successes in combating diseases and controlling infectious environments.

6.1.4 Combating diseases

From the colonial era to the turn of the twentieth century, American people were exposed to and died from various infectious diseases. Lacking scientific understanding and effective prevention and treatment

early twentieth century. But the practical method of producing hybrid corn on a large scale and its economical use by farmers was actualized in the 1930s.

[23] In colonial America, for example, textile-weaving was a home-based artisan activity. From spinning to weaving, most procedures were man-powered and labor intensive. With the Industrial Revolution, a series of inventions of new textile machines (like the spinning jenny in 1764 and the spinning mule in 1779) and a shift of the source of power to water and, later, steam power significantly reduced men's work intensity and time.

techniques for these infectious diseases, most populations were exposed to a series of health insults from birth to death. Endemic infections such as smallpox, yellow fever, and diphtheria struck suddenly and caused devastating deaths throughout the eighteenth century. Cholera, scarlet fever, measles, whooping cough, typhus, typhoid fever, and tuberculosis were the main causes of deaths until the late nineteenth century (Duffy 1971).

According to the 1850 US federal vital statistics (the first census of mortality), about 47 percent of total deaths resulted from these infections, which accounted for only 1.8 percent of deaths in 2005 (US Bureau of the Census 1856; Centers for Disease Control 2008a).[24] In 1850, 217 white infants (340 black infants) out of 1,000 births died within their first year mostly because of harmful diseases while the infant death rate in 2005 is 0.57 percent for white population (1.3 percent for black population).[25] Without doubt, rampant infections were the main reason for low life expectancy before the twentieth century. Life expectancy at birth in 1850 was around 40 years for the white population (23 years for the black population), which is only half of the level of the white population's life expectancy at birth in 2000 (a third of the level for the black population) (Table 6.8). These public health indicators gradually improved in 1860–1870, but they declined again in 1880. This suggests that epidemiological environments got worse until the 1880s, which is well explained by sanitary problems due to rapid population growth as a result of immigration and urbanization. In rural areas, parasitic diseases such as malaria and hookworm and other infectious diseases were prevalent until the late nineteenth century without enough medical knowledge on their pathogens and effective eradication efforts.

The malaria example illustrates how the health of a population had been hurt under contaminated environments in the period before germ

---

[24] The leading causes of infant death today are congenital malformations and disorder related with low birth weight.

[25] Despite the dramatic decline in infant mortality during the twentieth century, the US infant mortality rate was still higher than those of other developed countries. The infant mortality rate in 2009 was 6.26 out of 1,000 live births in the US, 4.85 in the UK, and 3.33 in France (CIA World Factbook 2010). Studies have suggested that this is related to the increase of the percentage of preterm birth in the US and that the preterm birth is more prevalent among the non-Hispanic black population (Centers for Disease Control 2008b).

Table 6.8 *Summary of vital statistics, 1850–2000*

	Crude death rate (per 1,000 population)			Infant mortality (per 1,000 births)		Life expectancy at birth (years)		Cause of death (per 100,000 population)			
Year	All	White	Non-white	White	Black	White	Black	Selected infections	Cardiovascular	Diabetes	Neoplasm
1850	18.7			216.8	340.0	39.5	23.0				
1860	18.8			181.3		43.6		551.2			
1870	18.8			175.6		45.2		499.7			
1880	19.8			214.8		40.5		505.1			
1890	19.4			150.6		46.8		373.6			
1900	17.2	17.0	25.0	119.8	170.3	49.6	41.8	279.3	345.2	11.0	64.0
1910	14.7	14.5	21.7	96.5	142.6	54.6	46.2	209.8	371.9	15.3	76.2
1920	13.0	12.6	17.7	82.1	135.6	54.9	45.3	144.8	364.9	16.1	83.4
1930	11.3	10.8	16.7	60.1	99.5	61.4	48.1	84.0	414.4	19.1	97.4
1940	10.7	10.4	13.8	43.2	72.9	64.2	53.1	48.6	485.7	26.6	120.3
1950	9.5	9.4	10.8	26.8	43.9	69.1	60.8	23.2	510.8	16.2	139.8
1960	9.5	9.4	10.0	22.9	44.3	70.6	63.6	6.3	521.8	16.7	149.2
1970	9.4	9.4	9.4	17.8	32.6	71.7	64.1	2.6	496.0	18.9	162.8
1980	8.7	8.9	7.8	10.9	22.2	74.4	68.1	0.9	436.4	15.4	183.9
1990	8.6	8.8	7.3	7.6	18.0	76.1	69.1	0.7	368.3	19.2	203.2
2000	8.6	9.0	6.9	5.8	14.6	77.4	71.7	0.4	348.0	24.0	200.3

Sources: Crude death rate and cause of death for 1860–1890 are the values for Massachusetts obtained from US Bureau of the Census 1975a, Part 1, Series B193. The others are nation-level values obtained mostly from population censuses. The data and detailed information on sources are available from Carter *et al.* 2006, Vol. 1, Series Ab952, Ab955, Ab958 (crude death rate), Series Ab9–Ab10 (infant mortality), Series Ab647 and Ab653 (life expectancy at birth), and Series Ab929, Ab931, Ab934, and Ab936 (cause of death). Tuberculosis, diphtheria, typhoid fever, and measles were selected for calculating deaths by infections.

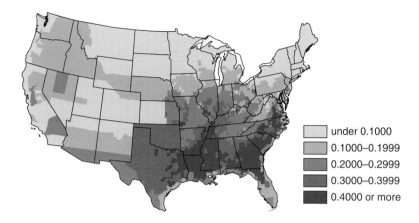

Source: Hong 2007a.

Figure 6.2 Estimated annual probability of contracting intermittent and remittent fevers by county in the 1850s

theory was widely accepted. As is now well known, malaria is a parasitic infection transmitted by mosquitoes. It was imported to America by European immigrants and African slaves beginning in the early seventeenth century. As more people moved west and as steamboats traveled more extensively along the Mississippi River, malaria prevailed not only in the south, but also in many parts of the Old Northwestern regions until the mid nineteenth century, as presented in the diagram in Figure 6.2, which shows the estimated annual probability of contracting intermittent and remittent fevers by county in the mid nineteenth century.[26] Before the malaria pathogen was discovered in the late nineteenth century, people thought that malarial fever came from malignant air, and they could not establish effective prevention. The medical history of the US Civil War reports that malarial fevers killed about 10,000 recruits in the Union Army troops. It was even more astonishing

[26] Nineteenth-century physicians generally classified fever by its pattern and type. In particular, "intermittent" and "remittent" fevers – terms physicians used before the word *malaria* came into use – have been considered to represent "malarial" fever. Hong (2007a) estimated the risk of these fevers using the correlation between annual fever incidence rate in nineteenth-century US forts and environmental factors, including temperature, precipitation, and elevation variables.

that about 1,300,000 recruits contracted malarial fevers during the Civil War (US Surgeon General's Office 1888).

Although quinine, the only treatment for malarial fever at that time, was introduced in the late seventeenth century, it did not completely cure infected malaria patients, so fevers frequently reoccurred whenever the afflicted were malnourished and weakened, and repeated infections caused serious nutritional deficit. In particular, malaria was rampant during the planting and harvest seasons. By rendering farmers bed-ridden in those seasons, malaria caused great economic loss. Quinine might get farmers back into the workforce, but their labor productivity could not resume as before. Although malaria retreated into the south, mainly because of agricultural drainage beginning in the 1870s, the regular malaria afflictions continued, bringing with them poverty and public health problems in the south until the 1920s, when eradication campaigns began (Humphreys 2001).

How did malaria undermine nutritional status and subsequent health? Besides malaria, all kinds of infections are closely associated with nutritional losses and, subsequently, with immune disorders. According to studies in nutritional science, more energy is needed for sustenance and stimulation of the immune response system during infection. If food supply is inadequate, this causes protein energy malnutrition (PEM), which is a critical factor in the susceptibility to infection. PEM also undermines the linear growth of children, leading to a further reduction in food intake and nutrient absorption, to catabolic nutrient losses, and to increased metabolic requirements. Subsequently, PEM and deficiencies in nutrients diminish and impair immune functions – both acquired immunity and innate host defense mechanisms – by reducing leptin concentrations. In the end, this increases susceptibility to major infectious diseases, particularly among children. This mechanism also implies that malnutrition itself can cause various infections and other health problems. A number of studies have demonstrated that nutritional deficiencies in childhood can have permanent adverse effects on cognitive performance and on the immune system, and are highly correlated with mortality from diarrhea, pneumonia, measles, and malaria – the principal causes of death of children in developing countries (Scrimshaw and San Giovanni 1997; Scrimshaw 1998; Woodward 1998; Caulfield, Richard, and Black 2004; Schaible and Kaufmann 2007).

However, not everyone had the same experience within disease environments. The effects of specific infectious diseases varied across race and nativity. For instance, African-American slaves experienced a different plantation environment to whites. Living in crowded nurseries in their early years, black children were frequently exposed to contagious diseases. They were also vulnerable to hookworm because of the sandy soil and warm climate of southern plantations. Because white children had less contact with those infections than black children, the difference in living conditions led to disparities in physical development due to malnutrition by infections (Coelho and McGuire 1999). In addition, the black population had different physiological characteristics from the white population: because of the sickle-cell trait, many African-Americans were more resistant or immune to malarial fevers than were white farm workers.[27] Consequently, slaves who survived southern environments in their early years might be more resistant to those harmful environments in adulthood than white farmers because of acquired immunity or physiological differences.

The spread of diseases was largely affected by urbanization and industrialization in the nineteenth and early twentieth centuries. While many cities had built water systems by the late nineteenth century, few of them had simultaneously constructed sewer systems to remove water waste. Most water waste from homes and factories was disposed of in the street and in rivers, without sanitary treatments. This polluted the reservoir of drinking water, which was not effectively purified until the early twentieth century. Accordingly, the incidence of waterborne diseases, such as typhoid, increased (Troesken 2004). The urban mortality penalty – people who spent their early years in large cities died faster than otherwise – was very substantial throughout the nineteenth century (Cain and Hong 2009).

High population density in large cities also made infections more contagious, and disease outbreaks were made worse by influxes of immigrants. Notably, the cholera epidemics in New York City in 1832 began with European immigrants entering the city. These epidemics killed about 3,000 people within six weeks. To curb the

---

[27] A person who survives malaria infections may be immune to subsequent infection only when he or she has been frequently and intensively infected with malaria in previous years. Sickle-cell mutation is a typical example of the malaria immunity gene that is found among people in some areas of Africa (Humphreys 2001).

outbreak of infectious diseases, large cities built quarantine centers, but these did not provide complete solutions to prevent disease contagions. The influenza pandemic of 1918 is a more recent example, which was worldwide. In Europe, the spread of the disease was accelerated by wartime migration of civilians and soldiers and overcrowding on public transport and in communities (Barry 2005). The death rate of American young adults (ages 20–40) from influenza and pneumonia was 20 times higher in 1918 than in previous years (Taubenberger and Morens 2006). It was studied that cohorts who were *in utero* during the pandemic had experienced the aftereffects throughout the life course such as reduced educational attainment, increased rates of physical disability, lower income, and lower socioeconomic status (Almond 2006).

So far we have explored various disease environments that Americans suffered and died from in the past. How could they then conquer those infectious environments and the high risk of mortality? Previous research has emphasized two main points: improvements in diet and improvements in sanitary reform. The role of diet was first suggested by Thomas McKeown. He argued that the decline of mortality after 1700 owed more to improved diet and increased standards of living than to medical interventions or targeted public health reforms. Although his argument has been controversial among researchers, it has been revealed that many types of infectious diseases are closely related to nutrition, including cholera, measles, tuberculosis, and respiratory diseases (Harris 2004b). Although it seems to be difficult to make a clear distinction between the role of improvement in diet and the success of public health intervention, the US incidence of tuberculosis declined from 105.1 per 100,000 population in 1930 to 4.6 in 2006 (Carter *et al.* 2006; Centers for Disease Control 2007b). The decline was affected by the improvement in the population's diet.[28]

In addition to diet, much attention has been paid to public health reforms, improved personal hygiene, and advances in medical knowledge. By the late nineteenth century, most large cities began to discuss

---

[28] Tuberculosis has long been associated with poverty, malnutrition, and overcrowding. Thus, the dramatic decline in the disease in the UK and other developed countries – which began before the introduction of BCG vaccination – has been attributed to improvements in those socioeconomic risk factors. On the other hand, Kunitz (2007) argues that the decline of the disease is also related with changes in the virulence of the tubercle bacillus.

public health policies at the board of health or the health department. They introduced new technologies for purifying drinking water, and sewer systems were established to reduce the threat to drinking water supplies. In the 1910s, the hookworm eradication campaign by the US Public Health Service and the Rockefeller Foundation was successful in the southern states (Bleakley 2007). In the 1920s, they turned their attention to malaria eradication. With the acceptance of germ theory, the importance of personal hygiene (including washing hands and boiling drinking water) was championed. These public health reforms were largely based upon advances in medical knowledge. With the discoveries of pathogens of various infections, strategic prevention became feasible. Vaccination virtually eliminated previously common infectious diseases, including diphtheria, tetanus, poliomyelitis, smallpox, measles, mumps, and rubella. The introduction of antibiotics and antimicrobial medicines also played a key role in controlling infectious diseases (Centers for Disease Control 1999a; Centers for Disease Control 1999b; Cutler and Miller 2005).

Since infants and children are generally the most vulnerable to infectious environments, this age group was most affected by these public health improvements. The environmental difference and sanitary conditions also explain a large disparity in infant death between urban and rural areas that did not disappear until the early twentieth century. In 1900, the urban infant mortality rate was 179.9 per 1,000 births, while the rural infant mortality rate was 117.4 per 1,000 births. The health condition of urban infants also depended on the quality of milk supplied. According to Rochester (1923), one of the main causes of infant death in urban areas was diarrhea, which was largely caused by intake of contaminated milk. As urban areas expanded, urban residents needed to bring milk from farther rural farms to feed infants, and the railroad could not provide fresh milk until refrigeration was introduced. It was reported that the number of bacteria in milk increased geometrically on the way to the cities. This partially explains the difference in infant mortality rates between urban and rural areas, and why infant deaths in urban areas were highest in summer and among the low-socioeconomic classes that could not afford to maintain fresh milk (Lee 2007).

In addition to the difference between urban and rural rates, disparities in the infant mortality rate prevailed within cities. Figure 6.3 and Table 6.9 present the changes in disparities in infant mortality during the twentieth century by the neighborhoods of six of the largest

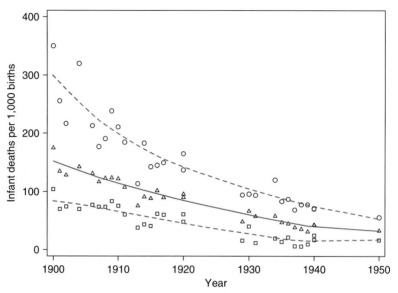

Source: Center for Population Economics website (www.cpe.uchicago.edu).
Notes: The symbol of circle, triangle, or square denotes, respectively, the maximum,
mean, and minimum value of infant mortality rates among wards in each city
in a given year. The dashed and solid curves are lowess fit curves for three
types of data. This diagram shows that between 1900 and 1950 more than
80 percent of the difference in the infant mortality rate between the worst
and best wards of six large cities had disappeared.

Figure 6.3 Preliminary findings on trends in disparities in infant death rates of
the wards of six large US cities, 1900–1950

US cities in 1900. We are using wards averaging about 30,000 people
as the unit of observation.[29] Figure 6.3 has three sets of observations:
The maximum infant death rates across about 120 wards of six large
cities are clustered around the top line; the minimum infant death rates
are clustered around the bottom line; and the line in the middle
represents the average. The main point of this figure is to show how
wide the range in infant death rates was at the beginning of the period
in 1890, for example, the infant mortality rate of the worst ward in
New York City was 562 per 1,000 births, while that of the best ward

[29] But such large units tend to mask disparities since they tend to combine both rich and
poor neighborhoods. We hope eventually to conduct the analyses at the level of
census districts, which average about 8,000 individuals, and are more homogeneous
with respect to socioeconomic status and health conditions than wards.

Table 6.9 *Disparity in infant mortality rate among wards of selected US large cities, 1890–1930 (infant deaths per 1,000 births)*

	Late nineteenth century					Early twentieth century				
City	Year	Mean	S.D.	Best	Worst	Year	Mean	S.D.	Best	Worst
New York	1890	369.8	84.7	234.3	562.0	1930	56.9	15.4	35.0	98.0
Chicago	1890	294.5	73.3	142.3	525.4	1931	52.4	20.6	9.5	127.1
Philadelphia	1890	312.2	99.0	162.1	677.3	1940	48.6	37.9	21.1	282.9
St. Louis	1890	294.9	126.2	170.0	671.8	1931	57.4	21.6	11.8	93.4
Boston	1890	346.8	80.4	177.6	514.6	1930	66.3	15.8	40.1	95.7
Baltimore	1890	409.7	120.0	286.3	768.0	1931	69.2	29.7	13.9	146.2
Buffalo	1890	306.8	82.8	232.0	546.0	1934	55.2	17.2	32.4	111.0
St. Paul	1890	246.6	69.3	142.9	402.4	1930	46.3	14.7	29.2	76.9
Newark	1890	410.4	98.9	295.9	678.9	1940	45.4	17.4	24.6	85.4

Sources: US Bureau of the Census 1896 for 1890 and Center for Population database (www.cpe.uchicago.edu) for the other years in the early twentieth century.
Notes: At that time, each city was divided into 10–30 wards (a smaller administrative unit of city). The table reports average, standard deviation, lowest, and highest infant mortality rate among wards in each large city.

was 234.3 (Table 6.9). This is closely related with disparities in socio-economic status and with unequal sanitary conditions among wards.

As public health interventions became effective in the early twentieth century, the United States observed a dramatic decline in infant mortality and a large improvement in the disparities between rural and urban populations. The overall level declined from 229 deaths per 1,000 births in 1850 to 69 in 1930. After the 1920s, the infant mortality rates of some large cities were lower than those in rural places. The intra-urban disparities were also dramatically reduced. By 1940, the differential between the best and the worst wards had declined to about 60 per 1,000. During the period of 1890–1940, the spread between the best and the worst wards diminished by 73 percent. For example, the infant mortality rate of the worst ward in New York City around 1930 was 98 per 1,000, while that of the best ward was 35 per 1,000.[30]

[30] The first point to be noted about changes and disparities in the twentieth century is that the range of differences in exposure to disease has narrowed greatly over the course of the century. The disparities we observe today are much smaller than they used to be. From the perspective of 1900 we are currently engaged in fine-tuning, not in gross corrections of disparities.

6.2 Changing bodies and the escape from premature death, sickness, and poverty

A key element in technophysio evolution theory is the use of anthropometric and demographic data for assessing the level of chronic malnutrition and the trends that we have reviewed so far. The study of the associations between change of body size and mortality, morbidity, and labor productivity is another important element of the theory. In this section, we introduce the American experience of physiological and economic changes that technological advances have brought about.

6.2.1 Changes in height and BMI under technological advances

One view of the economic impact on height is that increasing standards of living brought about by economic growth guarantee a stable upward trend in the average height of a population. This argument basically relies upon the impact of economic growth on food intake and real income. However, some counterevidence has been found for the period of industrialization in the United States and in Britain (Fogel *et al.* 1983; Floud, Wachter, and Gregory 1990). In the American case, the average height of native-born free males shrank by 4.4 cm (or 1.7 inches), beginning in the 1830s and lasting until the 1890s (Table 6.10). Since industrialization was expanding across the nation and the economy was growing during the period, the decline in height has been seen as problematic.

This paradox was first examined from the aspect of diet, for example as a major factor in the height decline of West Point cadets in the antebellum

That is the result one gets when looking at differences in crude death rates. What happens if one looks at the ratio? The ratio of the crude death rates between the worst and best wards was 3.56 (310 ÷ 87) in 1900 but in 1940, the ratio was 5.61 (73 ÷ 13). Using ratios, it appears that disparities in health were exacerbated between 1900 and 1940, since ratios imply that disparities increased by 58 percent. Which is the better measure of changes in disparities, changes in differences in crude death rates or changes in the ratios? The change in differences is consistent with the very large increase in life expectancy, the sharp decline in morbidity from a series of diseases that were deadly to infants, and the widespread improvement in housing and living standards generally.

Ratios give the wrong measure because of a mathematical artifact. When denominators are relatively small, a small change in the denominator can have a big effect on the value of the ratio. In the case of Figure 6.3, a modest improvement of conditions in the healthy wards obscures the huge improvement of conditions in the most unhealthy wards, when ratios are the measure of choice.

Table 6.10 *Height by sex and race, 1760–1980 (cm)*

	Males				Females			
Year	Native-born average	White	Black (slave)	Hispanic	Native-born average	White	Black (slave)	Hispanic
1760	172.3		169.0				158.4	
1770	172.8		169.5 (169.4)				159.5 (159.6)	
1780	173.2		170.1 (169.7)				158.7 (159.3)	
1790	172.9		169.8 (169.5)				159.0 (159.3)	
1800	172.9		170.4 (170.4)				158.9 (159.9)	
1810	173.0	174.7	170.3				158.6	
1820	172.9	173.8	170.8				158.1	
1830	173.5	174.2	170.1				157.6	
1840	172.2	173.7	169.6				156.6	
1850	171.1							
1860	170.6							
1870	171.2							
1880	169.5							
1890	169.1							
1900	170.0							
1910	172.1	174.6	173.8	170.0	160.5	160.6	160.7	158.2
1920	173.1	176.3	174.4	171.8	161.7	161.9	162.3	158.5
1930	175.8	177.4	175.2	172.3	162.6	163.1	162.9	159.7
1940	176.7	178.5	177.3	172.0	163.1	163.8	164.0	159.7
1950	177.3	178.8	177.9	172.3	163.1	164.0	164.2	159.7
1960	177.9	179.2	177.2	172.6	164.2	164.7	164.0	160.2
1970	177.4	179.5	177.6	172.3	163.6	164.9	164.3	160.8
1980	179.1	179.7	179.1	173.8	164.3	165.4	164.3	161.0

Sources: Fogel 1986, p. 511 and Carter *et al.* 2006, Vol. 2, Series Bd653, Bd654, Bd665, Bd666, Bd699, Bd670. Heights in italics were calculated from Union Army veterans' datasets from the Center for Population Economics of the University of Chicago (heights in 1810–1840) or the National Health Interview Survey (NHIS) datasets (heights in 1910–1980).

Notes: Parentheses denote data for slaves as opposed to free blacks.

period. Komlos (1987) pointed out that meat production did not keep pace with population growth, emphasizing reduced caloric intake. Although his argument was disputed among researchers (specifically, whether the decline in meat production was statistically significant), the general trend of food production prior to the Civil War was not favorable.[31] Rapid population growth by urbanization and immigration had fettered food supplies per capita for major foodstuffs, though their gross levels were increasing. The increased food price also led to disparities in food consumption stemming from increasing income inequality.[32]

In order to look at a simple long-run relationship between diet and height, Figure 6.4 shows a scatter plot of the average height of native-born males against daily caloric intake per capita around birth year from 1800 to 1980, which is estimated in Table 6.6.[33] The scatter plot presents the effect of diet in early life on physical growth over the past two centuries.

At a glance, no clear trend is found from the diagram; even the correlation between diet and height throughout the nineteenth century looks negative. For a better understanding of the scatter plot, a linear regression line between two variables together with its 90 percent confidence interval was estimated using the two periods of 1800–1840 and 1940–1970, when the levels of diet and height were relatively stable. This upward trend line means that height increased with food intake from the early nineteenth century to the late twentieth century. Under this long-run trend, as Komlos suggested, a considerable decline in adult height prior to the Civil War – especially for the 1850–1860 cohorts – seems to be highly related to reduced caloric intake. But beginning at the 1870 cohort, diet and height divert from the positive trend until 1940. In particular, the 1880–1900 cohort seems to have been well fed, but their heights were among the shortest since 1800. This is not clearly explained solely by diet and food consumption. There must be another factor on the side of claims on food intake that substantially reduced the positive impact of diet on height in the second half of the nineteenth century and the early twentieth century.

---

[31] See Gallman (1995; 1996) and footnote 20 for the critiques.

[32] According to the estimate of Steckel and Moehling (2001), the inequality measured by the Gini coefficient increased by 27 percent in 1820–1900. Also see Figure 6.12.

[33] This approach measures a relationship between food intake and height at the population level, though individual diet level largely depends on parental income and earnings.

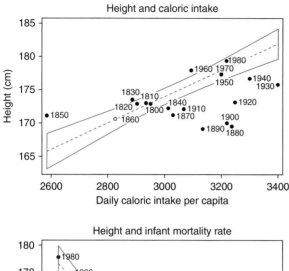

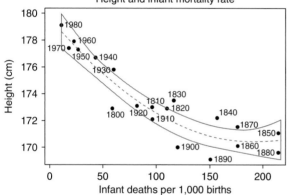

Sources: Table 6.6 for daily caloric intake per capita; Table 6.8 for infant mortality rate; and Table 6.10 for height.

Notes: Each scatter plot presents the long-run relationship between average adult height of native-born males and estimated daily caloric intake per capita around birth year, and infant mortality rate (IMR) of white population around birth year. Caloric intake and IMR were used as measures of the levels of diet and disease environments, respectively. IMR in 1800–1840 was imputed using the correlation between life expectancy at age 10 in 1850–1980 (Haines 1979; Fogel 1987) and infant mortality rates in the same period ($r = -0.9791$). The dashed line in the first diagram is the linear regression line for 1800–1830 and 1950–1980. The dashed curve in the second diagram is the quadratic regression line for all the sample years. The box in each diagram indicates the 95 percent confidence interval.

Figure 6.4 The relevance of adult height of native-born males to daily caloric intake per capita and infant mortality rate around birth year, 1800–1980

Another line of research has paid more attention to environmental impacts on height. Some studies have offered evidence that early exposure to infectious diseases and unhealthy conditions – driven by industrialization, urbanization, and immigration – increasingly required young people to use their energy for combating diseases, and that exposure to some diseases like diarrhea can reduce the efficiency with which food is converted into nutrients; this resulted in the deterioration of the final height of the population during the nineteenth century (Haines, Craig, and Weiss 2003; Hong 2007a).

In the bottom panel of Figure 6.4, we plot the scatter of average height of native-born males born in 1800–1980 against the infant mortality rate in their birth years. Infant mortality is generally considered to be a good indicator of prevailing epidemiological and socioeconomic environments because this age group is most vulnerable to infections and unhealthy conditions.[34] Since the height variable is estimated for the cohort of the year, the infant mortality rate represents the status of epidemiological and socioeconomic environments around the year.[35] The scatter plot suggests first that the substantial declines in height over 1850–1860 can be explained by the factors associated with the high level of the infant mortality rate as well as the low level of per capita diet. Second, the environmental factors associated with the infant mortality rate also account for the continuous declines in height after the Civil War until 1900, which were out of the trend of the relationship between diet and height.[36]

---

[34] Note that the infant mortality rate is also partly affected by the level of diet.

[35] One may have some reservations about whether the infant mortality rate can be a measure of prevailing environmental conditions because it depends on not only sanitary and epidemiological conditions but also on other factors such as diet and socioeconomic conditions. An alternative measure of environmental conditions is the rate of death from infectious diseases. Table 6.8 reports the mortality rate caused by some major infections including tuberculosis, diphtheria, typhoid fever, and measles in 1860–2000. The correlation coefficient of the infant mortality rate and the rate from selected infections is estimated at 0.9840. This implies that the use of the infant mortality rate is effective. The British case discussed in Chapter 4 suggests that the British infant mortality rate (shown in Figure 4.3 of Chapter 4) declined considerably as British expenditures on improving sanitary conditions increased substantially in the 1890s and early 1900s (shown in Figure 4.8 of Chapter 4).

[36] The height of the 1890 and 1900 cohorts seems to be shorter than this trend implies. This deviation may suggest that environments in that period were much worse than is measured by the infant mortality rate.

The diagrams imply that diet and environment are key factors in determining nutritional status in early life. Changes in two components – the reduction in per capita food availability in the antebellum period and the worsened environments in the late nineteenth century – account for the decline in height. Urbanization and increasing population were the risk factors that caused problems in diet level and environments. But it is hard to separate the two components because they are closely related. The effects of the lack of caloric intake can be aggravated by nutrition-related diseases like diarrhea, measles, and pneumonia. Similarly, people are more susceptible to infections when they are poorly nourished.

The debate about the decline in population height during the nineteenth century was opened up by studies of slave height, which had been studied to resolve the dispute over the material treatment of slaves and the efficiency of slavery. Margo and Steckel (1982) found that American male slaves were, on average, two to three inches taller than British or western European adult males in the nineteenth century, although slaves were slightly more than one inch shorter than northern white males.[37] This difference in average height by race and country has been considered to be evidence that the material conditions of slavery (regarding diet and work routine) were above the European standard. That is, it was thought that slaves were well fed, and their workload was not excessive. Further supporting this argument, it was also found that slave height was increasing in 1830–1860 while the free population's height was decreasing during the same period (Fogel *et al.* 1983; Komlos and Coclanis 1997).[38]

Although the decline in adult height was observed during the nineteenth century, the long-run trend of height since 1700 has been upward among all races and ethnic groups. Moreover, the disparities in height between white and black populations have been substantially narrowed

[37] Around 1800–1810, the estimated adult height was as follows: 174.7 cm for American white males, 170.4 cm for American male slaves, and about 168 cm for British males (Table 6.10 of this chapter and Table 2.5 of Chapter 2).
[38] There are some complexities to consider in the issue of slave height and health other than food intake and labor intensity. As we discussed in the previous section, African-American slaves possessed different physiological characteristics than the white population. They experienced different living conditions and different disease environments. For a better understanding of the lifetime health of slaves and the African-American population, more scholarly investigation is necessary on how slaves physiologically reacted to various disease environments in the south.

(Table 6.10). The gap in height between white and black males was about 4.4 cm in 1810, but is negligible today. This improvement implies that the disparities in food intake, exposure to infectious environments, and work conditions by race have been reduced in the same way as the disparity in height has declined over the centuries.

On the other hand, nutritional status in adulthood is affected by work conditions and labor intensity as well as diet and environments (and child labor also prevailed during the industrializing period). Many researchers have used BMI (= kg ÷ m²) to measure the nutritional status of adults. The first diagram in Figure 6.5 shows the trend of average BMI of white males at ages 40 to 59 between 1870 and 2000. The values in 1870–1910 were measured from Union Army veterans' datasets, and those in 1970–2000 were calculated from the National Health Interview Survey (NHIS) datasets. The average BMI levels in 1920–1960 were imputed using cohort average height trends in Table 6.10 and weight trends over time. Since observed average weight in 1870–1910 and 1970–2000 increased proportionally over the years, the trend of BMI was more affected by the trend in height. Thus, the fluctuation of the BMI trend in 1910–1970 reflects the fluctuation of cohort height in 1850–1910.

The other three diagrams in Figure 6.5 show the relationship of American white males' BMI at ages 40–59 to the level of per capita caloric intake, environments (proxied by infant mortality rate), and work level, measured by weekly hours worked in manufacturing. Regarding the effects of food intake on weight and BMI, the increase of BMI in 1870–1980 is not closely related to the increase in per capita daily caloric intake but it is correlated more strongly with the reduction of contaminated environments and work hours. Not only have working hours declined substantially throughout the twentieth century, but the type of work became more sedentary, and so required less energy. People also became less exposed to infectious diseases. Thus, given a similar level of food intake in 1870–1980 and given the metabolic requirement (BMR), people gained more weight relative to height. The recent large increase of BMI in 1980–2000 (6 percent) is highly connected to increased food intake during the period (22 percent).[39]

---

[39] While the adult height of white males at ages 40 to 59 increased less than 1 cm (less than 1 percent change) over two decades, their average weight increased about 6 kg (a change of 7 percent).

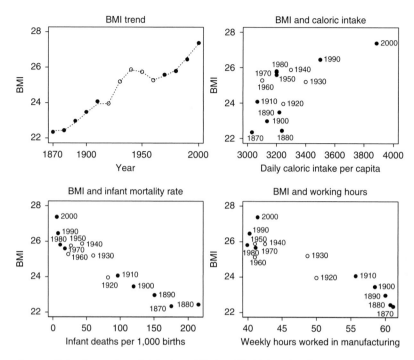

Sources: Union Army veterans' datasets and National Health Interview Survey datasets for BMI; Table 6.6 for daily caloric intake per capita; Table 6.7 for working hours; and Table 6.8 for infant mortality rate.
Notes: Each scatter plot presents the long-term relevance of average BMI of (non-Hispanic) white males to estimated daily caloric intake per capita, infant mortality rate of the white population, and average weekly hours worked in manufacturing. The BMI level in closed circles was measured from Union Army veterans' datasets and National Health Interview Survey datasets. The BMI level in open circles was imputed reflecting the year trend of cohort average of height and weight in other years. The dotted line of BMI trend denotes the estimated BMI trend.

Figure 6.5 The relevance of average BMI of white males at ages 40 to 59 to daily caloric intake per capita, infant mortality rate, and working hours in the examination year, 1870–2000

6.2.2 Issues in birth weight

An increasing number of recent studies have called attention to low birth weight (defined as weight less than 2,500 grams) and its relevance to later health outcomes. They have revealed that birth weight influences later body composition and musculoskeletal development (Sayer and Cooper 2005). Low birth weight is highly related with the development of cardiovascular diseases, type 2 diabetes, kidney problems, and other adverse health outcomes in later ages (Barker 1995; Barker 1998). Consequently, the determinants of birth weight and of having a baby with low birth weight have been of serious concern. Researchers have examined parental factors, especially maternal education, nutritional status (as proxied by maternal height), income, ethnicity, behaviors (drug exposure and smoking), and infections during pregnancy (notably malaria infections) as key risk factors.[40]

Low birth weight is a leading cause of infant mortality. As Figure 6.6 illustrates, a large proportion of perinatal deaths (death within one month after birth) in the early twentieth century occurred among low-birth-weight babies and 21.2 percent of infant deaths in 1900 resulted from premature birth, while infectious and contagious diseases were responsible for 44.5 percent (US Bureau of the Census 1906). Throughout the twentieth century, the perinatal mortality rate has declined significantly, primarily due to medical advances. The reduction in the number of deaths associated with premature births accounts for 20 percent of the decrease of the infant mortality rate between 1900 and 2004, while the prevention of infectious diseases explains 47 percent of the decline.[41] But birth weight is still an issue today because perinatal death accounts for 36.7 percent of infant deaths in 2004, though its absolute number declined during the twentieth century.

Some studies have found that developing countries generally have a lower level of mean birth weight and a higher proportion of low-birth-weight babies than developed countries (Fogel 2004b; UNICEF and WHO 2004). It has been argued that economic growth is related to national or regional levels of birth weight (Ward 1993). From the point of view of technophysio evolution, the results of these studies imply that the elimination of chronic malnutrition can increase birth weight by enhancing the level of maternal nutrition (and intrauterine nutrition), and that the increased birth weight can improve physiological conditions in later ages.

Contrary to those findings of disparities in mean birth weight among countries, however, the long-term trend in birth weight of the US

---

[40] See Costa (1998b; 2004) and Goldin and Margo (1989).

[41] Note that the infant mortality rate is 129.16 per 1,000 in 1900 and 6.76 in 2004; 44.5 percent of infant deaths in 2004 resulted from deaths associated with premature birth, and infectious diseases caused 2.9 percent of infant deaths (Centers for Disease Control 2007a). Therefore, the contribution of the reduction of premature deaths is calculated as 20.34 percent, calculated from $(129.16 \times 0.212 - 6.76 \times 0.367) \div (129.16 - 6.76) \times 100$. Similarly the contribution of the deterioration of infectious diseases is estimated as 46.80 percent, calculated from $(129.16 \times 0.445 - 6.76 \times 0.029) \div (129.16 - 6.76) \times 100$.

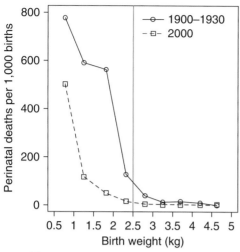

Sources: Historical birth records at Johns Hopkins University
Hospital in Baltimore for 1900–1930; and US National Birth
Certificate data for 2000.
Notes: Perinatal death is defined here as death that occurred
within one month after birth. Birth weight below 2,500 g (denoted
by the vertical line in the diagram) is considered as low birth weight.

Figure 6.6 Perinatal mortality by birth weight

population is still unclear and needs to be investigated further. As
Figure 6.7 presents, US mean birth weight was stable during the twentieth
century. The proportion of low-birth-weight babies among white populations has fluctuated around 5.5 percent and around 11 percent for
black populations. Compared with the remarkable changes in height
and longevity during the same period, the US trends in birth-weight
variables do not have a strong association with the elimination of chronic
malnutrition and economic growth.[42] This implies that the proportion of
low-birth-weight babies or perinatal conditions may have had little

---

[42] There are several possibilities. First, if the current level of average birth weight or
the distribution of low-birth-weight babies is optimal, the United States reached
the optimal level by the late nineteenth century. Second, birth weight might not be
determined by national food production and disease environments. Third, the
intrauterine environments during pregnancy can be protective from external
environments.

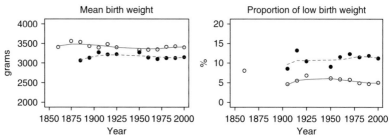

Sources: Goldin and Margo 1989 for 1848–1873 (Philadelphia's almshouse hospital records); Ward 1993 for 1875–1900 (New England Hospital records for white population and Boston Lying-in Hospital records for black population); Johns Hopkins Hospital baby records at the Center for Population Economics for 1900–1930; and National Birth Certificates for 1950–2000.
Note: The solid and dotted curves denote the lowess fit curves for white and black population, respectively.

Figure 6.7 Trends in average birth weight and proportion of low-birth-weight (< 2,500 g) babies, white population (open circle) and black population (closed circle)

association with adult height in the US, and that the association between infant mortality and adult height was primarily related to the association between post-perinatal mortality and adult height. Thus, our findings suggest that the long-term impact of environmental conditions in the post-neonatal period may be just as important in shaping lifelong health as impaired fetal development.

6.2.3 Body size and relative risk of mortality

So far, we have looked into how technological changes in food intake, work level, and disease controls have influenced the trends in nutritional status measured by height and BMI. Another key aspect of the technophysio evolution theory is that the physical change has led to escape from premature death and poor health and has established the secular increase in life expectancy. This hypothesis is described theoretically in Chapter 2 using Waaler surfaces and the analysis of iso-mortality curves. To examine the American experience, we employ a simple version of the Waaler surface in Figure 6.8, looking at the relationship between relative mortality risk and height and BMI.

In order to obtain the evidence for nineteenth-century America, we used the dataset of Union Army veterans developed by the Center for

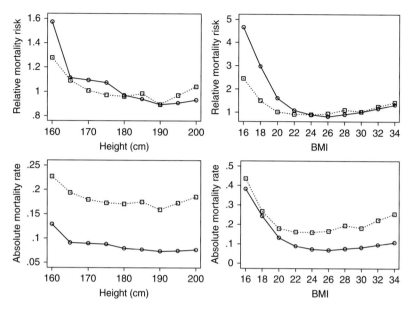

Sources: Union Army veterans' datasets at the Center for Population Economics and National Health Interview Survey datasets.
Notes: In both datasets, height and weight were measured at ages 40 to 59. The period of risk was 10 years. We used 61,171 modern American white males in the 1986–1992 NHIS (National Health Interview Survey) datasets which are linked to the 1986–2002 NDI (National Death Index). We used Union Army veteran samples whose heights and weights were measured at ages 40 to 59.

Figure 6.8 Comparison of relative and absolute mortality risk by height and BMI at ages 40–59, modern American non-Hispanic white males (solid) and Union Army veterans (dotted)

Population Economics at the University of Chicago. Out of 35,570 white veterans sampled, we have searched for those who were examined for pension purposes at ages 40 to 59.[43] Mortality risk is then measured by 10-year mortality after the examination year, relative to the sample average. To seek comparable evidence for current years, we used modern American non-Hispanic white males found in the 1986–1992 NHIS datasets which are linked to the National Death Index (NDI). We used 61,171 males between ages 40 to 59 and a 10-year mortality risk.

---

[43] Because their average birth year was 1840, the average year of examination for this sample is 1890.

The graphs on the left side of Figure 6.8 first show that the risk of premature death depends greatly on height. Although the absolute mortality rate declined by half throughout the twentieth century at all the height levels, the probability of dying within 10 years for very short persons (less than 162.5 cm) at ages 40 to 59 was 30 percent higher than the average figure among the sample of Union Army veterans and 60 percent higher than the average for white males in American today. In both periods, the mortality risk decreases with height up to around 190 cm, and then increases slightly again.[44] Considering the change of average height between two periods – from 173.3 cm (Union Army veterans) to 178.6 cm (modern American non-Hispanic white males) – this suggests that the escape from premature death in the twentieth century was achieved partly through improved nutritional status in the growing years. The graphs also have a modern implication and suggest that the mortality risk of today's population can be additionally improved by enhancing nutritional status in childhood.

Second, BMI is also highly connected to mortality risk, as presented on the right side of Figure 6.8. In both samples of Union Army veterans and the NHIS, those at the low BMI level – less than 19 – were exposed to greater than twice the mortality risk than the sample average. The relative risk for the low BMI group is much greater for the twentieth century because the reduction in the absolute mortality rate over the past century was more substantial for the high BMI group. This disproportionate decline in mortality rate by BMI resulted in shifts of the curve and the optimal BMI level that minimizes mortality risk. The optimal level is estimated as 24.11 for Union Army veterans and as 25.58 for modern American non-Hispanic white males. The change of optimal level reflects advances in medical technology in the twentieth century. Individuals with high BMI levels generally have a greater risk of various chronic disorders, such as cardiovascular diseases and diabetes. But advances in medicine have prolonged the lives of those at risk; otherwise, their average life expectancy would have been much less with the low level of medical technology in the nineteenth century.

In addition to the shift of optimal BMI, there was a significant shift in the BMI distribution of the population over time (Figure 6.9). The mean

---

[44] From two datasets, the optimal height that minimizes relative risk of 10-year mortality is estimated as 185.5 cm for Union Army veterans and 191.9 cm for modern American white males.

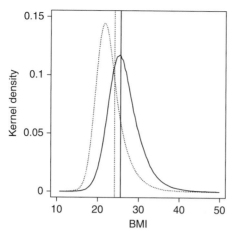

Sources: The BMI distribution (kernel density) was estimated from the 1986–1992 National Health Interview Survey datasets and the Union Army veterans' datasets. *Notes:* The mean (standard deviation) BMI of Union Army veteran is 22.97 (3.38) and that of modern American non-Hispanic white males is 26.54 (3.97). The vertical lines denote the optimal BMI level that minimized the 10-year mortality risk: 25.6 for modern American white males and 24.1 for Union Army veterans. These optimal levels were estimated from the analysis in Figure 6.8.

Figure 6.9 Shift of BMI distribution and optimal BMI level, modern American non-Hispanic white males (solid) and Union Army veterans (dotted)

(standard deviation) BMI of Union Army veterans was 22.97 (3.38), and that of modern American non-Hispanic white males is 26.54 (3.97). Clearly, the body size of a majority of Union Army veterans (71.6 percent) was below the estimated optimal BMI level (24.11) in the late nineteenth century and so carried a high risk of mortality. Over the twentieth century, people became taller, but they gained more weight in adulthood relative to height due to improvements in diet, environments, and work conditions. The increase in BMI level means a greater reduction in mortality rate. This supports the significance of improving nutritional status in reducing premature death.

However, the current trend of BMI change provides another implication for modern Americans. According to the analysis of two samples, the average BMI of American white males has increased by about 15.7 percent throughout the twentieth century, while the estimated optimal BMI level has increased by 6.1 percent. In other words, the body size of American adult males has increased by more than twice the rate of the change in medical technologies. This rapid growth of weight relative to height was helpful in reducing mortality risk at least until the middle of the twentieth century. Remarkably, about half of the BMI increase occurred during the last two decades of the twentieth century. This means that American body size is rapidly moving toward overweight and obesity.

6.2.4 The relevance of disease and disability to body size

Technological changes have led to a large reduction in premature death throughout the twentieth century. Some scholars have insisted that this would increase the morbidity rates of the elderly because, due to the mortality decline, larger numbers of weaker persons could survive to later ages (Riley and Alter 1996). However, the long-term study by Fogel, Costa, and Kim (1993) showed that age-specific chronic disease rates at older ages have decreased over the twentieth century. A comparison of the prevalence of selected chronic diseases between Union Army veterans and modern American veterans shows that all major chronic disorders were more than twice as prevalent in 1910 as they were in 1997–2006 (Table 6.11). The exposure to chronic malnutrition and infectious environments explains why people in the past had poor health over their lifetimes and died earlier (Costa 2008). Reduced exposure to infectious environments has led to a significant decline in the age-specific prevalence of chronic diseases during the twentieth century (Fogel 2004a).

The relevance of body size to relative mortality risk can be clarified by looking at the connection between body size and relative morbidity risk. Premature death is closely related to poor health driven by nutritional deficiency and environmental insults over the life cycle. It is therefore to be expected that the relationship between body size and the risk of poor health will be similar to that which we found between body size and mortality risk.

In seeking nineteenth-century evidence, we use Union Army veterans' lifetime health records to calculate the relative likelihood of being diagnosed with specific chronic diseases at the time of the physical examination date that occurred at ages 40 to 59. We used the four types of chronic diseases that most afflicted veterans in old ages: cardiovascular, respiratory, gastrointestinal, and liver/spleen/gallbladder-related diseases. As the graphs in the left-hand side of Figure 6.10 show, the development of those

Table 6.11 *Comparison of the prevalence of selected chronic conditions among Union Army veterans in 1910, veterans in 1983, veterans in NHIS, 1985–1988, and veterans in NHIS, 1997–2006*

Chronic disorder	1910 Union Army veterans	Age-adjusted 1983 veterans	NHIS 1985–1988 veterans	NHIS 1997–2006 veterans
Musculoskeletal	67.7	47.2	42.5	34.2
Digestive	84.0	48.9	18.0	1.9
Diarrhea	31.9	4.2	1.4	2.5
Genitourinary	27.3	32.3	8.9	2.1
Central nervous, endocrine, metabolic, or blood	24.2	29.1	12.6	6.2
Heart	76.0	39.9	26.6	19.4
Respiratory	42.2	28.1	26.5	15.1

Sources: Fogel, Costa, and Kim 1993 for veterans in 1910, 1983, and 1985–1988; and the National Health Interview Survey datasets for 1997–2006.

chronic conditions is highly related to body size and nutritional status. The risk of morbidity was generally lowest in the tall group. The relative risk decreases with BMI up to the level of 25–26 for all the selected diseases, which was slightly above the optimal BMI minimizing mortality risk, and then increases again beyond the point. Because a majority of nineteenth-century populations were at short height levels and low BMI levels, the observed relationship implies that deterioration in nutritional status caused by disease exposure and lack of caloric intake considerably affected lifetime health and longevity in the nineteenth century.[45]

Many researchers have provided supporting evidence. Using the dataset of the Union Army veterans, Costa (2000) has revealed that their experiences of infections during the Civil War were responsible for developing chronic diseases in old ages. For example, those who

---

[45] This relationship can be interpreted with a different causality. Individuals who suffer from those chronic disorders may have short height and low BMI due to nutritional loss. Thus, the above explanation is less applicable for those at the high BMI levels who also have a high risk of mortality and morbidity relative to the sample average.

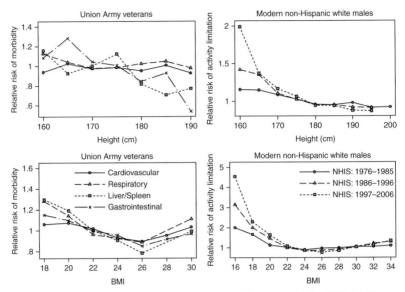

Sources: Estimated from the Union Army veterans' datasets and the 1976–2006 NHIS datasets.
Notes: The risk is relative to sample average. The legends of diagrams in the upper panels follow those in the lower panels.

Figure 6.10 Relative morbidity risk by BMI among Union Army veterans at ages 40–59 and relative risk of activity limitation by BMI among modern American non-Hispanic white males at ages 40–59

suffered from tuberculosis, typhoid fever, and rheumatism in the war developed more heart-related diseases in old ages by 14 percent, 12 percent, and 11 percent, respectively. Similarly, Hong (2007b) has investigated veterans who lived in malaria-endemic counties in their early years and found them more likely to have developed various chronic conditions. From modern data, it has been well documented that exposure to infectious diseases *in utero* and during infancy and childhood has a significant, adverse impact on rates of mortality and on the prevalence of chronic diseases and disabilities in middle and late ages (Barker 1995; Barker 1998).

The same implication is found from data on modern Americans. For modern evidence, we use white males aged 40 to 59 in three NHIS datasets of three different periods: 1976–1985, 1986–1996, and 1997–2006. Instead of specific chronic conditions, we examined the risk of having any health problems that limit life activities as a measure of relative morbidity risk. Compared with the results of Union Army veterans, the diagrams of modern Americans in Figure 6.10 look much more like the relationship between body size and mortality risk. For all the NHIS samples, the relative risk of limitation of activity decreased with height, and it has a quadratic relationship with BMI whose threshold level is around 25–26.

6.2.5 Labor productivity, inequalities, and generational effects

From an economic perspective, the significance of technophysio evolution theory lies in the capacity for the elimination of chronic malnutrition and the escape from poor health to increase labor productivity and income and to reduce economic inequalities. At the macro level, this will lead to economic growth, greater production of goods and services, and new technological developments, which will initiate a new path of technophysio evolution.

The contribution of changes in physiological factors to economic development and growth can be described in various ways. Changes in health, diet, and clothing and housing can significantly influence the efficiency with which ingested energy is converted into work. Mechanical advances accelerate this efficiency improvement. Reduction of environmental risks increases the proportion of ingested energy available for work by requiring less energy for combating diseases and enhancing the efficiency of absorbing nutrients. Moreover, changes in diet pattern can result in increased thermodynamic efficiency – denoted as "Atwater factors" in Chapter 2 – by producing more energy from the unit of food that can be metabolized. Finally, as people become less susceptible to chronic conditions and early death, they can spend more time working and participating in other economic activities, including leisure (Fogel 2004b).

By examining Union Army veterans who survived to 1900 and are found in the 1900 US Federal Census manuscripts, we have found a high correlation between BMI and labor force participation rate in 1900 as a measure of economic productivity (Figure 6.11). The labor force participation rate of those at the low BMI levels was only one-third of the average rate. The BMI level that maximizes labor force participation is similar to the optimal BMI that minimizes mortality and morbidity risk. The same pattern is found for modern American white males – not only for labor force participation, but also for the risk of poverty. The graph of earnings and wealth in Figure 6.11 also shows

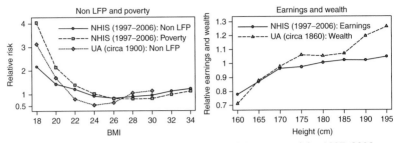

Sources: Estimated from the Union Army veterans' datasets and the 1997–2006 NHIS datasets.

Notes: Each BMI group's relative risk of non-LFP is measured by the group's proportion of population not in the labor force divided by the average LFP rate of the entire sample. The poverty rate is calculated as the proportion of samples whose reported earnings are below each year's poverty line. Each BMI group's relative risk of poverty is measured by the group's poverty proportion divided by the average poverty rate of the entire sample. We use modern Americans at ages 40 to 59. For nineteenth-century comparison, we searched for Union Army veterans in the 1900 US federal census, and used the variable of occupation in the census records. To look into the relationship between height and wealth in the nineteenth century, we searched for veterans found in the 1860 US federal census, and use the sum of real estate and personal property wealth. Their height was measured at the time of enlistment.

Figure 6.11 Comparison of relative risk of low economic productivity (non labor force participation and poverty) by BMI and relative wealth and earnings by height, modern non-Hispanic white American males and Union Army veterans

that low levels of wealth in 1860 and earnings in 1997–2006 can be linked to short height driven by malnutrition in early life.[46]

These findings imply that physiological improvement could be a leading factor in economic growth over the centuries. But the role of economic factors in inducing physiological improvement is not always consistent, as was seen during the mid nineteenth century. Economic growth in the nineteenth century was very costly because economic booms caused rapid population growth, internal and external migration, urbanization, sanitation problems, and rampant diseases; all these reduced people's productivity and their ability to accumulate human capital. One lesson of technophysio evolution theory is that standards of living cannot be measured only by economic variables. The theory suggests that a

---

[46] Lee (2005) also reveals a strong impact of veterans' wartime health on their wealth accumulation between 1860 and 1870. For the mid nineteenth century, Hong (2007b) suggests that people who migrated into malaria-endemic counties between 1850 and 1860 accumulated less wealth than those who moved to low-malaria areas.

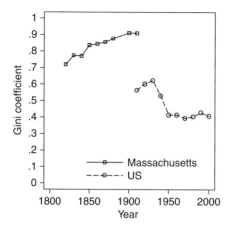

Sources: Steckel and Moehling 2001 for Massachusetts in 1820–1910; Plotnick *et al.* 2000 for 1913–1990; and United Nations 2006 for 2000.

Figure 6.12 US trend of economic inequality

measurement of economic growth that omits the close interaction between rapid technological change and the changes in human physiology is inappropriate (Steckel 1995b; Engerman 1997; Fogel 2004c).

Another cost in the nineteenth century was the increase in inequality. Some estimates of Gini coefficients suggest that economic inequality was increasing throughout the nineteenth century as much as disparities in living conditions and mortality by socioeconomic classes were increasing (Figure 6.12) (Steckel and Moehling 2001). In general, people in low socioeconomic groups were more likely to be exposed to infectious environments. Their access to better diets was also limited by low income. Inequalities in economic and ecological status and the lack of public health interventions led to a large disparity in nutritional status, accelerating the paradox of the "antebellum puzzle" in mid-nineteenth-century America.

Reducing inequalities is significant because economic inequality can cause subsequent disparities in body size, mortality, morbidity, and economic productivity over generations. An increasing number of studies has paid attention to the role of intergenerational effects in determining lifetime health and nutritional status. As is well documented over the centuries, pregnancy outcomes (including birth weight and infant mortality rate) largely depend on parental income and occupational and educational levels. These factors also affect children's physical growth in early life and their health outcomes in later life. Although parents' genes will determine, to some extent, how tall a person *can* be, the nutrition during the growing years will influence how tall a person *will* be. For these reasons, height is an early indicator of mortality, morbidity, and labor productivity in late life.

6.3 Recent trends and future prospects

The cohort of the late nineteenth century benefited substantially from secular improvements in nutritional status and so experienced physiological and economic progress. Economic development and growth along with improved public health conditions led to more technological advances in food production, its distribution, work conditions, and disease controls in the twentieth century. This affected the nutritional status of the next generation and initiated a new phase of technophysio evolution.

In the area of crop production, advances in biotechnology and genetic engineering introduced artificial fertilizers, accelerated the breeding process, and increased crop yields. For example, average yields of corn per acre have increased from 40 bushels in 1900 to 150 bushels in 2001. National per capita production of meat and dairy products has been enough to satisfy the level of national demand and consumption. As diet patterns have changed (such as the diversion from grains as the primary source of calories), various foodstuffs have been produced or imported. Today, the sum of caloric intake from grains, meats, and dairy products is less than 50 percent, while it was 80–90 percent of the diet at the end of the nineteenth century.

Because of mechanical advances and improved individual health, twentieth-century American workers have been more productive than were their ancestors. The increased real income due to high labor productivity also led to transitions in the labor market. Most of all, workers now retire from work earlier than they did in the nineteenth century (Costa 1998a). As Figure 6.13 illustrates, the labor force participation rate of males aged 65 and older dropped from 63.1 percent to 17.7 percent between 1900 and 2000. This rate also declined by 27 percent for the men aged 45 to 64. Compared with the trend for men, women's labor force participation increased more than twice throughout the mid twentieth century as women's opportunities to participate in economic activities expanded. But this trend has slowed since the 1980s. The labor force participation of women aged 65 and older did not change much throughout the twentieth century.

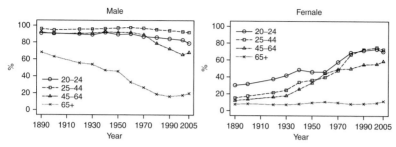

Sources: US Bureau of the Census 1975b for 1890–1970 and US Bureau of the Census 2007 for 1980–2005.

Figure 6.13 US trend in labor force participation rate by age group, 1890–2005

Additionally, individuals in the labor force have worked fewer but more efficient hours. Today, workers are working 30 percent fewer hours on average than workers in 1900. Reflecting the increase in productivity, real hourly wages have risen 14 times between 1910 and 2000 (Table 6.7). Consequently, modern Americans have devoted more of their energy and time to physiological development and human capital accumulation than their ancestors. According to Fogel's (2000) estimates, the hours that the household head spent on leisure activities in a day increased from 1.8 hours in 1880 to 5.8 hours in 1995, and this figure is expected to be 7.2 hours in 2040 (Table 6.12) . Similarly, the proportion of consumption related to leisure increased from 18 percent of total income in 1875 to 68 percent in 1995.

Advances in medical technology have been more dramatic during the twentieth century than in any previous period. Most of all, the improvements in sewage treatment, drinking water purification and fluoridation, and plumbing technology led to better sanitary conditions and reduced the threat from waterborne diseases (Troesken 2004; Cutler and Miller 2005). Antibiotics such as penicillin (discovered in 1928) reduced deaths and morbidity from bacterial diseases. The success of vaccination campaigns reduced children's deaths from infectious diseases – especially from smallpox, polio, and measles (Centers for Disease Control 1999b). The skill of diagnosis has become more accurate with the invention of X-ray technology, computerized tomography (CT), and, more recently, magnetic resonance imaging (MRI). Advances in organ transplantation have lowered the disability rate and extended life span.

Table 6.12 *US trends in consumption and daily time use*

Distribution of consumption (%)			Activity	Daily time use								
				circa 1880		circa 1995		circa 2040				
Consumption class	1875	1995		Hours	%	Hours	%	Hours	%			
Food	49	5	Sleep	8.0	33.3	8.0	33.3	8.0	33.3			
Clothing	12	2	Meals and essential hygiene	2.0	8.3	2.0	8.3	2.0	8.3			
Shelter	13	6	Chores	2.0	8.3	2.0	8.3	2.0	8.3			
Health care	1	9	Travel to and from work	1.0	4.2	1.0	4.2	0.5	2.1			
Education	1	5	Work	8.5	35.4	4.7	19.6	3.8	15.8			
Other	6	7	Illness	0.7	2.9	0.5	2.1	0.5	2.1			
Leisure	18	68	Residual for leisure activities	1.8	7.5	5.8	24.2	7.2	30.0			

Source: Fogel 2000.

6.3.1 *From undernutrition to overnutrition*

With this unprecedented progression of food intake, work level, and disease controls, the changes in body size have been remarkable. The average final height of members of the native-born white (black) adult male cohort born in 1980 is 5.1 cm (5.3 cm) greater than that of the cohort born in 1910; the average height of a native-born white (black) woman increased 4.8 cm (3.6 cm) over the century. Most achievement had been realized by the mid twentieth century (Table 6.10). Table 6.13 shows recent trends in American height, weight, and BMI by sex and age group between two periods, 1971–1974 and 1999–2002. Although a secular improvement of nutritional status (proxied by adult height) is detected for the groups aged 40 or over, the increase in height over 1971–2002 was small for the groups of ages less than 40. Compared with the slight change in height in the late twentieth century, the change in body weight has been greater – it considerably increased the average level of BMI. It is noteworthy that childhood weight and BMI increased to the same degree as that of adults.

Using modern American non-Hispanic white men at ages 40 to 59, we have estimated the modern optimal BMI to be 25.58, which minimizes the 10-year mortality risk as described in the previous section. It has also been shown that morbidity risk is minimized and economic productivity is maximized at this level. If the estimated optimal level can be applied to all of the male population at the same age intervals, the trend found in Table 6.13 suggests that average American males had achieved optimal body size in the 1970s, but that they have become overweight in recent years. From the estimated U-shaped relationships between BMI and health indicators, the recent trend implies that the number of American males who are likely to bear the high risk of mortality, morbidity, and poverty is increasing.

We have emphasized the balance between food intake and claims on it as the determinant of malnutrition. In the eighteenth and nineteenth centuries, "undernutrition," which is caused by lack of nutritional supplies, the demands of combating diseases, and occupations consisting of heavy work was a great concern. But today, "overnutrition," the opposite type of malnutrition, is the issue of the day. An increasing number of studies have indicated obesity as the main risk factor for chronic diseases, including type 2 diabetes, hypertension, heart disease, stroke, and some cancers (US Surgeon General's Office 2009). Some suggest that childhood obesity could lower the US life expectancy (Olshansky *et al.* 2005).

Table 6.13 *Recent trends in height, weight, and BMI by sex and age group, 1971–1974 and 1999–2002*

Ages	Height (cm)			Weight (kg)			BMI		
	1971–1974	1999–2002	Change (%)	1971–1974	1999–2002	Change (%)	1971–1974	1999–2002	Change (%)
(a) Male									
2–4	98.5	98.8	0.24	15.6	16.0	2.56	16.0	16.4	2.29
5–9	124.0	125.8	1.44	25.0	28.1	12.47	16.0	17.4	8.48
10–14	153.0	154.7	1.10	44.6	50.1	12.23	18.8	20.5	9.17
15–19	175.2	175.5	0.19	68.5	74.4	8.58	22.2	24.0	8.09
20–29	177.1	176.7	-0.23	77.1	83.4	8.17	24.5	26.6	8.57
30–39	176.1	176.4	0.17	81.0	86.0	6.17	26.1	27.5	5.36
40–49	175.5	177.2	0.97	80.7	89.1	10.41	26.2	28.4	8.40
50–59	174.0	175.8	1.03	78.7	88.8	12.83	26.0	28.7	10.38
60–74	171.8	174.4	1.51	75.2	87.1	15.82	25.4	28.6	12.60
(b) Female									
2–4	97.3	97.9	0.55	14.9	15.5	3.57	15.7	16.1	2.55
5–9	124.0	124.3	0.26	25.0	27.2	8.87	16.0	17.2	7.24
10–14	152.5	154.3	1.18	45.6	51.5	12.89	19.3	21.3	10.34
15–19	163.0	162.6	-0.25	58.1	63.8	9.74	21.9	24.0	9.87
20–29	162.8	162.8	0.00	60.9	71.1	16.75	23.0	26.8	16.52
30–39	162.9	163.0	0.06	65.6	74.1	12.96	24.7	27.9	12.96
40–49	162.3	163.4	0.68	67.6	76.5	13.17	25.7	28.6	11.28
50–59	160.4	162.3	1.18	67.4	76.9	14.09	26.2	29.2	11.45
60–74	158.6	160.0	0.88	66.5	74.9	12.63	26.5	29.2	10.19

Sources: Centers for Disease Control 2004 and the National Health and Nutrition Examination Surveys and (NHANES).

Today's obesity issue is closely related to changes in diet pattern and lifestyle. The fast food industry thrived throughout the second half of the twentieth century, producing cheaper, higher-calorie foods. Americans consume much more fat and oil than they did a hundred years ago. Their occupations have become more sedentary, and automation of their environment has led them to move less. Modern Americans are threatened not by nutritional deficit, but by the balance of nutritional status and its quality, for which they pay more through consuming high-quality nutrients, exercise, and nutrition-related education. The increasing prevalence of obesity and obesity-related chronic diseases is a particularly critical issue in recent years for black-female, low-income, and minority groups (Must *et al.* 1999; Cutler, Glaeser, and Shapiro 2003; Finkelstein, Ruhm, and Kosa 2005).

The association between body size, death, and sickness is still significant today. In Figure 6.14, we estimated the relationship between BMI and relative risk of mortality, morbidity, and poverty by race and sex, using modern American men and women at ages 40 to 59 as found in recent NHIS datasets. For men, the shape of relative mortality, morbidity, and poverty curves by BMI is almost identical across race. Thus, the long-term implications found from white males may be applicable to the other race groups. Although the curves for women have greater variation across race, the overall implication is similar to that which is found for men; women's optimal BMI level is estimated to be 22–26, depending on race. Around these levels, the risk of activity limitation and poverty is also minimized.

Another feature of the curves for women is that the risk of early death, disease, and poverty increases more rapidly with BMI than does that of men. According to Table 6.13, the recent increase in weight and BMI was greater in women than it was in men. Even the average BMI level of female adults is slightly greater than that of male adults' average in recent years. This implies that a considerable proportion of female populations are overweight, and on average the risk of premature death and disease for women is increasing faster than for men.

6.3.2 Health inequality by sex, race, and income

Throughout the twentieth century, Americans enjoyed large reductions in economic and health inequalities of real income, homelessness, life expectancy, and height (Fogel 2004b). Regarding economic inequalities, the Gini coefficient that reached 0.623 in 1930 declined to 0.408 by

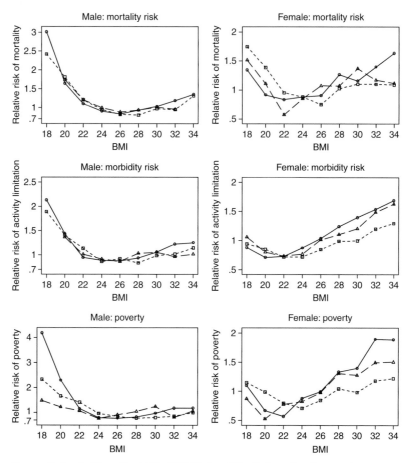

Source: Estimated from the 1986–1992 National Health Interview Survey datasets.
Notes: Mortality risk was measured by 10-year mortality from the survey year. Morbidity risk was measured by the risk of having an activity limitation that indicates whether persons were limited in their activities due to one or more chronic conditions. The relative risk of poverty at each BMI group is interpreted as the proportion of samples whose earnings are below the poverty line of each year relative to sample average.

Figure 6.14 Relative risk of mortality, morbidity, and poverty by BMI among modern Americans at ages 40–59 in 1986–1992, non-Hispanic white (solid), Hispanic (dashed), and black (small dashed)

2000. Health disparities by race and income have also declined greatly. The gains of the lower classes have been much greater than those experienced by the population as a whole. For example, life expectancy at birth of a black man (woman) increased by 106 percent (121 percent) between 1900 and 2000, while that of a white man (woman) increased by 60 percent (63 percent). In looking at this from an economic perspective, technological changes in the twentieth century have lowered the marginal cost for increasing additional units of nutritional status. Over the twentieth century, people have been able to access various foodstuffs at affordable prices. Many diseases that were costly to prevent at the turn of the twentieth century can be treated and prevented cheaply today. This cost reduction has lowered economic and health gradients in socioeconomic status.

As lifetime income has increased and the cost of caloric intake has decreased, consumption patterns have changed over the years. Compared with nineteenth-century Americans, modern Americans spend less of their income on food, clothing, and housing, but invest more in health and education (Table 6.12). Consequently, national health expenditure as a proportion of GDP has increased from 3.5 percent in 1930 to 16.2 percent in 2005 (Figure 6.15). Many studies also suggest that the demand for health care will increase in the future (Fogel 2008). The rapid increase

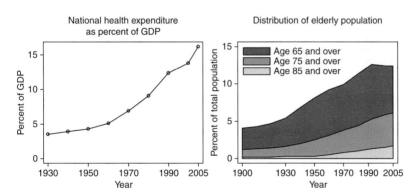

Sources: National health expenditure – US Bureau of the Census 1975b for 1930–1970 and US Bureau of the Census 2007 for 1980–2005; Distribution of elderly population – US Bureau of the Census 2002 for 1900–2000 and US Bureau of the Census 2007 for 2005.

Figure 6.15 US trends in national health expenditure and distribution of elderly population

in the demand for health care is highly related to the increasing population of elderly people; this is partly because the need for health care rises
with age and partly because current generations of older people demand
more health care than previous generations. As Figure 6.15 shows, the
proportion of the population aged 65 and over has doubled during the
twentieth century. Although older people are healthier than their historical counterparts and their recent disability rate has decreased, they still
demand more health care.

Although the twentieth century was prosperous for the lower classes,
we continue to observe considerable economic and health gradients
across socioeconomic status. Table 6.14 describes various disparities
in health indexes among American adults by sex, race, ethnicity, and
income in recent years. First, it shows that women are more limited by
various health disorders than men. In particular, about 10 percent more
women than men suffer from functional limitation (difficulty doing
sensory and physical activities due to health problems).[47] Second, disparities by race and ethnicity depend on the type of health indicators.
Non-Hispanic white adults suffer more from functional limitation, but
in terms of activity limitation, the black population has the poorest
average health status. Although disparities in chronic disorders vary
by kinds of diseases, heart-related diseases (heart problems, hypertension, heart stroke) and diabetes – which have become grave concerns
in recent years – are more prevalent among Hispanic and black populations. It is therefore more startling and worrying that the proportion of
Hispanic populations that are not covered by health insurance is three
times higher than that of the non-Hispanic white population. The black
population holds 30 percent less health insurance coverage than the
white population. Third, body size also varies by race and ethnicity.
Hispanic and black adults generally have higher BMIs than white

---

[47] According to the NHIS questionnaires, *functional limitation* considers the ability
to perform the specific sensory and physical activities including reading an
ordinary newspaper (with glasses if normally used), hearing normal conversation
(using aids if normally used), having speech understood, lifting or carrying 10
lbs., walking, climbing, and getting in and out of bed or chairs. *Activity limitation*
means any difficulty in performing major activities such as (1) working or
keeping house for persons aged 18–69 and (2) the capacity to bathe, shop, eat,
dress, and so forth without the help of another person. Thus, the prevalence of
functional limitation is higher than that of activity limitation. The NHIS dataset
shows that the disparity in function limitation between males and females is
substantial, but in activity limitation is very small.

Table 6.14 *Health disparities by sex, race, and income among Americans at ages 20–64 in 1997–2006*

	Males			Females				
	White	Hispanic	Black	White	Hispanic	Black	Below poverty line	Above poverty line
(a) General health status								
Average self-reported health score (1: Excellent ~ 5: Poor)	2.04	2.19	2.29	2.09	2.32	2.41	2.62	2.06
Functional limitation (%)	24.64	15.05	22.50	32.37	23.28	31.54	38.44	26.27
Activity limitation (%)	10.72	6.65	13.18	11.67	7.72	13.87	23.39	9.15
(b) Chronic disorders (%)								
Heart problem	14.06	10.52	12.04	8.43	7.50	11.27	11.90	10.47
Hypertension	7.11	9.91	14.07	7.51	12.16	19.62	13.72	8.68
Heart stroke	3.19	4.04	5.76	2.74	2.32	5.50	3.76	3.15
Lung problem	8.85	5.15	7.56	10.14	7.28	11.41	11.83	8.69
Diabetes	8.06	14.27	11.27	7.83	15.05	14.18	12.45	9.12
Musculoskeletal problem	40.09	35.91	33.40	47.01	42.26	43.28	41.84	43.76
Nervous	7.64	7.17	7.69	11.00	8.76	9.11	9.59	9.10
Genitourinary problem	1.64	3.49	4.20	1.89	3.80	2.73	2.97	2.09
Cancer	4.04	0.85	1.66	6.89	2.35	3.02	4.24	4.39
Hearing problem	3.57	3.00	1.68	2.57	2.75	1.79	3.30	2.83
Vision problem	5.65	7.85	7.10	5.07	7.36	6.58	8.26	5.60
Weight problem	2.31	2.57	2.03	4.07	3.67	3.64	4.37	3.32

Table 6.14 (*cont.*)

	Males			Females				
	White	Hispanic	Black	White	Hispanic	Black	Below poverty line	Above poverty line
(c) Insurance								
Not covered (%)	14.96	46.85	25.74	12.69	39.55	20.54	44.23	16.85
(d) Body size								
Height(cm): Mean	178.94	172.69	177.97	164.22	160.29	164.00	167.17	170.22
Height(cm): S.D.	6.54	6.87	7.27	6.25	5.94	6.38	9.40	9.75
BMI: Mean	27.02	27.50	27.45	25.70	26.99	28.29	27.04	26.65
BMI: S.D.	4.16	4.18	4.53	5.35	5.20	5.80	5.48	4.90

Source: Calculated from the 1997–2006 National Health Interview Survey datasets.
Notes: Self-reported health score is rated on a five-point scale: 1 (excellent), 2 (very good), 3 (good), 4 (fair), and 5 (poor). Functional limitation indicates whether sample adults had difficulty doing any of several specific activities because of a health problem. Activity limitation indicates whether persons were limited in their activities due to one or more chronic conditions.

adults. Black women especially are more likely to be highly overweight, which can be connected to a high risk of mortality and morbidity.

Finally, the variance in the health gradient is greater over income level than over sex, race, or ethnicity. Individuals whose earnings are below the poverty line have adverse indicators of health status: more functional and activity limitations, more chronic disorders, less insurance coverage. They are shorter, but have higher BMIs than individuals above the poverty line, which implies that the lower classes are experiencing overnutrition, which is another type of malnutrition. The health disparity by income is closely related with the difference in diet and environments or living conditions by income. As observed a century ago, poor people still live in less-healthy environments and are largely excluded from the consumption of high-quality nutrients. High health care costs can also fetter their health. Although modern individuals are not exposed to the battery of infectious diseases that affected past generations, the introduction of new infections and increases in some chronic diseases related to nutrition continue to be of concern. Ultimately, a population's health status depends on how easily people can access medical services; this is more effective today than it was in the past. The lower socioeconomic classes are damaged by the high costs of medical care. This may cause physiological disparities in the near future, if we extrapolate from current trends shown in Table 6.14.

So far the maximal capacity of human longevity has been restricted by limited diet and lifetime health insults. But human beings may live up to 130 years if they are well fed and if there are no health insults over the lifetime.[48] Similarly, we can reach the optimal body size and therefore minimize adverse health outcomes over the lifetime. The American experience of technophysio evolution over the past three centuries suggests that nutritional status – especially measured by body size – can be related to the risk of death, sickness, and poverty. Over the centuries, Americans have achieved remarkable improvements in longevity by escaping from undernutrition, defined as deficiency in nutritional status. Today, overnutrition and obesity are concerns. Inequalities in death, chronic disorders, activity limitation, body size, and access to better nutritional and medical services are still observed among various

---

[48] The belief is based on a series of works by Leonard Hayflick. He demonstrated that cultured human cells have a limited capacity for replication, and so eventually enter a senescence phase (the *Hayflick limit*).

socioeconomic groups. Thus, eliminating this new type of malnutrition and reducing these inequalities are the American challenges for the twenty-first century.

Appendix F

In Tables F.1 and F.2, we estimate the size distribution of caloric consumption per consuming unit in the United States at the beginning of the nineteenth century, and the distribution of physical activity level (PAL) among American adult males in the same period. The estimations

Table F.1 *Computing the factor to convert caloric consumption per capita to caloric consumption per equivalent adult male in the United States, 1830*

		Average caloric consumption at given ages as a proportion of that of those aged 20–39			
Age intervals (1)	Proportion of persons in each age interval in 1830 (2)	Males (3)	Females (4)	Both sexes combined 0.5*([3] + [4]) (5)	Age-specific caloric consumption per equivalent adult males (2) * (5) (6)
0–4	0.1800	0.4413	0.4367	0.4390	0.0790
5–9	0.1456	0.7100	0.6667	0.6884	0.1002
10–14	0.1243	0.9000	0.8000	0.8500	0.1057
15–19	0.1111	1.0167	0.7833	0.9000	0.1000
20–39	0.2872	1.0000	0.7333	0.8667	0.2489
40–49	0.0688	0.9500	0.6967	0.8234	0.0566
50–59	0.0430	0.9000	0.6600	0.7800	0.0336
60–69	0.0253	0.8000	0.5867	0.6934	0.0175
70+	0.0147	0.7000	0.5133	0.6067	0.0089
Factor for converting to consumption per equivalent adult male (Σ Column 6)					0.7504

Sources: Column 2: computed from Historical Statistics of the United States Millennial Edition Online Database. Columns 3 and 4: computed from FAO/WHO 1971.
Note: Entries in Column 5 may not always be equal to 0.5 × Col. 3 + 0.5 × Col. 4 because of rounding errors.

Table F.2 *The distribution of PAL among American adult males circa 1800*

					Distribution B	
					Consumed	
Decile	BMI	Stature (m)	Weight (kg)	kcal for BMR	(kcal)	PAL
(1)	(2)	(3)	(4)	(5)	(6)	(7)
Highest	27.66	1.85	94.76	2,129	6,307	2.96
9th	25.12	1.80	81.75	1,930	5,120	2.65
8th	23.90	1.78	75.69	1,837	4,597	2.50
7th	22.97	1.76	71.20	1,768	4,221	2.39
6th	22.17	1.74	67.39	1,710	3,910	2.29
5th	21.43	1.73	63.89	1,656	3,631	2.19
4th	20.68	1.71	60.45	1,604	3,364	2.10
3rd	19.88	1.69	56.81	1,548	3,088	1.99
2nd	18.92	1.67	52.51	1,482	2,773	1.87
1st	17.18	1.62	45.04	1,368	2,251	1.65

Notes: It is assumed that the log of BMI is normally distributed with mean = 22 and standard deviation = 3 [BMI~LN (22, 3)], and that stature is normally distributed with mean = 1.735 m and standard deviation = 0.066 m [Stature~N (1.735, 0.0662)]. Column 4: Col. 2 × (Col. 3 squared), Column 5: computed from Equation (A.7) in Chapter 2, Column 6: the distribution B assumes $s/\overline{X} = 0.3$ (medium egalitarianism), and Column 7: Col. 6 ÷ Col. 5.

require the factor that converts caloric consumption per capita to caloric consumption per consuming unit. The conversion factor is calculated at 0.7504 using the population distribution by age group in the 1830 census (the detailed age distribution is not available until 1830) and assuming that the age distribution did not change much in 1800–1830.

The estimated average caloric consumption per consuming unit is 3,934 kcal (= per capita calories in 1800 ÷ conversion factor). In Table F.2, the size distribution of caloric consumption per consumption unit is estimated for the medium level of egalitarianism (distribution B in Table 2.3) as we did for Britain and France in Chapter 2. In calculating the PAL, we assume that average height is 173.5 cm and average BMI is 22. Tables F.1 and F.2 are comparable with the tables for Britain and France reported in Chapter 2. The details about these analyzing tools are discussed in Chapters 2 and 3.

7 | Conclusion

We are taller, heavier, healthier, and longer lived than our ancestors; our bodies are sturdier, less susceptible to disease in early life and slower to wear out. These changes have occurred in all parts of the world and are continuing to occur, though not all at once and not all at the same speed; they have accumulated, generation by generation, and together constitute a major and surprising change to the human body. It is not as dramatic as the evolutionary changes that produced *Homo sapiens*, but it has occurred far more rapidly, within the course of about twelve to fifteen generations, from the beginning of the eighteenth century.

This book has described, and sought to explain, these changes and their causes and consequences. Its central thesis is that, over those generations, the process, which we have called technophysio evolution, has allowed many – although certainly not yet all – parts of the world to escape from hunger and disease. This has allowed men, women, and children to live longer and healthier lives and, at the same time, to enhance their own productivity and thus to contribute to the ability of our societies and economies to produce more material goods, to enjoy more leisure, and to nurture healthier and more productive succeeding generations. The process of industrialization that began in western Europe in the eighteenth century has allowed human beings to reach further toward the achievement of the potential which resides in every human body; economic growth and human ingenuity have given us the technological potential to underpin that achievement and to ensure that it continues.

The size, shape, and capacity of the human body in the developed world today are thus signs, visible all around us, of what has been achieved. But they are also signs of what has not been achieved and of what still may be achieved. First, the disparity that exists between the human body in the rich nations of the world and in the poor nations is a sign of the human potential that the world still fails to use. The stunted and wasted bodies that are still so visible in many parts of the

364

developing world are not from a different race; they are the bodies of human beings who have been starved and deprived of care and have therefore, despite their best efforts, been unable to achieve their full potential, either physical or cognitive. Many were born to mothers who had themselves been so deprived, as had their grandmothers. The task of ensuring that millions of people do, in future, achieve their potential, is huge; but so also are the possible gains.

The size of that task is unknown. We can assess, through measures such as stature, life expectancy, and morbidity, the gap that currently exists between best practice in the developed world and the relative and absolute deprivation of people in the developing world. We can also assess what would be required to bring average performance in the developed world up to the standard of the Netherlands, currently the tallest country. We can recognize that there are still many deprived people even within the richer countries. But we do not know what possibilities still exist to improve best practice in the developed world, to raise best and average practice to and beyond that of the Netherlands, and then to extend that to the rest of the world.

This concluding chapter considers, therefore, what has been achieved and what is likely to be achieved. Some may consider that such an approach is excessively Panglossian, or that at least it exhibits an attachment to what used to be called the Whig interpretation of history: that history shows a constant improvement toward some ideal of human perfection. There are, of course, penalties to economic growth and its consequences – not least climate change – and, as the current "obesity epidemic" shows, it is possible for plenty to lead to over-consumption. In the future, as in the past, there are likely to be obstacles to continued improvement in the shape of the consequences of urbanization and the difficulty of organizing food supplies to many billions of people. However, this book concludes that technophysio evolution has benefited, and will continue to benefit, the human condition and that further significant gains in height, infant mortality, and life expectancy are likely to be possible.

7.1 What has been achieved and is now in prospect?

What is the scale of the changes that have occurred to the human body in developed nations? At the beginning of the seventeenth century, average male height in the United Kingdom – the richest country at the time – was about 165 cm, male life expectancy at birth was about 33 years, and about 50 percent of the male population was literate – an inadequate measure of cognitive achievement, but all that we know. Three hundred years later, males in the United Kingdom were more than 10 cm taller, their life expectancy had more than doubled to over 70, and 100 percent of the population was literate (Steckel and Floud 1997b, p. 424).

Similar changes occurred in other nations. The average male in the Netherlands in 1800 was 164 cm tall and lived 34.1 years; in 1950, he was 178 cm tall and lived over 71 years. In 2008, he was 180.8 cm tall and in 2009, lived to 76.8 years. In the United States, the average male in 1800 was 173 cm tall and lived nearly 47 years; even so, by 1950, he was over 177 cm and lived over 68 years. In 2006, he was 176.3 cm tall and in 2009, lived to 75.65 years. The most spectacular growth in stature, among developed nations, appears to have been achieved in Norway, where average male height in 1761 is estimated to have been about 159 cm – about the height of some African bushmen tribes today – and is now just under 180 cm. Our knowledge of female heights is patchy and generally inadequate, but we can assume that similar increases have occurred (Harris 2009).

These changes are testament to the economic growth that has occurred in all these countries. Floud (1984) and Steckel (1983) have both documented the close relationship between height and measures of per capita income, while Steckel also emphasized the importance of the distribution of income; for a given level of income, the more equal countries tend to have higher average stature. But spectacular although these changes in stature and life expectancy are, they probably significantly underestimate the changes that are currently under way. This is because both average height and average life expectancy today are at least in part the legacy of economic, social, and health conditions achieved over fifty years ago, when the people who are now dying were born, when their stature was established, and when they began to have children whose heights, mortality, and morbidity they have influenced.

But much has changed over those fifty years. The real per capita income of the United States has risen, measured in $ of 2000, from $6,769 to $38,262, an increase of over 5.6 times; the real per capita income of the United Kingdom has risen, measured in £ of 2003, from £5,123 to £20,790, an increase of 4 times; the real per capita income of

Japan, a late industrializer, has risen, measured in ¥ of 2000, from ¥522 to ¥4,388, a rise of 8.4 times. Even more spectacular growth is currently being achieved: for example, in China. All these increases are much greater than had occurred in previous fifty-year periods, so it is reasonable to expect that the results – in terms of extended life, improved physical health, and greater stature – will similarly show even more rapid changes in the immediate future than has been the case in the past century or two. Changes can also be expected, to much the same degree, in the other countries of the industrialized world, which have experienced similar rates of growth.

Fears have sometimes been expressed that the rise in life expectancy, seen in all developing countries, will not be paralleled by increases in the numbers of years of healthy life, so that people will face longer periods of ill health in later life, with consequent burdens on those caring for them and on medical services. Recent evidence suggests otherwise. In 2000–2002, UK females aged 65 could expect to live a further 19 years, 14 years of which would be in good health; by 2004–2006, they could expect to live a further 19.7 years and be healthy for 14.5 years of them. UK males of 65 in 2000–2002 could expect to live a further 15.9 years, 11.9 of them in good health; in 2004–2006, they could expect to live 16.9 years and be healthy for 12.8 of them. In the United States in 2002, males and females at age 60 could expect 15.3 and 17.9 healthy years, respectively. Across the whole age range, healthy life expectancy has risen along with life expectancy, while the incidence of disability has fallen and estimated disability-free life expectancy has risen (Smith 2009).

It is also reasonable to expect, on the basis of the studies reported in Chapter 1, that these increases in nutritional status and its correlates will have been accompanied by improvements in cognitive ability. Increases in educational attainment have been observed in many developed countries, but their cause is often contentious. They have been attributed, for example, to improved teaching but also to "dumbing down," a decline in test requirements. It has also recently been argued that, although there are some signs of a link between nutrition and measured intelligence in the past, this association cannot now be observed (Flynn 2009; Smith 2009). However, it still seems likely that a widespread improvement in nutritional status will have had positive effects on cognitive development in infancy and on consequential ability to learn and that, in conjunction with improvements in teaching methods and educational technology, it will have contributed to improvements in attainment and, subsequently, to enhanced productivity. Many of the results of this are likely to be still to come.

7.2 Will these improvements continue?

The simplest answer to this question is: we do not know. However, it is possible to speculate that there are some factors in modern societies in the developed world which may inhibit or constrain further improvements. In a number of countries, including the United States and the United Kingdom, recent decades have seen an increase in income inequality, which may act as a brake on further improvements in average nutritional status as a result of economic growth, although it is unlikely that it will entirely outweigh the positive effects of that growth. But there are certainly some social groups – for example, some parts of the black and minority ethnic populations in the United States, the United Kingdom, and other countries – that have failed to share equally in the rewards of economic growth and whose morbidity, mortality, and stature have not grown as rapidly as in the population as a whole. However, this is not true of all such groups, which suggests that social policies of various kinds might be successful in mitigating the effects of such inequality.

More puzzling is the potential impact of what can best be called "overconsumption." The most obvious change to the appearance of human bodies in developed countries in the past two or three decades has been the rise in the numbers of the overweight and obese. This is so recent a phenomenon that textbooks on human growth published in the 1970s do not mention it. But the "obesity epidemic," often attributed to the availability of cheap food and, in particular, processed fast food, is now a feature of many developed countries. At least one-quarter of the population of the United States is obese,[1] although obesity is concentrated in the lower social classes and the more deprived sections of

---

[1] "In 2008, only one state (Colorado) had a prevalence of obesity less than 20 percent. Thirty-two states had a prevalence equal to or greater than 25 percent; six of these states (Alabama, Mississippi, Oklahoma, South Carolina, Tennessee, and West Virginia) had a prevalence of obesity equal to or greater than 30 percent." The most obese state was Mississippi, at 32.8 percent (Centers for Disease Control 2009). Obesity is defined by a body mass index of 30 or greater.

society in developed countries.[2] Linked as it is to the rising incidence of diseases such as diabetes, obesity is predicted by some medical experts to become a major cause of enhanced morbidity and premature death in future decades (see Offer 2001; Offer 2006, pp. 138–169; Komlos and Baur 2004).

The fact that the phenomenon is so recent, and that it still affects a small proportion of the populations of most developed countries other than the United States (typically less than 10 percent), makes these predictions rather hazardous and certainly speculative.[3] The evidence on the link between BMI and mortality, discussed in Chapters 2 and 3 above, shows that the base of the U-shaped curve that links the two is quite flat and elongated, so that BMI has to be very high (or very low) before mortality is significantly affected. But the Waaler curves discussed in those chapters were derived from a Norwegian population in which there were very few obese people, and it is certainly possible that the consequences of much more widespread overweight and obesity and the change to social customs in activities such as physical exercise will have more serious consequences than the curves suggest.

The Waaler curves are important evidence in another context. It has often been suggested that there "must be" some limit to human physical size and to life expectancy. The Waaler curve linking height to mortality does indeed show a V-shape in which mortality appears to rise for male heights above about 188 cm. If this effect were to be confirmed, such enhanced mortality would act as a brake on average human size. But since the average height of males in most developed countries today is

---

[2] The same source (Centers for Disease Control 2009) comments that "Blacks had 51 percent higher prevalence of obesity and Hispanics had 21 percent higher obesity prevalence compared with whites."

[3] It is important to note that the summary of this document (FAO/WHO/UNU 2002) concludes as follows: "The study has revealed considerable variation between populations in both stature and weight. It is not clear how much of this variation is due to adverse environmental factors. Privileged groups in some populations follow growth curves close to the US 50th centile while their less privileged compatriots are smaller. However, in view of our very limited knowledge of the genetic structure of these populations, we cannot assume that the mean for the whole population would necessarily reach our 50th centile curves if nutrition were improved. We have even less basis for making this assumption for those countries where even privileged members of the population are small in stature and weight. Thus in general, we can only study populations as they are and any attempt to predict what they might be like in other circumstances is hazardous."

still less than 180 cm, it is likely that this effect, if it exists, will take some time to have any effect.[4] In the case of mortality, most demographers and actuaries have predicted that at some time expectation of life will cease to rise. However, in fact it has risen, as Oeppen and Vaupel (2002) have shown, remorselessly and remarkably regularly, for two centuries, and the rise shows no signs of stopping; this has led some to speculate that an upper limit for human life expectancy may be as much as 130 years. It is safest, at least for historians, to conclude that we do not know.

7.3 What is still to be achieved?

Even if the extent of future change in the human body in the developed world remains a matter of speculation, there are likely to be significant changes among the remainder – the majority – of the human race. In the developing world, the evidence is plain to see in the stunted and wasted bodies of children and adults, while the statistics of morbidity, mortality, and literacy tell the same story, periodically documented in the *Human Development Report* of the United Nations. Recall that Dutch men are now 180.8 cm tall (STATLINE 2010); by contrast, men in Cameroon are 170.6 cm tall (Kamadjey *et al.* 2006), in rural India 161.2 cm (Venkaiah *et al.* 2002), in Peru 164.0 cm (Instituto Nacional de Salud [Peru] 2006), and in the Philippines 163.5 cm (Food and Nutrition Research Institute 2003).

In 2002, the joint FAO/WHO/UNU expert consultation gathered data from 380 anthropometric studies published since 1960. Average heights and weights from many countries were reported and compared to the current US standard, which was taken as representative of developed nations; the majority of European nations, for example, lie consistently between the 40th and 60th centiles of the US distribution. By contrast, the statures of males in Liberia, Sudan, Benin, Ethiopia, Liberia, and Nigeria follow growth curves approximating to the 10th

---

[4] Batty *et al.* 2009 survey a large number of relevant surveys and cohort studies to explore the relationship between height and mortality from coronary heart disease (CHD), stroke, and cancers. They find a negative relationship between height and CHD and stroke, but a positive relationship between height and many cancers. They cite one study, the original Whitehall study (p. 146, table 4), showing that a 15 cm increase in height has a hazard ratio of 0.76 for CHD, 0.93 for stroke, and 1.06 for all cancers (1.22 for prostate and 1.13 for colon cancer).

US centile, while those of Uganda, Somalia, and Tanzania begin as children at the 40th to 50th centile but fall in adulthood to the 3rd to 10th centile. (It is noticeable that white South Africans and privileged Nigerians follow the 50th centile.) African weights show a similar pattern. In Asia, poorer Indian populations are best represented by a curve following the 5th centile, while males in the Philippines, Singapore, Thailand, Indonesia, and New Guinea begin at the 20th centile but drop gradually to the 3rd. The rural poor of South American countries are also closest to the 3rd centile (FAO/WHO/ UNU 2002).

While the authors of this study are properly cautious about making predictions on the basis of these data,[5] the historical evolution of stature suggests that the reduction of poverty and disease would increase human potential. There is room for argument, certainly, about whether better organization of the economy, or better governance, could alleviate this poverty or could have done so in recent decades in areas such as sub-Saharan Africa. As Sen and others have demonstrated, many famines which were previously attributed to the forces of nature can be shown to have been predominantly man-made or, at least, avoidable by human action. But the focus of this book has been on the long-term course of human nutritional status and, within such a perspective, short-term crisis mortality has had little effect. In the long term, what we observe is that many parts of the developing world have not yet attained standards – for example, in the provision of clean water and effective sewage disposal – which have been the norm in the developed world for over a century and which, together with adequate food supplies, account for the improvements which have been documented in this book.

Improvements are, of course, now taking place in areas of the world such as China and India, which are both experiencing rapid economic growth that is already raising the average nutritional status of their populations and being accompanied by lower morbidity and rising life expectancy. But other areas of the world still lag behind. This is not because of doubts about the efficacy of intervention to promote nutritional status, particularly in infancy and childhood – it has been amply demonstrated in the many trials of food supplements and public health

---

[5] See footnote 3 above.

improvements on which we have drawn. However, this knowledge has not, for many reasons, been translated into action.

7.4 Possible constraints

As this book illustrates, there is a powerful and self-reinforcing dynamic within technophysio evolution as it affects successive generations and improves nutritional status over many years, but there are other factors which can potentially limit or even halt that evolution.

The first of these is growth of population, outrunning the world's capacity to produce the food needed to sustain continued improvements in nutritional status. The fear that this would occur has become known as Malthusian, after its best-known exponent, the Rev. Thomas Malthus, who wrote during the first century of the period which we have identified as the initial stages of technophysio evolution. In the event, his and many others' fears proved to be unjustified, because of that evolution; but this does not mean that it could not happen at some time in the future.

There are, however, a number of grounds for doubting that this will occur. The first is that there is abundant evidence that economic growth, particularly operating through greater education and through improvements in the position of women, leads quite rapidly to a declining birth rate. In the modern world, this occurs partly through what Malthus described as the prudential check – an increase in marriage age – but principally through a voluntary check which he did not foresee, widespread artificial contraception. Populations in the developed world are now, in general, failing to reproduce themselves and are expected during the next decades to experience some of the effects of an increase in the average age of their populations. It can be expected that, as economic growth increases in countries such as China and India, reproduction rates will decrease, even without compulsory measures such as the Chinese "one-child" policy. Fertility rates are already below replacement in China and in urban India.

But there are also grounds for arguing that, given a better organization of the world's agricultural resources, sufficient food could be produced to meet any likely future population. This is a highly contentious statement, since it is often argued that the world could not produce, for example, the amount of animal protein which would be required were the whole world population to adopt the current consumption patterns of the developed world. However, there are still many areas of Africa, Asia, and Latin America that have very low agricultural productivity by the standards of other parts of the world; the adoption, in those areas, of the best practice which is already being used in developed nations, would be likely to improve output, even without any gains from the (so far largely hypothetical) genetic modification of crops and animals. The world's food supply is now being produced using less land than was used to feed a much smaller population in 1950, so that the potential for extensive as well as intensive agriculture still remains.

Much of the cost of food is accounted for by transport, packaging, and retailing costs, which increase as populations move from the land. Rising agricultural productivity in the developed world in the eighteenth and nineteenth centuries was accompanied by a movement of population from the land and the growth of towns and cities. Urbanization is happening again today, particularly in the developing world, and with the same results. At least initially, urban populations are outrunning the infrastructure, as the slums, barrios, and tent cities of so many rapidly growing cities now testify. Even if wages are higher in the cities than on the land, the costs of survival and the impact of disease and overcrowding are even greater. It is likely that this process, in the nineteenth century, was responsible for the decline in average male heights which occurred for several decades in the United States, in England, and in other European countries. The decline in average nutritional status, which it signifies, may well be occurring today in cities across the world, from Mexico City to Shanghai. Even if there is no actual decline, the evidence of similar cities in the past suggests that social conditions in the big cities are limiting and hampering the growth, both physical and cognitive, of children and young people. These problems were, in the past, solved by societal and governmental will to provide the appropriate infrastructure in the form of water supply and water disposal facilities, power supplies, and public health education. The fact that the problems were solved, albeit after a number of decades, in the nineteenth and early twentieth centuries, suggests that they could be solved again in the twenty-first.

An unresolved question, which could affect all these predictions, is whether man-made climate change would affect the possibility of such solutions. While economists such as Stern (2007; 2009) have argued that adjustments to the effects of climate change could well be accommodated within expected rates of economic growth, and that technological changes could indeed contribute to such growth, it is not clear whether the world's political and economic systems will make this possible. If they do not, climate scientists predict that there will be major changes, some positive and some negative, within world agriculture, whose total effect is very difficult to forecast but which could well negate optimistic predictions, such as those in previous paragraphs, about world agricultural capacity.

Those predictions could also be negated by major changes to the world's mortality regime. The AIDS epidemic is already one of the factors severely limiting African productivity and, although some success has come from the use of anti-retroviral drugs, they are expensive and may at some point stimulate drug resistance. Although, once again, the question is hotly disputed, it is certainly not clear that the world is currently winning the fight against AIDS, and there is always a danger from more conventional, but more rapidly lethal, epidemic diseases, now spread easily and rapidly by globalized air transport.

Finally, it is impossible to ignore the continued potential of armed conflict to disrupt social and economic systems and to divert vast resources to preparing for or deterring warfare, terrorism, or the disputes about control over natural resources that seem likely to become more common in a world of growing population, climate change, and pressure on resources such as water supplies. The September 11 attacks, Iraq, Afghanistan, and Darfur are just the most recent, and certainly not the last, manifestations of the ability of relatively small groups of people, disaffected for whatever reason, to disrupt the lives of tens of millions. Although it is sometimes argued that war, and military expenditure in time of war and peace, stimulates technological change, it has rarely assisted improvements in average nutritional status and the technophysio evolution that is the subject of this book.

7.5 Conclusion

The fact that a book on anthropometric history can sensibly conclude with speculations on world demography, urbanization, and climate change is a reflection of how much has been learned in the thirty years since the creation of this branch of historical enquiry. The endeavor began with limited objectives, to establish the health of the inhabitants of North America and Europe in the eighteenth century, at the beginning of the period of mass migration. It has mushroomed into a study of the long-term development of human society, drawing upon skills and insights developed in statistics, anthropology, human biology, economics, demography, genetics, psychology, and many other disciplines. It has been characterized by methodological innovation in the estimation of average heights from incomplete samples; technologies new to history have been deployed in the collection and analysis of unusually large and complex data sets; teams of scholars from many different backgrounds have combined their skills.

The central fact that has made all this possible, and that gives it a continuing interest and importance in areas far beyond history, is the plasticity, flexibility, and responsiveness of the human body. Initial assertions of this fact were met with incredulity; it was disputed either that the body had changed or that it had done so in ways which were systematically related to the human environment. Yet, as the evidence has accumulated, it has continued to show the ways in which the size and shape of the human body has responded to apparently tiny changes in nutrition, disease, work demands, warmth, or even love. It has shown also that these changes are both immediate and part of, as well as constrained by, generational changes by which the size, shape, and nutritional status of an individual reflect in part the nutritional status of his or her parents and grandparents. It has been the particular contribution of anthropometric history to give historical flesh to these insights of epidemiologists and human biologists and to show how they relate to changes in the economy, to agriculture, education, and technological change and, overall, to the shape and nature of modern economic growth.

References

Acheson, D. 1998. *Independent Inquiry into Inequalities in Health*. London: The Stationery Office.

A'Hearn, B. 2003. Anthropometric evidence on living standards in northern Italy, 1730–1860. *Journal of Economic History* 63: 351–381.

Aitchson, J., Brown, J. 1966. *The Lognormal Distribution*. *University of Cambridge, Department of Applied Economics Micrographs no. 5*. Cambridge University Press.

Åkerman, S., Högberg, U., Danielsson, M. 1988. Health, height and nutrition in early modern Sweden. In *Society, Health and Population during Demographic Transition*, ed. Brändström, A., Tedebrand, L. Stockholm: Almqvist and Wiksell International.

Allen, R. 1994. Agriculture during the Industrial Revolution. In *The Economic History of Britain since 1700*, ed. Floud, R., McCloskey, D. Cambridge University Press.

2001a. The great divergence in European wages and prices from the Middle Ages to the First World War. *Explorations in Economic History* 38: 411–477.

2001b. Wages, prices and living standards: The world-historical perspective. www.economics.ox.ac.uk/Members/robert.allen/WagesPrices.htm.

2004. Agriculture during the Industrial Revolution, 1700–1850. In *The Cambridge Economic History of Modern Britain, Volume 1*, ed. Floud, R., Johnson, P. Cambridge University Press.

2007. Pessimism preserved: Real wages in the British industrial revolution. Oxford University Department of Economics Working Paper 314.

2009. *The British Industrial Revolution in Global Perspective*. Cambridge University Press.

Almond, D. 2006. Is the 1918 influenza pandemic over? Long-term effects of in-utero influenza exposure in the post-1940 U.S. population. *Journal of Political Economy* 114: 672–712.

Alter, G. 2004. Height, frailty, and the standard of living: Modeling the effects of diet and disease on declining mortality and increasing height. *Population Studies* 58: 265–279.

Alter, G., Neven, M., Oris, M. 2004. Stature in transition: A microlevel study from nineteenth-century Belgium. *Social Science History* 28: 231–247.

Alter, G., Riley, J. 1989. Frailty, sickness and death: Models of morbidity and mortality in historical populations. *Population Studies* 43: 25–45.

Andersen, O. 1979. The development in Danish mortality. In *The Fifth Scandinavian Demographic Symposium*, ed. Brunborg, H., Sørenson, K, 9–23. Oslo: Scandinavian Demographic Society.

Angell-Andersen, E., Tretli, S., Bjerknes, R., Forsén, T., Sørensen, T. I., Eriksson, J. G., Räsänen, L., Grotmol, T. 2004. The association between nutritional conditions during World War II and childhood anthropometric variables in the Nordic countries. *Annals of Human Biology* 31: 342–355.

Antonov, A. 1947. Children born during the siege of Leningrad in 1942. *Journal of Pediatrics* 30: 250–259.

Appleby, A. 1979. Diet in sixteenth-century England: Sources, problems, possibilities. In *Health, Medicine, and Mortality in the Sixteenth Century*, ed. Webster, C., 97–116. Cambridge University Press.

Arcaleni, E. 2006. Secular trend and regional differences in the stature of Italians, 1854–1980. *Economics and Human Biology* 4: 24–38.

Arora, S. 2001. Health, human productivity and long-term economic growth. *Journal of Economic History* 61: 699–749.

2005. On epidemiological and economic transitions: A historical view. In *Health and Economic Growth: Findings and Policy Implications*, ed. López-Casasnovas, G., Rivera, B., Currais, L., 197–238. Cambridge: MIT Press.

Baird, D. 1974. The epidemiology of low birth weight: Changes in incidence in Aberdeen, 1948–72. *Journal of Biological Science* 6: 323–341.

1975. The interplay of changes in society, reproductive habits and obstetric practice in Scotland between 1922 and 1972. *British Journal of Preventive and Social Medicine* 29: 135–146.

Ballagh, J. 1902. *A History of Slavery in Virginia*. Baltimore: Johns Hopkins Press.

Barker, D. 1992. *Fetal Origins of Adult Disease*. London: British Medical Journal.

1995. Fetal origins of coronary heart disease. *British Medical Journal* 311: 171–174.

1998. *Mothers, Babies, and Health in Later Life*. Edinburgh: Churchill Livingstone.

Barker, D., Clark, P. 1997. Fetal undernutrition and disease in later life. *Reviews of Reproduction* 2: 105–112.

Barker, D., Eriksson, J., Forsén, T., Osmond, C. 2002. Fetal origins of adult disease: Strength of effects and biological basis. *International Journal of Epidemiology* 31: 1235–1239.

Barker, D., Osmond, C. 1986. Infant mortality, childhood nutrition, and ischaemic heart disease in England and Wales. *Lancet* 1: 1077–1081.

Barnes, D. 1930. *A History of the English Corn Laws from 1660 to 1846.* London: George Routledge and Sons.

Barro, R. 1996. Health and economic growth: Paper prepared for the Pan American Health Organisation. www.paho.org/English/HDP/HDD/ barro.pdf.

Barry, J. 2005. *The Great Influenza: The Story of the Deadliest Pandemic in History.* New York: Penguin.

Baten, J. 1999. *Ernährung und wirtschaftliche Entwicklung in Bayern (1730–1880).* Stuttgart: Franz Steiner Verlag.

2000a. Economic development and the distribution of nutritional resources in Bavaria, 1797–1839: An anthropometric study. *Journal of Income Distribution* 9: 89–106.

2000b. Heights and weights in the eighteenth and nineteenth centuries: An international overview. *Jahrbuch für Wirtschaftsgeschichte* 61–73.

2001. Climate, grain production and nutritional status in southern Germany during the eighteenth century. *Journal of European Economic History* 30: 9–47.

Baten, J., Murray, J. 1997. Bastardy in South Germany revisited: An anthropometric synthesis. *Journal of Interdisciplinary History* 28: 47–56.

2000. Heights of men and women in nineteenth-century Bavaria: Economic, nutritional and disease influences. *Explorations in Economic History* 37: 351–369.

Batty, G., Shipley, M., Gunnell, D., Huxley, R. 2009. Height, weight and health: An overview with new data from three longitudinal studies. *Economics and Human Biology* 7: 137–152.

Baxter, J. 1875. *Statistics, Medical and Anthropological, of the Provost-Marshall-General's Bureau, Derived from Records of the Examination for Military Service in the Armies of the United States during the Late War of the Rebellion of over a Million Recruits, Drafted Men, Substitutes, and Enrolled Men.* Washington, DC: Government Printing Office.

Behrman, J., Alderman, H., Hoddinott, J. 2004. Malnutrition and hunger. In *Global Crises, Global Solutions,* ed. Lomborg, B. Cambridge University Press.

Bell, F., Millward, R. 1998. Public health expenditures and mortality in England and Wales 1870–1914. *Continuity and Change* 13: 221–249.

Ben-Shlomo, Y., Kuh, D. 2002. A life-course approach to chronic disease epidemiology: Conceptual models, empirical challenges and disciplinary perspectives. *International Journal of Epidemiology* 31: 285–293.

Bengtsson, T., Lindström, M. 2000. Childhood misery and disease in later life: The effects on mortality in old age of hazards experienced in early life, southern Sweden, 1760–1894. *Population Studies* 54: 263–277.

Bennett, M. 1955. The food economy of the New England Indians, 1605–75. *Journal of Political Economy* 63: 369–396.

Bennett, M., Pierce, R. 1961. Change in the American national diet, 1879–1959. *Food Research Institute Studies* 2: 95–119.

Berlanstein, L. 1998. The working people of Paris, 1871–1914. In *Classics in Anthropometric History*, ed. Komlos J., Cuff T., 298–306. St. Katharinen, Germany: Scripta Mercaturae Verlag.

Bernard, R. [1969] 1975. Peasant diet in eighteenth-century Gévaudan. In *European Diet from Pre-Industrial to Modern Times*, ed. Forster E., Forster R., 19–46. New York: Harper & Row.

Bidwell, P., Falconer, J. 1941. *History of Agriculture in the Northern United States: 1620–1860*. Washington: Carnegie Institution of Washington.

Bielicki, T., Hulanicka, B. 1998. Secular trend in stature and age-at-menarche in Poland. In *Secular Growth Changes in Europe*, ed. Bodzsár, E., Susanne, C., 263–279. Budapest: Eötvös University Press.

Björklund, J., Stenlund, H. 1995. Real wages in Sweden, 1870–1950: A study of six industrial branches. In *Labour's Reward: Real Wages and Economic Change in 19th and 20th-Century Europe*, ed. Scholliers P., Zamagni V., 253–257. Aldershot: Edward Elgar.

Black, A., Coward, W., Cole, T. J. 1996. Human energy expenditure in affluent societies: An analysis of 574 doubly-labeled water measurements. *European Journal of Clinical Nutrition* 50: 72–92.

Blayo, Y. 1975. La mortalité en France de 1740 à 1829. *Population* 30: 123–142.

Bleakley, H. 2007. Disease and development: Evidence from hookworm eradication in the American south. *Quarterly Journal of Economics* 122: 73–117.

Blodget, S. 1964. *Economica: A Statistical Manual for the United States of America*. New York: Kelley.

Bloom, D., Canning, D., Sevilla, J. 2001. The effect of health on economic growth: Theory and evidence. NBER Working Paper 8587.

Blum, J. 1978. *The End of the Old Order in Rural Europe*. Princeton University Press.

Bodzsár, E. 1998. Secular growth changes in Hungary. In *Secular Growth Changes in Europe*, ed. Bodzsár, E., Susanne, C., 175–205. Budapest: Eötvös University Press.

Bok, D. 2010. *The Politics of Happiness: What Government can Learn from New Research on Well-Being*. Princeton University Press.

Boonen, C. 2004. A European social model: The way forward in health care. *World Hospitals and Health Services* 40: 46–48.

Bossuyt, N., Gadeyne, S., Deboosere, P., Van Oyen, H. 2004. Socio-economic inequalities in health expectancy in Belgium. *Public Health* 118: 3–10.

Botting, B. 1997. Mortality in childhood. In *Health Inequalities: Decennial Supplement*, ed. Drever, F., Whitehead, M., 83–94. London: The Stationery Office.

Bourgeois-Pichat, J. 1965. The general development of the population of France since the eighteenth century. In *Population in History: Essays in Historical Demography*, ed. Glass, D., Eversley, D., 476–506. Chicago: Aldine Publishing Co.

Boyd, M. 1941. A historical sketch of the prevalence of malaria in North America. *American Journal of Tropical Medicine* 21: 223–244.

Breakwell, C., Bajekal, M. 2005. Review of sources and methods to monitor healthy life expectancy. *Health Statistics Quarterly* 26: 17–22.

British Medical Association. 2003. *Childhood Immunisation: A Guide for Healthcare Professionals*. London: British Medical Association. www.-bma.org.uk/images/childhoodimm_tcm41–20002.pdf.

British Nutrition Foundation. 2003. Healthy eating: A whole diet approach. www.nutrition.org.uk/home.asp?siteId=43&sectionId=325&subSectionId=320&parentSection=299&which=1.

Broad, J. 1999. Parish economies of welfare, 1650–1834. *Historical Journal* 42: 985–1006.

Brønnum-Hansen, H. 2005. Health expectancy in Denmark, 1987–2000. *European Journal of Public Health* 15: 20–25.

Brown, J. 1988. Coping with crisis? The diffusion of waterworks in late-nineteenth-century German towns. *Journal of Economic History* 48: 307–318.

2000. Economics and infant mortality decline in German towns, 1889–1912: Household behavior and public intervention. In *Body and City: Histories of Urban Public Health*, ed. Sheard, S., Power, H., 166–193. Aldershot: Ashgate.

Bruland K. 2004. Industrialisation and technical change. In *The Cambridge Economic History of Modern Britain, Volume 1*, ed. Floud, R., Johnson, P. Cambridge University Press.

Brundtland, G., Liestøl, K., Walløe, L. 1980. Height, weight and menarcheal age of Oslo schoolchildren during the last sixty years. *Annals of Human Biology* 7: 307–322.

Brunt, L. 2001. The advent of the sample survey in the social sciences. *Journal of the Royal Statistical Society, Series D (The Statistician)* 50: 179–189.

Burgmeijer, R., Wieringen, J. 1998. Secular changes of growth in the Netherlands. In *Secular Growth Changes in Europe*, ed. Bodzsár, E., Susanne, C., 233–262. Budapest: Eötvös University Press.

Burnett, J. 1979. *Plenty and Want*. London: Scholar Press.

Cain, L., Hong, S. C. 2009. Survival in the 19th century cities: The larger the city, the smaller your chances. *Explorations in Economic History* 46: 450–463.

Cambois, E., Robine, J.-M., Hayward, M. 2001. Social inequalities in disability-free life expectancy in the French male population, 1980–91. *Demography* 38: 513–524.

Cameron, N. 1979. The growth of London schoolchildren 1904–1966: An analysis of secular trend and intra-county variation. *Annals of Human Biology* 6: 505–525.

2003. Physical growth in a transitional economy: The aftermath of South American apartheid. *Economics and Human Biology* 1: 29–42.

Carey, J. 2001. Life span: A conceptual overview. In *Life Span: Evolutionary, Ecological and Demographic Perspectives*, ed. Carey, J., Tuljiapurkar, S. New York: Population Council.

Carr, L. 1992. Emigration and the standard of living: The seventeenth century Chesapeake. *Journal of Economic History* 52: 271–291.

Carrier, L. 1923. *The Beginning of Agriculture in America*. New York: McGraw-Hill.

Carter, S. 2006. *Historical Statistics of the United States: Earliest Times to the Present*. New York: Cambridge University Press.

Carter, S., Gartner, S., Haines, M., Olmstead, A., Sutch, R., Wright, G. 2006. Historical Statistics of the United States Millennial Edition. http://hsus.cambridge.org/HSUSWeb/HSUSEntryServlet.

Case, A., Paxson, C. 2008. Stature and status: Height, ability, and labour market outcomes. *Journal of Political Economy* 116: 491–532.

2009. Early life health and cognitive function in old age. *American Economic Review Papers and Proceedings* 992: 104–109.

Caselli, G. 1991. Health transition and cause-specific mortality. In *The Decline of Mortality in Europe*, ed. Schofield, R., Reher, D., Bideau, A., 68–96. Oxford: Clarendon Press.

Caselli, G., Capocaccia, R. 1989. Age, period, cohort and early mortality: An analysis of adult mortality in Italy. *Population Studies* 43: 133–153.

Caulfield, L., Richard, S., Black, R. 2004. Undernutrition as an underlying cause of malaria morbidity and mortality in children less than five years old. *American Journal of Tropical Medicine and Hygiene* 71: 55–63.

Cavelaars, A., Kunst, A., Geurts, J., Crialesi, R. 2000. Persistant variation in average height between countries and between socio-economic groups: An overview of 10 European countries. *Annals of Human Biology* 27: 407–421.

Centers for Disease Control. 1999a. CDC on infectious diseases in the United States, 1900–99. *Population and Development Review* 25: 635–640.

1999b. CDC on vaccines and children's health: United States 1900–98. *Population and Development Review* 25: 391–395.

2004. Mean body weight, height, and body mass index, United States 1960–2002. *Advance Data from Vital and Health Statistics* 347.

2006. Overweight and obesity. www.cdc.gov/nccdphp/dnpa/obesity/index. htm.

2007a. Deaths: Final data for 2004. *National Vital Statistics Report* 55: 1–120.

2007b. Trends in tuberculosis incidence: United States, 2006. *MMWR* 56: 245–250.

2008a. Infant mortality statistics from the 2005 period linked birth/infant death data set. *National Vital Statistics Report* 57: 1–32.

2008b. Recent trends in infant mortality in the United States. *NCHS Data Brief* 9.

2009. U.S. obesity trends. *CDC Online* www.cdc.gov/obesity/data/trends.html.

Chamla M. 1983. L'évolution recente de la stature en Europe occidentale (périod 1960–1980). *Bulletins et Mémoires de la Société d'Anthrologie de Paris* 10: 195–224.

Chandra R. 1975. Antibody formation in first and second generation offspring of nutritionally deprived rats. *Science* 4211: 289–290.

Charlton, J., Murphy, M. 1997. Trends in all-cause mortality: 1841–1994. In *The Health of Adult Britain, 1841–1994. Volume 1, Chapters 1–14*, ed. Charlton, J., Murphy, M., 30–57. London: Office for National Statistics.

Charlton, J., Quaife, K. 1997. Trends in diet, 1841–1994. In *The Health of Adult Britain, 1841–1994. Volume 1. Chapters 1–14*, ed. Charlton, J., Murphy, M., 93–113. London: Office for National Statistics.

Chartres, J. 1985. The marketing of agricultural produce. In *The Agrarian History of England and Wales. Volume V: 1640–1750; II: Agrarian Change*, ed. Thirsk, J., 406–502. Cambridge University Press.

Christensen, K., Doblhammer, G., Rau, R., Vaupel, J. 2009. Ageing populations: The challenges ahead. *Lancet* 374: 1196–1208.

Chrzanowska, M., Koziel, S., Ulijaszek, S. 2007. Changes in BMI and the prevalence of overweight and obesity in children and adolescents in Cracow, Poland, 1971–2000. *Economics and Human Biology* 5: 370–378.

CIA World Factbook. 2010. Available online at www.cia.gov/library/publications/the-world-factbook/.

Cinnirella, F. 2008. Optimists or pessimists? A reconsideration of nutritional status in Britain, 1740–1865. *European Review of Economic History* 12: 325–354.

Clark, G. 2001. Farm wages and living standards in the industrial revolution, England, 1670–1850. *Economic History Review* 54: 477–505.

2005. The condition of the working class in England, 1209–2004. *Journal of Political Economy* 113: 1307–1340.

2007. *A Farewell to Alms: A Brief Economic History of the World*. Princeton University Press.

Clark, G., Huberman, M., Lindert, P. 1995. A British food puzzle, 1770–1850. *Economic History Review* 2: 215–237.

Clarkson, L. 1975. *Death, Disease, and Famine in Pre-Industrial England*. New York: St. Martin's Press.

Coale, A., Demeny, P. 1966. *Regional Model Life Tables and Stable Population*. Princeton University Press.

Coelho, P., McGuire, R. 1999. Biology, diseases, and economics: An epidemiological history of slavery in the American south. *Journal of Bioeconomics* 1: 151–190.

Cole, G., Postgate, R. [1938] 1956. *The Common People, 1746–1946*. London: Methuen.

Cole, T. 2000a. Galton's midparent height revisited. *Annals of Human Biology* 27: 401–405.

2000b. Secular trends in growth. *Proceedings of the Nutrition Society* 59: 317–324.

2003. The secular trend in human physical growth: A biological view. *Economics and Human Biology* 1: 161–168.

Coleman, D., Salt, J. 1992. *The British Population: Patterns, Trends and Processes*. Oxford University Press.

Colquhoun, P. 1814. *Treatise on the Wealth, Power, and Resources of the British Empire*. London: Joseph Mawmay.

Cook, D., Strachan, D. 1999. Summary of effects of parental smoking on the respiratory health of children and implications for research. *Thorax* 54: 357–366.

Costa, D. 1993. Height, weight, wartime stress and older-age mortality: Evidence from the Union Army records. *Explorations in Economic History* 30: 424–449.

1998a. *The Evolution of Retirement: An American Economic History 1880–1990*. University of Chicago Press.

1998b. Unequal at birth: A long-term comparison of income and birth weight. *Journal of Economic History* 58: 987–1009.

2000. Understanding the twentieth-century decline in chronic conditions among older men. *Demography* 37: 53–72.

2002. Changing chronic disease rates and long-term declines in functional limitation among older men. *Demography* 39: 119–137.

2004. Race and pregnancy outcomes in the twentieth century: A long-term comparison. *Journal of Economic History* 64: 1056–1086.

2008. Why were older men in the past in such poor health? In *Health in Older Ages: The Causes and Consequences of Declining Disability among the Elderly*, ed. Cutler, D., Wise, D. University of Chicago Press.

Costa, D., Steckel, R. 1997. Long-term trends in health, welfare, and economic growth in the United States. In *Health and Welfare during Industrialization*, ed. Steckel, R., Floud, R. University of Chicago Press.

Costa-Font, J., Gil, J. 2008. Generational effects and gender height dimorphism in contemporary Spain. *Economics and Human Biology* 6: 1–18.

Crafts, N. 1980. Income elasticities of demand and the release of labor by agriculture during the British industrial revolution. *Journal of European Economic History* 9: 153–168.

1982. Regional price variations in England in 1843: An aspect of the standard-of-living debate. *Explorations in Economic History* 19: 51–70.

1985a. *British Economic Growth during the Industrial Revolution*. Oxford University Press.

1985b. English workers' living standards during the Industrial Revolution: Some remaining problems. *Journal of Economic History* 45: 139–144.

1997. The human development index and changes in the standard of living: Some historical comparison. *European Review of Economic History* 1: 299–322.

Crafts, N., Harley, C. 1992. Output growth and the Industrial Revolution: A restatement of the Crafts-Harley view. *Economic History Review* 45: 703–730.

Craig, L., Goodwin, B., Grennes, T. 2004. The effect of mechanical refrigeration on nutrition in the United States. *Social Science History* 28: 325–336.

Crawford, S. 1992. The slave family: A view from the slave narratives. In *Strategic Factors in Nineteenth Century American Economic History: A Volume to Honor Robert W. Fogel*, ed. Goldin, C., Rockoff, H. University of Chicago Press.

Cutler, D. 2001. The reduction in disability among the elderly. *Proceedings of the National Academy of Sciences* 98: 6456–6457.

Cutler, D., Glaeser, E., Shapiro, J. M. 2003. Why have Americans become more obese? *Journal of Economic Perspectives* 17: 93–118.

Cutler, D., Miller, G. 2005. The role of public health improvements in health advances: The twentieth-century United States. *Demography* 42: 1–22.

Dalstra, J., Kunst, A., Geurts, J., Frenken, F., Mackenbach, J. 2002. Trends in socio-economic health inequalities in the Netherlands, 1981–99. *Journal of Epidemiology and Community Health* 56: 927–934.

Dangour, A., Farmer, A., Hill, H. L., Ismail, S. J. 2003. Anthropometric status of Kazakh children in the 1990s. *Economics and Human Biology* 1: 43–53.

Dasgupta, P. 1993. *An Inquiry into Well-being and Destitution.* Oxford: Clarendon Press.

1997. Nutritional status, the capacity for work, and poverty traps. *Journal of Econometrics* 77: 5–37.

Dasgupta, P., Ray, D. 1990. Adapting to undernourishment: The biological evidence and its implications. In *The Political Economy of Hunger. Volume 1: Entitlement and Well-Being*, ed. Drèze, J., Sen, A., 191–246. Oxford: Clarendon Press.

Dasgupta, P., Weale, M. 1992. On measuring the quality of life. *World Development* 20: 119–131.

Davey Smith, G., Gunnell, D., Ben-Shlomo, Y. 2001. Life-course approaches to socio-economic differentials in cause-specific adult mortality. In *Poverty, Inequality and Health: An International Perspective*, ed. Leon, D., Walt, G., 88–124. Oxford University Press.

Davey Smith, G., Hart, C., Upton, M., Hole, D., Gillis, C., Watt, G., Hawthorne, V. 2000. Height and risk of death among men and women: Aetiological implications for associations with cardiorespiratory disease and cancer mortality. *Journal of Epidemiology and Community Health* 54: 97–103.

Davidson, S., Passmore, R., Brock, J. F., Truswell, A. S. 1979. *Human Nutrition and Dietetics*, seventh edition. Edinburgh: Churchill Livingstone.

Davies, D. 1795. *The Case of Labourers in Husbandry Stated and Considered.*

De Beer, H. 2004. Observations on the history of Dutch physical stature from the late-Middle Ages to the present. *Economics and Human Biology* 2: 45–55.

de Vries, J. 1976. *The Economy of Europe in an Age of Crisis, 1600–1750.* Cambridge University Press.

1984. *European Urbanisation, 1500–1800.* London: Methuen.

1994. The industrial revolution and the industrious revolution. *Journal of Economic History* 54: 249–270.

2008. *The Industrious Revolution: Consumer Behavior and the Household Economy, 1650 to the Present.* Cambridge University Press.

Deane, P., Cole, A. 1967. *British Economic Growth, 1688–1959: Trends and Structure.* Cambridge University Press.

Del Panta, L. 1997. Infant and child mortality in Italy, eighteenth to twentieth century: Long-term trends and territorial differences. In *Infant and Child Mortality in the Past*, ed. Bideau, A., Desjardins, B., Brignoli, H., 7–21. Oxford: Clarendon Press.

Demoulin, F. 1998. Secular trend in Europe. In *Secular Growth Changes in Europe*, ed. Bodzsár, E., Susanne, C., 109–134. Budapest: Eötvös University Press.

Department for Work and Pensions. 2002. *Simplicity, Security and Choice: Working and Saving for Retirement (Cm. 5677)*. London: HMSO.

2006. *Security in Retirement: Towards a New Pension System: Summary*. London: HMSO.

Department of Environment, Food and Rural Affairs. 2001. Household consumption of selected foods by income group of head-of-household (GB). https://statistics.defra.gov.uk/esg/publications/nfs/default.asp.

Department of Health. 2004. *Health Survey for England 2003: Trends*. www. dh.gov.uk/en/Publicationsandstatistics/PublishedSurvey/ HealthSurveyForEngland/Healthsurveyresults/DH_4098913.

2006. *Forecasting Obesity to 2010*. London: Department of Health.

Doblhammer, G., Kytir, K. 2001. Compression or expansion of morbidity? Trends in healthy-life expectancy in the elderly Austrian population between 1978 and 1998. *Social Science and Medicine* 52: 385–391.

Dobson, M. 1997. *Contours of Death and Disease in Early-Modern England*. Cambridge University Press.

Doll, R., Hill, A. 1950. Smoking and carcinoma of the lung: Preliminary report. *British Medical Journal* 221: 739–748.

Dowler, E., Seo, Y. 1985. Estimates of food supply v. measurement of food consumption. *Food Policy* 10: 278–288.

Drabble, M. 1985. *The Oxford Companion to English Literature*. Oxford University Press.

Drake, M. 1969. *Population and Society in Norway, 1735–1865*. Cambridge University Press.

Drukker, J., Tassenaar, V. 1997. Paradoxes of modernisation and material well-being in the Netherlands during the nineteenth century. In *Health and Welfare during Industrialization*, ed. Steckel, R., Floud, R. University of Chicago Press.

Drummond, J., Wilbraham, A. 1958. *The Englishman's Food: A History of Five Centuries of English Diet*. London: Jonathan Cape.

Duffy, J. 1971. *Epidemics in Colonial America*. Baton Rouge: Louisiana State University Press.

Dunnell, K. 1997. Are we healthier? In *The Health of Adult Britain 1841–1994. Volume 2, Chapters 15–27*, ed. Charlton, J., Murphy, M., 173–181. London: Office for National Statistics.

Dupâquier, J. 1979. *La Population Française aux xviie et xviiie Siècles*. Paris: Presses Universitaires de France.

1989. Demographic crises and subsidence crises in France, 1650–1725. In *Famine, Disease, and the Social Order in Early Modern Society*, ed. Walter, J., Schofield, R. Cambridge University Press.

Durnin, J., Passmore, R. 1967. *Energy, Work, and Leisure*. London: Heinemann.

Dyer, C. 1983. English diet in the later Middle Ages. In *Social Relations and Ideals: Essays in Honour of R. H. Hilton*, ed. Aston, T., Cross, P., Dyer, C., 191–216. Cambridge University Press.

Eden, F. 1797. *The State of the Poor* (three volumes). Reprinted 1954.

Edwards, C., Gorsky, M., Harris, B., Hinde, P. R. A. 2003. Sickness, insurance and health: Assessing trends in morbidity through friendly society records. *Annales de Démographie Historique* 1: 131–167.

Elstad, J. 2005. Childhood adversities and health variations among middle-aged men: A retrospective life-course study. *European Journal of Public Health* 15: 51–58.

Eltis, D. 1982. Nutritional trends in Africa and the Americas: Heights of the Africans, 1819–1839. *Journal of Interdisciplinary History* 12: 453–475.

Emery, H. 1998. Review of James C. Riley, "Sick, not Dead: The Health of British Workingmen during the Mortality Decline." *EH Net, H-Net Reviews, July 1998* www.h-net.msu.edu/reviews/showrev.cgi?path=17775899999635.

Engerman, S. 1997. The standard of living debate in international perspective; measures and indicators. In *Health and Welfare during Industrialization*, ed. Steckel, R., Floud, R. University of Chicago Press.

Eveleth, P., Tanner, J. 1976. *Worldwide Variation in Human Growth*. Cambridge University Press.

1990. *Worldwide Variation in Human Growth*, second edition. Cambridge University Press.

FAO. 1977. *The Fourth World Food Survey: FAO Food and Nutrition Series no. 10*. Rome: FAO.

1983. *A Comparative Study of Food Consumption Data from Food Balance Sheets and Household Surveys. Statistics Division, Economic and Social Development Paper 34*. Rome: FAO.

2010. FAO Country Profiles. www.fao.org/countryprofiles/default.asp?lang=en.

FAO/WHO. 1971. *Energy and Protein Requirements: Report of a Joint FAO/WHO Ad-Hoc Expert Committee. FAO Nutrition Meetings Report Series no. 52. WHO Technical Report Series no. 522*. Rome: FAO/WHO.

FAO/WHO/UNU. 1985. *Energy and Protein Requirements: Report of a Joint FAO/WHO/UNU Expert Consultation. Technical Report Series no. 724*. Geneva: WHO.

2002. *Joint FAO/WHO/UNU Expert Consultation on Energy and Protein Requirements*. Meeting EPR 81/8 of 2002.

FAOSTAT Consumption Database. http://faostat.fao.org/site/345/default.aspx.

Federico, G. 2003. Heights, calories and welfare: A new perspective on Italian industrialisation, 1854–1913. *Economics and Human Biology* 1: 289–308.

Feinstein, C. 1995. United Kingdom, 1780–1990. In *Labour's Reward: Real Wages and Economic Change in 19th and 20th-Century Europe*, ed. Scholliers, P., Zamagni, V., 258–266. Aldershot: Edward Elgar.

1998. Pessimism perpetuated: Real wages and the standard of living in Britain during and after the Industrial Revolution. *Journal of Economic History* 58: 625–658.

Finch, C., Crimmins, E. 2004. Inflammatory exposure and historical changes in human life spans. *Science* 305: 1736–1739.

Finkelstein, E., Ruhm, C., Kosa, K. M. 2005. Economic causes and consequences of obesity. *Annual Review of Public Health* 26: 239–257.

Fitzpatrick, R., Chandola, T. 2000. Health. In *Twentieth-Century British Social Trends*, ed. Halsey, A., Webb, J., 94–127. Basingstoke: Macmillan.

Flinn, M. 1965. *Report on the Sanitary Condition of the Labouring Population of Great Britain by Edwin Chadwick, 1842*. Edinburgh University Press.

1974. The stabilization of mortality in pre-industrial western Europe. *Journal of European Economic History* 3: 285–318.

1981. *The European Demographic System, 1500–1820*. Baltimore: Johns Hopkins University Press.

Flora, P., Alber, J. 1982. Modernisation, democratisation and the development of welfare states in western Europe. In *The Development of Welfare States in Europe and America*, ed. Flora, P., Heidenheimer, A., 37–80. New Brunswick and London: Transaction Publishers.

Flora, P., Kraus, F., Pfenning, W. 1987. *State, Economy and Society in Western Europe, 1815–75: A Data Handbook in Two Volumes. Volume II: The Growth of Industrial Societies and Capitalist Economies*. Frankfurt: Campus Verlag.

Floris, G., Sanna, E. 1998. Some aspects of secular trends in Italy. In *Secular Growth Changes in Europe*, ed. Bodzsár, E., Susanne, C. Budapest: Eötvös University Press.

Floud R. 1984. Measuring the transformation of the European economies. Centre for Economic Policy Research Working Paper 33.

1994. The heights of Europeans since 1750: A new source for European economic history. In *Stature, Living Standards and Economic Development: Essays in Anthropometric History*, ed. Komlos, J. University of Chicago Press.

1998. Height, weight, and body mass of the British population since 1820. National Bureau of Economic Research Historical Paper 108.

Floud, R., Harris, B. 1997. Health, height and welfare: Britain 1700–1980. In *Health and Welfare during Industrialization*, ed. Steckel, R., Floud, R., 91–126. University of Chicago Press.

Floud, R., Wachter, K. 1982. Poverty and physical stature: Evidence on the standard of living of London boys 1770–1870. *Social Science History* 6: 422–452.

Floud, R., Wachter, K., Gregory, A. 1990. *Height, Health and History: Nutritional Status in the United Kingdom, 1750–1980*. Cambridge University Press.

1993. Measuring historical heights: Short cuts or the long way round: A reply to Komlos. *Economic History Review* 46: 145–154.

Flynn J. 2009. Requiem for nutrition as the cause of IQ gains: Raven's gains in Britain 1838–2008. *Economics and Human Biology* 7: 18–27.

Fogel R. 1964. *Railroads and American Economic Growth*. Baltimore: Johns Hopkins University Press.

1986a. Long-term changes in nutrition and the standard of living. Presented at Research topics for section B7 of the Ninth International Economic History Congress, Berne, Switzerland.

1986b. Nutrition and decline in mortality since 1700: Some preliminary findings. In *Long-Term Factors in American Economic Growth*, ed. Engerman, S., Gallman, R. University of Chicago Press (for NBER).

1987. Biomedical approaches to the estimation and interpretation of secular trends in equity, morbidity, mortality, and labor productivity in Europe, 1750–1980. Typescript, Center for Population Economics, University of Chicago.

1989. *Without Consent or Contract, Volume 1*. New York: W.W. Norton.

1991. The conquest of high mortality and hunger in Europe and America: Timing and mechanisms. In *Favorites of Fortune: Technology, Growth, and Economic Development since the Industrial Revolution*, ed. Landes, D., Higgonet, P., Rosovsky, H. Cambridge: Harvard University Press.

1992a. The body mass index of adult male slaves in the U.S. c. 1836 and its bearing on mortality rates. In *Without Consent or Contract, Volume 2*, ed. Fogel, R., Galantine, R., Manning, R. New York: W.W. Norton.

1992b. Egalitarianism: The economic revolution of the twentieth century. Typescript, Center for Population Economics, University of Chicago.

1992c. Second thoughts on the European escape from hunger: Famines, chronic malnutrition, and mortality rates. In *Nutrition and Poverty*, ed. Osmani S. Oxford: Clarendon Press.

1993a. A comparison of biomedical and economic measures of egalitarianism: Some implications of secular trends for current policy. Presented at the Workshop on Economic Theories of Inequality, Stanford University, March 11–13.

1993b. New sources and new techniques for the study of secular trends in nutritional status, health, mortality, and the process of aging. *Historical Methods* 26: 5–43.

1994. Economic growth, population theory, and physiology: The bearing of long-term processes on the making of economic policy. *American Economic Review* 84: 369–395.

1997. New findings on secular trends in nutrition and mortality: Some implications for population theory. In *Handbook of Population and Family Economics Volume 1A*, ed. Rosenzweig, M., Stark, O., 435–486. Amsterdam: Elsevier.

2000. *The Fourth Great Awakening and the Future of Egalitarianism*. University of Chicago Press.

2004a. Changes in the process of aging during the twentieth century: Findings and procedures of the Early Indicators project. *Population and Development Review* 30 (suppl.): 19–47.

2004b. *The Escape from Hunger and Premature Death, 1700–2100: Europe, America, and the Third World*. Cambridge University Press.

2004c. Technophysio evolution and the measurement of economic growth. *Journal of Evolutionary Economics* 14: 217–221.

2008. Forecasting the cost of U.S. health care in 2040. NBER Working Paper 14361.

Fogel, R., Costa, D. 1997. A theory of technophysio evolution, with some implications for forecasting population, health care costs and pension costs. *Demography* 34: 49–66.

Fogel, R., Costa, D., Burton, J. 2008. Early Indicators of Later Work Levels, Disease, and Death (Grant application submitted to the National Institute on Aging).

Fogel, R., Costa, D., Kim, J. M. 1993. Secular trends in the distribution of chronic conditions and disabilities at young adult and late ages, 1860–1988: Some preliminary findings. Presented at NBER Summer Institute, Economics of Aging Program.

Fogel, R., Engerman, S. 1974a. *Time on the Cross: Evidence and Methods, A Supplement*. Boston: Little, Brown.

1974b. *Time on the Cross: The Economics of American Negro Slavery*. Boston: Little, Brown.

1992. The slave diet on large plantations in 1860. In *Without Consent or Contract: Evidence and Methods*, ed. Fogel, R., Galantine, R., Manning, R. New York: W.W. Norton.

Fogel, R., Engerman, S., Floud, R. C., Friedman, G., Margo, R. A., Sokoloff, K., Steckel, R. H., Trussell, T. J., Villaflor, G. A., Wachter, K. W. 1983. Secular changes in American and British stature and nutrition. *Journal of Interdisciplinary History* 14: 445–481.

Fogel, R., Galantine, R., Manning, R. L. 1992. *Without Consent or Contract, Volume 2, Evidence and Methods*. New York: W.W. Norton.

Food and Nutrition Research Institute. 2003. Philippine facts and figures: Part II. Anthropometric facts and figures. www.fnri.dost.gov.ph/files/fnri %20files/nns/factsandfigures2003/anthropometric.pdf.

Franklin, J. 1969. *From Slavery to Freedom*. New York: Alfred A. Knopf, Inc.

Fraser, P., Fleming, D., Murphy, M., Charlton, J., Gill, L., Goldacre, M. 1997. Morbidity statistics from health service utilisation. In *The Health of Adult Britain 1841–1994. Volume 1. Chapters 1–14*, ed. Charlton, J., Murphy, M., 58–73. London: Office for National Statistics.

Fredriks, A., Van Buren, S., Burgmeijer, R., Meulmeester, J., Beuker, R., Brugman, E., Roede, M. J., Verloove-Vanhorick, S. P., Wilt, J. M. 2000. Continuing positive secular growth change in the Netherlands, 1955–97. *Pediatric Research* 47: 316–323.

Freeman, J., Cole, T., Chinn, S., Jones, P., White, E., Preece, M. 1995. Cross-sectional stature and weight reference curves for the UK, 1990. *Archives of Disease in Childhood* 73: 17–24.

Fridlizius, G. 1989. The deformation of cohorts: Nineteenth-century mortality decline in a generational perspective. *Scandinavian Economic History Review/Economy and Society* 37: 3–17.

Frijhoff, W., Julia, D. 1979. The diet in boarding schools at the end of the ancién regime. In *Food and Drink in History: Selections from the Annales Economies, Sociétés, Civilisations, Volume 5*, ed. Forster, R., Ranum, O. Baltimore and London: Johns Hopkins University Press.

Galeson, D. W. 2000. The settlement and growth of the colonies: Population, labor, and economic development. In *The Cambridge Economic History of the United States, Volume 1: The Colonial Era*, ed. Engerman, S., Gallman, R., 207–243. New York: Cambridge University Press.

Gallman, R. 1960. Commodity output, 1839–1899. In *Trends in the American Economy in the Nineteenth Century*, ed. Parker, W., 13–71. Princeton University Press.

1971. The statistical approach: Fundamental concepts applied to history. In *Approaches to American Economic History*, ed. Taylor, G., Ellsworth, L., 63–86. Charlottesville: University Press of Virginia.

1995. Pork production and nutrition during the late nineteenth century: A weight issue visited yet again. *Agricultural History* 69: 592–606.

1996. Dietary change in antebellum America. *Journal of Economic History* 56: 193–201.

Galloway, P. 1986. Differentials in demographic responses to annual price variations in pre-revolutionary France: A comparison of rich and poor areas in Rouen, 1681–1787. *European Journal of Population* 2: 269–305.

Galobardes, B., Lynch, J., Davey Smith, G. 2004. Childhood socioeconomic circumstances and cause-specific mortality in adulthood: Systematic review and interpretation. *Epidemiologic Reviews* 26: 7–21.

2008. Is the association between childhood socioeconomic circumstances and cause-specific mortality established? Update of a systematic review. *Journal of Epidemiology and Community Health* 62: 387–390.

Garcia, J., Quintana-Domeque, C. 2007. The evolution of adult height in Europe: A brief note. *Economics and Human Biology* 5: 340–349.

General Register Office. 1953. *The Registrar-General's Statistical Review of England and Wales for the Year 1949. Supplement on General Morbidity, Cancer and Mental Health.* London: HMSO.

Goldin, C., Margo, R. 1989. The poor at birth: Birth weights and infant mortality at Philadelphia's almshouse hospital, 1848–1873. *Explorations in Economic History* 26: 360–379.

Gorsky, M., Harris, B., Hinde, P. R. A. 2004. Health and sickness in the late-nineteenth and twentieth centuries: The Hampshire Friendly Society and its records. Presented at Economic History Society Conference, Royal Holloway and Bedford New College, London.

Goubert, P. 1973. *The Ancien Régime.* New York: Harper Torchbooks.

Gould, B. 1869. *Investigations in the Military and Anthropological Statistics of American Soldiers.* Cambridge University Press.

Grantham, G. 1992. Urban provisioning zones before the industrial revolution. Photocopy, Institut National de la Recherche Agronomique and McGill University.

1993. Divisions of labour: Agricultural productivity and occupation specialization in pre-industrial Europe. *Economic History Review* 46: 478–502.

Grigg, D. 1995. The nutritional transition in western Europe. *Journal of Historical Geography* 21: 247–261.

Groenewegen, P., Westert, G., Boshuizen, H. 2003. Regional differences in healthy life expectancy in the Netherlands. *Public Health* 117: 424–429.

Gruenberg, E. 1977. The failures of success. *Milbank Quarterly* 55: 3–24.

Grundy, E. 1994. The health and health care of older adults in England and Wales, 1841–1994. In *The Health of Adult Britain 1841–1994. Volume 2. Chapter 15–27,* ed. Charlton, J., Murphy, M., 182–203. London: Office for National Statistics.

Gunnell, D., Whitley, E., Upton, M. N., McConnachie, A., Davey Smith, G. 2003. Associations of height, leg-length and lung function with cardiovascular risk factors in the Midspan Family Study. *Journal of Epidemiology and Community Health* 57.

Gutiérrez-Fisac, J., Gispert, R., Solà, J. 2000. Factors explaining the geographical differences in disability-free life expectancy in Spain. *Journal of Epidemiology and Community Health* 54: 451–455.

Haines, M. 1979. The use of model life tables to estimate mortality for the United States in the late-nineteenth century. *Demography* 16: 289–312.

Haines, M., Craig, L., Weiss, T. 2003. The short and the dead: A new look at the "antebellum puzzle" in the United States. *Journal of Economic History* 63: 385–415.

Harding, S., Bethune, A., Maxwell, R., Brown, J. 1997. Mortality trends using the longitudinal study. In *Health Inequalities: Decennial Supplement*, ed. Drever, F., Whitehead, M., 143–155. London: The Stationery Office.

Hardy, A. 2001. *Health and Medicine in Britain since 1860*. Basingstoke: Palgrave.

Harris, B. 1993. The demographic impact of the first World War: An anthropometric perspective. *Social History of Medicine* 6: 343–366.

1994. Health, height and history: An overview of recent developments in anthropometric history. *Social History of Medicine* 7: 297–320.

1995. *The Health of the Schoolchild: A History of the School Medical Service in England and Wales*. Buckingham: Open University Press.

1997a. Growing taller, living longer? Anthropometric history and the future of old age. *Ageing and Society* 17: 491–512.

1997b. Heights and weights of British schoolchildren, 1908–50. Computer file. UK Data Archive, March 1997: SN: 3546.

1998. Gender, height and mortality in nineteenth- and twentieth-century Britain: Some preliminary reflections. In *The Biological Standard of Living in Comparative Perspective*, ed. Komlos, J., Baten, J., 413–448. Stuttgart: Franz Steiner Verlag.

2000. Height and nutrition. In *The Cambridge World History of Food*, ed. Kiple, K., Ornelas, K., 1427–1438. Cambridge University Press.

2001. "The child is the father to the man." The relationship between child health and adult mortality in the 19th and 20th centuries. *International Journal of Epidemiology* 30: 688–696.

2004a. *The Origins of the British Welfare State: Society, State and Social Welfare in England and Wales, 1800–1945*. Basingstoke: Palgrave.

2004b. Public health, nutrition and the decline of mortality: The McKeown thesis revisited. *Social History of Medicine* 17: 379–407.

2008. Gender, health and welfare in England and Wales since industrialization. *Research in Economic History* 26: 157–204.

2009. Anthropometric history, gender and the measurement of wellbeing. In *Gender and Wellbeing in Europe: Historical and Contemporary Perspectives*, ed. Harris, B., Gálvez, L., Machado, H., 59–84. Farnham: Ashgate.

Harris, B., Gálvez, L., Machado, H., eds. 2009. *Gender and Well-Being in Europe: Historical and Contemporary Perspectives*. Farnham: Ashgate Publishing.

Harris, B., Hinde, P., Gorsky, M. 2009. *The Health and Morbidity of Friendly Society Members in the Late-Nineteenth and Twentieth Century: Full Research Report ESRC End of Award Report, RES-062-23-0324.* Swindon: ESRC.

Hassan, J. 1985. The growth and impact of the British water industry in the nineteenth century. *Economic History Review* 38: 531–547.

Hattersley, L. 1997. Expectation of life by social class. In *Health Inequalities: Decennial Supplement*, ed. Drever, F., Whitehead, M., 73–82. London: The Stationery Office.

Hauspie, R., Vercauteren, M., Susanne, C. 1997. Secular change in growth and maturation: An update. *Acta Paediatrica Scandinavica* Supplement 423: 20–27.

Heckscher, E. 1954. *An Economic History of Sweden.* Cambridge University Press.

Heintel, M., Sandberg, L., Steckel, R. H. 1998. Swedish historical heights revisited: New estimation techniques and results. In *The Biological Standard of Living in Comparative Perspective*, ed. Komlos, J., Baten, J., 449–458. Stuttgart: Franz Steiner Verlag.

Heirmeyer, M. 2009. Height and BMI values of German conscripts in 2000, 2001 and 1906. *Economics and Human Biology* 7: 366–375.

Hémardinquer, J. 1970. *Pour une Histoire de L'alimentation.* Paris: Colon.

Hennock, E. 1957. Urban sanitary reform a generation before Chadwick? *Economic History Review* 10: 113–120.

2000. The urban sanitary movement in England and Germany, 1838–1914: A comparison. *Continuity and Change* 15: 269–296.

Henry, L. 1987. Mortalité des hommes et des femmes dans le passe. *Annales de Démographie Historique* 87–118.

Hermanussen, M., Burmeister, J., Burkhardt, V. 1995. Stature and stature distribution in recent West German and historic samples of Italian and Dutch conscripts. *American Journal of Human Biology* 7: 507–515.

Heyberger, L. 2007. Toward an anthropometric history of provincial France, 1780–1920. *Economics and Human Biology* 7: 366–375.

Higman, B. 1984. *Slave Populations of the British Caribbean, 1807–1834.* Baltimore: Johns Hopkins University Press.

Himmelfarb, G. 1983. *The Idea of Poverty: England in the Early Industrial Age.* New York: Random House.

Hobsbawm, E. 1963. The standard of living during the Industrial Revolution: A discussion. *Economic History Review* 16: 120–148.

Hodne, F., Grytte, O., Alme, J. 1995. Norway, 1850–1950. In *Labour's Reward: Real Wages and Economic Change in 19th and 20th-Century Europe*, ed. Scholliers, P., Zamagni, V., 238–248. Aldershot: Edward Elgar.

Hoffman, P. 1988. Institutions and agriculture in Old Regime France. *Politics and Society* 16: 241–264.

1991. Land rents and agricultural productivity: The Paris Basin, 1450–1789. *Journal of Economic History* 51: 771–805.

1998. Agricultural productivity and the food supply in France, 1500–1815. In *The Biological Standard of Living in Comparative Perspective*, ed. Komlos, J., Baten, J., 509–525. Stuttgart: Steiner Verlag.

Hofsten, E., Lundström, H. 1976. *Swedish Population Theory: Main Trends from 1750 to 1970*. Stockholm: Norstedts Tryckeri.

Hohls, R. 1995. Germany, 1850–1985. In *Labour's Reward: Real Wages and Economic Change in 19th and 20th-Century Europe*, ed. Scholliers, P., Zamagni, V., 210–219. Aldershot: Edward Alder.

Holderness, B. 1989. Prices, productivity, and output. In *Agrarian History of England and Wales VI: 1750–1850*, ed. Mingay, G., 84–189. Cambridge University Press.

Hong, S. C. 2007a. The burden of early exposure to malaria in the United States, 1850–1860: Malnutrition and immune disorders. *Journal of Economic History* 67: 1001–1035.

2007b. The health and economic burdens of malaria: The American case. Dissertation, University of Chicago.

Horrell, S., Humphries, J., Voth, H.-J. 2001. Destined for deprivation: Human capital formation and intergenerational poverty in nineteenth-century England. *Explorations in Economic History* 38: 339–365.

Horrell, S., Meredith, D., Oxley, D. 2009. Measuring misery: Body mass, ageing and gender inequality in Victorian London. *Explorations in Economic History* 46: 93–119.

Hoskins, W. 1964. Harvest fluctuations and English economic history, 1480–1619. *Agricultural History Review* 12.

1968. Harvest fluctuations and English economic history, 1620–1759. *Agricultural History Review* 16: 15–31.

Hubbard, W. 2000. The urban penalty: Towns and mortality in nineteenth-century Norway. *Continuity and Change* 15: 331–350.

Hufton, O. 1974. *The Poor of Eighteenth-Century France*. Oxford: Clarendon Press.

1983. Social conflict and the grain supply in eighteenth-century France. *Journal of Interdisciplinary History* 14: 303–331.

Humphreys, M. 2001. *Malaria: Poverty, Race, and Public Health in the United States*. Baltimore: Johns Hopkins University Press.

Humphries J. 1991. "Bread and a pennyworth of treacle": Excess female mortality in England in the 1840s. *Cambridge Journal of Economics* 15: 451–473.

2010. *Childhood and Child Labour in the British Industrial Revolution.* Cambridge University Press.

Imhof, A. 1981. Women, family and death: Excess mortality of women in child-bearing age in four communities in nineteenth-century Germany. In *The German Family: Essays on the Social History of the Family in Nineteenth- and Twentieth-Century Germany,* ed. Evans, R., Lee, W., 148–174. London: Croom Helm.

1990. *Lebenserwartungen in Deutschland vom 17. bis 19. Jahrhundert (Life Expectancies in Germany from the 17th to the 19th Century).* Weinheim: VCH, Acta Humaniora.

1994. *Lebenserwartungen in Deutschland, Norwegen und Schweden im 19. und 20. Jahrhundert.* Berlin: Akademie Verlag.

INED. 1977. Sixième rapport sur la situation démographique de la France. *Population* 32: 253–338.

Instituto Nacional de Salud (Peru). 2006. Reporte Epidemiologico INS 2006. www.ins.gob.pe/insvirtual/images/boletin/pdf/reporteepidemiologico INS2006–22.pdf.

International Obesity Taskforce. 2002. *Obesity in Europe: The Case for Action.* London: International Obesity Taskforce.

Jablonski, M., Rosenblum, L., Kunze, K. 1988. Productivity, age, and labor composition changes in the U.S. *Monthly Labor Review* 111.

Jackson, R. 1996. The heights of rural-born English female convicts transported to New South Wales. *Economic History Review* 49: 584–590.

Jaeger, U. 1998. Secular trend in Germany. In *Secular Growth Changes in Europe,* ed. Bodzsár, E., Susanne, C. Budapest: Eötvös University Press.

James, W. 2008. The epidemiology of obesity: The size of the problem. *Journal of Internal Medicine* 263: 336–352.

Jamison, D., Lau, L., Wiang J. 2004. Health's contribution to economic growth in an environment of partially-endogenous technical progress. Disease Control Priorities Project 10.

2005. Health's contribution to economic growth in an environment of partially-endogenous technical progress. In *Health and Economic Growth: Findings and Policy Implications,* ed. López-Casasnovas, G., Rivera, B., Currais, L., 67–91. Cambridge: MIT Press.

Janssen, F., Kunst, A. 2005. Cohort patterns in mortality trends among the elderly in seven European countries, 1950–1999. *International Journal of Epidemiology* 34: 1149–1159.

Johannisson K. 1994. The people's health: Public health policies in Sweden. In *The History of Public Health and the Modern State,* ed. Porter, D., 165–182. Amsterdam: Rodopi.

Johansson, S. 1991. The health transition: The cultural inflation of morbidity during the decline of mortality. *Health Transition Review* 1: 39–65.

1992. Measuring the cultural inflation of morbidity during the decline in mortality. *Health Transition Review* 2: 77–87.

1994. Food for thought: Rhetoric and reality in modern mortality history. *Historical Methods* 27: 101–125.

John, A. 1989. Statistical appendix. In *The Agrarian History of England and Wales. Vol. VI. 1750–1850*, ed. Mingay, G., 973–1131. Cambridge University Press.

Johnson, D. 2000. Population, food, and knowledge. *American Economic Review* 90: 1–14.

Johnson, P., Nicholas, S. 1995. Male and female living standard in England and Wales 1812–57: Evidence from criminal height records. *Economic History Review* 48: 470–481.

1997. Health and welfare of women in the United Kingdom 1785–1920. In *Health and Welfare during Industrialization*, ed. Steckel, R., Floud, R., 201–249. University of Chicago Press.

Johnston, L., Williamson, S. 2008. What was the U.S. GDP then? Available online at www.measuringworth.org/usgdp/.

Jones, E., Falkus, M. 1990. Urban improvement and the English economy in the seventeenth and eighteenth centuries. In *The Eighteenth Century Town: A Reader in English Urban History 1688–1820*, ed. Borsay, P., 116–158. London and New York: Longman.

Jones, M. 1992. *American Immigration*. University of Chicago Press.

Jones, P. 1988. *The Peasantry in the French Revolution*. Cambridge University Press.

Jones, S. 2000. *Almost Like a Whale: The Origin of Species Updated*. London: Anchor.

Jousilahti, P., Tuomilehto, J., Vartiainen, E., Eriksson, J., Puska, P. 2000. Relation of adult height to cause-specific and total mortality: A prospective follow-up study of 31,199 middle-aged men and women in Finland. *American Journal of Epidemiology* 151: 1112–1120.

Kajantie, E., Osmond, C., Barker, D., Forsén, T., Phillips, D., Eriksson, J. 2005. Size at birth as a predictor of mortality in adulthood: A follow-up of 350,000 person-years. *International Journal of Epidemiology* 34: 655–663.

Kalėdienė, R., Petrauskienė, J. 2004. Healthy life expectancy – An important indicator for health policy development in Lithuania. *Medicina (Kaunas)* 40: 582–588.

Kamadjey, R., Edwards, R., Atanga, J.S., Kiawi, E.C., Unwin, N., Mbanya, J.C. 2006. Anthropometry measures and prevalence of obesity in the urban adult population of Cameroon: An update from the Cameroon Burden of Diabetes Baseline Survey. *BMC Public Health* 6: 228.

Karlberg, J. 1989. A biologically-oriented mathematical model (ICP) for human growth. *Acta Paediatrica Scandinavica* Supplement 350: 70–94.

Karpinos, B. 1958. Height and weight of selective service registrants processed for military service WWII. *Human Biology* 40: 292–321.

Kearns, G. 1988. The urban penalty and the population history of England. In *Society, Health, and Population during the Demographic Transition*, ed. Brandström, A., Tedebrand, L.-G., 213–236. Stockholm: Almqvist and Wisksell International.

Kermack, W., McKendrick, A., McKinlay, P. L. 1934. Death rates in Great Britain and Sweden: Some general regularities and their significance. *Lancet* 1: 698–703.

Kiil, V. 1939. *Stature and Growth of Norwegian Men during the Past Two Hundred Years*. Oslo: I Kommisjon Hos. Jacob Dybwad.

Kim, J. 1993. Waaler surfaces: A new perspective on height, weight, morbidity, and mortality. Typescript, University of Chicago.

1995. The health of the elderly, 1990–2035: An alternative forecasting approach based on changes in human physiology, with implications for health care costs and policy. Typescript, University of Chicago.

1996. Waaler surfaces: The economics of nutrition, body build, and health. Dissertation, University of Chicago.

Kimhi, A. 2003. Socio-economic determinants of health and physical fitness in southern Ethiopia. *Economics and Human Biology* 1: 55–75.

King, G. (1696) 1973. Natural and political observations and conclusions upon the state and condition of England, 1696. In *The Earliest Classics*, ed. Laslett, P. Farnsborough: Gregg.

King, P. 1991. Customary rights and women's earnings: the importance of gleaning to the rural labouring poor, 1750–1850. *Economic History Review* 44: 461–76.

King, S., Tomkins, A., eds. 2003. *The Poor in England 1750–1850: An Economy of Makeshifts*. Manchester University Press.

Klasen, S. 1998. Marriage, bargaining and intrahousehold resource allocation: Excess female mortality among adults during early German development, 1740–1860. *Journal of Economic History* 58: 432–467.

Knight, I., Eldridge, J. 1984. *The Heights and Weights of Adults in Great Britain: Report of a Survey Carried Out on the Behalf of the Department of Health and Social Security among Adults aged 16–64*. London: HMSO.

Komlos, J. 1987. The height and weight of West Point cadets: Dietary change in antebellum America. *Journal of Economic History* 47: 897–927.

1989. *Nutrition and Economic Development in the Eighteenth Century Habsburg Monarchy: An Anthropometric History*. Princeton University Press.

1990. Stature, nutrition and the economy in the eighteenth-century Habsburg monarchy. Dissertation, University of Chicago.

1991. On the significance of anthropometric history. *Revista di Storia Economica* 11: 97–109.

1993a. Further thoughts on the nutritional status of the British population. *Economic History Review* 46: 363–366.

1993b. The secular trend in the biological standard of living in the United Kingdom, 1730–1860. *Economic History Review* 46: 115–144.

1994. The nutritional status of French students. *Journal of Interdisciplinary History* 24: 493–508.

2003. An anthropometric history of early-modern France. *European Review of Economic History* 7: 159–189.

2004. How to (and how not to) analyze deficient height samples: An introduction. *Historical Methods* 37: 160–173.

2007. Anthropometric evidence on economic growth, biological well-being and regional convergence in the Hapsburg monarchy, c. 1850–1910. *Cliometrica* 1: 211–237.

Komlos, J., Baten, J., eds. 1998. *The Biological Standard of Living in Comparative Perspective*. Stuttgart: Franz Steiner Verlag.

Komlos, J., Baur, M. 2004. From the tallest to (one of) the fattest: The enigmatic fate of the American population in the 20th century. *Economics and Human Biology* 2: 57–74.

Komlos, J., Coclanis, P. 1997. On the puzzling cycle in the biological standard of living: The case of antebellum Georgia. *Explorations in Economic History* 34: 433–459.

Komlos, J., Cuff, T., eds. 1998. *Classics in Anthropometric History*. St. Katharinen, Germany: Scripta Mercaturae Verlag.

Komlos, J., Kim, J. 1990. Estimating trends in historical heights. *Historical Methods* 23: 116–120.

Kramer, M. 1987. Determinants of low birth weight: Methodological assessment and meta-analysis. *Bulletin of the World Health Organisation* 65 663–737.

Kuh, D., Hardy, R., Langenberg, C., Richards, M., Wadsworth, M. E. J. 2002. Mortality in adults aged 26–54 years related to socioeconomic conditions in childhood and adulthood: Post war birth cohort study. *British Medical Journal* 325: 1076–1080.

Kunitz, S. 2007. *The Health of Populations: General Theories and Particular Realities*. Oxford University Press.

Kunitz, S., Engerman, S. 1992. The ranks of death: Secular trends in income and mortality. *Health Transition Review* 2: 29–46.

Kuznets, S. 1966. *Modern Economic Growth: Rate, Structure and Spread.* New Haven and London: Yale University Press.

Labrousse, C. 1944. *La Crise de L'économie Française a la Fin de L'ancien Régime et au Debut de la Révolution.* Paris: Presses Universitaires de France.

Lader, D. 2009. *Drinking: Adults' Behavior and Knowledge in 2008: A Report on Research using the National Statistics Opinions (Omnibus) Survey Produced on Behalf of the NHS Information Centre for Health and Social Care.* Newport: Office for National Statistics.

Lancet. 2001. An overstretched hypothesis? *Lancet* 357: 405.

Landers, J. 1993. *Death and the Metropolis: Studies in the Demographic History of London 1670–1830.* Cambridge University Press.
    2000. Review article. *Continuity and Change* 15: 466–468.

Landes, D. 1969. *The Unbound Prometheus: Technological Change and Industrial Development from 1750 to the Present.* Cambridge University Press.

Laslett, P. 1971. *The World We Have Lost.* London: Methuen and Co. Ltd.

Law, C. 1967. The growth of urban population in England and Wales, 1801–1911. *Transactions of the Institute of British Geographers* 41: 125–143.

Layard, R. 2006. *Happiness: Lessons from a New Science.* London: Penguin.

Le Roy Ladurie, E. 1979a. The conscripts of 1868: A study of the correlation between geographical mobility, delinquency and physical stature, and other aspects of the situation of young Frenchmen called to do military service in that year. In *The Territory of the Historian*, ed. Le Roy Ladurie, E., 33–60. Brighton: Harvester Press.
    1979b. *The Territory of the Historian.* Great Britain: Redwood Burn.

Lee, C. 2005. Wealth accumulation and the health of Union Army veterans, 1860–1870. *Journal of Economic History* 65: 352–385.

Lee, K.-S. 2007. Infant mortality decline in the late 19th and early 20th centuries: The role of market milk. *Perspective in Biology and Medicine* 50: 585–602.

Lee, W. 1979. Germany. In *European Demography and Economic Growth*, ed. Lee, W., 144–195. London: Croom Helm.

Lee, W., Vögele, J. 2001. The benefits of federalism? The development of public health policy and health care systems in nineteenth-century Germany and their impact on mortality reduction. *Annales de Démographie Historique* 1: 65–96.

Leon, D. 2001. Common threads: Underlying components of inequalities in mortality between and within countries. In *Poverty, Inequality and Health: An International Perspective*, ed. Leon, D., Walt, G., 58–87. Oxford University Press.

Leon, D., Davey Smith, G., Shipley, M., Strachan, D. 1995. Adult height and mortality in London: Early life, socioeconomic confounding, or shrinkage? *Journal of Epidemiology and Community Health* 49: 5–9.

Liestøl, K., Rosenberg, M. 1995. Height, weight and menarchael age of schoolgirls in Oslo: An update. *Annals of Human Biology* 22: 199–205.

Lindert, P., Williamson, J. 1982. Revising England's social tables, 1688–1812. *Explorations in Economic History* 19: 385–408.

1983b. Reinterpreting England's social tables: 1688–1913. *Explorations in Economic History* 20: 94–109.

1985. English workers' real wages: Reply to Crafts. *Journal of Economic History* 45: 145–153.

Lindgren, G. 1998. Secular growth changes in Sweden. In *Secular Growth Changes in Europe*, ed. Bodzsár, E., Susanne, C., 319–333. Budapest: Eötvös University Press.

Lipson, E. 1971. *The Economic History of England, Volume 3, The Age of Mercantilism*. London: Adam and Charles Black.

Lipton, M. 1983. Poverty, undernutrition, and hunger. World Bank Staff Working Papers no. 597.

Livi-Bacci, M. 1991. *Population and Nutrition: An Essay in European Demographic History*. Cambridge University Press.

2000. *The Population of Europe: A History*. Oxford: Blackwell.

Ljung, B.-O., Bergsten-Brucefors, A., Dindgren, G. 1974. The secular trend in physical growth in Sweden. *Annals of Human Biology* 1: 245–256.

Logan, T. 2006. Is the calorie distribution log normal? Evidence from the nineteenth century. *Historical Methods* 39: 112–122.

Logan, W., Brooke, E. 1957. *The Survey of Sickness 1943–1952*. London: HMSO.

López-Casasnovas, G., Rivera, B., Currais, L. 2005. Introduction: The role health plays in economic growth: Findings and policy implications. In *Health and Economic Growth: Findings and Policy Implications*, ed. López-Casasnovas, G., Rivera, B., Currais, L., 1–16. Cambridge: MIT Press.

Loudon, I. 1992. *Death in Childbirth: An International Study of Maternal Care and Maternal Mortality 1800–1950*. Oxford: Clarendon Press.

Lumey, L. 1998. Reproductive outcomes in women prenatally exposed to undernutrition: A review of findings from the Dutch famine birth cohort. *Proceedings of the Nutrition Society* 57: 129–135.

Macaulay, T. B. 1848. *The History of England*. London: J M Dent and Sons Ltd.

Mackenbach, J., Bakker, M., Kunst, A., Diderichsen, F. 2002. Socioeconomic inequalities in health in Europe: An overview. In *Reducing Inequalities in Health: A European Perspective*, ed. Mackenbach, J., Bakker, M., 3–24. London: Routledge.

Macnicol, J. 1998. *The Politics of Retirement in Britain, 1878–1948.* Cambridge University Press.

Maddison, A. 1982. *Phases of Capitalist Development.* Oxford University Press.

1995. *Monitoring the World Economy 1820–1992.* Paris: Organisation for Economic Cooperation and Development.

2001. *The World Economy: A Millennial Perspective.* Paris: Organisation for Economic Cooperation and Development.

2003. *The World Economy: Historical Statistics.* Paris: Organisation for Economic Cooperation and Development.

Malthus, T. 1993. *An Essay on the Principle of Population. Edited with an Introduction by Geoffrey Gilbert.* Oxford and New York: Oxford University Press.

Mankiw, N. G., Romer, D., Weil, D. 1992. A contribution to the empirics of economic growth. *Quarterly Journal of Economics* 107: 407–437.

Manton, K. 1982. Changing concepts of morbidity and mortality in the elderly population. *Milbank Quarterly* 60: 183–244.

Manton, K., Corder, L., Stallard, E. 1997. Chronic disability trends in elderly United States populations: 1982–94. *Proceedings of the National Academy of Sciences* 94: 2593–2598.

Manton, K., Gu, X. 2001. Changes in the prevalence of chronic disability in the United States black and nonblack population above age 65 from 1982 to 1999. *Proceedings of the National Academy of Sciences* 98: 6354–6359.

Manton, K., Gu, X., Lamb, V. 2006. Long-term trends in life expectancy and active life expectancy in the United States. *Population and Development Review* 32: 81–105.

Margo, R. 2000. The labor force in the nineteenth century. In *The Cambridge Economic History of the United States, Volume II: The Long Nineteenth Century*, ed. Engerman, S., Gallman, R. New York: Cambridge University Press.

Margo, R., Steckel, R. 1982. The heights of American slaves: New evidence on slave nutrition and health. *Social Science History* 6: 516–538.

Marmot, M. 2004. *Status Syndrome: How Your Social Standing Directly Affects Your Life Health and Life Expectancy.* London: Bloomsbury.

Marmot, M., Shipley, M., Rose, G. 1984. Inequalities in death-specific explanations of a general pattern? *Lancet* 1: 1003–1006.

Marshall, J. 1968. *The Old-Poor Law, 1795–1834.* London: Macmillan.

Martinez-Carrión, J. 1994. Stature, welfare and economic growth in nineteenth-century Spain: The case of Murcia. In *Stature, Living Standards, and Economic Development: Essays in Anthropometric History*, ed. Komlos, J. University of Chicago Press.

Martinez-Carrión, J., Moreno-Lázaro, J. 2007. Was there an urban height penalty in Spain, 1840–1913? *Economics and Human Biology* 5: 144–164.

Martinez-Carrión, J., Perez-Castejón, J. 2002. Creciendo con desilgualdad. Niveles de vida biológicos en la España rural mediterránea desde 1840. In *El Nivel de Vida en la España Rural, Siglos XVIII-XX*, ed. Carrión, J., 405–460. San Vicente: Universidad de Alicante.

Mathias, P. 1957. The social structure in the eighteenth century: A calculation by Joseph Massie. *Economic History Review, Second Series* 10: 35–45.

1975. Preface. In *The Standard of Living in Britain in the Industrial Revolution*, ed. Taylor, A. J. London: Methuen.

2001. *The First Industrial Nation: An Economic History of Britain, 1700–1914*. London: Routledge.

McCance, R., Widdowson, E. 1960. *The Composition of Foods*. London: HMSO.

McClelland, P. D., Zeckhauser, R. 1982. *Demographic Dimensions of the New Republic: American Interregional Migration, Vital Statistics, and Manumissions, 1800–1860*. Cambridge University Press.

McCusker, J., Menard, R. 1985. *The Economy of British America, 1607–1789*. Chapel Hill and London: University of North Carolina Press.

McKeown, T. 1976. *The Modern Rise of Population*. London: Edward Arnold.

McMahon, S. 1981. Provisions laid up for the family: Toward a history of diet in New England, 1650–1850. *Historical Methods* 14: 4–21.

1985. A comfortable subsistence: The changing composition of diet in rural New England. *William and Mary Quarterly* 42: 25–65.

McNay, K., Humphries, J., Klasen, S. 1998. Death and gender in Victorian England and Wales: Comparisons with contemporary developing countries. University of Cambridge Department of Applied Economics Working Paper.

2005. Excess female mortality in nineteenth-century England and Wales: A regional analysis. *Social Science History* 29: 649–681.

McWilliams, J. 2005. *A Revolution in Eating: How the Quest for Food Shaped America*. New York: Columbia University Press.

Mennell, S. 1985. *All Manners of Food*. London: Basil Blackwell.

Mercer, A. 1985. Smallpox and epidemiological-demographic change in Europe: The role of vaccination. *Population Studies* 39: 287–307.

1990. *Disease, Morality and Population in Transition: Epidemiological-Demographic Change in England since the Eighteenth Century as Part of a Global Phenomenon*. Leicester University Press.

Metzer, J. 1992. Rational management, modern business practices, and economies of scale in antebellum southern plantations. In *Without*

Consent or Contract: Markets and Production: Technical Papers Volume 1, ed. Fogel, R., Engerman, S. New York: W.W. Norton.

Michel, J-P. 2002. Vieillissement en bonne santé: l'experience suisse. *Comptes Rendus Biologies* 325: 693–696.

Miguel, E. 2005. Health, education, and economic development. In *Health and Economic Growth: Findings and Policy Implications*, ed. López-Casasnovas, G., Rivera, B., Currais, L., 143–168. Cambridge: MIT Press.

Millward, R. 2000. Urban government, finance and public health in Victorian Britatin. In *Urban Governance: Britain and Beyond since 1750*, ed. Morris, R., Trainor, R., 47–68. Aldershot: Ashgate.

Millward, R., Bell, F. 1998. Economic factors in the decline of mortality in late 19th and 20th century Britain. *European Review of Economic History* 2: 263–288.

2001. Infant mortality in Victorian Britain: The mother as medium. *Economic History Review* 54: 699–733.

Millward, R., Sheard, S. 1995. The urban fiscal problem, 1870–1914: Government expenditure and finance in England and Wales. *Economic History Review* 2: 501–535.

Ministère du Travail. 1977. *Sixième Rapport sur la Situation Démographique de la France*. Paris: Ministère du Travail.

Mironov, B. 2007. Birth weight and physical stature in St. Petersburg: Living standards of women in Russia, 1980–2005. *Economics and Human Biology* 5: 123–143.

Mitchell, B. 1988. *British Historical Statistics*. Cambridge University Press.

2003. *International Historical Statistics: Europe, 1750–2000*. Basingstoke: Palgrave.

Mitchell, B., Deane, P. 1962. *Abstract of British Historical Statistics*. Cambridge University Press.

Mokdad, A., Ford, E., Bowman, B., Dietz, W., Vinicor, F., Bales, V., Marks, J. 2003. Prevalence of obesity, diabetes and obesity-related health risk factors, 2001. *Journal of the American Medical Association* 289.

Mokyr, J. 1983. *Why Ireland Starved: A Quantitative and Analytical History of the Irish Economy 1800–1850*. London: George Allen & Unwin.

1988. Is there still life in the pessimist case? Consumption during the industrial revolution, 1790–1850. *Journal of Economic History* 43: 69–92.

1990. *The Lever of Riches: Technological Creativity and Economic Progress*. New York and Oxford: Oxford University Press.

2004. Accounting for the Industrial Revolution. In *The Cambridge Economic History of Modern Britain, Volume 1*, ed. Floud, R., Johnson, P. Cambridge University Press.

Mokyr, J., O'Gráda, C. 1991. Height of the British and the Irish 1800–1815: Evidence from recruits to the East India Company army. Typescript, Northwestern University.

Morand, O. F. 2005. Economic growth, health and longevity in the very long term: Facts and mechanisms. In *Health and Economic Growth*, ed. López-Casasnovas, G., Rivera, B., Currais, L. Cambridge, Mass.: MIT Press.

Morell, M. 1983. Food consumption among inmates of Swedish hospitals during the eighteenth and early nineteenth centuries. Presented at Colloquium on the Standard of Living in Europe since 1850, Uppsala University, Sweden.

Murphy, K., Welch, F. 1990. Empirical age-earning profiles. *Journal of Labor Economics* 8: 202–229.

Murray, C., Chen, L. 1992. Understanding morbidity change. *Population and Development Review* 18: 481–503.

 1993. Understanding morbidity change: Reply to Riley. *Population and Development Review* 19: 812–815.

Murray, J. 2003. Social insurance claims and morbidity estimates: Sickness or absence? *Social History of Medicine* 16: 225–245.

Must, A., Spadano, J., Coakley, E. H., Field, A. E., Colditz, G., Dietz, W. H. 1999. The disease burden associated with overweight and obesity. *Journal of the American Medical Association* 282: 1523–1529.

Mutafova, M., Van de Water, H., Perenbloom, R., Boshuizen, H., Maleshkov, C. 1996. Occupational handicap-free life expectancy in Bulgaria, 1976–92, based on the data of the Medical Expert Commissions. *Social Science and Medicine* 43: 537–542.

National Health Service Information Centre. 2008. *Health Survey for England 2007: Latest Trends*. www.ic.nhs.uk/pubs/hse07trends.

Nelson, M., Rogers, J. 1994. Cleaning up the cities: Application of the first comprehensive Public Health Law in Sweden. *Scandinavian Journal of History* 19: 17–39.

Ng, K., Virts N. 1989. The value of freedom. *Journal of Economic History* 49: 958–965.

NHS. 2010. NHS Database. www.nhsdatabase.com/.

Nicholas, S., Oxley, D. 1993. The living standards of women during the industrial revolution, 1795–1820. *Economic History Review* 46: 723–749.

 1996. Living standards of women in England and Wales, 1785–1815: New evidence from Newgate prison records. *Economic History Review* 49: 591–599.

Nicholas, S., Steckel, R. 1991. Heights and living standards of English workers during the early years of industrialization. *Journal of Economic History* 51: 937–957.

Nordhaus, W. D., Tobin, J. 1972. Is growth obsolete? In *Economic Growth: Fiftieth Anniversary Colloquium*, 1–80. New York: National Bureau of Economic Research.

O'Brien, P., Keyder, C. 1978. *Economic Growth in Britain and France 1780–1914: Two Paths to the Twentieth Century*. London: George Allen and Unwin.

Oddy, D. 1970. Working-class diets in late nineteenth-century Britain. *Economic History Review* 23: 314–323.

   1990. Food, drink, and nutrition. In *The Cambridge Social History of Britain 1750–1950, Volume 2*, ed. Thompson, F., 251–278. Cambridge University Press.

   2003. *From Plain Fare to Fusion Food: British Diet from the 1890s to the 1990s*. Woodridge: Boydell.

OECD. 2005. *Health at a Glance*. Paris: OECD.

Oeppen, J., Vaupel, J. 2002. Broken limits to life expectancy. *Science* 296: 1029–1031.

Offer, A. 2001. Body weights and self-control in the United States and Britain since the 1950s. *Social History of Medicine* 14: 79–106.

   2003. Economic welfare measurements and human well-being. In *The Economic Future in Historical Perspective*, ed. David, P. A., Thomas, M. Oxford: Oxford University Press for the British Academy.

   2006. *The Challenge of Affluence: Self-Control and Wellbeing in the United States and Britain since 1950*. Oxford University Press.

Office for National Statistics. 1999. *Cancer Survival Trends in England and Wales, 1971–1995: Deprivation and NHS Region*. London: The Stationery Office.

   2002. *Mortality Statistics: Cause. Review of the Registrar General on Deaths by Cause, Sex and Age, in England and Wales, 2001*. London: Office for National Statistics. www.statistics.gov.uk/downloads/theme_-health/Dh2_28/DH2No28.pdf.

   2004a. *Stillbirths and Infant Deaths by Age at Death, 1921 to 2002*. www.statistics.gov.uk/STATBASE/expodata/files/10406733081.csv.

   2004b. *Mortality Statistics: General. Review of the Registrar-General on Deaths in England and Wales, 2002*. London: Office for National Statistics. www.statistics.gov.uk/downloads/theme_health/DH1_35_2002/DH1no35.pdf.

   2005. Cancer Survival: England and Wales, 1991–2001: Twenty Major Cancers. www.statistics.gov.uk/statbase/ssdataset.asp?vlnk=7898.

   2009a. *Mortality Statistics:Deaths Registered in 2008*. London: Office for National Statistics. www.statistics.gov.uk/downloads/theme_health/DR2008/DR_08.pdf.

2009b. Statistical Bulletin: Infant and Perinatal Mortality 2008: Health Areas, England and Wales. www.statistics.gov.uk/pdfdir/ipm0909.pdf.

Olmstead, A., Rhode, P. 2008. *Creating Abundance: Biological Innovation and American Agricultural Development*. Chapel Hill: University of North Carolina.

Olshansky, S., Passaro, D., Hershow, R. C., Layden, J., Carnes, B., Brody, J., Hayflick, L., Butler, R., Allison, D., Ludwig, D. 2005. A potential decline in life expectancy in the United States in the 21st century. *New England Journal of Medicine* 352: 1138–1145.

Olshansky, S., Rudberg, M., Carnes, B., Cassel, C., Brody, J. 1991. Trading off longer life for worsening health: The expansion of morbidity hypothesis. *Journal of Aging and Health* 3: 194–216.

Olson, J. 1992. Clock time versus real time: A comparison of the northern and southern agricultural years. In *Without Consent or Contract, Volume 3, Markets and Production: Technical Papers Volume 1*, ed. Fogel, R., Engerman, S., 216–240. New York: W.W. Norton.

Onland-Moret, N., Peeters, P., van Gils, C., Clavel-Chapelon, F., Key, T., Tjønneland, A., Trichopoulou, A., Kaaks, R., Manjer, J., Panico, S., Palli, D., Tehard, B., Stoikidou, M., Bueno-De-Mesquita, H. B., Boeing, H., Overad, K., Lenner, P., Quirós, J., Chirlaque, M. D., Miller, A., Khaw, K., Riboli, E. 2005. Age at menarche in relation to adult height. *American Journal of Epidemiology* 162: 623–632.

Oren, L. 1974. The welfare of women in laboring families. In *Clio's Consciousness Raised: New Perspectives on the History of Women*, ed. Hartman, M., Banner, L., 222–244. New York: Harper Torchbooks.

Orr, J. 1937. *Food, Health, and Income: Report on a Survey of Adequacy of Diet in Relation to Income*. London: Macmillan.

Osmani, S., Sen, A. 2003. The hidden penalties of gender inequality: Fetal origins of ill-health. *Economics and Human Biology* 1: 105–121.

Otero, A., Zunzunegui, M., Rodriguez-Laslo, A., Aguilar, A., Lazaro, P. 2004. Volumen y tendencias de la dependencia asociada al envejecimiento en la población española. *Revista Española de Salud Pública* 78: 201–213.

Owen, J. 1976. Workweeks and leisure: An analysis of trends, 1948–1975. *Monthly Labor Review* 99: 3–8.

1988. Work-time reduction in the United States and western Europe. *Monthly Labor Review* 111: 41–45.

Papadimtriou, A. 1998. Growth and development of Greek children in the twentieth century. In *Secular Growth Changes in Europe*, ed. Bodzsár, E., Susanne, C., 161–173. Budapest: Eötvös University Press.

Parliamentary Papers. 1849a. *An Account of the Imports of the Principal Articles of Foreign and Colonial Merchandise, of the Consumption of*

Such Articles, and of the Customs Duties Received Thereon, in the Year 1848, Compared with the Imports, Consumption and Receipts of the Preceding Year. PP 1849 (67) I, 1.

1849b. *Return of Wheat, Barley and Oats, and of Flour and Meal, Imported into the United Kingdom, Cleared for Consumption and Exported in Each Year from 1792 to 1848, with Average Annual Price, and the Duty Per Quarter.* PP 1849 (443) I, 393.

1851. *An Account of the Imports of the Principal Articles of Foreign and Colonial Merchandise, of the Consumption of Such Articles, and of the Customs Duties Received Thereon, in the Year Ending 5th January 1851, Compared with the Imports, Consumption and Receipts of the Preceding Year.* PP 1851 (21) liii, 1.

1853. *An Account of the Imports of the Principal Articles of Foreign and Colonial Merchandise, of the Consumption of Such Articles, and of the Custom Duties Received Thereon, in the Year Ending 5th January 1853, Compared with the Imports, Consumption and Receipts of the Preceding Year.* PP 1853-3 (117) xcviii, 1.

1864. *Sixth Report of the Medical Officer of the Privy Council, with Appendix, 1863.* PP 1864 (3416) xxvii 1.

1917. *The Food Supply of the United Kingdom: A Report Drawn Up by a Committee of the Royal Society at the Request of the President of the Board of Trade.* PP 1916 Cd 8421 ix, 211.

Paukert, F. 1973. Income distribution at different levels of development: A survey of evidence. *International Labor Review* August-September: 97–125.

Perenboom, R., van Herten, L., Boshuizen, H., van den Bos, G. 2005. Life expectancy without chronic morbidity: Trends in gender and socioeconomic disparities. *Public Health Reports* 120: 46–54.

Peterson, S., Peto, V. 2004. *Smoking Statistics 2004.* London: British Heart Foundation Health Promotion Research Group.

Plotnick, R., Smolensky, E., Evenhouse, E., Reilly, S. 2000. The twentieth-century record of inequality and poverty in the United States. In *The Cambridge Economic History of the United States, Volume III: The Twentieth Century*, ed. Engerman, S., Gallman, R., 249–300. New York: Cambridge University Press.

Pooley, C. 1992. *Housing Strategies in Europe, 1880–1930.* Leicester University Press.

Popkin, B., Udry, J. R. 1998. Adolescent obesity increases significantly in second and third generation US immigrants: The National Longitudinal Study of Adolescent Health. *Journal of Nutrition* 128: 701–706.

Porter, R. 1991. Cleaning up the Great Wen: Public health in eighteenth-century London. In *Living and Dying in London*, ed. Bynum, W.,

Porter, R., 61–75. London: Wellcome Institute for the History of Medicine.

1997. *The Greatest Benefit to Mankind: A Medical History of Humanity from Antiquity to the Present.* London: HarperCollins.

Post, J. 1977. *The Last Great Subsistence Crisis in the Western World.* Baltimore: Johns Hopkins University Press.

Power, A. 1993. *Hovels to High Rise: State Housing in Europe since 1850.* London: Routledge.

Prebeg, Z., Jureša, V., Kujundžič, M. 1995. Secular growth changes in Zagreb schoolchildren over four decades, 1951–91. *Annals of Human Biology* 22: 99–110.

Preston, S., van de Walle, E. 1978. Urban French mortality in the nineteenth century. *Population Studies* 32: 275–297.

Prince, J., Steckel, R. 2003. Nutritional success on the Great Plains: Nineteenth-century equestrian nomads. *Journal of Interdisciplinary History* 33: 353–384.

Pullar, P. 1970. *Consuming Passions: Being an Historic Inquiry into Certain English Appetites.* Boston: Little, Brown.

Quenouille, M., Boyne, A., Fisher, W. B., Leitch, I. 1951. Statistical studies of recorded energy expenditure in man. *Commonwealth Bureau of Animal Nutrition* 17.

Ransom, R., Sutch, R. 1977. *One Kind of Freedom: The Economic Consequences of Emancipation.* New York: Cambridge University Press.

Rasmussen, W. 1960. *Readings in the History of American Agriculture.* Urbana: University of Illinois Press.

Rau, R., Soroko, E., Jasilionis, D., Vaupel, J. 2008. Continued reductions in mortality at advanced ages. *Population and Development Review* 14: 747–768.

Razzell, P. 1965. Population change in eighteenth-century England: A reinterpretation. *Economic History Review* 18: 312–332.

1977. *The Conquest of Smallpox: The Impact of Inoculation on Smallpox Mortality in Eighteenth-Century Britain.* Sussex: Caliban.

1994. The growth of population in eighteenth-century England: A critical reappraisal. In *Essays in English Population History*, ed. Razzell, P., 173–206. London: Caliban.

1998. The conundrum of eighteenth-century English population growth. *Social History of Medicine* 11: 469–500.

Reay, B. 2004. *Rural Englands: Labouring Lives in the Nineteenth Century.* Basingstoke: Palgrave.

Rebato, E. 1998. The studies on secular trend in Spain: A review. In *Secular Growth Changes in Europe*, ed. Bodzsár, E., Susanne, C., 279–317. Budapest: Eötvös University Press.

Regidor, E., Dominguez, V., Navarro, P., Rodriguez, C. 1999. The magnitude of difference in perceived general health associated with educational level in the regions of Spain. *Journal of Epidemiology and Community Health* 53: 288–293.

Richards, M., Hardy, R., Kuh, D., Wadsworth, M. 2001. Birth weight and cognitive function in the British 1946 birth cohort: Longitudinal population based study. *British Medical Journal* 322: 199–203.

Rickards, L., Fox, K., Roberts, C., Fletcher, L., Goddard, E. 2002. *Living in Britain, no. 31: Results from the 2002 General Household Survey.* London: The Stationery Office.

Ridley, M. 2004. *Evolution.* Malden, Mass.: Blackwell.

Riggs, P. 1994. The standard of living in Scotland 1800–50. In *Stature, Living Standards and Economic Development: Essays in Anthropometric History*, ed. Komlos, J., 60–75. Chicago: University of Chicago Press.

Riley, J. 1989. *Sickness, Recovery and Death: A History and Forecast of Ill-Health.* Basingstoke: Macmillan.

　　1993. Understanding morbidity change: Comment on an article by Murray and Chen. *Population and Development Review* 19: 807–811.

　　1994. Height, nutrition and mortality risk reconsidered. *Journal of Interdisciplinary History* 24: 465–492.

　　1997. *Sick, Not Dead: The Health of British Workingmen during the Mortality Decline.* Baltimore: Johns Hopkins University Press.

Riley, J., Alter, G. 1989. The epidemiologic transition and morbidity. *Annales de Démographie Historique* 199–213.

　　1996. The sick and the well: Adult health in Britain during the health transition. *Health Transition Review* 6 (suppl.): 19–44.

Robine, J.-M., Cambois, E., Romieu, A. 1999. L'évolution de l'espérance de vie sans incapacité. *Médecine/Sciences* 15: 1450–1453.

Robine, J.-M., Romieu, I., Cambois, E. 1999. Health expectancy indicators. *Bulletin of the World Health Organisation* 77: 181–185.

Robinson, S., Lader, D. 2007. *Smoking and Drinking Among Adults, 2007.* Newport: Office for National Statistics.

Rochester, A. 1923. *Infant Mortality.* Washington, D.C.: Government Printing Office.

Rolland-Cachera, M., Cole, T., Sempe, M., Tichet, J. 1991. Body mass index variations: Centiles from birth to 87 years. *European Journal of Clinical Nutrition* 45: 13–21.

Rona, R. 1998. Secular trend of stature and body mass index in Britain in the twentieth century. In *Secular Changes in Europe*, ed. Bodzsár, E., Susanne, C., 335–349. Budapest: Eötvös University Press.

Rose, M. 1971. *The Relief of Poverty, 1834–1914: Studies in Economic History.* London: Macmillan.

Rosenberg, M. 1988. Birth weights in three Norwegian cities. *Annals of Human Biology* 15: 275–288.

Rowan, S. 2003. Implications of changes in the United Kingdom social and occupational classifications in 2001 on infant mortality statistics. *Health Statistics Quarterly* 17: 33–40.

Ruel, M., Rivera, J., Habicht, J., Martorell, R. 1995. Differential response to early nutrition supplementation: Long-term effects on height at adolescence. *International Journal of Epidemiology* 24: 404–412.

Sala-i-Martin, X., Doppelhofer, G., Miller, R. 2004. Determinants of long-term growth: A Bayesian averaging of classical estimates (BACE) approach. *American Economic Review* 94: 813–835.

Salaman, R. 1949. *The History and Social Influence of the Potato*. Cambridge University Press.

Samaras, R., Elrick, H., Storms, L. 2003. Is height related to longevity? *Life Sciences* 72: 1781–1802.

Samaras, T., Elrick, H., Storms, L. 2004. Is short height really a risk factor for coronary heart disease and stroke mortality? A review. *Medical Science Monitor* 10: 63–76.

Sandberg, L. 1989. Swedish height fluctuations during the eighteenth and nineteenth centuries in relation to the experience of other European countries and the United States. In *Auxology '88: Perspectives in the Science of Growth and Development*, ed. Tanner, J., 187–197. London: Smith-Gordon.

Sandberg, L., Steckel, R. 1987. Heights and economic history: The Swedish case. *Annals of Human Biology* 14: 101–109.

1997. Was industrialisation hazardous to your health? Not in Sweden! In *Health and Welfare during Industrialization*, ed. Steckel, R., Floud, R., 127–160. University of Chicago Press.

Saugstard, L. 1979. Infant death rate and infant mortality 1840–1900 in Norway, Sweden and Denmark and England and Wales with particular attention to the relationship between mortality and population density-urbanisation. In *The Fifth Scandinavian Demographic Symposium*, ed. Brunborg, H., Sørenson, K., 83–97. Oslo: Scandinavian Demographic Society.

Sawyer, M. 1976. Income distribution in OECD countries. *OECD Economic Outlook: Occasional Studies* July: 3–36.

Sayer, A., Cooper, C. 2005. Fetal programming of body composition and musculoskeletal development. *Early Human Development* 81: 735–744.

Schaible, U., Kaufmann, S. 2007. Malnutrition and infection: Complex mechanisms and global impacts. *PLoS Medicine* 4: e115.

Schoeller, D. 1990. How accurate is self-reported dietary energy intake? *Nutrition Reviews* 48: 373–379.

Schoeni, R., Freedman, V., Martin, L. 2008. Why is late-life disability declining? *Milbank Quarterly* 86: 47–89.

Schofield, R. 1994. British population change, 1700–1871. In *The Economic History of Britain since 1700*, ed. Floud, R., McCloskey, D., 60–95. Cambridge University Press.

Schofield, R., Reher, D. 1991. The decline of mortality in Europe. In *The Decline of Mortality in Europe*, ed. Schofield, R., Reher, D., Bideau, A., 1–17. Oxford: Clarendon Press.

Scholliers, P. 1995. A century of real industrial wages in Belgium, 1840–1939. In *Labour's Reward: Real Wages and Economic Change in 19th and 20th-Century Europe*, ed. Scholliers, P., Zamagni, V., 106–137. Aldershot: Edward Elgar.

Schultz, T. P. 2002. Wage gains associated with height as a form of health human capital. *American Economic Review* 92.

2003. Wage rentals for reproducible human capital: Evidence from Ghana and the Ivory Coast. *Economics and Human Biology* 1: 331–366.

2005. Productive benefits of health: Evidence from low-income countries. In *Health and Economic Growth*, ed. López-Casasnovas, G., Rivera, B., Currais, L., 257–286. Cambridge, Mass.: MIT Press.

Schumpeter, E. 1960. *English Overseas Trade Statistics, 1697–1808*. Oxford University Press.

Schwarz, L. 1985. The standard of living in the long run: London 1700–1860. *Economic History Review* 38: 21–41.

Scrimshaw, N. 1998. Malnutrition, brain development, learning, and behavior. *Nutrition Research* 18: 351–379.

Scrimshaw, N., San Giovanni, J. 1997. Synergism of nutrition, infection, and immunity: An overview. *American Journal of Clinical Nutrition* 66: 464S-477S.

Segers, Y. 2004. Nutrition and living standards in industrializing Belgium (1846–1913). *Food and History* 2: 153–178.

Sen, A. 1981. *Poverty and Famines: An Essay on Entitlement and Deprivation*. Oxford: Clarendon Press.

1999. *Development as Freedom*. Oxford University Press.

Shammas, C. 1983. Food expenditures and economic well-being in early modern England. *Journal of Economic History* 43: 89–100.

1984. The eighteenth-century English diet and economic change. *Explorations in Economic History* 21: 254–269.

1990. *The Pre-Industrial Consumer in England and America*. Oxford: Clarendon Press.

Sheridan, R. 1973. *Sugar and Slavery: An Economic History of the British West Indies, 1623–1775*. Kingston, Jamaica: University of the West Indies Press.

Shlomowitz, R. 1990. Convict workers: A review article. *Australian Economic History Review* 30: 67–88.

1991. Convict transportees: Casual or professional criminals? *Australian Economic History Review* 31.

Sicsic, P. 1995. France, 1820–1940. In *Labour's Reward: Real Wages and Economic Change in 19th and 20th-Century Europe*, ed. Scholliers, P., Zamagni, V., 206–209. Aldershot: Edward Elgar.

Sihvonen, A.-P., Kunst, A., Lahelma, E., Valkonen, T., Mackenbach, J. 1998. Socioeconomic inequalities in health expectancy in Finland and Norway in the late-1980s. *Social Science and Medicine* 47: 303–315.

Silventoinen, K., Lahelma, E., Rahkonen, O. 1999. Social background, adult body-height and health. *International Journal of Epidemiology* 28: 911–918.

Silventoinen, K., Zdravkovic, S., Skytthe, A., McCarron, P., Herskind, A., Koskenvuo, M., de Faire, U., Pedersen, N., Christensen, K., Kapiro, J. 2006. Association between height and coronary heart disease mortality: A prospective study of 35,000 twin pairs. *American Journal of Epidemiology* 163: 615–621.

Simpson, J. 1995. Spain, 1800–1950. In *Labour's Reward: Real Wages and Economic Change in 19th and 20th-Century Europe*, ed. Scholliers, P., Zamagni, V., 250–252. Aldershot: Edward Elgar.

Slicher Van Bath, B. H. 1963. *The Agrarian History of Western Europe, A.D. 500–1850*. London: Edward Arnold.

Smith, B. 1981. The material lives of laboring Philadelphians, 1750 to 1800. *William and Mary Quarterly* 38: 163–202.

Smith, M. 2009. Better health at older ages: Trends in healthy and disability-free life expectancy. Presented at Insurance, Sickness, and Old Age: Past Experiences and Future Prospects, University of Southampton, April 15–16.

Smith, M., Edgar, G., Groom, G. 2008. Health expectancies in the United Kingdom, 2004–06. *Health Statistics Quarterly* 40: 77–80.

Smith, P. K., Bogin, B., Varela-Silva, M., Loucky, J. 2003. Economic and anthropological assessments of the health of children in the Maya immigrant families in the US. *Economics and Human Biology* 1: 145–160.

Smolensky, E. 1971. The past and present poor. In *The Reinterpretation of American Economic History*, ed. Fogel, R., Engerman, S. New York: Harper and Row.

Southall, H., Garrett, E. 1991. Morbidity and mortality among early-nineteenth century engineering workers. *Social History of Medicine* 4: 231–252.

Srinivasan, T. 1992. Undernutrition: Concepts, measurement, and policy implications In *Nutrition and Poverty*, ed. Osmani, S. Oxford: Clarendon Press.

Statistics Denmark. 2009. *Statistical Yearbook 2009*. Copenhagen: Statistics Denmark.

Statistics Norway. 2000. *Historical Statistics 1994*. Oslo: Statistisk Sentralbyrå. Available online at www.ssb.no/english/subjects/00/histstat/.

STATLINE. 2010. Key figures of the population forecasts 2008–2050. *Centraal Bureau voor de Statistiek (Statistics Netherlands)*. http://statline.cbs.nl/StatWeb/publication/?DM=SLEN&PA=03766ENG&D1=11-12&D2=0&D3=0-2,7,12,17,22,27,32,37,l&LA=EN&VW=T.

Steckel, R. 1983. Height and per capita income. *Historical Methods* 16: 1–7.

1986. A peculiar population: The nutrition, health, and mortality of American slaves from childhood to maturity. *Journal of Economic History* 46: 721–741.

1995a. Percentiles of modern height standards for use in historical research. NBER Working Paper Series on Historical Factors in Long-Run Growth 75.

1995b. Stature and the standard of living. *Journal of Economic Literature* 33: 1903–1940.

2003. Net nutrition over the past millennium: Methodology and some results for northern Europe. Presented at the Annual Conference of the Economic History Society, University of Durham, April 2003.

Steckel, R., Floud, R. 1997a. Conclusions. In *Health and Welfare during Industrialization*, ed. Steckel, R., Floud, R., 423–449. University of Chicago Press.

eds. 1997b. *Health and Welfare during Industrialization*. University of Chicago Press.

Steckel, R., Moehling, C. 2001. Rising inequality: Trends in the distribution of wealth in industrializing New England. *Journal of Economic History* 61: 160–183.

Steckel, R., Rose, J. 2002. *The Backbone of History: Health and Nutrition in the Western Hemisphere*. Cambridge University Press.

Štefančič, M., Tomoazo-Favnik, T. 1998. Fifty-two years of secular trend in Ljublijana schoolchildren. In *Secular Growth Changes in Europe*, ed. Bodzsár, E., Susanne, C., 281–295. Budapest: Eötvös University Press.

Stein, Z., Susser, M., Saenger, G., Marolla, F. 1975. *Famine and Human Development: The Dutch Hunger Winter of 1944–5*. New York: Oxford University Press.

Stern, N. 2007. *The Economics of Climate Change: The Stern Review*. Cambridge University Press.

2009. *Blueprint for a Safer Planet: How to Manage Climate Change and Create a New Era of Progress and Prosperity*. London: The Bodley Head.

Stigler, G. 1954. The early history of empirical studies of consumer behavior. *Journal of Political Economy* 52: 95–113.

Strauss, F., Bean, L. 1940. Gross farm income and indices of farm production and prices in the United States, 1869–1937. Technical Bulletin 703. US Department of Agriculture Cooperating with the National Bureau of Economic Research.

Strauss, J., Thomas, D. 1998. Health, nutrition, and economic development. *Journal of Economic Literature* 36: 766–817.

Su, D. 2009. Risk exposure in early life and mortality at older ages: Evidence from Union Army veterans. *Population and Development Review* 35: 275–295.

Suhrcke, M., McKee, M., Arce, R., Tsolova, S., Mortensen, J. 2005. *The Contribution of Health to the Economy in the European Union.* Luxembourg: European Communities.

Susanne, C., Bodzsár, E., Bielicki, T., Hauspie, R., Hulanicka, B., Lepage, Y., Rebato, E., Vercauteren, M. 2001. Changement séculaire de la croissance et du développement en Europe. *Antropo* 0: 71–90.

Sutch, R. 1976. The care and feeding of slaves. In *Reckoning with Slavery*, ed. David, P., Gutman, H., Sutch, R., Temin, P., Wright, G. New York: Oxford University Press.

Szreter, S. 1988. The importance of social intervention in Britain's mortality decline, c. 1850–1914: A reinterpretation of the role of public health. *Social History of Medicine* 1: 1–37.

1997. Economic growth, disruption, deprivation, disease and death: On the importance of the politics of public health for development. *Population and Development Review* 23: 693–728.

2001. Review of Robert Woods, *The Demography of Victorian England and Wales. Social History of Medicine* 14: 562–563.

Szreter, S., Mooney, G. 1998. Urbanisation, mortality and the standard of living debate: New estimates of the expectation of life at birth in nineteenth-century British cities. *Economic History Review* 51: 84–112.

Tanner, J. 1962. *Growth at Adolescence, With a General Consideration of the Effects of Hereditary and Environmental Factors upon Growth and Maturation from Birth to Maturity.* Oxford: Blackwell.

1978. *Foetus into Man: Physical Growth from Conception to Maturity.* London: Open Books Publishing.

1981. *A History of the Study of Human Growth.* Cambridge University Press.

1990. *Foetus into Man: Physical Growth from Conception to Maturity.* Cambridge University Press.

Tanner, J., Hayashi, T., Preece, M., Cameron, N. 1982. Increase in length of leg relative to trunk size in Japanese children and adults from 1957 to 1977: Comparison with British and with Japanese Americans. *Annals of Human Biology* 9: 411–423.

Tanner, J., Whitehouse, R., Takaishi, M. 1966. Height, weight, height velocity, weight velocity: British children, 1965. *Archives of Disease in Childhood* 41: 454–471, 613–635.

Taubenberger, J., Morens, D. 2006. 1918 influenza: The mother of all pandemics. *Centers for Disease Control* www.cdc.gov/ncidod/EID/vol12no01/05-0979.htm.

Temin, P. 1991. Free land and federalism: American economic exceptionalism. In *Is America Different? A New Look at American Exceptionalism*, ed. Shafer, B., 71–93. Oxford University Press.

Thatcher, A. 1992. Trends in numbers and mortality at high ages in England and Wales. *Population Studies* 46: 411–426.

   1997. Trends and prospects at very high ages. In *The Health of Adult Britain 1841–1994. Volume 2. Chapter 15–27*, ed. Charlton, J., Murphy, M., 204–210. London: Office for National Statistics.

Thirsk, J. 2002. Review of ME Turner, JV Beckett and B Afton, *Farm Production in England 1700–1914*. *Economic History Review* 55: 355–356.

Thompson, E. 1963. *The Making of the English Working Class*. New York: Vintage.

   1967. Time, work-discipline and industrial capitalism. *Past and Present* 38: 56–97.

Tilly, C. 1975. Food supply and public order in modern Europe. In *The Formation of National States in Western Europe*, ed. Tilly, C., 380–455. Princeton University Press.

Tilly, L. 1971. The food riot as a form of political conflict in France. *Journal of Interdisciplinary History* 2: 23–57.

Toutain, J. 1971. La consommation alimentaire en France de 1789 à 1964. *Economies et Sociétés, Cahiers de l'I.S.E.A* 5: 1909–2049.

Towne, M., Rasmussen, W. 1960. Farm gross product and gross investment in the nineteenth century. In *Trends in the American Economy in the Nineteenth Century*, ed. Parker, W., 255–315. Princeton University Press.

Townsend, P., Davidson, N., Whitehead, M. 1988. *Inequalities in Health: The Black Report and the Health Divide*. Harmondsworth: Penguin.

Treurniet, H., Hoeymans, N., Giksen, R., Poos, M. 2005. Gezondheid en ziekte in Nederland: Het Nationaal Kompas Volksgezondheid als informatiebron. *Nederlands Tijdschrift voor Geneeskunde* 149: 226–231.

Troesken, W. 2004. *Water, Race, and Disease*. Cambridge: MIT Press.

Trussell, J., Steckel, R. 1978. The age of slaves at menarche and their first birth. *Journal of Interdisciplinary History* 3: 477–505.

Trussell, J., Wachter, K. 1984. Estimating covariates of height in truncated samples. National Bureau of Economic Research Working Paper 1455.

Turner, M., Beckett, J., Afton, B. 2001. *Farm Production in England 1700–1914*. Oxford University Press.

Twarog, S. 1997. Heights and living standards in Germany, 1850–1939: The case of Württemberg. In *Health and Welfare during Industrialization*, ed. Steckel, R., Floud, R., 285–330. University of Chicago Press.

Uauy, R. 1985. Commentary. In *Clinical Nutrition of the Young Child*, ed. Brunser, O. *et al.*, 96–98. New York: Raven Press.

Ulijaszek, S. 2003. Trends in body size, diet and food availability in the Cook Islands in the second half of the 20th century. *Economics and Human Biology* 1: 123–137.

UNICEF, WHO. 2004. *Low Birthweight: Country, Regional and Global Estimates*. UNICEF.

United Nations. 2006. *Human Development Report 2006*. United Nations Development Programme.

United States Senate. 1893. Wholesale prices, wages, and transportation. In *Senate Report 1394, Fifty-Second Congress, Second Session*. Washington, DC: Government Printing Office.

US Bureau of the Census. 1856. *Statistical Report on the Sickness and Mortality in the Army of the United States*. Washington, DC: A.O.P. Nicholson, Printer.

  1896. *Report on Vital and Social Statistics in the United States at the Eleventh Census: 1890*. Washington, DC: US Government Printing Office.

  1906. *Special Reports: Mortality Statistics 1900 to 1904*. Washington, DC: US Government Printing Office.

  1975a. *Bicentennial Edition: Historical Statistics of the United States, Colonial Times to 1970*. Washington, DC: US Government Publishing Office.

  1975b. *Historical Statistics of the United States, Colonial Times to 1970*. Washington, DC: US Government Printing Office.

  2002. *Demographic Trends in the 20th Century: Census 2000 Special Reports*. Washington, DC: US Government Printing Office.

  2007. Statistical Abstract of the United States: 2007 Edition. www.census.gov/compendia/statab/.

US Department of Agriculture. 1939. *Agricultural Statistics, 1939*. Washington, DC: United States Department of Agriculture.

  1952. *Conversion Factors and Weights and Measures for Agricultural Commodities and their Products*. Washington, DC: United States Department of Agriculture Production and Marketing Administration.

  1953. *Consumption of Food in the United States, 1909–1952. Agriculture Handbook no. 62*. Washington, DC: US Government Printing Office.

  1992. *Weights, Measures and Conversion Factors for Agricultural Commodities and their Products, Agricultural Handbook no. 697*. Washington, DC: United States Department of Agriculture.

2009. Nutrient Availability. Online Database available at www.ers.usda. gov/Data/FoodConsumption/NutrientAvailIndex.htm.

US Department of Agriculture Agricultural Marketing Service. 1958. *Livestock and Meat Statistics, 1957. Statistical Bulletin 230.* Washington, DC.

US Department of Agriculture Human Nutrition Research Division Agricultural Research Service. 1960. *Heights and Weights of Adults in the United States. Home Economics Report 10.* Washington, DC.

US Department of Health and Human Services. 1987. *Anthropometric Reference Data and Prevalence of Overweight.* Washington, DC: Government Printing Office.

US Department of Interior. 1883. Report on the Statistics of Wages in Manufacturing Industries. In *1880 Census, Volume 20.* Washington, DC: Government Printing Office.

US National Center for Health Statistics. 1965. *Weight, Height, and Selected Body Dimensions for Adults: United States 1960–62. Series 11, no. 8.* Washington, DC.

1977. *Dietary Intake Findings: United States, 1971–1974. Data from the Health and Nutrition Examination Survey. Health Resources Administration, Public Health Service, U.S. Department of Health, Education, and Welfare. Series 11 no. 202.* Washington, DC.

US Surgeon General's Office. 1888. *The Medical and Surgical History of the War of the Rebellion, 1861–65: Volume 5.* Washington, DC: Government Printing Office.

2009. Overweight and Obesity: Health Consequences. www.surgeongeneral. gov/topics/obesity/calltoaction/fact_consequences.htm.

Usher, D. 1980. *The Measurement of Economic Growth.* Oxford: Blackwell.

Valkonen, T., Sihvonen, A.-P., Lahelma, E. 1997. Health expectancy by level of education in Finland. *Social Science and Medicine* 44: 801–808.

Vallin, J., Meslé, F. 2001. Tables de mortalité francaise 1886–1997 et projections jusqu'en 2102. www.ined.fr/publications/cdrom_vallin_mesle/ contenu.htm.

Van de Walle, E. 1979. France. In *European Demography and Economic Growth,* ed. Lee, W., 123–143. London: Croom Helm.

Van Oers, J. 2002. *Health on Course? Key Messages from the 2002 Dutch Public Health Status and Forecasts Report.* Bilthoven: National Institute for Public Health and the Environment.

Van Oyen, H., Tafforeau, J., Roelands, M. 1996. Regional inequalities in health expectancy in Belgium. *Social Science and Medicine* 43.

Van Wieringen, J. 1978. Secular growth changes. In *Human Growth: A Comprehensive Treatise,* ed. Falkner, F., Tanner, J., 445–473. New York: Plenum.

1986. Secular growth changes. In *Human Growth: A Comprehensive Treatise*, ed. Falkner, F., Tanner, J., 307–331. New York: Plenum.

Van Wieringen, J., Wafelbakker, F., Verbrugge, H., De Haas, J. 1971. *Growth Diagrams 1965 Netherlands: Second National Survey on 0–24 Year Olds*. Leiden: Netherlands Institute for Preventive Medicine.

Venkaiah, K., Damayanti, K., Nayak, M., Vijayaraghavan, K. 2002. Diet and nutritional status of rural adolescents in India. *European Journal of Clinical Nutrition* 56: 1119–1125.

Verbrugge, L. 1984. Longer life but worsening health: Trends in health and mortality of middle-aged and older persons. *Milbank Memorial Fund Quarterly* 62: 475–519.

Vermaas, A. 1995. Netherlands, 1850–1939. In *Labour's Reward: Real Wages and Economic Change in 19th and 20th-Century Europe*, ed. Scholliers, P., Zamagni, V., 234–237. Aldershot: Edward Elgar.

Viazzo, P. 1997. Alpine patterns of infant mortality in perspective. In *Infant and Child Mortality in the Past*, ed. Bideau, A., Desjardins, B., Brignoli, H. Oxford: Clarendon Press.

Vignerová, J., Bláha, P. 1998. The growth of the Czech child during the past forty years. In *Secular Growth Changes in Europe*, ed. Bodzsár, E., Susanne, C., 233–262. Budapest: Eötvös University Press.

Vignerová, J., Humeníkova, L., Brabec, M., Riedlová, M., Bláha, P. 2007. Long-term changes in body weight, BMI and adiposity rebound among children and adolescents in the Czech Republic. *Economics and Human Biology* 5: 409–425.

Vlastovsky, V. 1966. The secular trend in the growth and development of children and young persons in the Soviet Union. *Human Biology* 38: 219–230.

Vögele, J. 1998. *Urban Mortality Change in England and Germany, 1870–1913*. Liverpool University Press.

Vögele, J., Woelk, W., Fehlmann, S. 2000. Decline of the urban penalty: Milk supply and infant welfare centres in Germany, 1890s to 1920s. In *Body and City: Histories of Urban Public Health*, ed. Sheard, S., Power, H., 194–213. Aldershot: Ashgate.

Von Tunzelmann, N. 1979. Trends in real wages, 1750–1850, revisited. *Economic History Review second series* 32: 33–49.

Voth, H.-J. 1995. Height, nutrition, and labor: Recasting the "Austrian Model". *Journal of Interdisciplinary History* 25: 627–636.

2000. *Time and Work in England, 1750–1830*. Oxford University Press.

2001. The longest years: New estimates of labor input in England, 1760–1830. *Journal of Economic History* 61: 1065–1082.

Waaler, H. 1984. Height, weight, and mortality: The Norwegian experience. *Acta Medica Scandinavia Supplement* 679: 1–51.

Wachter, K. 1981. Graphical estimation of military heights. *Historical Methods* 14: 31–42.

Wachter, K., Trussell, J. 1982. Estimating historical heights. *Journal of the American Statistical Association* 77: 279–303.

Wadsworth, M. 1997. Health inequalities in the life course perspective. *Social Science and Medicine* 44: 859–869.

Wadsworth, M., Hardy, R., Paul, A., Marshall, S., Cole, T. 2002. Leg and trunk length at 43 years in relation to childhood health, diet, and family circumstances: Evidence from the 1946 National Birth Cohort. *International Journal of Epidemiology* 31: 383–390.

Wald, N., Nicolaides-Bouman, A. 1991. *UK Smoking Statistics*. Oxford University Press.

Walter, J., Schofield, R. 1989. Famine, disease and crisis mortality in early modern society. In *Famine, Disease and the Social Order in Early Modern Society*, ed. Walter, J., Schofield, R., 1–76. Cambridge and New York: Cambridge University Press.

Ward, W. P. 1988. Hospitalization, birth weight, and nutrition in Montreal and Vienna 1850–1930. In *Society, Health and Population during the Demographic Transition*, ed. Bräandström, A., Tedebrand, L. Stockholm: Almqvist and Wiksell International.

1993. *Birth Weight and Economic Growth: Women's Living Standards in the Industrializing West*. Chicago: University of Chicago Press.

Warnes, A. 2006. The future life course, migration, and old age. In *The Futures of Old Age*, ed. Vincent, J., Phillipson, C., Downs, M., 208–217. London: Sage.

Waterlow, J. 1994. Summary of research in the area of linear growth retardation. *European Journal of Clinical Nutrition* 48 (supplement 1): S211.

Watt, B., Merrill, A. 1950. Consumption of foods: Raw, processed, prepared. In *Agricultural Handbook no. 8*. US Department of Agriculture. Washington, DC: Government Printing Office.

Webb, E., Kuh, D., Pajak, A., Kubinova, R., Malyutina, S., Bobak, M. 2008. Estimation of secular trends in adult height, and childhood socioeconomic circumstances in three eastern European populations. *Economics and Human Biology* 6: 228–236.

Weber, A. 1899. *The Growth of Cities in the Nineteenth Century: A Study in Statistics*. Ithaca: Cornell University Press.

Weir, D. 1984. Life under pressure: France and England, 1670–1870. *Journal of Economic History* 44: 27–47.

1989a. Markets and mortality in France, 1600–1789. In *Famine, Disease, and the Social Order in Early Modern Society*, ed. Walter, J., Schofield, R. Cambridge University Press.

1989b. Tontines, public finance, and revolution in France and England, 1688–1798. *Journal of Economic History* 49: 95–124.

1997. Economic welfare and physical well-being in France, 1750–1990. In *Health and Welfare during Industrialization*, ed. Steckel, R., Floud, R., 161–200. University of Chicago Press.

Weiss, T., Craig, L. 1993. Agricultural productivity growth during the decade of the Civil War. *Journal of Economic History* 53: 527–548.

Whiteside, N. 1987. Counting the cost: Sickness and disability among working people in an era of industrial recession. *Economic History Review* 40: 228–246.

Widding, J. 2006. The implementation of the 1857 Public Health reform in Uppsala and Gävle. Presented at the Sixth European Social Science History Conference, March.

Wilkinson, R. 1996. *Unhealthy Societies: The Afflictions of Inequality*. London: Routledge.

Wilkinson, R. and Pickett, K. 2009. *The Spirit Level: Why Equality is Better for Everyone*. London: Allen Lane.

Williams, S. 2005. Earnings, poor relief and the economy of makeshifts: Bedfordshire in the early years of the New Poor Law. *Rural History* 16: 21–52.

Williamson, J. 1985. *Did British Capitalism Breed Inequality*. Boston: Allen and Unwin.

Williamson, J. G. 1981. Urban disamenities, dark satanic mills and the British standard of living debate. *Journal of Economic History* 41: 75–83.

1982. Was the industrial revolution worth it? Disamenities and death in 19th century British towns. *Explorations in Economic History* 19: 221–245.

Wilmoth, J., Deegan, L., Lundström, H., Horiuchi, S. 2000. Increase of maximum life span in Sweden, 1861–1999. *Science* 289: 2366–2368.

Wilson, C. 1973. *Food and Drink in Britain: From the Stone Age to Recent Times*. London: Constable.

Winblad, I., Jääskeläinen, M., Kivelä, S.-L., Hiltunen, P., Laippala, P. 2001. Prevalence of disability in three birth cohorts at old age over time spans of 10 and 20 years. *Journal of Clinical Epidemiology* 54: 1019–1024.

Wohl, A. 1984. *Endangered Lives: Public Health in Victorian Britain*. London: Methuen.

Wood, B., Carter, J. 2000. Towns, urban change and local government. In *Twentieth Century British Social Trends*, ed. Halsey, A., 412–433. Basingstoke: Macmillan.

Woods, R. 1985. The effects of population redistribution on the level of mortality in nineteenth-century England and Wales. *Journal of Economic History* 45: 645–651.

2000. *The Demography of Victorian England and Wales*. Cambridge University Press.

2009. *Death before Birth: Fetal Health and Mortality in Historical Perspective*. Oxford University Press.

Woods, R., Shelton, N. 1997. *An Atlas of Victorian Mortality*. Liverpool University Press.

Woodward, B. 1998. Protein, calories, and immune defenses. *Nutrition Reviews* 56: S84–S92.

Woodward, D. 1981. Wage rates and living standards in pre-industrial England. *Past and Present* 91: 28–45.

World Bank. 1987. *World Development Report 1987*. Oxford University Press.

World Health Organisation. 2006. European Health for All Database (HFA-DB). http://data.euro.who.int/hfadb.

Wrigley, E. A. 1987a. *People, Cities and Wealth: The Transformation of Traditional Society*. Oxford: Blackwell.

1987b. Urban growth and agricultural change: England and the continent in the early modern period. In *People, Cities, and Wealth: The Transformation of Traditional Society*, ed. Wrigley, E. A., 157–193. Basil Blackwell.

1998. Explaining the rise in marital fertility in England in the "long" eighteenth century. *Economic History Review* 51: 435–464.

2004. British population during the "long" eighteenth century. In *The Cambridge Economic History of Modern Britain*, ed. Floud, R., Johnson, P. Cambridge University Press.

Wrigley, E. A., Davies, R., Oeppen, J., Schofield, R. 1997. *English Population History from Family Reconstitution*. Cambridge University Press.

Wrigley, E. A., Schofield, R. 1981. *The Population History of England, 1541–1871: A Reconstruction*. Cambridge: Harvard University Press.

Zamagni, V. 1995. Italy, 1890–1946. In *Labour's Reward: Real Wages and Economic Change in 19th and 20th-Century Europe*, ed. Scholliers, P., Zamagni, V., 213–233. Aldershot: Edward Elgar.

Zellner, K., Ulbricht, G., Kromeyer-Hauschild, K. 2007. Long-term trends in body mass index of children in Jena, eastern Germany. *Economics and Human Biology* 5: 426–434.

Index